THE ROUGH GUIDE TO

Guitar

WITHDRAWN

Dave Hunter

ROUGH GUIDES

www.roughguides.com

Credits

The Rough Guide to Guitar

Editing: Matthew Milton
Design: Diana Jarvis
Layout: Jessica Subramanian, Matthew Milton
Picture research: Matthew Milton, Carmen McCulloch
Proofreading: Jason Freeman
Production: Erica Pepe, Rebecca Short

Rough Guides Reference

Director: Andrew Lockett
Editors: Kate Berens, Peter Buckley, Tom Cabot, Tracy Hopkins, Matthew Milton, Joe Staines

Publishing Information

Distributed by the Penguin Group:
Penguin Books Ltd, 80 Strand, London WC2R 0RL
Penguin Group (USA), 375 Hudson Street, New York 10014, USA
Penguin Group (Australia), 250 Camberwell Road, Camberwell, Victoria 3124, Australia
Penguin Group (NZ), 67 Apollo Drive, Mairangi Bay,
Auckland 1310, New Zealand

Rough Guides is represented in Canada by Tourmaline Editions Inc.,
662 King Street West, Suite 304, Toronto, Ontario, M5V 1M7

Printed in Singapore by Star Standard

320 pages; includes index

A catalogue record for this book is available from the British Library

ISBN: 978-1-84836-585-8

1 3 5 7 9 8 6 4 2

Contents

Introduction

Over the past 120 years the guitar has evolved from being a minority status instrument – it was associated almost solely with folkies and vagabonds, and often derided by "serious" musicians – to being the most popular musical instrument in the world. This might be reason enough to pick one up, even if it wasn't enormously rewarding and just plain fun. The guitar's runaway popularity lies in its combination of accessibility and versatility. If you want to make a whole lot of music on one instrument, the guitar is your best bet.

Virtually any type of music can be played on the guitar. Its ability to carry full chords enables it to accompany a singer single-handedly, or add to a driving rhythm section in a band. At the same time, the many ways a guitar can project single-note lines – playing the role of a saxophone, a trumpet, a violin or even a synthesizer – make it an adept soloist too. When it comes to virtuosity on the instrument, the sky truly is the limit, and the best guitarists are up there with the most accomplished musicians in the world.

Yet the guitar is also one of the easiest instruments to learn the basics on – it's as rewarding to strum a handful of chords at a campfire singalong as it is to wail away in the spotlight on stage. In short, much of the guitar's beauty and appeal is that you can make of it what you want. But where do you begin? That's where the *Rough Guide to Guitar* comes in.

This book will help you progress from a beginner to an intermediate or advanced player, and give you a good understanding of the instrument in the process. It'll tell you everything you need to know to pick up the instrument and start playing straight away, while offering tips and techniques that will benefit more experienced guitarists.

Along the way, it covers all the crucial facts about guitars themselves, both acoustic and electric, as well as the gear that accompanies them – from amplifiers and effects pedals to all the cables and accessories that connect them. And, because so many musicians are taking advantage of the boom in home-recording technology, the book also provides a quick primer in recording techniques, as well as coaching you in how to put a band together, and how to tackle your first live shows once you do.

Most of all, though, the *Rough Guide to Guitar* tries to make the instrument fun. Rather than a dry tone and a laborious approach, this book aims to deliver the information you need to get you where you want to go. It doesn't skimp on the details and the inside information but we've tried to keep things accessible and easy to understand for players who haven't yet strummed their first string.

More than anything, this book revels in the fact that playing the guitar is simply a blast. It's a hobby that just about anyone can enjoy, and which can quickly become so much more. If you never progress beyond learning half a dozen chords that let you noodle away on a few simple songs, there's plenty in here to ease you into a lifetime of guitar-playing pleasure; if you plan to take it to the limit, the *Rough Guide to Guitar* will take you a long way down that path.

Three chords (or less) playlist

1 **Johnny B. Goode**
Chuck Berry

2 **Twist and Shout**
The Beatles (or the Isley Brothers)

3 **That'll Be the Day** Buddy Holly

4 **All Along the Watchtower**
Bob Dylan (or Jimi Hendrix)

5 **Whole Lotta Love** Led Zeppelin
(just two chords!)

6 **Folsom Prison Blues** Johnny Cash

7 **No Woman No Cry** Bob Marley

8 **All Apologies** Nirvana

9 **Pride and Joy** Stevie Ray Vaughan

10 **Blue Suede Shoes** Elvis Presley

11 **Guitars, Cadillacs** Dwight Yoakam
(two chords)

12 **Tumbling Dice** The Rolling Stones

13 **Shook Me All Night Long** AC/DC

14 **Gloria** Them (with Van Morrison)

15 **Born in the USA** Bruce Springsteen
(two chords)

16 **Desire** U2

17 **Save It For Later** The Beat

18 **Wild Thing** The Troggs

19 **La Bamba** Ritchie Valens

20 **Bad Moon Rising** Creedence
Clearwater Revival

To give you a taste of how far a little knowledge of the guitar can take you, here's a list of twenty well-known songs that can be played with just three simple chords (and although a few might use more than this for flavour, you can play them just fine with three, and sometimes fewer). From here, we'll tackle the basics and beyond, and have you – by the end of the next chapter – playing a song on the guitar with a mere twenty minutes-worth of effort. Enjoy!

Acknowledgements

The author wishes to thank the editors of this book, Matt Milton and Peter Buckley, its designer Diana Jarvis and its typesetter, Jessica Subramanian, for their stellar work and attention to detail. Additionally, thanks go out to his editors and colleagues at *Guitar Player* and *Vintage Guitar* magazines, to Nigel Osborne and Tony Bacon at Jawbone, and to his wife Jess and children Freddie and Flo for their constant support.

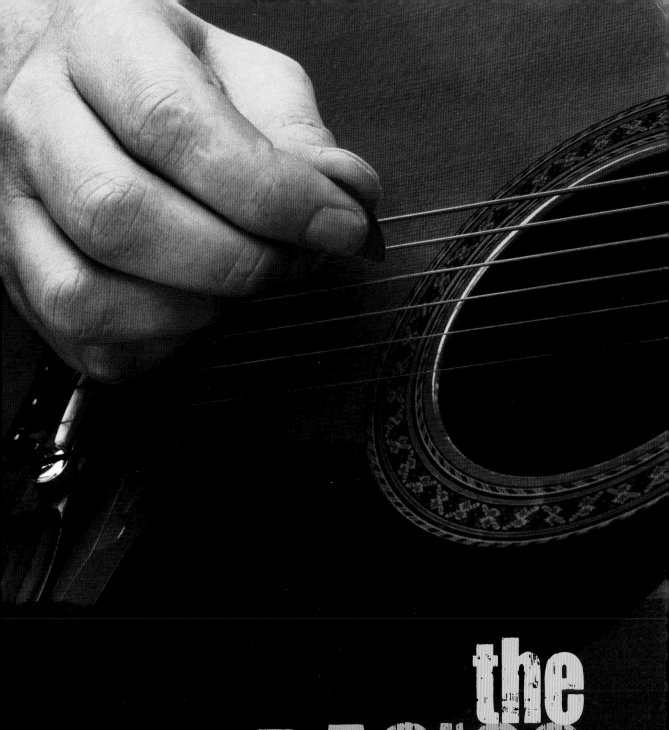

the BASICS

More than almost any other musical instrument, playing the guitar well goes hand in hand with understanding how it works. Or at least it should. Too often, however, players hinder their progress by failing to grasp the basics about the guitar itself. Not knowing how the instrument works will sometimes frustrate otherwise promising players.

So in this chapter we'll look at the basic function and components of the guitar. We'll also get into the basics – playing a few simple chords, and showing you the common notation systems used in this book and others, to help you develop further under your own steam. It's a quick-start guide of sorts – these subjects will be covered in far greater depth later on in the book.

All of this might at first sound a little over-the-top. After all, you don't necessarily need to understand how to tune a piano, much less repair or re-string one, in order to successfully play it – you just sit down and put your fingers on the keys. The guitar is truly an oddball contraption, however; and the electric guitar in particular is a rather complex electromechanical gizmo. Acoustic and electric guitars both require frequent retuning, occasional restringing, periodic minor adjustments, and routine maintenance, aside from any repairs necessitated by damage or abuse.

Sure, you can play the guitar without knowing the first thing about any of this, but you'd end up stopping so often that you wouldn't get far. Understanding the basics will help your own playing efforts, while increasing your enjoyment of the instrument.

The guitar produces sound through an interaction of physical vibrations, a phenomenon called "resonance". Minor adjustments at various points of the instrument will help not only to maximize the sound, or tone, of any given guitar, but will also help to put it in optimum playing condition, making playing it as easy as possible on the hand and fingers. Let's briefly explore the ways in which the instrument produces its sound, with reference to the annotated diagrams of each type of guitar later in this chapter, while discovering a few of the physical attributes that contribute to its feel.

THE ACOUSTIC GUITAR

An acoustic guitar is one with a hollow body, which produces its sound directly into the air, without further aid of electronics or amplification. Many acoustic guitars made today do include some kind of electronics to help them be heard by larger audiences, but can still be played entirely acoustically, or "unplugged", and be heard perfectly adequately in a small to medium-sized room.

For our purposes here, we'll discuss the breed of acoustic guitar known more specifically as a steel-string flat-top guitar (as pictured overleaf), which remains the world's most popular type of guitar, but classical guitars – which, outwardly, are roughly similar other than their nylon strings – are also popular, and acoustic steel-string archtop guitars still exist, too, instruments made in the image of the "jazz boxes" that were popular in the 1930s and 40s.

BASIC COMPONENTS

Pluck a string on a flat-top acoustic and the movement of this length of wire transfers vibrations into the wooden top of the guitar, which in turn amplifies the note represented by these vibrations – makes it louder – and transmits it, via sound waves in the open air, to the ear of anyone present to listen. This appears simple enough, but in order to function optimally the guitar needs to incorporate a number of minor paradoxes.

Its top (or soundboard), which is ideally made from a fillet of solid wood, most often spruce, needs to be thin enough to vibrate well. Given the tension that the strings are put under when tuned to their respective pitches, however, this top also requires further support systems to keep it from bowing and warping and being pulled from the body. If it were thick enough to support itself entirely, the top would be too rigid to resonate freely (and thus, too stiff to produce a good tone and adequate volume).

The outwardly visible support and anchor mechanism for the strings at the body end is the bridge, normally seen as a rectangle of darker wood through which the strings pass, via six "buttons". These buttons, actually called bridge pins, fit into holes in the bridge, and hold the ends of the strings (which are wound around little metal hoops, or "ball ends") in place, in a thin wooden bridge block mounted beneath the top. On their way to these holes, the strings pass over a thin strip of rigid bone or synthetic material, known as the saddle, and this serves as the termination point of the "speaking length" of the string, that is, the portion that vibrates and creates the sound. The saddle, being denser and harder than the wood itself, also helps to transmit the strings' vibrations into the bridge and, thereby, the top of the guitar, which is where we came in.

If the bridge and its components help to anchor the strings in the guitar top and to keep them from pulling free from that thinner wood, the top still requires further supports to help it maintain its relatively flat position within the body, and its structural integrity overall. These supports are called braces, and are glued to the underside of the top in a pattern that helps to strengthen it without overly impeding its ability to resonate. These braces are carved from long strips of light but strong wood, and are usually laid out in some form of an "X" pattern that crosses between the soundhole and the bridge. Other additional braces help to reinforce the "X", and there is often further support around the soundhole itself.

While the soundhole, by name and function, serves as one place where sound is emitted from the body, it is as much of an air vent as it is a "sound hole" per se. A large proportion of any flat-

top acoustic guitar's sound emanates directly from the outside of the top, while the sound coming from the soundhole is a blend of the top's inward vibrations with the vibrations of the back and sides of the body of the guitar.

In higher-quality guitars these are also made from thin slices of solid wood, usually mahogany or rosewood but sometimes maple or other varieties, while entry-level guitars will often incorporate laminated woods here to save in constructional costs. While these parts of the guitar aren't attached directly to the strings, they still vibrate in sympathy with the top, and contribute something to the overall tone of the instrument.

The condition and adjustment of any guitar – what is called the set-up – affects both its sound and its playing feel. There are usually far more adjustment points on electric guitars, but acoustic guitars have a handful of places at which the playing feel can be fine-tuned, too. We have already looked at the bridge's relationship to the sound, but it also has a role in the feel of strings under the fingers. The bridge saddle needs to be of a certain height to give the strings clearance over the front edge of the bridge itself, but if it's much higher than necessary this raises the strings uncomfortably high over the neck, making them difficult to press down. (The strings' height over the neck is often referred to as a guitar's "action", a low height equating with an "easy action", and so forth.) Although often simpler in their design, the bridges on most acoustic guitars are more difficult to adjust than those on electric guitars.

Lowering the string height by lowering the bridge saddle requires removing that saddle from its slot and sanding away some of the material from its underside; it's a simple enough adjustment in principle, but one best undertaken by a professional to avoid any risk of making the saddle uneven, or too short altogether.

Of course, the strings must be anchored at both ends, and this fact implies that there are at least two places where string height, and therefore playing feel, might be adjusted. At the far end of the neck the strings pass over a solid, slotted piece of bone or synthetic material on their way to the tuners, and this nut – as it's called – forms the other termination point for the speaking length of the strings.

A nut that is cut too high will lift the strings uncomfortably high off the neck, while a nut that is too low, or which has string slots that have worn down too far, will leave the strings buzzing on the frets. Nut adjustment isn't easily undertaken by the player, but the occasional need for it is worth being aware of. And this also brings us full circle to the issue of tone. The nut also must be in good condition if it is going to provide a clean, solid anchor at the neck-end of the guitar for the strings to vibrate freely and to sustain well. Meanwhile, a nut that is secure, and which has well-cut slots, also does a better job of transferring string vibration into the neck, which in turn transfers it to the body, where it contributes to the overall sonic blend of the instrument.

The guitar's neck plays a big part in its performance, and in its playing feel in particular. The flatter wood on the front of the neck that provides the playing surface onto which you press down the strings is called the fretboard, and the pieces of wire inlaid across it are called the frets. The frets provide precise termination points for the strings that you press down behind them, and thereby contribute to any note you play other than one that is played "open", or unfretted. The condition both of the frets and of the wood beneath them will contribute to the guitar's playing feel, as well as to its ability to yield a clean, clear tone. Low or worn frets will often lead to buzzing strings; they can be replaced, but if you're trying out a second-hand guitar with frets that are already worn too low, it might be difficult to tell if it performs adequately in the first place. Also, the general shape of the back of the neck (referred to as its "profile"), and the way it feels in the player's hand, plays an enormous part in the playing feel of any guitar. This is something that can't really be adjusted, and it behooves any player to begin by selecting a guitar with a neck that feels "just right" in their own hand, rather than trying to make do with a guitar that has a neck that they are never quite comfortable with.

Beyond all of the above, other components and bits of hardware pertain more to their own function than to the tone or playing feel of the instrument. The tuners should rotate freely and smoothly so that you can raise or lower each string to pitch, but they are rarely so loose that they will actually slip and affect tuning stability, unless they really are shot and in need of replacement. Many acoustic guitars also carry a pickguard (or scratchplate) mounted to the body beneath the soundhole, to help protect it from being scuffed or scratched by a pick (plectrum) while the player is strumming. Most acoustic guitars will also carry at least one strap button. This is mounted in the heel block at the bottom of the body, and used to attach one end of a strap used to play the guitar while standing. Some acoustics will have a second strap button mounted in the neck heel, while others assume the player will continue the time-tested practice of attaching the other end of the strap with a string tied around the headstock beyond the nut.

THE ELECTRIC GUITAR

Any guitar intended to produce its sound through an amplifier via the magnetic pickups attached to the instrument itself is considered an electric guitar. All will produce a little sound when unplugged, and some will even have hollow or partly hollow bodies and be almost as loud as actual acoustic guitars, but if they carry one or more pickups and are primarily intended to be played plugged-in, they are electric guitars nonetheless.

Electrics have many of the same basic components of acoustic guitars, although these are often notably different in design and construction to suit their differing functions in the sturdier bodies afforded by most electric guitars. The archetypal electric guitar is the "solidbody electric" (as pictured opposite), and that's the kind we'll examine here, since it takes us to the pole furthest from the acoustic that we have just discussed. Other types of electrics – hollowbody, semi-acoustic, semi-solid – will be discussed in detail in the following chapter.

BASIC COMPONENTS

The body of a solidbody electric guitar doesn't need to resonate in the same way as that of an acoustic in order to create this guitar's sound, since any significant volume produced by it is created by the amplifier that it is plugged into. The design and construction of its body, and of the electric guitar as a whole, does contribute to its tonal character, however, and different types tend to sound and perform quite differently, depending upon the woods used, the way the neck is set into the body, and the hardware and electrical components mounted onto them. Woods that are popular in the manufacture of electric guitar bodies include ash, alder, mahogany and maple, but many others are used, too – a far greater range of timbers than are commonly used in acoustic guitar-making. Some electrics have carved or contoured tops, while others use simple, flat "slabs" of wood. Most electric guitars will also carry some form of pickguard (or scratchplate) to help protect the top of the body top from scratch marks caused by the use of a pick. On some styles of electric guitars, these are fairly large and elaborate, and also help to hold other components that are mounted to them.

With the electric guitar, the electrical components mentioned above are clearly at the heart of matters: I have already mentioned the pickups, and these play a crucial role in translating the sound of the plucked string on an electric into the note that comes out of a speaker at the far end of many metres of wire. Any electric guitar has at least one pickup, and some prominent models have as many as three. A pickup is a passive magnetic device made from a coil of thin wire wrapped around (or positioned above) a magnet or magnets. As such it requires no actual electricity to function, but itself produces a low-voltage signal when a vibrating guitar string disturbs the magnetic field above it and induces a charge in the coil. It is this simple but rather magical interaction that changes an audible note into an invisible electrical signal that travels down a length of wire to be reproduced in an amplifier. Given the important role that the pickup(s) play in creating the sound of any electric guitar, it stands to reason that different types will contribute to different guitar tones, and we'll cover this in more detail later. It's worth being aware, meanwhile, that pickups of even the same type will produce slightly different tones depending on where they are positioned on the body, a pickup near the bridge being relatively brighter sounding than one mounted near the end of the neck.

An electric guitar will also carry an array of volume and tone controls and, if it has more than one pickup, a pickup-selector switch, which allows the player to change between pickups to achieve different sounds. Using these in combination, the player has some control over the sound the guitar produces, and different types of electric guitars will carry different control complements, depending upon the designer's intentions. Although some guitars do carry active preamps or active EQ sections that require an onboard nine-volt battery to power them, these are still in the minority; it's worth noting early on, if you're new to the electric guitar, that no mains electricity passes through the instrument at all, and it is merely connected – at the output jack – by a cable that carries its passive, low-voltage signal to an amplifier... where electricity is put to work to make things louder.

The solid body used to make this type of electric guitar also means the instrument offers a firmer base for mounting heavier, more versatile hardware. Like an acoustic guitar, an electric guitar also uses a bridge and bridge saddles, but on the solidbody electric this is more likely to be machined from some form of metal, often with a series of small bolts, nuts, or thumbscrews for adjusting saddle position and height, all of which works to afford far greater user-adjustment of the playing feel of the instrument. Guitars with simple means of adjustments like this allow players themselves to lower string height to produce an easier playing feel, or action. As we discovered while examining the acoustic guitar, the way in which an electric guitar's bridge is positioned can also impact the sound of the instrument. On some electric guitars, the strings are actually anchored in a separate piece of hardware called a tailpiece, and from there they pass over the saddles mounted in an independent bridge. On others, saddle and tailpiece are one and the same.

Many guitars employ a piece of hardware called a vibrato unit (vibrato bridge, vibrato tailpiece, whammy bar), which is usually anchored in position by use of a spring or springs, and which can be moved with a vibrato arm in order to produce a pitch-bending, or "vibrato" effect. Players who like to use this effect will intentionally choose guitars equipped with vibrato units, while some types can be added after purchase as a modification. Players who don't use them much will often still play guitars that carry vibrato units if they like other aspects of the way the guitar feels and sounds – they can simply ignore the vibrato arm if they choose, or even remove it from the bridge. Others will opt for one of the many types of guitars that come standard without a vibrato unit. None is better or worse than the other; like so many guitar-related choices, it is merely a matter of taste and playing preference.

Another notable distinction of the electric guitar is that the neck on most will offer easy access to a far greater number of frets. This is because a solid body enables the maker to attach the neck much higher up its length and still attain a strong joint that is able to resist the tension of the strings. Some electric guitar necks are glued in place, while others are held in place with a number of bolts or screws. The necks on many electric guitars carry a separate, glued-on fretboard into which the frets are laid, while, unlike acoustic guitars, some others have their neck and fretboard carved out of one and the same piece of wood (usually maple, when this is the case). Many electric guitars carry a standard nut of bone or synthetic material that differs little from the nut on any acoustic guitar, while some – those with vibrato units in particular – employ nuts made out of a slippery graphite or Teflon-impregnated material to help strings slide back into place more easily when the vibrato is used, and others still have more complex mechanical nuts that use little rollers or ball bearings to help the strings return to pitch. The tuners on an electric guitar are generally similar to those on many acoustic guitars, although many electrics also use more advanced tuner designs, which occasionally include units that lock or clamp the strings in place so fewer winds around the tuning post are required. Whereas many acoustic guitars are manufactured with only one strap button, almost all electric guitars will have two, one at the "tail" and one on the upper "horn" (the forward curve of the upper part of the guitar's body).

TWENTY-MINUTE GUITAR TUTOR

THREE CHORDS... AND YOU'RE PLAYING!

You're probably itching to get your hands on the thing and just play something. Further and more detailed instruction in a range of playing styles and techniques will follow, but let's jump in right now and find out just how easy it can be to at least play a few chords, and even to make a song out of them.

We'll do this by learning to read and play three simple chord boxes. You'll encounter many more of these diagrams in the learn-to-play section in Chapter 3, and they provide an easy guide to where to place your fingers to shape certain chords. For this tutorial, however, we'll stick to a "quick start" method and just jump right in, without going into too much detail about them – they're not actually all that complicated.

For now, we'll simplify the method used to show the chord changes of a song, to get you playing quickly. Each chord diagram opposite represents a section of the neck of the guitar, with the six horizontal lines depicting the strings (lowest/heaviest string at the bottom), while the vertical lines depict the frets (in these instances, the far-left bar represents the nut at the bottom of the fretboard, while the line after it represents the first fret, and so on).

The dots show you where to place your fingers to obtain the notes that make up each chord. Be aware that – as indicated in the diagrams – you don't place your fingertips right on the frets, but *slightly behind them* (that is, on the nut-side of the fret where you want the note to sound). You need to apply enough pressure to hold the string down to the fingerboard so that the note sounds without buzzing, but not so much pressure that your fingertips hurt and your hand begins to ache. Even so, your hand will probably ache a little after a few minutes of this unfamiliar activity, but with

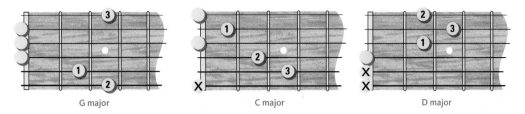

G major   C major   D major

just a little practice each day your muscles will soon get used to it. And your fingertips will develop calluses that will likewise reduce the initial pain of holding down the strings.

Practise forming the chords and holding down the fretted notes firmly, while gently sounding one string at a time in a downward picking motion, before trying to move on and change chords, or to play the entire piece. Take your time with it, and get your hands familiar with the effort needed, which is likely to feel awkward if this is the first time you have played the guitar.

Note that each of the three chords you are learning here – G, C and D – is formed by a combination of fretted and open strings – the latter meaning strings that are sounded without pressing any fingers down on them at all. The blue circles in the diagram indicates that this string is to played open, while an "X" indicates a string that should not be sounded at all. Sounding a string indicated by an "X" will produce a note that jars with the chord you are attempting to play, and it's worth learning right now that you don't need to strum all six strings all the time in order to successfully play a chord. As such, you'll see that our G chord is the only one that uses all six strings. The C chord uses five strings, and the D chord only uses four strings.

The three chords you are playing represent the most common chords used in the scale of G major, and the intervals between them are the most common chord changes in any key. That's to say, if you played other songs in different major keys into G Major, the three chords that are most important to playing them would fall in these same relative positions on the scale. As such, you will find that these three basic chords can be used to play countless tunes. Knowing these three chords will let you play the majority of the songs listed in this book's introduction.

Let's get started by playing one easy, universally known tune, the hymn "Amazing Grace" (shown overleaf). This song is in 3/4 time, otherwise known as waltz time, which means there are three beats to each measure of music. These beats have been written out for you in the song: strum the chord that is indicated above each measure three times per measure. For the time being, you will probably find it easier to strum lightly but quickly with the flesh of the side of your thumb, brushing it in a downward motion from the first played string to the last string in the chord (remembering to skip any "X" strings). Strumming in time to a specific rhythm takes some getting used to, so practise your downward strums until they are fluid and even, before actually jumping in and playing the song.

It's a classic that has been recorded by thousands of artists, including Aretha Franklin, Johnny Cash, Al Green, Sufjan Stevens, Bryan Ferry and even the Dropkick Murphies. A quick search on YouTube, iTunes, Spotify or any music-hosting website should find you a version to listen to, in case you need any further pointers as to how the song sounds. Once you've got that one down, we'll move on, to gain a more thorough grounding in the systems and symbols used to represent guitar music. Further along, in Chapter 3, we'll learn a wide variety of chords and explore a range of playing styles.

Amazing Grace (trad.)

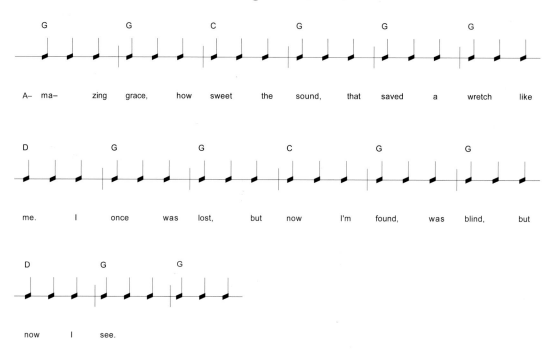

A–	ma–	zing	grace,| how	sweet	the	sound,| that	saved	a	wretch	like

| me. | I | once | was | lost, | but | now | I'm | found,| was | blind, | but |

| now | I | see. |

NOTATION, TAB & CHORD BOXES

Learning to read standard musical notation fluently requires a lot of study, and a lot more space than this book can accommodate. Fortunately for guitarists, however, we have our own simplified system known as tablature (or "tab" for short), which can be easily explained.

The majority of any learning guitarist's playing will revolve around using chord boxes of the type you have just encountered. But in Chapter 3 we'll also touch upon some basic single-note

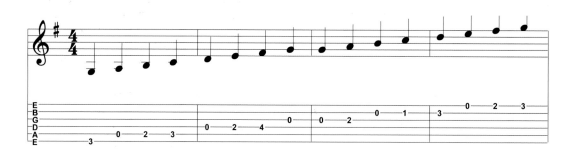

When playing a song using a pick, hold it firmly (but not too tightly) between thumb and forefinger.

playing, and tab makes this much easier for the non-music-reader to grasp. Also, in addition to applying your understanding of tab and chord boxes to the playing instructions here, you can take this widely used system of guitar notation with you to other guitar-tutor books, and to all the thousands of tabbed-out songs and riffs online: the sky's the limit in terms of genres and playing styles that tab can help you to learn..

Tab is easy to grasp because it is a logical visual representation of where notes can be found on the guitar. It uses six horizontal lines to represent the six strings, beginning with the lowest (low E, in standard tuning) at the bottom, which reflects the "upside-down" way in which the strings are viewed by the player who is looking down at them. Instead of the traditional dot that notation uses to represent notes, the tab lines carry numbers, with each number representing the fret at which you should place your finger on that string to produce the desired note (strings that should be played open – that is, unfretted – will be represented with a "o"). To help you remember where you are (and which way is up), the notes of the open strings are written along the left end of the tab lines.

In the example opposite, the G major scale is shown in both notation and tab. The three on the lowest line indicates that you place your finger just behind the 3rd fret on the low E string (the top string, or thickest string on your guitar) to produce a low G note. The "o-2-3" on the next line up indicate the A, B and C notes on the A string, and onward up to the G octave on the open G string (the fourth line up).

In addition to the string lines and fret numbers, tab uses a number of symbols and terms to instruct you on the nuances of finger movement necessary to play any given piece of music with the correct "feel". The string lines and fret numbers alone might provide the correct notes of any given piece, but without applying the necessary playing techniques such as the glisses (slides), bends, hammer-ons and pull-offs, alongside the picking directions and techniques, the phrase you play isn't likely to come out sounding anything like its composer intended.

Picking symbols

When a composer or tutor feels that the direction of your pick motion is important to the correct playing feel of a particular phrase, the pick stroke will be indicated by two types of symbols. This doesn't happen all the time, but will be included when a certain starting point, or pick direction, is required for a proper execution of the piece.

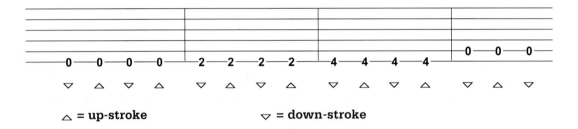

$\triangle$ = up-stroke $\triangledown$ = down-stroke

Gliss

Short for glissando, gliss is the term used to indicate a steady slide between notes, and is indicated by a little arch symbol in notation and an arch or a diagonal adjoining line between notes in tab (sometimes accompanied by, or replaced by, "Sl" for "slide"). A gliss can go either up or down. Today, in modern music this is also simply referred to as a slide (or finger slide), though in standard notation the term gliss is still usually seen.

To perform a gliss, simply play the first note, then slide the same finger along the required number of frets to hit the second note indicated. A gliss can also be used to slide into our out of a note (from or to an unspecified pitch), which is indicated by a gliss symbol placed before or after a single note/number with no note or number preceding or following as a starting/ending point.

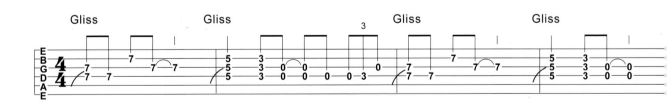

Bends

A string bend is indicated in a manner similar to a gliss. An arch symbol connects a note to the note that you should bend up to. You shouldn't move your finger from the starting fret to the second fret indicated in the bend, but stay in the same fret and push the string upwards – bending the string – to reach the same note you would play if you were to move to the fret number indicated.

In tab, a bend is often accompanied by further instructions: a number telling you how many notes up (or down) you are supposed to bend;

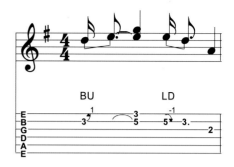

and an abbreviation such as "BU" ("bend up") or "BD" ("bend down"). Sometimes, durational information will be given – telling you precisely when a note is to be bent and then returned to its starting point.

If a "BD" follows a "BU" bend, the tab is telling you to bring the string back down. Alternatively, you might find this instruction illustrating a slightly more advanced technique that is called a "pre-bend" (sometimes noted by the initials "PB"). This requires you to play the first note of a phrase by bending the string *before* plucking the note, then picking the note and bending down (releasing) the string to the *second* fret number indicated, to hit the second note. (In other words, your finger is only ever placed at the fret indicated by the second number in the phrase, but bends up from there to achieve the starting note.)

On some occasions, when the pre-bent note isn't intended to be sounded on its own but merely indicates the starting point for the bend down, the instruction will be included in parentheses: (PB) or (BD). The instruction "LD" will also be used in some of these circumstances, to indicate that you are to "let down" the string.

Hammer-ons & pull-offs

Not all notes have to be sounded using your right hand. Your left hand can sound notes entirely on its own. Hammering on, for example, is a technique in which you sound a string by placing your finger down hard (hammering) on the string. Pulling off a string is almost like doing the opposite: swiftly removing your finger from a string, and doing so hard enough to generate a note. The pair

are generally indicated by a linking arch symbol and the absence of a picking symbol.

In the example below, hammered-on notes are shown in the tab with the letter "H", and pulled-off notes by the initials "Po". Some phrases might begin with a picked note, followed by a hammer-on and then pull-off notes. You can usually determine which technique is required by observing the direction of the musical phrase: ascending notes will be hammered, descending notes will be pulled off. You're likely to hear a pull-off or two in an acoustic blues solo, while pretty much any heavy metal guitar solo will feature any number of hammer-ons and pull-offs.

Rake

This one is a little like a normal strum with your pick. However, a rake is a strum in which you sweep the pick smoothly across the strings, hitting each string individually – but in rapid succession. It is indicated by a wavy vertical line. To make it even clearer, this symbol is usually accompanied by the initial "R".

Harmonics

Notes that are played by gently damping the string directly above the 12th, 5th or 7th fret are called "natural harmonics". (There are plenty of other harmonics, but those three frets are the easiest to sound harmonics at.) All that's required is a very light touch of the finger – the string is not to be pressed down so that it actually touches the fretboard. Harmonics are recognizable for their high, muted, ringing tone and are indicated by diamond-shaped (rather than round or oval) notes in the stave of standard notation, sometimes with the instruction "nat harms" above them, and/or the instruction "Nh - - - -" above the tab. You can see one at the very end of the example below.

Artificial harmonics are notes played by fretting a string with the left hand and damping it with a finger of the right hand twelve frets higher than the fretted note. They're indicated in standard notation by placing the fretted note in parentheses and the damped (harmonic) note above it, with a "T" followed by the number of the fret above which you should damp the string. In the tab, this is sometimes indicated by a number for the fret, followed by another in parentheses for the damping position above it, which might also have an "Ah" indicator above.

Gliss

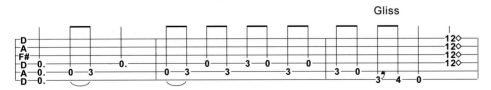

Half notes, quarter notes, eighth notes and triplets

Plenty of the exercises in this book use nothing but quarter notes (known as "crotchets" in classical music) and eighth notes (known as "quavers"). The G major scale shown on p.12 uses only quarter notes – there are four of them to every bar. There are, unsurprisingly, eight eighth notes to every bar, as you can see in the second bar of the "Harmonics" example given at the bottom of the opposite page. Half notes (known as "minims") have a duration of two beats. They are held for twice the length of a quarter note. You can see one in the second bar of the example below: the half note follows after four eighth notes (two sets of two). In the guitar tabs in this book, half notes are distinguishable from quarter notes by the fact that they only have a tiny little stump of a cut-off stem; the quarter notes have a full-length stem. Eighth notes have a short, curled "crook" to them when displayed individually, but are also often grouped into pairs. There are examples of both paired and individual eighth notes in the tab in the middle of the opposite page, illustrating the "Rake".

This example also shows a set of triplets. These are notes that are clustered into three-note groupings, with each note given equal rhythmic value. That's to say, no matter what the rhythmic value of the phrase might otherwise be, if the notes are triplets, their total note-length must be

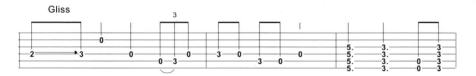

divided by three. This might sound complicated, but is a lot simpler in practice. Try counting "one, two, one, two" out loud, while clapping steadily along in unison. Then, without altering your spoken "one, two, one, two" count, try to clap over it in threes – three claps on "one" and three claps on "two". You are now clapping triplets. In written notation, they are joined together by a bracket above the stave of standard notation and the numeral "three" to indicate their status as triplets. Sextuplets are much less common, but when they appear they are accompanied by a "six" in the bracket above … along with a lot of attention from the tabloid press, and, very likely, their own reality TV show. The example below shows a particularly busy piece of tab, with both a gliss and a triplet (in the first bar).

Chord boxes

We have already encountered chord boxes in the "Twenty-Minute Guitar Tutor" earlier in this chapter. In Chapter 3, we will learn many more chords using the same system, and most of these will be more advanced than the first position G, C, and D chords that you have already mastered (all of

C7 barre chord (beginning at the 3rd fret)

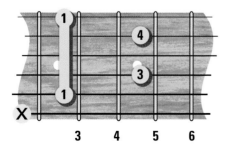

A major (note the guitar's nut on the left)

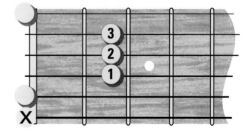

D minor 7

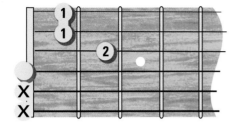

G major barre chord (beginning at the 3rd fret)

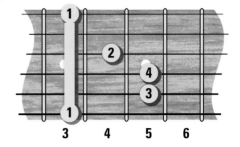

which are played at the first three frets from the nut, at the bottom of the neck).

Chords in this position, or near it, are easy to locate because the nut – the strip of white on the left of the chord-box diagram – provides an obvious reference point. You will eventually encounter chords further up the neck, however, and to help you locate these, a number will be placed beside the left edge of the box to indicate the fret at which such chords begin. When chords are played further up the neck, you need to play close attention to the "X" and blue "O" symbols at the top of the chord box that indicate unplayed and open strings respectively. Playing unwanted open strings in chords further up the neck is even more likely to make your chord sound all wrong.

When learning more advanced chords, you will also encounter "barre chords". These might at first appear to be impossible to play – requiring more fingers than you have on one hand. But they can be played by placing your forefinger all the way across a fret – holding all six strings down in one go with just one finger – while you use your other fingers to fret the other notes. In effect, it's like using your index finger as a kind of capo. The barre portion of the chord will often be indicated with a solid line across the strings at the required fret, rather than a series of dots, to help make this clear. They're initially very tough to play, and your left-hand's index finger will take a while to get used to them. But we'll come back to barre chords later.

the
INSTRUMENT

When the guitar-bug bites, it infects many people in different ways: there's the challenge of learning to play the thing, but there's also the inevitable fascination with the instrument itself. Many people make a hobby out of collecting guitars and related equipment, and get as much out of it as they do making music on the instrument. There is a great deal to this outwardly simple but actually rather complex instrument. We touched on some of it in Chapter 1 and we'll dig deeper here, delving into the differences between a range of types of electric and acoustic guitars – how different parts of the instrument help to shape their sound, and how you can learn to identify the right guitar for you – and providing a few lessons in maintaining and modifying your instrument.

None of the following should imply that you need to go out and buy a number of different guitars. If you're happy with just one that feels right to you, so much the better. Many great professionals have made careers out of playing just one guitar (even if they inevitably own spares). On the other hand, if you start with just one guitar that works well for you as you learn to play, you might find that a burgeoning interest in this fascinating six-string leads you to experiment with other makes and models, and there's definitely something fun and exciting about building a small collection of beautifully made objects – which also happen to make music.

If you're new to the big, bright, beautiful world of the guitar, the many variations on the otherwise simple theme of body, neck, and six steel strings can be rather overwhelming. Some instruments will appear straightforward enough to fit a child's mind's-eye image of a guitar, while others will carry a dazzling array of controls, switches and gizmos, the functions of which you can only guess at. Fear not – none of this is rocket science. The *Rough Guide to Guitar* will lead you through the minefield, and reveal the groovy little secrets behind that knob, this lever, and the other switch. In the course of this chapter, more space will be spent discussing the electric guitar, simply because its shapes and styles are far more varied than those of the acoustic guitar. Put a different way, sure, many different types of acoustic guitar exist, but the vast majority follow very similar templates and have similar components (even if their shapes are somewhat different). Electric guitars, on the other hand, are all over the map – so much so that many barely appear to have come from the same planet.

That said, the acoustic is where it all started. We'll take in the variations of wood types and body designs in greater depth than in Chapter 1, while also touching on acoustic designs that are new to us at this stage, such as the nylon-string classical guitar and the archtop acoustic guitar.

Guitar design has come a long way, as the wacky retro forms made by Danelectro show.

ACOUSTIC GUITARS

The most obvious factor of any acoustic guitar's design is the sheer size of its body. A flat-top acoustic guitar's volume-producing capability, and its low-end response and high-end clarity in particular, is in direct correlation to its body size and its overall internal dimensions. Given two equally well-made acoustic guitars – one large, one small – the bigger one should put out more volume and hit you with heavier low notes. The smaller guitar will be a little quieter and sweeter, but (ideally) with clear highs and good balance and articulation.

While size is the most obvious factor in acoustic guitar design, however, it certainly isn't the be all and end all, and there's a lot more to it than a simple "size equals volume". Any good acoustic guitar should be at least loud enough for the listener in a medium-sized room to hear it clearly, so a player's choice of one type of guitar over another comes down to many other considerations. Certain styles of music might indeed demand a big, booming guitar with a lot of punch, but in many other situations the small yet articulate flat-top might win the day.

Many makers have their own designations, but the different sizes of acoustic guitars mentioned here are generally referred to – in ascending order, from small to extra large – as parlour, concert, grand concert, and jumbo. In 1916 Martin developed a body type for the Ditson company (adopted under the actual Martin name in the early 1930s) that would become known as the dreadnought, and this wide-waisted, square-shouldered style has become one of the most popular types of flat-top acoustic guitar in the world.

The Gibson Super Jumbo: a big guitar with a big sound.

The 1930s saw Gibson produce its own oversized flat-top, one with more rounded body lines, that would become known as the Super Jumbo (model designation J-200 or SJ-200).

The top (soundboard)

Whatever an instrument's size, the majority of design factors of an acoustic guitar work towards a perfect ratio of strength to lightness. The lighter – or more to the point, thinner – a guitar's top (soundboard) is, the more it will vibrate when a string is plucked, and convert the string's own vibration into acoustic volume. At the same time, however, this soundboard has to be strong enough to withstand the force of the tight, tuned-up steel strings pulling upon it, which represents around 175lb. of pressure on the average flat-top.

If you make a guitar's top thick enough to withstand this string pull all on its own you won't get much sound out of it at all, so luthiers use braces glued to the underside of the top to strengthen it, which enables the use of a soundboard that is thin enough to vibrate freely.

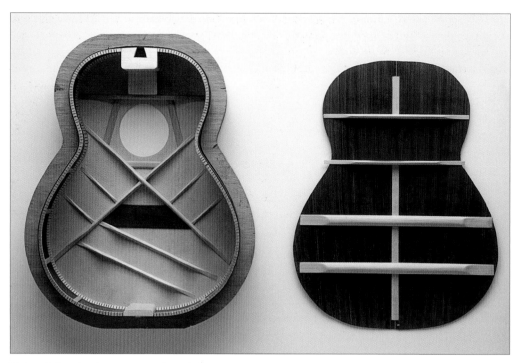

You can see how the X-brace system works inside this acoustic guitar (cut in half).

Some entry-level guitars are made with simple parallel braces that run from the end pin to the neck heel either side of the soundhole, while others have something called "ladder braces" that run side to side across the underside of the top. The standard for quality bracing patterns was established as far back as 1850, however, when C.F. Martin developed a pattern known as "X-bracing" – as shown in the picture overleaf. The X-brace greatly increases a soundboard's strength without excessively hampering its ability to vibrate freely, and it remains far and away the preferred bracing system for flat-top acoustics today. (Nylon-string classical guitars have different structural requirements and use other patterns, which we will look at below.)

As the name implies, X-bracing uses two braces carved from light but strong wood that cross each other in an X pattern somewhere on the bridge side of the soundhole. This technique also employs a number of small struts glued at other points around the top, to add further support. Where that crossing of the X occurs, the acuteness of the angles it forms, and the number and positioning of the supportive struts, are factors that vary widely, and are often part of a respected guitar-maker's secret tonal recipe.

Many manufacturers – whether it's Taylor, Martin, Gibson or Santa Cruz – will use a wide variety of different X-bracing patterns across their range, tailoring the braces to suit the model of guitar and the tone they would like it to produce. In addition to this, some makers will "scallop" braces by shaving some wood away from their sides, a practice that reduces the weight of these support beams, while retaining the majority of their strength.

While certain design standards for "the quality flat-top guitar" have certainly been established, different makers use many variations on the template to enhance different sonic goals. A big dreadnought or jumbo-sized acoustic that will be used mostly for booming rhythm playing might benefit from a top made from slightly thicker wood and heavier bracing, one that can withstand the stress of aggressive strumming, project a lot of volume when driven hard, and resist the vibrational distortion that a thinner, lighter top might succumb to when whacked in anger at a beer-soaked pub gig night after night.

At the other end of the scale, a smaller-bodied concert or parlour guitar designed for fingerstyle playing might require a thin top and carefully designed light bracing so that the soundboard is livelier and the strings don't have to be hit hard to produce adequate volume. These guitars will still produce a little less volume than a big jumbo-bodied flat-top, but they don't have to be played as hard to achieve their potential and for players of this style of music their added clarity and woody richness make for a fair trade-off.

In between these, a big-bodied dreadnought designed to excel at flatpicking for speedy bluegrass soloists might use scalloped braces and a slightly thinner top; a medium-bodied flat-top such as a grand concert model intended to excel at hybrid (pick and fingers) picking – while also being suitable for strummed rhythm – might employ a slightly more rigid top than a fingerstyle guitar of a similar size.

The bridge

We have already seen how the braces within the guitar do the real work of supporting the top. But the bridge also plays its part. The bridge on a flat-top, usually made from rosewood or ebony, provides a conduit for the strings from the top of the guitar into their secure positions, where they are held in place inside the bridge block beneath it by the bridge pins that pass through the individual string holes.

As such, its purpose is twofold: to securely hold the ball-ends of these strings (which would certainly pull through the thinner wood of the top without the support of this bridge and bridge block); and to spread the string vibration across the important centre section of the top. Even with the support of the bridge and the braces beneath the top, some guitars will exhibit some apparent mild warping of the soundboard between the bridge and the end of the body when the strings are up to full tension.

This slight curvature, known as a "belly", is natural in thin-topped instruments, and isn't a matter for concern unless it approaches extremes. "Bellying" tends to only become a problem on very old guitars.

The parlour guitar is an instrument particularly favoured by blues, folk and country players – in fact, any players who specialize in fingerstyle guitar playing – for its evenness of tone.

Cutaways

Many contemporary flat-tops are made with what's called a cutaway in the body, a feature seen more commonly on electric guitars prior to the 1980s or so. A cutaway is a rounded carving in the treble side of the upper bout (near the high-strings side of the neck/body joint) that allows the player to reach frets higher up the neck.

More traditional styles of flat-tops, and those that are still intended to be played purely acoustically, are still often made without a cutaway, and some players consider that this modern feature might hamper the sonic performance of an upmarket guitar ever so slightly (although in practice this would be difficult to detect).

Acoustic pickups

Built-in pickups and onboard preamps are also popular on many new models of acoustic guitar. Unlike the magnetic pickups used on electric guitars, which we examined briefly in Chapter 1 (and which we'll look at more closely later), the pickups on acoustic guitars are usually made from piezo-electric sensors mounted beneath the bridge saddle or the underside of the top.

Magnetic pickups are also sometimes used for acoustic guitars, but these are more common as an after-sales add-on by a guitarist, and can be mounted into the soundhole without much trouble. While many such pickups are passive, meaning they can be plugged directly into an amplifier or sound system, others benefit from the inclusion of a battery-powered preamp, which is either mounted in the guitar itself, or contained in a separate floor unit to be positioned at the player's feet.

Up the neck

The *feel* of any guitar neck in the player's hand is something each guitarist will have their own opinion on. Neck construction, on the other hand – in particular the way in which the neck is attached to the body – is an objective consideration and another important factor in any flat-top's design. While the neck/body joint does play a part in transferring resonance and string vibration – makers argue at length over

A cutaway guitar lets a guitarist get their left hand right up to the top of the neck with the minimum of fuss. (This one here's a 12-string.)

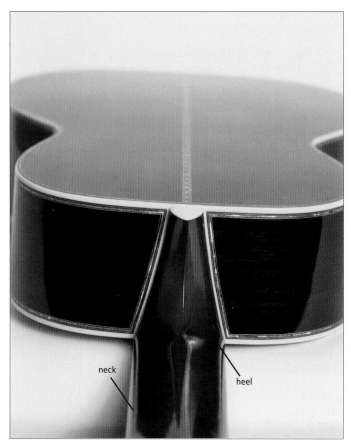

neck

heel

Happiness is a well-glued neck.

the tonal merits of their respective techniques – it's more interesting to look at the neck with respect to maintenance and set-up issues.

For many years, the standard was a glued-in neck using a dovetailed or mortise-and-tenon joint (think of a tongue extending from the neck-end into a pocket in the body). These continue to proliferate today. But plenty of adventurous manufacturers have used variations on a bolted- or pinned-in neck joint for an acoustic guitar. The argument behind these runs that many acoustic guitars will need some neck adjustment in their lifetime regardless of how well the neck/body joint is constructed, and so a removable attachment will make that work a lot less painful when the time comes. Variations on the removable neck are used by highly respected makers both large and small, from Taylor to Froggy Bottom – neither of whom are likely to be accused of building guitars that are tonally inferior to those with glued-in necks.

The majority of flat-tops made today have necks that attach to the body at the 14th fret, usually with a further six frets laid over the top of the body, taking the fingerboard up to the soundhole. But up through the first third of the twentieth century or so, the 12th-fret neck joint was the norm, and some players and manufacturers still prefer this variation. It gives you fewer frets to work with – which would seem to make the 12-fret neck more a negative than a positive. But attaching the neck at the 12th fret shifts the speaking length of the strings further into the body, resulting in a bridge that is centred further into the "meat" of the lower bout (the bottom of the guitar's body). Some players feel this gives such guitars a fuller, richer tone, or at least one that's different from a similar guitar with a 14-fret neck joint.

Most modern acoustic guitars benefit from a support rod inside the neck, known as a "truss rod", which helps to counteract the tension of the strings upon the neck. In most decent-quality flat-tops manufactured today, this truss rod is adjustable, and can be set to correct mild forward or reverse curvature of the neck that might set in with time and changing atmospheric conditions.

The tuners used on acoustic flat-tops are broadly similar in principle and function to those used on electric guitars, and you will find more detail on the subject in that section in this chapter.

Top woods

The wood used to construct the top of your acoustic guitar is the most tonally important piece of timber in the entire instrument. Apart from budget options for beginners, any acoustic guitar ought to at least have a solid top, which costs more than a laminated (plywood) top. Fortunately the range of entry-level models carrying solid tops is wider today than ever before, and these instruments are also more affordable in real terms than they were even ten years ago. Automated, computer-numeric-controlled (CNC) cutting and routing machines have made it much easier for companies to manufacture comfortable-playing and decent-sounding acoustic guitars at entry-level prices. The player entering the market today is in a much better position, value-for-money-wise, than their parent or grandparent might have been twenty or forty years ago.

In the discussion of acoustic guitar-making, the use of the term solid wood can be a bit confusing. When we talk about "solid" woods in acoustic guitars, we're still talking about very thin pieces of wood – cuts of a thinness that could be used as a veneer in other types of construction or furniture making – but they are sawn from solid timber and used all on their lonesome (though glued side-to-side to make up an adequate width), without being glued back-to-back with other cuts of wood to form a laminated, or ply, wood stock. The term can be confusing, since there's a lot of empty space inside an acoustic guitar such as, for example, a Martin D-28 that's made from solid spruce and solid rosewood. The top, back and sides of a guitar like that, however thin, are indeed made from solid wood.

Spruce

For well over a century and a half, spruce has been the most popular top wood for flat-top acoustic guitars. Spruce is light, strong and rigid – all qualities required in a resonant soundboard – and it has a round, sweet tonal character and an appealing high-end response, with good clarity and definition. The most common form of spruce used today is Sitka spruce, a wood that accentuates a guitar's fundamental notes boldly, and which presents a bright, loud voice. The rarest and most prized variety is eastern red spruce, also known as Adirondack spruce, or sometimes as Appalachian spruce. Along with its darker, slightly amber appearance, it has a rich voice, delicious complexity, and excellent volume. This is the wood of the most prized pre-World War II flat-tops.

Few old-growth stocks remain, and any new guitars built with it will be very expensive. Another highly prized variety of spruce with a lighter grain is Englemann spruce. It has a tonality that is more harmonically complex than Sitka, but is mellower and less forceful along with it.

Any good piece of spruce should exhibit a tight, fairly straight grain, although some appealing irregularities do occur in perfectly good samples. In fact, a sample of

The Martin D-28: a guitar made from solid spruce and rosewood that really sings.

spruce doesn't have to have a straight grain to sound good, but since most reputable makers will select samples that exhibit those qualities anyway they have become known as the signs of a better grade of guitar. A spruce top generally takes some playing-in to reach maturity and reveal its full tone. (Note that braces on the finer acoustic guitars are often made from spruce, too.)

Cedar

Several flat-top makers have also made good use of cedar, also known as western red cedar, although it is far more common in classical guitar-making. Cedar is usually heard as being rich, open and well defined, perhaps with a mellower bass, a little less clarity, and sometimes a warmer overall tone than spruce. It is a wood that reveals its voice more quickly on young guitars, rather than requiring quite as much playing-in as spruce does.

Cedar tops will occasionally distort more quickly when played hard, but the fact that some good cedar can sound relatively louder than spruce without aggressive strumming helps to counteract this impression. It has a darker appearance than spruce.

Mahogany

Better known for its use in the back, sides, and neck of an acoustic guitar, mahogany is occasionally used as a top wood, too – usually in an all-mahogany-bodied flat-top. Such guitars were traditionally lower-end options (albeit from some excellent makers), but can sound perfectly good for many players' needs. A mahogany soundboard tends to be less "open" sounding than one of spruce or cedar, but usually has a pronounced mid-range element and a punchy voice.

Body woods

Traditionally, the same variety of wood is used for both the back and sides of an acoustic guitar. Although the guitar's top plays the lead role in the instrument's tone, many manufacturers agree that the body wood does play a part in shaping and fine-tuning its voice. Lower-priced acoustics with solid tops will often still use laminated wood for the back and sides, although this usually contains thin layers of the same tonewoods discussed below. When used as part of a laminated "sandwich" made from two or more different woods, the tonal characteristics of these species are lessened.

Decently made guitars with solid tops and laminated backs and sides can still sound very good, but the use of a solid back and sides indicates a jump into the premier league, construction-wise – and is another step beyond the tonal improvement that a solid top represents over a ply top. The presence of solid tonewoods here also indicates a better-constructed guitar overall, and that takes you further up the quality ladder. In the better flat-tops, the characteristics of the wood used in the guitar's back and sides will be clearly present in its overall tone. It will usually make itself heard as a degree of seasoning in the low end, in the guitar's overall presence, and in the harmonic complexity of the instrument.

Mahogany

Although it is the more affordable of the two most common body woods, mahogany nevertheless is found in many of the world's finest flat-top guitars. It has a voice that is bright, clear and tight, and provides excellent volume and projection, with a round, woody mid-range.

Rosewood

Often used for upgraded or high-end models, rosewood contributes excellent depth, warmth and dimension to the overall voice of a good acoustic guitar. It offers a bold, rich low end, and presents a detailed yet balanced mid-range. East Indian rosewood is the most common variety used in guitar-making today, although some manufacturers will also use Madagascar rosewood in their top models. Both possess similar tonal traits, although Madagascar is considered by some makers to offer more of the good stuff, and to be closer in sound and appearance to the legendary king of rosewoods, Brazilian rosewood.

The latter is now on the C.I.T.E.S. list of endangered species and is therefore barred from importation. Guitars that boast Brazilian rosewood will be either those made quite some years ago (usually before 1969), or, if new, instruments made with old stocks of rosewood imported to Europe or North America before the wood hit the endangered list.

Ovangkol

This African wood has been making inroads into flat-top guitar manufacture in recent years, and has become popular as a back-and-sides wood with a number of large manufacturers – Larrivee and Taylor among them. Sporting a deep, textured, interlocking grain and a colour that runs from yellowish brown to a deep chocolate, ovangkol yields a voice that blends the rich lows of rosewood with the ringing highs of maple.

Maple

A hard, rigid wood, maple is used far less often than mahogany or rosewood, but is an important ingredient in a few noteworthy flat-tops, such as the post-war Gibson J-200 (SJ-200) or the Guild F-50. Maple contributes a distinctive brightness and definition to a guitar's overall tone, and enhances cutting power and sustain.

Koa

Traditionally used in Hawaiian-style acoustic steel guitars (known as such because they are played with a bar slide, or "steel"), where it is sometimes used for soundboards too, this luscious, honey-coloured wood is an exotic choice that is employed for its look as much as – or more than – its sound. It doesn't make for a particularly loud guitar, but has a clear, bright tone with a little mid-range honk that appeals to certain players.

Other woods

While the woods listed above probably account for more than ninety percent of acoustic flat-top guitars out there, some manufacturers do use more exotic or uncommon tonewoods such as walnut, cherry, bubinga, Australian blackwood, ebony, oak, imbuia, sapele and others. Each of these has its own distinctive tonal qualities, but the more unusual among them are often selected on grounds of look than tone.

Neck & fingerboard woods

The vast majority of the necks on flat-top acoustic guitars are made from mahogany. This wood's useful blend of strength and rigidity with a reasonable density and weight makes it an excellent choice for this critical part of the instrument. Some flat-tops do have maple necks, especially those made with maple back and sides (as mentioned above), where a darker mahogany neck would look awkward and out of place. Maple is one of the hardest and most stable woods used in guitar-making, but also often proves one of the heaviest. As used in guitar necks it is seen far more often in electric guitars, though frequently in archtop acoustics too. Having lately become a popular wood for guitar backs and sides, ovangkol is occasionally also used for the necks of acoustic guitars.

Rosewood is far and away the most popular variety of wood for the fingerboards (fretboards) of flat-top acoustics. It wears reasonably well, and is often said to attribute a slight warmth and roundness to the instrument's tone, even in this limited application. Many high-end guitars have traditionally been made with ebony, largely because it is harder wearing and its dark, almost glossy black appearance gives a more exotic look to a deluxe instrument. Ebony's density is also believed to lend extra sharpness and definition to a guitar's tone, which is noticeable in the higher frequencies in particular.

CLASSICAL GUITARS

Through its associations with a musical form that is often assumed to be more noble and cultured than the various genres of popular music that feature other types of guitars, the classical guitar has attained an elevated status among fretted six-string instruments, yet is often misunderstood and underappreciated. Any discussion of the classical guitar in a book that is likely to be read by many newcomers to the instrument really ought to begin with a brief explanation of what a classical guitar is *not*.

Learners are often advised to purchase a classical guitar because the nylon strings will be easier on the fingers, but such advice is misleading, and can often result in frustration. A classical guitar (or concert guitar, as they are called in classical circles) does indeed use nylon strings, but a proper classical has a neck and fingerboard that are significantly flatter and wider than those of the average steel-string flat-top guitar.

This can make it more difficult for the beginner – and the younger player in particular – to wrap their fingers around the neck and successfully shape chords. With this in mind, it's often more productive to persist with a more comfortable-feeling steel-string guitar. It might hurt your fingertips more at the start, but it will become comfortable in a short time as your calluses develop, and it will be easier to fret and shape chords on than a wide-necked classical guitar once your digits have hardened a bit.

There is also a breed of guitar known as the nylon-string folk guitar, and these are often made without the extreme neck proportions of the true classical guitar. It might indeed be easier for the beginner to get to grips with one of these. With this in mind, though, remember that millions of players around the world have overcome any early difficulties presented by steel strings and learned to play the instrument to their satisfaction, and if the sound that led you to an initial interest in the guitar is that of a steel-stringed instrument – as it so often is – the softer, gentler tone of a nylon-string folk guitar might not prove entirely satisfying. It's there as an option, even so, and worth being aware of.

With this caveat behind us, let's look briefly at the genuine classical guitar. Although its sound can initially be dwarfed by the bright, aggressive thrang of the steel-string flat-top, a good classical guitar offers degrees of tonal depth and nuance that set it among the most elevated of the six-strings. Mellow, rich and warm when played gently, it is also capable of surprising attack and dynamics when plucked more vigorously. Despite having been rendered more of a one-genre

Charlie Byrd was a virtuoso jazz guitarist who preferred to play a classical guitar, rather than an archtop or semi-acoustic.

instrument than almost any other type of guitar, it is a surprisingly versatile performer, capable of projecting many moods and voices.

With that in mind, it's worth mentioning that classical guitars have made notable inroads into other types of music: classically trained guitarist Charlie Byrd introduced the nylon-string concert guitar to the jazz world in the late 1950s and early 60s, pop-jazzer Earl Klugh employed one for his mellow instrumental excursions in the 70s and 80s, former Fleetwood Mac guitarist Lindsey Buckingham and Sting sideman Dominic Miller have both flown the classical flag in their rock-pop-fusion excursions, and country picker *extraordinaire* Chet Atkins moved from steel-string electric and acoustic guitars to a thin-bodied electric classical model to preserve his brittle fingernails.

Body woods & design

Many of the woods used in classical guitar construction echo those of the steel-string flat-top, but there are also some notable variations. Spruce is a popular wood for the top (also called a "table" in classical guitar-making), but cedar is a more widely used alternative here than in the steel-string world. The fact that cedar requires less breaking in to reach its full potential offers a clear advantage in an instrument with a relatively low string tension in the first place, and this slightly softer wood's natural tonal characteristics also suit the genre well.

Rosewood remains a popular wood for back and sides, the endangered Brazilian rosewood being, again, the most highly prized. Many makers also use mahogany, although it is less frequently seen in high-end classical guitars and more often a component of lower- and mid-level instruments (which still includes many makes and models of fine quality). Cypress has also been used by many luthiers, and this light yet strong timber is particularly popular with variations of the classical guitar intended for flamenco-style playing, where minimum weight and maximum resonance are valued (more of which below). Some exotic body-wood alternatives include walnut, wenge, pau ferro, zebrawood, bubinga, American cherry, black acacia and cocobolo.

While the X-brace has become standard in steel-string flat-top construction, there tends to be more variation in classical guitar bracing systems, with many new makers becoming particularly adventurous. Way back in the 1850s Antonio de Torres, known as the father of the modern classical guitar, established a "fan strut" bracing system. It uses a series of individual braces radiating from the soundhole outward toward the guitar's bridge and beyond, in a fan-like pattern, and it remains popular today. Others use a range of latticework bracing systems, employing extremely thin braces that cover a larger proportion of the underside of the guitar's top.

Neck & fingerboard

The mahogany neck and rosewood fingerboard proliferates in the lower strata of classical guitars, but high-end designs very often feature cypress necks, echoing the use of Spanish cypress in many parts of the great classical designs from the nineteenth century. An ebony fingerboard is also considered a near-universal feature of any better classical guitar, and this wood provides the combination of durability and tonal definition and clarity that this type of guitar demands.

More than the woods it uses, the classical guitar neck is distinguished from that of the steel-string flat-top by its design and dimensions. The traditional classical playing style, achieved with the thumb placed well behind the neck and the rest of the hand and fingers rotated more fully forward across the width of the fingerboard, requires that the instrument be made with a wide, flat fingerboard, and a relatively thin, flat neck. The fingerboard of a genuine classical guitar, therefore, can often approach 2" (51 mm) wide at the nut, where a standard steel-string flat-top will average around 1.75", and most electric from 1.6" to 1.7". The majority of classical guitars have necks that are attached to the body at the 12th fret, with a further six full frets on a fingerboard extension over the top of the body, and often another partial fret (rarely used in any but the most extreme performances) above and below the front curve of the soundhole.

Hardware & components

Classical guitars carry a minimum of extraneous components compared even to the more austere flat-tops. They require a nut at the end of a neck and a bridge at the body, of course, to anchor the speaking length of the strings, but the classical bridge is quite different from that of the steel-string flat-top. Rather than channelling the strings into the body through six holes, where they are anchored by bridge pins, the classical guitar's strings – which lack ball-ends – are threaded through holes in a portion of the top of the bridge called a "tie block", and twisted around themselves to anchor them behind the saddle.

Another difference is seen at the headstock of the classical guitar, which uses a slotted design with tuner keys extending at right angles backward from it, and posts that are anchored within the slots. Classical guitars do not typically feature pickguards. That's partly because the strumming and plucking techniques used to play them – which employ the fingertips and nails of the right hand – are rarely vigorous enough to scratch the guitar, and partly in an effort to minimize any extraneous material that might impede the resonance of the guitar's top.

FLAMENCO GUITARS

Although they appear to be much the same as classical guitars, given their nylon strings and general body shape, flamenco guitars are made with slightly different goals in mind. The instruments used for this percussive, extremely dynamic and occasionally aggressive style of guitar playing are – perhaps counter-intuitively – usually lighter and thinner than classical guitars, and are more likely to feature Spanish cypress or sycamore, and tops of spruce or cedar.

The bodies are generally a bit smaller than those of classical guitars, but given their lightness and quick response, they still achieve volume and projection, important qualities if they are to adequately accompany the often loud, nail-shoed dance that is part and parcel of flamenco's *raison d'être*.

Unlike a classical guitar, a genuine flamenco guitar does carry a form of scratchplate known as a golpeador, or "tap plate", required to protect the body from the percussive finger tapping that is part of the flamenco playing style (often this golpeador isn't noticed by the novice at first glance, since today they are frequently made from transparent plastic). Many flamenco guitars today have headstocks that resemble those of classical guitars, but some players and manufacturers alike still favour the old-fashioned friction pegs – wooden tuning keys much like those used on violins, which are held in place only by the friction of the holes into which the slightly cone-shaped posts are inserted.

ARCHTOP ACOUSTICS

The archtop guitar ruled the roost among professional players from the late 1920s to the 40s, but the wholly acoustic form of this instrument is rarely seen today outside the jazz world, and even there it's in the minority amid the many electrified variants that have evolved from it. While a few contemporary musicians outside the jazz world have rediscovered the warm, rich pleasures a good archtop acoustic can offer, few understand the significant differences between these guitars and their otherwise similarly shaped flat-top cousins. Much more than just a flat-top with f-holes instead of a round soundhole, an archtop acoustic guitar is designed and constructed very differently from the more popular breeds of acoustic guitar, and sounds quite different, too.

Orville Gibson, founder of the legendary Gibson guitar brand, single-handedly invented the archtop guitar in the 1890s, working in his back-room shop in Kalamazoo, Michigan, patterning it on existing archtop instruments such as the cello, mandocello, and violin. Several makers of flat-top guitars were already working in the US – C.F. Martin and Washburn being the most notable among them – but these instruments really were poor relations to the more popular mandolins, violins, and banjos, which retained their top-dog status through the first quarter of the following century.

Throughout the 1930s, however, guitars were replacing banjos as a preferred rhythm instrument on the bandstand, thanks in part to Gibson's development of pivotal new designs. Advances in pickups and amplification would soon take the wind out of the purely acoustic archtop guitar's sails (and sales), but it would remain dear to the hearts of many musicians playing the jazz music that had its heyday alongside that of this sultry six-string.

Archtop woods & design

Archtop and flat-top acoustic guitars do share some constructional techniques and material components, but they are really very different instruments. The thing they have most in common is their fretted neck, and even those are angled very differently. The top (soundboard) of a quality archtop acoustic is laboriously hand-carved into its arched shape, usually out of solid spruce, but cedar, redwood, and other light but strong woods are sometimes used.

This requires not only the skill to undertake the carving itself, but the ability to "tap tune" the top, a technique that involves literally tapping the wood with a knuckle as you carve it into an arch, in an effort to elicit a tone and resonance that will complement the final instrument. No two pieces of spruce will sound exactly alike – or can be carved exactly alike – due to the differences in grain, density, rigidity and so forth from one to the next, and the carving process continues to balance the wood's resonance as required, until the desired tap tone is achieved.

Whereas the flat-top produces its sound through the vibration of strings anchored within a bridge mounted to the top itself, the archtop receives its acoustic energy from strings loaded in a "trapeze tailpiece" (a semi-floating tailpiece anchored at the end of the body) and exerting their downward pressure on a "floating" bridge positioned toward the centre of the guitar's lower bout. (A floating bridge is one that is laid on the top and held in place by the strings' downward pressure alone, not by any pins, screws, or glue.)

These different arrangements result in different vibration patterns and, hence, different structural requirements. X-bracing is far and away the most popular bracing technique for flat-top acoustics, and is also used in many archtops, where the braces have to be carved to fit the profile of the

The eccentric punk-blues one-man-band that is Bob Log III, playing his old archtop acoustic (with fitted pickup). He accompanies himself with a very basic drum machine and plays a kick-drum and hi-hat with his feet.

underside of the curved top. Some makers and players believe X-bracing is better suited to solo, lead, and chord-melody playing, while parallel braces (tone bars) are advantageous to rhythm playing. Frequently an X-brace is coupled to a slightly thicker top, while the parallel braces support a thinner top that offers a louder and livelier response to the strummed chord.

High-end archtops use solid woods for their backs and sides, too – figured maple being the most desirable variety. The back is, traditionally, also carved into an arch, although some are also made with flat backs. While the move to amplification made the use of a laminated top entirely acceptable in many great acoustic-electric archtop models, lam-top archtops have never been praised for their properties as purely acoustic instruments. This is not to say that you can't elicit entirely satisfactory acoustic tones from an archtop made with a laminated top, but the full depth and nuance of an acoustic archtop is best exhibited by guitars with solid, carved-arch tops, and ideally solid-wood backs and sides as well.

The better archtop acoustics are likely to be made with maple necks to match their maple backs and sides, and fingerboards of either rosewood or ebony. Many examples do carry mahogany necks, too, particularly when the aesthetic continuity of a uniform wood grain isn't required. From the front, the neck of an archtop guitar will look very similar to that of a flat-top, and non-cutaway examples traditionally have similar 14th-fret neck/body joints. View it side-on, however, and its constructional differences emerge. The archtop's trapeze tailpiece and floating bridge raise the strings higher off the body at the bridge saddle than does the flat-top's flat, integral bridge and saddle, so the archtop's neck must be attached at a slight pitch, or downward angle. In addition to this, the fingerboard extension (the portion extending over the body) on many archtop guitars will "float". That is, it will not be glued to the body top itself, in order to raise it to the height required without impeding the vibration of the top.

A quality archtop will display warmth and fatness in the notes in both the high and low frequencies, with a woody depth and richness that is round and even, yet still punchy enough to provide good definition. It's a tone that is quite different from that of a good flat-top acoustic – not better, not inferior, but purely different – and is far less familiar to most ears today, too. Of course, any effort to project the sound of an archtop acoustic to anything but the most intimate of audiences will involve amplifying it in some way.

The purest means for recording or concert performance, in the tonal sense, is to strategically position a quality microphone (or several) in front of the guitar, but many artists also mount internal piezo pickups similar to those used to amplify flat-top acoustic guitars. Magnetic pickups are also used, where they are mounted in a "floating" fashion by attaching them to the end of the fingerboard or to the pickguard, so they don't touch and potentially dampen the vibrating top of the instrument (and herein lies the birth of the electric guitar). Despite its "jazz box" image, acoustic archtops can be found in the hands of everyone from country crooner Lyle Lovett, to Texas blueser Jimmie Vaughan, to Americana picker Kurt Wagner of Lambchop, to folk maestro David Rawlings of Gillian Welch and Old Crow Medicine Show.

ELECTRIC GUITARS

Conventional wisdom has it that any guitar newbie should start out on an acoustic. Perhaps this was simply because the acoustic came first. Or perhaps it's because beginners's acoustic guitars were for many years more affordable than good-quality electrics. In this postmodern age of the instrument, however, anything goes. If you have been drawn to the guitar primarily by a love of music played on the electric guitar, consider starting there (and vice versa).

There are many starter guitar-and-amp sets available today from reputable companies at extremely reasonable prices, and the quality of instruments and accessories in these is better today than ever before – in terms of playability in particular. Also, there are several affordable amp and effects simulators on the market that enable you to practise with headphones or earbuds, which also helps to forestall any protests from parents, housemates, or neighbours. In any case, any player who pursues their discovery of the instrument beyond the beginner stage is likely to want to explore both the acoustic and the electric breeds eventually, and it pays to know a little something about all of what's out there.

As we discovered in Chapter 1, there's a great diversity to the electric guitar market. There are more variables with the electric guitar than with the acoustic, although many of the crucial components do much the same thing (even if they look like entirely different pieces of hardware). In this section, we'll get into the real nitty-gritty details of the different types of pickups, bridges, tuners, body and neck woods, designs, controls and electronics that you'll find on a wide range of electric guitars. We'll discuss not only how they function, but how they form the unique sound and feel of many iconic electric guitars.

The electric guitar is an excellent example of an old adage, in that each and every instrument is much more than the sum of its parts. (It's also occasionally much *less*, when good components have been put together poorly.) Virtually every single item that is glued, screwed, inlaid or bolted into or onto an electric guitar has a role in determining its overall sound.

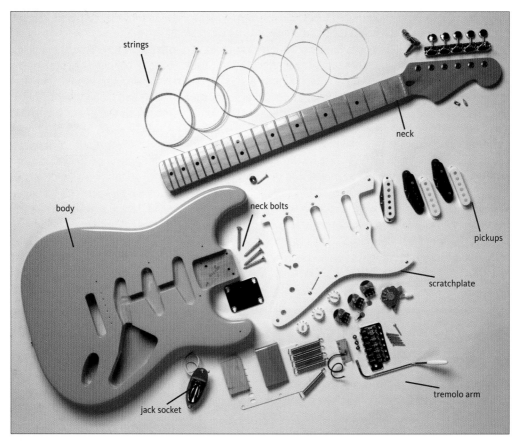

strings

neck

body

neck bolts

pickups

scratchplate

tremolo arm

jack socket

An electric guitar anatomy lesson. This is what your axe looks like in bits.

That said, there's also a degree of unquantifiable magic in the tone of any truly superlative electric guitar, and sometimes you just can't gauge the way the same woods and hardware components will conspire to make outwardly similar instruments sound and perform slightly differently. An analysis on paper can only ever get us in the ballpark, whereas the real game begins when you pick up as many different guitars as you can get your hands on and try them out for yourself.

Body woods

As with acoustic guitars, the different wood types used in the manufacture of electrics have different resonant properties, and help to shape the voice of any given instrument. While electric guitars are occasionally mistaken, usually by the uninitiated, as largely a plank of wood with a pickup bolted to it (the implication being that it's the pickup that matters most), the type and quality of wood used in that plank, and the way it is shaped and assembled, play an enormous part in determining the guitar's tone.

Every note is shaped in an interaction between string, hardware (nut and bridge, mainly), and wood, irrespective of its conversion into an electrical audio signal by the pickups, and the briefest glance at any electric guitar tells you that the wood accounts for the greatest mass of all of these components. Experienced players and guitar-makers alike can often even determine the quality of an electric guitar's tone by listening closely to the instrument unplugged, and although this sound will certainly be moulded by any electrical effects and amplification the guitar goes through further down the signal chain, its fundamental nature usually remains intact.

Many guitar-makers' wood selections – and many players' purchase decisions – are also influenced by the look of the wood a guitar is made with, so aesthetics certainly play a part here, too. Any given tonewood's sound is usually the first consideration, however, and samples that have a particular visual appeal are usually selected from among a batch of appropriate timber.

Mahogany

As popular a body wood in electric guitars as it is in acoustic flat-tops, mahogany has a warm, round and thick tone that is well balanced and offers good bite and definition, with a muscular mid-range. Good cuts of mahogany usually offer excellent tonal depth in well-made guitars, with highs and lows that are full but not overly pronounced or harsh.

This fairly dense, medium-to-heavy wood is harvested primarily in Africa and Central America. It can result in guitars with a wide range of body weights, depending upon timber stocks used, but light to medium-light examples are usually most prized by players. In its raw, unfinished state, mahogany has a light-brown hue with a fine, tight grain. The right translucent finishing process can give it a shimmering golden or bronze appearance under the right light, and it also takes translucent cherry finishes well. Mahogany is probably best known as the body wood of several Gibson solidbody models, and is often seen in guitars by other makers that follow that type. In addition to being used on its own, mahogany is also frequently paired with maple in multi-wood bodies.

Maple

A dense, hard, heavy wood harvested mostly (for use in guitar-making) from trees grown in both the northeastern and northwestern US and Canada, maple is usually used as one of two or more ingredients in multi-wood bodies (usually paired with mahogany. Some makers have also used all-maple bodies, but unless these are kept very thin the weight can be off-putting.

On its own, maple's sonic signature is tight, bright and precise; its highs can tend toward the harsh (in an all-maple configuration), while its lows are firm but not especially fat. A light-coloured wood with a varied grain, maple is also used as much for its appearance as for its sound. Some, though not all, examples of maple – known in the trade as curly maple – exhibit dramatic figuring that can be emphasized in the finishing process. The results are seen in the attractive flame, quilt and tiger-stripe patterns that appear in some high-end instruments.

Maple-mahogany

In examining this popular wood combination, it's impossible to avoid citing Gibson yet again, which used this pairing in the legendary Les Paul Standard, with a carved maple cap atop a mahogany body. Later makers such as Hamer, Paul Reed Smith, Dean, and many, many others have followed suit. This combination has become as much a classic as any single-wood template.

The mahogany-maple body offers a "best of both worlds" scenario, both tonally and visually. The maple adds some tightness and snap to the mahogany's tonal response, which adds depth and warmth to what an otherwise all-maple body might yield. Mahogany helps to lighten the load, while maple dresses up the package. All in all, it's easy to see why this collaboration has stayed with us for six decades and counting.

Ash

In its most prized form, as "swamp ash" harvested from the lowest portions of trees grown in the wetlands of the southern states of the US, this wood is light, sturdy, and tone enhancing. Ash trees with root systems below water level yield a wood that has expanded, taking on more water than most trees normally hold. It becomes light and resonant when the water in the expanded cells within the timber eventually dries out and is replaced with air. When players enthuse over the sound of an ash body, they are usually talking about swamp ash, and are referring to a tone that is twangy, open and sweet, with firm lows, pleasant highs and a slightly "scooped" mid-range.

This is very much the sound of the 1950s Fender Telecaster and mid-to-late 50s sunburst and blonde Fender Stratocaster, the bodies of which were made primarily with this wood – as well as of other later makers who have sought to emulate that sound.

Harder ash from trees grown farther north in the US has also been used for guitar-making, as has timber from the upper, and less waterlogged, portions of wetlands trees. This wood tends to be denser and heavier than swamp ash, and contributes to a brighter, harder tone that might be advantageous to more cutting, distorted guitar styles.

Alder

If ash is commonly regarded as first among Fender body woods, alder is certainly the second. When good supplies of light, well-seasoned swamp ash became scarcer in the late 50s and early 60s, Fender turned to alder – and for its opaque custom-colour guitars in particular, which didn't show ash's plainer grain beneath their nitrocellulose lacquer. It just so happens, though, that alder is a superb tonewood in its own right, and has found its place in the pantheon of legendary guitar components right beside its swampy predecessor.

If ash is the sound of the 50s Tele, alder is the sound of the early 60s Strat: its tone is bold, clear and full bodied, with chunky lower mids, tight lows and smooth highs. Ever since Fender's employment of it in the late 50s, this timber – sourced mostly from the northwestern US – has remained popular with many electric-guitar makers, used mainly in single-wood bodies, but also in some recent multi-wood designs.

Basswood

Although it is often associated with budget and mid-level guitars (wherein it first appeared as a replacement for pricier ash or alder), basswood (also known as American linden) is a good tonewood by any standards, and has recently received its due in many more thoughtful electric-guitar designs from high-end makers such as Suhr.

This light and relatively soft wood offers good tonal balance, with a full mid-range and a somewhat open and airy feel throughout the sonic spectrum. It is a fairly plain-looking wood, with little discernible grain, and its appearance in the final instrument really depends upon the finish applied to it.

Korina

A relative of mahogany, this African wood (generically known as limba) is lighter both in weight and appearance, and offers distinct tonal refinements as well. Many high-end contemporary manufacturers have made use of its admirable blend of resonance, warmth, sweetness and sustain, which was first heard on the short-lived (but enthusiastically revived) Gibson Flying V and Explorer of 1958–60. Korina is usually given a translucent finish, occasionally with a soft stain to bring out a vintage-yellow or golden hue in the wood.

Poplar

Traditionally used in flooring and furniture, this relatively soft breed of hardwood has surfaced in many budget-range, Asian-made electric guitars in recent years. Its inherent tone offers nothing particularly distinctive, but that also means it's a fairly malleable timber to work with, in sonic terms, and the results depend largely upon other factors of the instrument's construction.

Exotic alternatives

Given the scarcity of the best supplies of more traditional tonewoods, guitar-makers are always in search of suitable alternatives. Several other woods are used to make electric guitar bodies, some of which are rare woods that specific makers use for their tonal properties, others of which are largely decorative, and are added to bodies that are generally constructed out of more common tonewoods. Rosewood, a popular fingerboard wood, is occasionally used in bodies, and becomes a more exotic alternative in this application. Walnut, while not extremely exotic, has also been used for bodies and necks.

Fancier, and more unusual, types include wenge, koa, bubinga and purple heart, as well as some woods that are better associated with carpentry luthiery, such as oak and cherry.

The Gibson Flying V, originally made of Korina, seen in the more-than-capable hands of blues legend Albert King.

Neck & fingerboard woods

The first consideration in choosing wood to shape a guitar's neck from is clearly the strength offered by any given variety, but electric guitar necks do also contribute to the overall tone of the instrument. Any time a string is plucked, vibrational energy is transferred into the fingerboard and neck via either the nut or the frets, and from there is transferred into the body, where it becomes part of the overall sonic blend that the pickups send to the amplifier. As such, fingerboard woods also play their part, although they have less impact on any guitar's sound than the neck itself, which in turn has a smaller role than the body wood.

Most players will select a guitar for many other factors before considering the neck wood's tonal contribution, and if the neck feels right in the hand they aren't likely to baulk at a particular timber, as long as the rest of the guitar is to their liking. Fingerboard wood, on the other hand, does have a bigger "feel factor" and maple, rosewood and ebony all feel quite different to the fingertips.

Maple

This strong, dense wood was popular with makers of hollowbody archtop guitars long before the solidbody came to town. Ever since Leo Fender put it on his Telecaster (originally Esquire/ Broadcaster) in 1950, however, it has been associated with that instrument – largely because Fender generally feature it in a one-piece construction with integral maple neck and fingerboard. Used in this way, maple contributes added snap and brightness to an ash or alder-bodied guitar.

Topped with a fingerboard of a different wood, it will add tightness and cutting power to an instrument's tone. While the classic Fender maple neck/fingerboard was carved out of one piece of wood, with a truss rod inserted into a channel routed into the back, other makers (most notably Ernie Ball/Music Man) have constructed two-piece necks out of a single plank of maple, by slicing a fillet off the top, inserting the truss rod, and glueing the thin fingerboard back onto the neck.

Pairing a maple neck with a rosewood fingerboard serves to warm and sweeten its tonal characteristics somewhat, while adding some roundness to the lows and a smooth depth to the highs.

Mahogany

The other most popular neck wood is a little softer and lighter than maple – though still very strong – and is never used for fingerboards, other than in some very cheap beginner's instruments of years past. The tonal contribution of a mahogany neck is heard in its warmth, balance and mid-range presence. Although as mahogany necks are frequently paired with mahogany bodies, the sonic presence of this lesser plank of timber is likely to be buried within the bigger picture.

A mahogany neck will most often be paired with a rosewood fingerboard, where that added fillet of wood contributes some creaminess to the lows and complexity to the highs. Several guitars – some high-end models in particular – carry mahogany necks with ebony fingerboards. This dark, hard, extremely dense wood wears very well, and doesn't divot (scar, nick or wear away) under finger-and-string pressure as easily as rosewood does.

It also sounds somewhat different, however, and is characterized by a fast attack, firm lows and snappy, sizzling highs.

Pau ferro

This central American hardwood is fairly dense and hard, with a tight grain, and has seen increased use in recent years as a fingerboard wood. It offers some of ebony's smooth feel blended with rosewood's tonal depth and warmth. It has chunky lows, muscular lower mids and complex highs.

A neck is fitted into the body of a Strat-style electric.

BODY & NECK DESIGN

The way that any guitar is put together will have an enormous impact on its sound – more so than its woods, pickups, hardware and other components. Different body shapes, constructional techniques, neck joints and so on are combined with very specific sound and performance goals in mind, and better-made guitars are manufactured to consciously achieve the desired ends of their designers, rather than slapped together in a "let's see what this does" sort of fashion.

The different templates all have their different sounds, and it's worth learning something about the voice you can expect to hear from each. The best way to do this is to take a look at the characteristics of half a dozen of the classic templates of the electric guitar.

Bolt necks: Fender Teles & Strats

After experimenting with a few prototypes the year before, Fender released the first commercially successful mass-produced solidbody electric guitar in 1950. Other makers had experimented with the format, and the solidbody was seen by many as a desirable means of helping to cut the feedback problems that hollowbody electrics experienced at higher volumes, while also improving sustain and tonal definition. First briefly named the Esquire, then Broadcaster (while the Esquire name was given to the one-pickup version), Fender's ground-breaking solidbody has forever after been known as the Telecaster, the name it was given in mid 1951.

This model, and the Stratocaster that followed it in 1954, have come to typify the "bolt-neck tone", and while there are many other factors that contribute to their bright, cutting sound, their bolt-on necks (which are actually screwed on) do play a part in this sonic signature. A screwed-on neck – especially one of maple, attached to an ash or alder body carved from a single species of wood –

lends a snappy, percussive response to the guitar, with a slightly compressed feel as the pick initially attacks the strings, but an explosive response as the note bursts to life. This template also tends to have a slightly scooped mid-range, with firm lows and ringing, jangly highs.

Other elements of these Fender guitars – and those from other makers that have emulated them over the years – also contribute to this bright, twangy voice. The single-coil pickups on Telecasters and Stratocasters are very lively, while their bridges also enhance this ringing, bell-like treble, and even the 25.5" scale length on which the guitar is built (the length of the strings from saddle to nut) is a significant but oft-overlooked factor, reinforcing a bright and chimey response, but with full, firm lows.

While the Telecaster bridge's simple, stamped-steel base plate, its brass or steel saddles and its through-body stringing (more of which later) combine to lend a

AC/DC's lead guitarist Angus Young has played a Gibson SG (and dressed in school uniform) for the entire duration of his guitar-playing career.

sharp response and a lot of sustain to its tone, the Stratocaster's spring-loaded vibrato bridge gives it a slightly more compressed and forgiving feel under the pick, and a somewhat rounder, more springy tone as well. Their similar neck and body construction and their single-coil pickups mean both are bright, twangy, jangly electrics, but they are nonetheless very different guitars: both offer some versatile voices well beyond these easy categories.

Consider the facts that Jimmy Page used a Telecaster for many early Led Zeppelin recordings, that Bill Frisell uses one for eclectic jazz excursions, or that Jimi Hendrix turned a Stratocaster – originally designed for country and western artists – into one of the most sought-after rock guitars of all time, and you realize that nothing is set in stone.

Set necks: the Gibson Les Paul & SG

Released as Gibson's answer to the Fender Tele, the Les Paul is the other archetypal solidbody electric guitar. Although it was seen as radical at the time, its long-established manufacturer gave it many more traditional elements, details that echoed the archtop electrics that players were more familiar with. As such, the Les Paul emerged from the factory a very different instrument from the slab-bodied, bolt-neck guitars of Fender. The Les Paul had (and still has) a carved, arched maple top on a solid mahogany back, a glued-in mahogany neck (often called a "set neck"), and traditional decorative touches such as a raised pickguard and celluloid binding around its body top and rosewood fingerboard.

The body and neck construction gave this guitar a warmer, thicker sound from the start, with different sustain characteristics and a rounder, fatter tonal signature overall. It so happens that the Les Paul's slightly shorter 24.75" scale-length also enhanced this warm, round, slightly furry tone.

It all gave the Les Paul a different core tonality, which is to say its attack and dynamics are very different from those of the Tele or Strat. The glued-in neck transfers resonance between neck and body more freely and immediately, a phenomenon that often results in more fullness in the set-neck instrument. The mahogany neck and body also contribute to overall warmth and prominent mid-range, while the maple top enhances definition and cutting power. Having said that, all this warmth and thickness makes it difficult for a Les Paul-style guitar to achieve the brightness and clarity of a Tele or Strat-style guitar, and the scale and pickup choices fuzz things further.

The shorter scale makes the Les Paul easier to bend notes on, and its flatter fingerboard (12" rather than Fender's much rounder 7.25" radius) helps players push those blues notes to extremes.

In 1961 Gibson revamped the Les Paul design into an all-mahogany, double-cutaway body style (which would be renamed the SG a couple of years later). Although most other components remained the same or similar, this would bring a subtle but noticeable alteration to the model's sound. Perhaps a little less complex than the Les Paul tone, and with slightly less sustain, the SG tone is also slightly snappier, but still warm, thick and rich – a classic tone in its own right.

Both the Les Paul and SG provide further examples of genre-busting electrics: designed for the jazz, pop and dance band players of their day, they became archetypal blues-rock and even heavy metal instruments when players in the mid-to-late 60s rediscovered them and rammed them through cranked-up Marshall amps.

Semi-acoustics & archtop electrics

Earlier in this chapter we looked at some of the basic principles behind archtop acoustic guitars. Proper archtop electrics really just evolved out of them: guitarists in the 1930s began attaching pickups to their instruments in order to play them through the amplifiers that were becoming available, and manufacturers soon cottoned onto the trend – they started to offer guitars with pickups installed at the factory. Gibson's ES-150, released in 1936, was the first factory-fitted electric guitar from a major maker.

One would reasonably assume that the semi-acoustic electric guitar was, therefore, an evolutionary step on the road from fully acoustic archtop to solidbody, but in fact this variation only arrived some years after the solidbody had assaulted the market. Nevertheless, it is a stylistic halfway house between the full-bodied archtop and the solidbody electric.

The goals of feedback resistance and improved sustain led to the development of the solidbody electric, and this instrument was already gaining followers by the mid-50s, but the style, feel and tone of early solidbodies – derided as "planks" and "canoe paddles" by some traditional-minded players – still didn't fit many guitarists' image of what a guitar should be. They wanted the performance benefits of the solidbody designs, but also desired a more traditional instrument, with the outward appearance of the old "jazz box".

Gibson took an early stab at making the archtop both more comfortable and more feedback resistant with its "thinline" Byrdland and ES-350T models of 1955, but in 1958 it went a step further. By installing a centre block of solid wood between the arched front and back of its thinline, double-cutaway ES-335, Gibson established the semi-acoustic electric guitar. Its body retains some acoustic elements, but is also partially solid.

This combination gives the semi a warm, round, full tone that is somewhat reminiscent of the archtop jazz guitar, but also yields more snap and clarity along with it. As such, it's an extremely

Americana artist Devon Sproule's archtop is a crucial part of her warm, retro sound.

versatile design, and great players have used this type of guitar for everything from traditional jazz, to blues, rock and country.

Meanwhile, throughout the 50s Gibson and others had still been having success with their updates of the full-depth archtop electric, adding elements such as top-mounted (rather than floating) pickups and steel bridges to the brew, making them more suitable for the contemporary music of the day. In 1949 Gibson had introduced its ES-175 with a laminated top (which was an early bid to cut feedback from the archtop, rather than to merely cheapen its construction) and the more rigid laminated top was now the standard with many archtop electrics.

Gretsch, in particular, was an early front runner in the rock'n'roll boom of the 1950s and early 60s, and the company attained this position initially on the strength of fully hollow archtop electric models such as the 6120 Chet Atkins Hollowbody. Despite its snazzy translucent orange finish, deluxe fingerboard inlays, and vibrato tailpiece, the 6120 wasn't much different, in principle at least, from the jazz boxes that preceded it. But today the guitar screams rockabilly. Tonally, it blends good bite and twang with a little more warmth and breadth than most solidbodies can achieve.

Semi-solid & chambered guitars

The Gretsch company also brought us another successful model in the 1950s – one that introduced yet another category of instrument. The "chambered" or "semi-solid" electric was marketed simply as a solidbody at the time: the black Gretsch Duo Jet (Jet Fire Bird in red, Silver Jet in silver sparkle), released in 1953, looks outwardly like a solidbody electric with a body shape similar to that of a Les Paul, but its mahogany body and pressed-arched maple top actually conceal a number of hollow pockets.

This was done to simplify construction and reduce the weight of the guitar, and wasn't promoted as a design feature at the time. (In fact, the same guitar with a different finish became the subtly misleading Chet Atkins Solidbody model in 1955.) The Duo Jet and its siblings also have glued-in necks, but retain more archtop-like elements in their floating bridges and trapeze tailpieces. The combination of these ingredients, alongside the single-coil pickups they debuted with, produced a twangy, snappy tone that nevertheless had plenty of girth to it.

Very different from either the Fender or Gibson offerings of the day, the Duo Jet presented another classic sound of rock'n'roll, and they've been played by everyone from Bo Diddley, to Gene Vincent's guitarist Cliff Gallup, to LA's punkabilly grinder Billy Zoom (of the band X).

Several other makers have employed the chambering that arrived unseen in the Duo Jet. Rickenbacker introduced several models throughout the 50s and 60s. Fender debuted its own Telecaster Thinline in 1968, with chambered body and one F-hole (still with bolt-on neck and other traditional Tele appointments). And contemporary manufacturers such as Tom Anderson Guitarworks and G&L have made great use of the approach, producing semi-solid models with and without F-holes.

On the whole, adding some chambering to an otherwise solid body tends to introduce a little more roundness to the tone, alongside a slight mid-range honk.

Other contemporary electrics

While the US's Fender, Gibson, Gretsch and Rickenbacker, and Europe's Vox, Burns and Hofner, are all true classic electrics of the golden age of guitar design, it's the first two of these companies that became the most copied on the planet. And numerous creative manufacturers have drawn from

One of Gibson's 1960s guitars: the ES350T.

elements of the Gibson and Fender templates to produce excellent guitars that look and feel nothing like copies, and which have plenty of original and innovative twists of their own.

Upon its move to wide-scale manufacture in the 1980s, Paul Reed Smith (PRS) was often regarded as a hybrid of Gibson and Fender designs. The company's core models featured a 25" scale length,

a modified Fender-like vibrato in a carved, arched maple top, and humbucking pickups – with glued-in necks on its upmarket models and bolt-neck construction on its more affordable guitars.

Indeed, these elements, along with pickup switching that allowed a player to roll from humbucking to faux-single-coil tones – see overleaf – on the same guitar, did woo a great many players who were looking for a best-of-both-worlds instrument. Today, PRS offers instruments that appeal to the traditional Gibson-style player, others that provide much Fender-like versatility, and a little of everything in between. So it's impossible to pin the maker down to one core sound, unless, perhaps, that sound is defined as "modern, functional, versatile".

Not that PRS was the first to blend a little Fender with a little Gibson. From the mid-1970s several manufacturers – some of which started out as custom luthiers and parts manufacturers – mined the popular vein of guitars that came to be known as "superstrats". Charvel, Jackson and Kramer all made headway in the market by offering guitars with Strat-style bodies, necks and vibratos, with humbucking pickups (in the bridge position in particular) and other hot-rod elements. Major Japanese manufacturers Ibanez and Yamaha have taken up the cause, and today offer numerous models that particularly suit the needs of the "shredder" crowd that came into their own in the 1980s: the rock guitarists who push the boundaries of speed and technique, who have long been drawn to the superstrat configuration.

Plenty of other companies that started up well after the 60s have made, and continue to make, some very good guitars, examples of which occasionally echo designs from Fender or Gibson (and occasionally Gretsch or Rickenbacker too), but which, ultimately, have voices of their own, and resolutely refuse to be pigeonholed as copies of anything. It so happens that companies such as Dean, Hamer and Carvin in the US, and Eggle, Fret-King and Gordon-Smith in the UK, have tilted more toward Gibson in the details, but each offers thoroughly original instruments that run to many diverse styles and sounds besides the trad carved-top-and-humbuckers formula. On the other hand, makers such as Tom Anderson, G&L, Ernie Ball/Music Man, Don Grosh and John Suhr largely got their start emulating Fender styles, although most have diversified significantly.

In short, the sky really is the limit today, and there are plenty of excellent makers out there that are ready and willing to design any form of electric guitar that the player can possibly conceive. While ultra-modern incarnations win over many adventurous guitarists, however, the vast majority of players continue to be drawn to a handful of standards that were pretty much set in stone a good 55 years ago.

COMPONENTS OF THE ELECTRIC GUITAR

This section began by stating that any great electric guitar is much more than the sum of its parts. But those individual parts do make a difference, and they work toward shaping the sound of every guitar you will encounter. Beyond the value of understanding the components' contribution to the performance of different instruments, it's worth knowing a little bit about what each does and how it sounds in case you want to modify a guitar you might already own.

Pickups

A pickup translates the plucked string into a signal that can be reproduced by an amplifier. This component is the very heart of what makes an electric guitar electric. So crucial is the pickup, and so sensitive is its performance, that tiny alterations in the design of otherwise identical units will lead to clear differences of tone. Extreme differences in design can also lead to extreme differences of tone and yet, conversely, similar tones can be arrived at using very different techniques. Change the number of turns in the coil and you change its sound. Change the size of its magnet(s) and you change its sound. Change the material that the wire or the magnet(s) are made from and you change its sound. Get the picture?

The main talking points concern the types of magnets used, and the type, gauge and quantity of wire that the coil is wound with. Pickups are made with one or more long-bar magnets, or individual rod magnets for each string. These can be either old-school alnico or more modern ceramic magnets, and each style and each material has its own performance properties and its own sonic variables. Pickup coils are usually wound with between 42- and 44-gauge wire, but what is often considered more significant is the number of turns of wire used – more wire equating to a hotter, louder output.

Pickups are split into two broad camps, referred to as "single-coil pickups" and "humbucking pickups", and there are many different types within each category. Single-coil pickups employ just one coil to convert the string vibration sensed by the magnet(s) into an electrical signal. Humbucking pickups pair two coils wound to opposite polarities and positioned either side by side or stacked one above the other, so that when the signals from the two coils are summed together they retain the sound of the guitar but reject the hum that can be induced by external electrical sources.

These basic differences of format have their own different sounds, too, quite apart from any hum-rejecting considerations. Generally, the wider the pickup, the warmer and thicker its sound; the narrower a pickup, the brighter and more tightly defined its sound. Many other factors affect pickup performance, too, as mentioned above, but this description is the essential difference between humbuckers and single coils. While, for example, a Fender Stratocaster single-coil pickup and a Gibson Les Paul humbucking pickup are both very versatile designs, and are used by a wide range of players to make myriad styles of music, they are very different building blocks. For most savvy players, choosing between humbucker and single-coil is a starting point for your sound.

Fender-style single-coil pickups

Although pickups of roughly similar design had been around for some twenty years, Fender's early pickups established what we think of today as the single-coil sound. Leo Fender himself had used similar pickups on his lap-steel guitars of the late 1950s, but we know these units and their distinctive sounds from the Tele and Strat. First used on the Broadcaster in 1950 (renamed Telecaster in 1951), the Tele bridge pickup set the standard for bright-yet-meaty twang tones and became a staple of the country guitar sound, before going on to work its magic on countless great blues, rock, indie and alternative recordings over the years.

This pickup is made with six individual alnico rod magnets inserted into top and bottom fibre plates (known as coil formers), with several thousand turns of fine-gauge wire wound around them. In addition, any authentic Tele-style bridge pickup also has a copper-plated tin base plate mounted to its bottom, which serves to focus the magnetic field slightly, and to enhance its mid-range response. This simple yet effective design yields a lot of sparkle and definition but, in many instances, still offers enough output to help drive a tube amp into slight break-up. The Telecaster neck pickup is similarly constructed, but uses smaller fibre plates. It has no base plate, and its magnetic pole pieces are hidden beneath a metal cover.

Fender's Stratocaster pickup is constructed much like a Tele pickup, but is a little narrower and carries fewer turns of coil wire; it also lacks the Tele bridge pickup's base plate. These variations make the Strat pickup slightly brighter and snappier, and result in a little less output. While making this pickup sound a little thinner in the bridge position, the Stratocaster neck pickup tone is often considered one of the sweetest in electric guitar music, with its blend of rich warmth and steely articulation, and is a particular favourite of many blues players. The wiring of the Fender Stratocaster's three pickups is also noteworthy; originally, Fender made this guitar with a simple three-way switch that selected each pickup individually, but a five-way switch was added later.

Many players were making this a common modification before Fender finally introduced it, and it allows the added two combinations of bridge+middle and neck+middle. Both of Fender's archetypal single coils have become standards in the industry, and have been reproduced in both vintage-style and heavily modified units by a number of pickup makers.

Gibson-style P-90 single-coil pickup

Perhaps surprisingly, Gibson was making single-coil pickups well before Fender guitars even came into existence. The company's most popular example, the P-90 (also sometimes referred to as a

Other single coils

It's impossible to keep track of all the variations on the theme that clever pickup makers have come up with over the past sixty years, but a handful of other designs do warrant particular mention. Danelectro's bright, spanky "lipstick-tube pickup", which derives its name from the fact that original units really were built within two chromed lipstick covers, has won many fans over the years, and has been the subject of many reworkings from other manufacturers.

Fender's Jaguar and Jazzmaster pickups have plenty of followers – the latter in particular, which offers a slightly thicker tone than the other classic Fender designs, but still retains plenty of brightness and clarity. Burns's Tri-Sonic pickups have won kudos from many corners, and were even the choice of Queen's Brian May for his homemade "Red Special" guitar.

Gibson's simple Melody Maker pickup, which looks like a covered Fender single-coil but is actually made with a coil wound directly around an alnico bar magnet, has some devoted followers, too.

"soapbar" or "dogear" pickup in its two different mounting configurations) was introduced in 1946, but predecessors to it had existed since the late 30s. It is made with two alnico bar magnets mounted beneath a wide, flat coil wound with approximately ten thousand turns of 42-gauge wire, with six threaded, adjustable steel pole pieces that look like short bolts running through the centre of the coil.

The steel pole pieces give the P-90 more kick in the mid-range frequencies when compared to a Fender-style single coil, and also add a slightly gritty sizzle to its tone. The wide, fat coil also gives it more warmth and thickness although, being a single coil, it still has a bright edge to it. Having been the standard pickup on Gibson's great jazz guitars of the late 40s and early 50s, the P-90 appeared on the first Les Paul of 1952 and was retained until it was replaced by the new humbucker in 1957. It then remained in use on other popular Gibsons such as the Les Paul and SG Special and Junior, and the ES-330 and ES-125. This is another archetypal pickup that has been reproduced by countless other pickup manufacturers, and it remains enormously popular today.

Gretsch/DeArmond single-coil pickup

Gretsch guitars of the early to mid-50s used a single-coil pickup made by the DeArmond company, the Model 200, which Gretsch renamed the DynaSonic when it

Queen's Brian May, helped by his dad, made his own electric guitar using a British-made Burns Tri-Sonic pickup.

appeared on its original 6120, Duo Jet and other models. It's a pickup that's been copied by other makers far more rarely than those of Fender and Gibson, partly because of its extremely complex design. But it was no less responsible for the formative sounds of rock'n'roll.

It uses six alnico-rod pole pieces, and has a complicated "monkey-on-a-stick" adjustment mechanism that requires an individual screw, spring and harness. This enables the player to independently raise and lower each magnet to adjust the string-to-string output (these extra adjustment screws lead some people to assume they are humbucking pickups). Bright and well defined, the Model 200/DynaSonic can also give plenty of bite and snarl when played through a cranked amplifier.

Rickenbacker "toaster-top" single-coil pickup

Mention "jangle" in respect to guitar music and many people will picture a Rickenbacker in the hands of Roger McGuinn of The Byrds or George Harrison of The Beatles – each of which were equipped with that maker's own "toaster-top" pickups. These were named after the parallel indentations in their chromed covers: they might outwardly appear to be humbuckers, but are actually single-coil units, with a single row of six alnico-magnet pole pieces aligned down the centre of the coil, between the black inserts at either side of the cover.

Toaster-top pickups were wound with a very fine gauge of wire to a relatively low output, for a bright, chimey sound. Expose one to the wilder exploits of a player like Pete Townshend of The Who, who often used a Rickenbacker in the band's early days, and they can create plenty of meat and snarl as desired.

In 1969 Rickenbacker introduced a second notable single-coil unit, its "High-Gain" pickup, better known to players as the "button-top", thanks to the six rounded, button-like tops of its steel pole pieces. Made with a pair of ceramic magnets mounted beneath the coil, this was indeed a hotter pickup than the toaster-top. Although it has never been favoured as much by Rickenbacker purists, it has helped to make plenty of classic music on the guitars of Paul Weller of The Jam and Peter Buck of R.E.M., each of whom has used a later-model Rickenbacker from time to time.

Gibson humbucking pickup

Developed by Gibson engineers Seth Lover and Walter Fuller in 1955, and first used on a traditional electric guitar in 1957, the Gibson humbucker has remained the other standard pickup for more than fifty years. Original units made from 1957 to 1962 were referred to as "PAF humbuckers" because of the "Patent Applied For" stickers on their undersides, and although they were thicker and warmer-sounding than single-coil pickups of the day, they were not the hot, muddy pickups that some players think of humbuckers as being. Original PAFs, or good reproductions, offer a lot of clarity and note definition, yet are still fat and juicy sounding.

In the hands of Eric Clapton, Paul Kossoff, Jimmy Page and countless others, they established legendary rock and blues-rock tones that are still widely emulated today.

The traditional Gibson humbucker (and numerous units made in its image) uses side-by-side coils, as previously explained, which are wound in opposite directions and charged with opposite magnetic polarities. While helping to reject unwanted hum, this wide, low "magnetic window" also translates a broader range of frequencies into the electrical signal that the pickup sends to the amplifier.

Gretsch humbucking pickup

Developed virtually in parallel to Gibson's humbucker (although patented slightly later), Gretsch's own humbucking pickup follows the same electronic principles, while achieving a different tone along the way.

Wound with fewer turns of finer wire, and made with a slightly different magnet and pole-piece structure, Gretsch's so-called Filter'Tron humbucking pickup yields a brighter, snappier, chimier sound than Gibson's humbucker – which just so happens to perfectly suit the image of the Gretsch tone, following in the footsteps of the twangy yet meaty DeArmond single-coil unit that it superceded.

This is the tone of both the 6120 of Brian Setzer (rockabilly guitarist with the Stray Cats) and the White Falcon of Billy Duffy (guitarist with The Cult). A good Filter'Tron can roll from bright but gnarly rockabilly to grinding grunge rock with ease.

Hot humbucking pickup

On the heels of these classic templates, pickup manufacturers have made countless variations to account for players' requirements for increased output, improved sustain, more contemporary voicing and so on. Many do this by making what we might refer to generically as hot humbuckers: pickups with extra winds and/or stronger magnets that result in hotter signals being passed to the amplifier.

Companies such as DiMarzio and Seymour Duncan were the early leaders in the custom and modifications pickup business of the 1970s, and many other respected names have joined that long list today. Meanwhile, plenty of makers are still simply chasing the Holy Grail and trying to produce the best version of a classic, original-style PAF humbucker; very often these are the same companies that are also turning out hot contemporary-styled pickups.

Hot & noiseless single-coil pickups

The fat, crunch-inducing humbucker sound inevitably led many single-coil players to want to achieve the same tones. But without swapping guitars. The answer? Hot single-coil pickups, which have been a major retro-fit item since way back in the early 1970s. DiMarzio and Seymour Duncan developed early hot single-coils such as their SDS-one and Quarter Pounder, respectively, alongside their hot-humbucker endeavours, to offer Stratocaster and Telecaster players their own means of boosting output.

While that breed continues apace today, there has also been a major move toward "noiseless" single-coil pickups, which are essentially alternatively constructed humbucking pickups made to fit mountings meant for single-coils. In the early 80s, these two major names in pickup manufacture also patented designs for stacked humbuckers – pickups made with two coils, one on top of the other rather than side by side. They have then led the way through several further developments in the field. Others, such as Joe Barden and Bill Lawrence, have gained much respect and plenty of followers for their own individual approaches to the ultimate pickup.

As with electric guitars in general, there are so many variations of pickups on the market today that players can achieve, right from this most fundamental component, virtually any tonal response they might desire. Even so, new makers seem to join the race every week, and guitar-oriented web boards still blossom with questions such as "where can I find the most accurate vintage Strat-style pickup?" However far forward-looking designers will push the envelope, plenty of guitarists still want it the way it was done back in the early 1950s.

Electronics: controls & switches

The controls and switches through which a guitar's pickups are filtered on the way to the output jack can be ultra simple (such as the single volume and tone control on a Gibson Les Paul Junior) or extremely complex (as in the four switches and multiple volume and tone controls on a Fender Jaguar). By and large, however, the controls on 95 percent of guitars are fairly straightforward: either each pickup will have its own volume and tone control, or all will share a master tone and volume control, and there will be a switch to select either one pickup alone or two wired together. These allow the player some control over volume and EQ right from the guitar, without having to turn back to the amp every time an adjustment is required.

Note that the guitar's own volume control can only attain levels to the maximum of your volume setting on the amplifier, and is mainly used to turn the guitar down from its maximum potential volume. As such, some players set their amps for a driving lead tone, then turn the guitar's volume down to achieve a cleaner "rhythm" tone.

What's in a name?

The original big boys of the electric guitar industry, Fender, Gibson and Gretsch, and PRS after them, were for many years purely American-made brands, and as such – rightly or wrongly – helped to cultivate a "West is best" attitude in the guitar market that still persists today, to some extent, and elevated pricing to go along with it. When affordable Asian-made imports started to make a dent in these leading brands' sales figures, each eventually introduced their own Asian-made import to fight in the lower of the market, and they all maintain an entry-to-mid-level sister brand to this day.

Gibson acquired the New York-based Epiphone company way back in 1957, and manufactured Epiphone electrics in the Gibson factory in Kalamazoo, Michigan, from 1958 to 1969. After that time, however, production was moved to Japan, and Epiphone brand pricing was moved downward to the entry- and mid-level market. Today, Epiphone guitars are manufactured in a number of Asian countries and sold at a broad range of prices; most important to most new guitar buyers on a budget, they also parallel all of Gibson's most popular models, from the Les Paul and the SG to the Flying V and the ES-335 (the latter represented today by the Dot and the Sheraton II). The look and structure of these guitars hold up well in comparison to the US-made Gibson versions, while cost savings are made in the use of cheaper woods, pickups, and hardware, and of course in the more affordable Asian manufacture.

Fender launched its Squier guitars in the early 80s specifically to combat the rise in cheap imported copies of its Stratocaster and Telecaster models, and the brand has bloomed into a major entry-level line. Originally made in Japan, Squier guitars – like Epiphones – have, through the years, also been made in Korea, China and other Asian countries.

While the Japanese alternatives were originally seen as the "cheapos", Japanese manufacture now represents the high end of the Asian-made guitar market, and is saved for the more elite models of these brands. Since the mid-1980s the majority of Gretsch's high-end guitars (now called the Professional Collection) have been made in Japan, although the company's ownership and headquarters remains in the US, and the company's more affordable Electromatic Collection is manufactured in Korea and elsewhere. PRS, a major US-made alternative since the late 1980s, also recently introduced its own Asian-made range, the PRS SE series. True to form, these models often parallel popular high-end PRS guitars, but are manufactured to more affordable specifications.

Today, while these "support brands" all benefit from their associations with the big-name originals, it's also important to be aware that there are several different grades of budget-brand models, from the cream of the crop to entry level packages. It is likewise important to know what you're getting, and where it was made. As such, a Squier Stratocaster, an Epiphone Les Paul or a PRS SE Singlecut shouldn't be expected to represent the ultimate achievement of that model, which is still to be found wearing the Fender, Gibson and PRS brand names respectively, but they can present excellent value for money, and be very good playing and sounding instruments by any standards, for the guitarist whose budget falls in line with these more affordable options.

This proliferation of offshoot sister brands might have brought some confusion to the market, but if you take the time to investigate what you're buying, it can also deliver plenty of very good guitar options for the money.

Guitars with three pickups often have some compromise of options, since few practical switches exist capable of yielding the six potential individual and multi-pickup selections (or seven, if you include an all-three-together option), but clever makers have occasionally found ways around this. Other more complex switching arrays will include mini-toggle switches to choose between series, parallel and in/out-of-phase wiring of individual pickups; split-coil options (which can produce single-coil-style sounds from a humbucking pickup); and deluxe additions such as active preamps and EQ stages.

As plenty of players have discovered, however, the more switches and knobs there are to mess with, the more likely you are to flip your way into the wrong setting mid-song. The majority of the world's greatest guitarists kept it simple and traditional.

Bridges & tailpieces

As discussed briefly in Chapter 1, an electric guitar's bridge (in conjunction with its tailpiece if they are separate units), forms one of the most important coupling points between string and guitar body, and therefore is a crucial link in the tone chain. Any bridge-and-saddle unit performs multiple functions at once: ideally it will be at least slightly adjustable (although some are not) so that both string-height and intonation can be accurately set, and it also needs to be firm enough to aid resonance and sustain by adequately supporting the vibrating strings. To some extent these properties work against each other. Any part that moves freely for easy adjustment is, by nature, less stable than a firmly fixed part. But guitar-makers have found many ingenious ways around this conundrum at the heart of the perfect bridge.

The bridge and tailpiece tended to be, in the early days, specific proprietary designs of individual makers. Before after-market parts manufacturers began producing countless copies and updates of the common designs, guitar-makers tended to create their own style of bridge to suit the instrument. Today, as with pickups and virtually every other component, there is an enormous range of options on the market, many of which purport to be accurate reproductions of vintage originals, while others aim to improve upon the fifty-year-old templates. Here's a look at a handful of the seminal templates that most modern manufacturers have built upon in one way or the other.

The switch-tastic Fender Jaguar lets you flip between every possible pickup combination.

Floating bridge & trapeze tailpiece

Although it's seen less in rock and blues circles today, this is the set-up that gave birth to rock'n'roll on early archtop electrics, and is still in use on several new reissue-style Gretsch models. In its original configuration it was a two-piece wooden bridge – a height-adjustable rosewood or ebony saddle atop a base of the same material, which was held to the top of the guitar by the downward pressure of the strings. This piece of hardware gave a round, woody, acoustic tone to the instrument, and in many cases afforded somewhat limited sustain. Intonation adjustment on these was limited to a basic overall compromise, with no facility for tweaking individual strings.

Later modifications such as Gretsch's Roller Bar, Rocker and Melita bridges, and Gibson's Tune-o-matic bridge, used steel for the upper bridge/saddle piece, and the latter two offered individually adjustable saddles for each string. These advancements tended to enhance attack, sustain and high-frequency content, while also making it much easier to perfect an instrument's intonation.

Trapeze tailpieces, which are almost always partnered with floating bridges (except when a Bigsby vibrato is used) come in a variety of forms. All anchor at the tail-end of the guitar, with an extension into which the strings' ball-ends are anchored – that is, where they are lifted out above the body by the strings' tension. These tailpieces provide a simple means of anchoring the strings without attaching any more hardware directly to the guitar's top (soundboard).

Telecaster strings-through-body bridge

As the earliest mass-produced solidbody electric guitar, the Fender Telecaster also introduced one of the industry's more successful bridge designs. This simple yet ingenious contraption relies on strings that are anchored in ferules (small metal cups) in the back of the guitar's body, from which they pass through holes in the body to emerge through a steel bridge plate before taking a rounded right-angle turn over the bridge saddles and heading toward the neck. This simple configuration achieves excellent sustain, a firm attack and a bright ringing tone, yielding a sound that is virtually impossible to repeat with any other style of bridge, however similar the guitar might be otherwise.

The fact that a Telecaster's bridge pickup hangs from mounting bolts that are anchored in this bridge plate also adds to this unique guitar's mojo. Tele bridges originally had only three brass (later steel) saddles, using one saddle per pair of strings, and this necessitated a slight compromise in intonation adjustment. Many six-saddle variations have been developed, although countless name players continue to prefer the look and tone of the less versatile original.

Fender's non-vibrato (aka "hardtail") Stratocaster uses a variation of through-body stringing

The back of a Fender Telecaster: the strings are threaded through those six holes.

The wraparound bridge design.

with a cut-down Strat-style bridge unit, and countless other makers have developed their own variant of this much-vaunted original.

Wraparound bridge

After an awkward early variation of the trapeze tailpiece, which actually resulted in the strings wrapping under the bridge bar on the 1952 Les Paul, Gibson devised this simple one-piece, arched steel bar as an all-in-one bridge/tailpiece unit. The strings enter through the front edge of the bar, their ball-ends anchoring in holes drilled there, then they pass up and over the arched top of the bar, which forms the saddle.

U-shaped slots at either end of the bar hold it firmly in the wide "studs" (bolts) that are threaded into steel anchors in the body. The design affords very little adjustment, other than an overall height adjustment at either end and a slight backward-and-forward adjustment via a small screw behind each U-slot, but the wraparound bridge has nevertheless won many followers over the years, and remains popular today.

It was standard equipment on the 1952–55 Les Paul, and – for a much longer run – on the Les Paul and SG Junior and Special. Its plus points include solid anchoring, good sustain and excellent coupling between strings, bridge and body. The arched saddle top can add a slightly furry sizzle to the notes, but many players also like the way this thickens up their tone. In later years Gibson added a low ridge to the top of the bar to improve intonation, and several other makers have updated the design even further. Contemporary guitar and parts makers such as Paul Reed Smith, Wilkinson and TonePros have also modified the basic design to offer improved intonation and, in some cases, built-in adjustable saddles.

Stratocaster vibrato bridge

A handful of other vibrato designs existed before this unit, but Fender's Stratocaster bridge set the standard for vibrato bridges used on flat-faced solidbody guitars. Debuting on the Stratocaster of 1954, it ingeniously incorporated a smooth, stable vibrato function and six individual, fully adjustable string saddles all in the same piece of hardware. A steel "inertia block" mounted beneath the bridge's base plate helped to replace mass lost in the bridge's moving connection to the body via the six pivot screws at the front of the plate. It adds some weight and depth to the otherwise snappy, bright tone that this stamped-steel unit inspires.

Fender has modified this bridge in a number of ways itself: the variant on the American Standard

Stratocaster, with die-cast steel block saddles instead of bent stamped-steel saddles, and just two pivot posts, is enjoyed by many players. That said, countless big-name pros still swear by the vintage version circa 1954, and this is what you're hearing in the evocative vibrato action of Jimi Hendrix, Stevie Ray Vaughan, Hank Marvin, David Gilmour and so many others.

One of the most significant major modifications of this template from another maker arrived in the late 1970s as the Floyd Rose Vibrato. This system, which is usually coupled with a locking nut at the other end that clamps the strings tightly in place at the headstock, provides extended action for deeper "divebomb" style bends, along with individual fine-tuning of each string at the bridge itself (a feature necessitated by that locked nut).

A similar concept was offered by Kahler, as well as by several individual guitar makers (occasionally under licence from Floyd Rose or Kahler). In the 1980s, PRS developed its own proprietary vibrato bridge around the basic principles of the vintage Stratocaster unit, with modifications to improve

New or secondhand?

Traditionally, the used or secondhand market has been a fertile buying ground for newcomers looking to score a bargain on an entry-level guitar, as well as for more experienced players looking to move up. That remains largely true today as well. But the proliferation of "virtual shopping" means that extra care is required, especially when shopping sight-unseen for pre-owned guitars. The massive rise in online guitar sales – via secondhand and auction sites such as Craig's List and eBay, and through vintage guitar dealers in general – has brought a wider market to the average player, while simultaneously reducing the number of used guitars hanging on the walls of most local guitar shops.

The ease of online sales for the average guitar owner often means that selling a secondhand instrument directly to a buyer who might be hundreds of miles away (and therefore less likely to complain about its condition to your face) is preferable to selling it through the local classified ads, or on consignment in a local shop, where the retailer will take a hefty cut of the sale price. From the guitar shopper's perspective, this state of play means the old adage "buyer beware" carries more weight than ever.

As with buying new, it would still be preferable, in an ideal world, to examine and play a secondhand guitar first hand, as it were, but for all of the above reasons that isn't always possible. If you are buying a used instrument from an online source, ensure there is some form of guarantee in place to prevent sellers from offloading gear that is way below the described condition, and also insist on a money-back trial period when at all possible. Once the guitar is in your hands, apply all of the checks and criteria described in this chapter, and don't hesitate to ask to return the instrument for your money back if it doesn't meet your expectations.

When shopping for a used guitar in person, apply the checking and playing guidelines, and also look more closely at things such as fret wear, neck wear and/or damage, and any factor that impedes playability. While a used guitar might seem like a decent bargain as it stands, one major repair required to put it in playable condition – the installation of new frets, for example – might put its real cost way above the going rate for a similar guitar in better, ready-to-go condition. If a used guitar you are considering is believed to have any vintage value, you will also want to ascertain that the finish and all of the components are original.

That's something that you might require an expert's help with. A non-original finish can dent an otherwise collectible vintage guitar's value by as much as half, and swapped pickups or hardware can also take a bite out of its worth. There are still some good bargains to be had on the secondhand market in general, and hunting them down can be a lot of fun, but if you're tempted to wade into the vintage waters, proceed with extreme caution unless you really know what you're doing.

tuning stability and overall solidity of tone, and this unit has been a major feature on many of the company's popular guitars ever since. Today, parts makers offer hundreds of variations on the original, both in vintage and contemporary formats.

Gibson Tune-o-matic bridge & Stopbar tailpiece

Gibson president Ted McCarty himself designed the famous Tune-o-matic bridges (aka ABR-one) to improve upon the limited intonation-adjustment capabilities of its predecessor, the wraparound bridge, and this new piece of hardware fulfilled its task in spades. Conceived in 1954, it appeared first on the Les Paul Custom, then on the Les Paul Standard, and then on a range of other models the following year.

This bridge incorporated individual steel saddles for each string, which could be adjusted forwards or backwards by the simple turn of a screw, along with thumbwheels at each end for overall height adjustment.

On solidbody and semi-acoustic guitars, the mounting bolts onto which these thumbwheels were threaded were set directly into the top, while on hollowbody electrics the Tune-o-matic was still often used, but set into a "floating" wooden bridge base, where it was alternatively paired with a trapeze bridge.

Partnered with a stopbar tailpiece (also called a "stud" tailpiece, for its wide mounting studs) – which is really just a version of the wraparound bar bridge – the Tune-o-matic provided extremely efficient string-to-body coupling along with its adjustment flexibility, making it a gift to sustain, note articulation and overall tone. Several guitar and parts makers today offer their own renditions of the legendary Tune-o-matic bridge, in both original and modified form, and it has become another one of the solid foundations of electric guitar hardware.

The Tune-o-matic bridge and Stopbar.

Bigsby vibrato tailpiece

Although Paul Bigsby, inventor of the Bigsby Vibrato, did manufacture guitars for a time (including one of the first successful solidbody designs), his tailpiece is a little unusual for being known as a classic ingredient on the instruments of several other makers, most of whom prided themselves in otherwise designing and manufacturing virtually every other piece of hardware employed by their guitars.

Many players will tell you that a Gretsch without a Bigsby just doesn't look like a Gretsch, much less sound like one, but these smooth, efficient vibratos were also standard equipment on many Gibson, Guild and even Fender guitars, and remain so today.

The Bigsby's basic mechanism consists of a roller bar with six small studs onto which the strings' ball-ends are hooked before being pulled up and over the bar and on toward the bridge. When the vibrato arm is depressed, a single short, stout spring at one end provides resistance – and the unit's return-to-pitch capabilities – when you let the arm up again.

A Bigsby doesn't provide as much down-bend as a Fender Stratocaster vibrato, nor as much as modifications and updates of that format such as the Floyd Rose or the PRS vibrato bridge. But it does produce a smooth, steady wobble when used right, and one that many players find easier to manoeuvre mid-flight than some other designs.

They come in two basic types – one with roller bar only and another with a second tension bar, under which the strings pass on their way to the bridge – and they're sized for a wide range of solid, semi- and archtop guitars. Bigsby does make its own aluminium rocker bridge, but more often than not a guitar maker will pair it with a suitable bridge of their own design: a Tune-o-matic on a Gibson, a Melita or Rocker-bar bridge on a Gretsch and so on.

The Bigsby tremolo system is one feature on this tasty looking Epiphone Casino guitar.

The nut

Players unfamiliar with its subtle charms might pay little attention to that unassuming strip of white or black material at the thin end of the neck. But a guitar's nut represents one of your strings' essential bonding points with the wood of the guitar, and is, therefore, a first-team player in the tone stakes. In addition to holding the strings in position, the nut transfers their vibration into the neck, and thereby into the body, where it becomes part of the tonal mix.

As such, it is a major coupling point, in the same league as the bridge and the frets. Of course the nut is only responsible for neck-end string resonance and vibration for any strings played open, but even when a string is fretted the nut's quality and condition has major implications for tuning accuracy, return-to-pitch consistency after bending and vibrato use, and so forth. Good-sounding and hard-wearing nuts are made from a number of different materials. Many vintage guitars commonly had bone nuts, and this remains a popular material for upmarket electrics, but synthetic materials such as Corian, Delrin and Tusq are also big with makers and players.

All offer excellent density, a smooth, hitch-free finish when filed well, and excellent transference of vibrations when cut and seated properly. Guitarists who put a lot of heavy string bending or vibrato use into their playing are also often fond of modern alternatives that are impregnated with graphite and Teflon, because these become slicker the more the string slides across them, a quality that helps strings return to their correct pitch.

Other materials such as soft plastic, hollow plastic or aluminium are also used from time to time, and these are all generally considered inferior to the harder, denser nuts listed above. Guitars with such nuts can often still sound perfectly fine, although they can usually also be upgraded by a professional repairman to carry a nut of a better quality. Several makers, in the 6os in particular, followed a craze for a "nut that wasn't a nut", and built guitars with something called a "zero fret" – a fret located before the first fret, positioned just after the nut. The zero frets found on some guitars by Gretsch, Framus, Hofner, National and others, took string-ending duties away from the nut itself, rendering the nut's function one of string-guide and spacing functions only. There is some logic to the zero fret, as it gives open strings the same point of resonance transfer as fretted strings, although many players carry an unspecified bias against it.

Frets

The frets themselves are simple wire strips that form accurate points at which to stop the strings to form precise notes, but they are also an enormous link in the tone chain. In fact, much like neck shape and fingerboard design, the frets' size, shape and condition have multiple implications, affecting tone, feel and playability all at the same time.

A number of sizes, or "gauges", of fretwire are available, but they are commonly divided into narrow, medium-jumbo and jumbo (meaning thin, wide and wider), and are also available in different heights, too. And although we call it fret wire, most frets have a cross-section that looks much like a "T", but with a rounded, semi-circular (or sometimes rounded V-shaped) upper edge. Most fret wire is made from an alloy containing 18 percent nickel-silver (German silver), which itself is an alloy of nickel and copper – and no silver! A few makers today are also using stainless-steel fret wire, which is harder wearing, but also more difficult to shape and install.

Many players feel that wider frets transfer more vibration into the fingerboard, and therefore add a slightly fatter, rounder tone. They are also generally considered easier to bend, and are – for either or both of these reasons – a favourite of blues and heavy rock players. Narrower frets do, however, yield more precise noting, given that they are a finer, sharper stop-point for the strings, and provide a more definitive feel that many other players enjoy. As with so many aspects of guitar construction, fret preference is largely a matter of feel and taste. One factor is beyond question, though: frets need to be installed well; filed, sanded and polished well; and kept in good condition. Otherwise a guitar's tone and feel will both suffer.

Tuners

Also known as machine heads, tuning keys, tuning heads and tuning pegs, tuners perform the self-described task of bringing your strings up to tension, and thereby tuning the guitar – with your help, of course. They come in a wide range of makes, shapes, sizes and designs, but most follow the same basic form – the main differences being in how well they are made, and how efficiently they perform their job.

Although most tuners used on electrics today are fully enclosed, the simple open-back tuners on many more basic acoustic guitars (or the expensive Waverly tuners, which also dispense with covers) provide an easy look at how these little machines operate. Twist the tuner's button, or key, between finger and thumb and it rotates a worm gear on the end of its shaft, which turns a pinion gear on the end of the post onto which the string is wound. Simple as that.

The measure of efficiency of this piece of hardware is found in the ratio of button turns to post turns: for example, you need to turn the button fifteen times to produce one full rotation of the tuning post. Ratios between 12:1 and 18:1 are common: the higher the ratio the more precise the tuner. Traditional tuners have a hole or slot into which the string-end is inserted to start the wind, while many variations of "locking tuners" now also exist, which lock the string-end tightly in place against the tuning post, thereby requiring fewer turns to keep it secure and bring it up to pitch.

The goals of the better-made and more expensive tuners are tight, smooth gearing, tuning precision and longevity. Other than that, tuners don't necessarily have a direct effect on a guitar's tone, although their weight (or lack thereof) might contribute slightly to the mass of the headstock, and therefore the resonance of the neck, for better or worse.

And of course, loose or ill-fitting tuners might rattle or slip, causing unwanted noise and tuning failure. Several functional generic tuners exist, and you'll usually find these on more affordable instruments, but greater attention to detail is found in the tuners from brands such as Grover, Schaller, Sperzel, Kluson and Gotoh.

BUYING A GUITAR

For the new guitarist, the search for an electric or acoustic guitar that is "just right for you" can feel like a minefield. The double-bind position of not knowing much about the instrument, and perhaps not yet being able to play it very confidently can make you feel at a total disadvantage amidst all the elevated price tags and occasionally cloying salespeople. If you have thoroughly digested all that has come before in this chapter, you should already have a big leg up in the game. Knowing one end of a guitar from the other and understanding what all its component parts do – being able to walk the walk and talk the talk, essentially – should boost your confidence considerably. But there are still so many different makes and models out there that the choices can be baffling. Where do you begin?

Well, the best plan is to begin before the shopping trip. Do your research online and through manufacturers' catalogues, outline your requirements as far as sound, feel and general style (once again, using the information in this chapter as a guide), and write up a list with detailed notes that you can take along with you when you enter the lion's den. Determine a realistic budget, plan to stick to it, and define your requirements in an instrument, and you should come out on top of the game with a new or secondhand guitar that will do you proud.

Another good strategy is to take an experienced guitar-playing friend along with you. A player who knows their way around guitars from years of experience can be a real boon, even if they just help you to separate the wheat from the chaff during your early exploratory forays. Be sure that the friend in question understands what you want in a guitar (and isn't using your shopping trip as a vicarious means of landing a guitar that they want to play). Be clear about your budgetary limits, too. However reputable the shop where you end up doing business, it's a lot easier to trust a friend who suggests that spending just a little more for a different model will give you much more guitar for your buck than it is to trust a salesperson trying the same line.

The good news is that you can buy better entry-level guitars today, and for less money, than ever before. Vast improvements made in Asian guitar-manufacturing over the course of the past fifteen years have brought very playable, good-sounding electric and acoustic guitars into the hands of learners at prices that just weren't attainable twenty or thrity years ago. It's possible to purchase a good starter electric, for example, for less than $200 in the US or £200 in the UK, and the guitar will often be a much more competent instrument than your parent or grandparent might have acquired years ago for the equivalent cash.

It remains important, however, to check over any lower-priced guitar thoroughly, because instruments in this range, even those from larger name-brand makers, still sometimes don't have quite the consistency of manufacturing quality and final set-up that guitars costing three or four times their price will benefit from. As many brand new guitars are far from perfect, it's worth thoroughly checking any that you are considering and, when possible, selecting the best from a range of similar examples.

Buying online

If you are buying a new guitar online, as so often happens these days, ensure the purchase comes with a no-strings-attached trial period, with the option to return it within that time frame if it isn't suitable for any reason (you will usually have to foot the bill for shipping both ways, even so). Personally, I would still advise newer players to purchase a guitar in person when possible, as there's no substitute for checking a guitar over with your own hands, and playing it, before you lay down your hard-earned cash.

Also, as mentioned above, any dozen guitars of the same model from the same manufacturer, all selling at the same price in the same guitar store, will often exhibit some variation: they are made from wood, after all, which is an organic and imperfect material, and their final set-up is done by equally imperfect humans. For that matter, the same principles apply equally to upmarket guitars, too; any experienced player will tell you that of any ten pro-level guitars hanging on the wall, one or two might be magical, six or seven will be quite good, and one or two might be clunkers. This applies even more to entry-level instruments, so you will want to look them over thoroughly, play, play, and look some more, before you even pull out your wallet.

General condition

Neck

Is the neck straight, with perhaps just a little relief (bow) if necessary? (see p.66). Does the truss rod function properly? You – or a repairman – will need it to do so if a relief adjustment is required.

Check the condition of the frets carefully. The frets on a new guitar should not have any major divots (nicks) or worn spots (although you'll have to look out for these on any used guitar and judge whether they are significant), but you should still ensure that the frets have been crowned and polished well – that is, that their tops have been shaped cleanly. Also, make sure there are no sharp fret ends at the edges of the fingerboard. Sometimes frets are simply put in badly, too, so check that the guitar plays in tune all the way up the neck. A failure to do so often just means the intonation needs to be adjusted at the bridge, but will also be a sure sign of poor fret installation. If a guitar that you otherwise like does have some sharp fret ends, you might get the shop to agree to have its repair department file these for you to seal the deal.

If it's a bolt-on neck, grab the neck firmly and pull it back and forth to see if there is excessive side-to-side play that can't be eliminated by tightening the mounting screws. Also, will the mounting screws tighten fully when you try them? Stripped screw holes are a major problem, and one that's best avoided altogether. If it's a set neck, are there any signs of a faulty joint: cracks, excessive finish checking around the heel or strings that rise – or fall – drastically from the point of the neck joint to the bridge might be an indication of this.

Body

Check the general stability of the wood, especially any cracks if it's an acoustic, semi-acoustic or archtop in particular. Check for cracks around the jack or jack plate on an electric, one common point of stress. On acoustic flat-tops, check for excessive "belly" (upward bulging) on the top between the bridge and the end pin; note that some bellying is normal in many designs, but drastic bellying might be a sign of excessive string tension over a long period of time, and a sign that a used acoustic, in particular, has been strung with a string set that is too heavy for its top-bracing configuration.

Hardware

Is it all stable and functional? Do the tuners work, without slipping? (Note that poor tuning stability is usually not the fault of the tuners, although a tuner that is genuinely loose or slipping is a problem). Is the bridge secure, with sturdy saddles and slots that have been smoothly and accurately cut, and which – on a secondhand instrument – are not too worn out? Does it all

Vintage values

A lot of guitars for sale on the secondhand market today are described as vintage, and loosely speaking the term can, perhaps, be applied to any older guitar – pre-1980 being a reasonable guideline. However, "vintage" is usually used to describe a guitar that is of interest to collectors, and which possibly has some financial value above that of a mere "used" guitar. Several prized vintage Fender and Gibson electric guitars made in the 1950s and early 60s regularly sell for $20,000 to $50,000 and more on the collector's market, while a highly prized 1958–60 Gibson Les Paul Standard, in good original condition, can fetch the price of a comfortable three-bedroom house. Too often, though, unscrupulous dealers will use the vintage tag to lure a customer into paying over the odds for a beaten-up old instrument that is only going to be harder to play, and cost more in repairs down the road, than a serviceable new or newer-used model.

Can any guitar be worth five or even six figures? Well, the good old laws of supply and demand dictate that many of them certainly can. Just as a rare stamp, coin or antique vase might command a sale price at auction that seems far, far above its intrinsic worth, the scarcity and desirability of certain guitars makes them extremely collectible, and surprisingly valuable in the process. The knock-on effect from this is that examples of certain models that are just outside the genuinely collectible vintage period will often be awarded elevated prices, and inflated status, simply by association.

The distinctions can get very confusing. If you're ever tempted to move into the lower end of the vintage market simply to acquire a guitar that will be a solid, playable instrument – thinking that you might pick up a potential investment along the way – it's important to learn your subject inside out before putting up your cash, and to purchase from a respected and long-standing dealer whenever possible.

You're also likely to encounter a related breed of vintage instrument that is often referred to as "player's vintage", or just a "player's" guitar. Dealers and private sellers alike might promote a vintage guitar as a player's instrument because it has suffered some alteration from its original state. Typical changes include refinishes, changed pickups, extra body routes, non-original bridges and tuners and so forth. Also, with bolt-neck guitars, you will sometimes encounter instruments that have been put together from the parts of different guitars: a body from 1962 and a neck from 1967, with pickups from the early 70s, for example.

Serious guitar collectors maintain strict definitions of what is and isn't collectible, and any change from original will dent a vintage guitar's value, however slight – or even necessary – that change is. A desirable vintage guitar that has had a re-fret and a new nut to keep it in good playing condition will still be worth less than a similar model in similar condition, with original frets and nut, even if the latter is less playable than the former (it seems crazy, but that's the way it goes). In good condition, the refretted guitar might still be very collectible; give it a new finish and change its tuners and one of its volume pots, however, and it is far less collectible, and now worth perhaps only about fifty percent of the value of the all-original example. This is the player's guitar: it maintains some vintage value, but is more within reach of the gigging guitarist's bank account, can be taken out to clubs and bars without as much risk of loss or damage, and most of all, it should play great... even better, in many cases, than the all-original vintage example that has been untouched.

The trouble arises with old instruments that are described simply as player's guitars because they have been beaten and abused and modified over the years. To do well out of a "player's vintage" purchase, you need to know proper, collector's vintage guitars inside out in the first place, or know a friend who does. Keep in mind the original principles of the player's guitar, described above, that can sometimes make a good and genuine example of the breed an excellent way for a player to get his or her hands on a sweet old guitar. But if an instrument doesn't play well and has lost the better part of its investment value, buyer beware: that guitar is probably better headed for the parts drawer, unless it is going for a song.

move smoothly for intonation and height adjustment, where available? Are the nut slots in good condition – not over-worn – and spaced correctly?

Electronics

Are the pickups working in all positions? Is there any serious intermittency in switches or pots? Minor scratchiness is pretty easy to remedy with a squirt of contact cleaner, but bigger issues like shorts or bad pots/switches might be more frustrating to repair, although they aren't necessarily deal breakers if the price is right.

Faulty or intermittent pickups, on the other hand, are usually a more expensive proposition – a minimum of $40 or £40 (at least) each, plus installation costs, just for basic generic replacements.

Playability

Action

Is the action (string height) comfortable to play and, if not, can it be improved with a simple bridge adjustment and/or a half a turn of the truss rod either way?

Neck

Does the neck profile (shape) and thickness feel good in your hand? Is the string spacing appropriate to your playing style?

Playing comfort

Does the guitar feel good, when played both seated and standing? Are there any sharp edges on the bridge, frets or nut that hurt when you move your hand across them to play?

Sound

Ah, that intangible known as tone. It's the most ethereal of considerations, but something you should try to assess logically nevertheless. If an acoustic plays great, sounds great and seems generally solid – and the price is right – that's about all you need to know. With an electric, however, you will need to plug it into a decent amp to make this judgement. If the guitar feels great in your hands, but doesn't sound the way you'd hoped when plugged in, ask the salesperson if it's possible to adjust the amp to achieve the sound you are looking for, or to try another amp entirely. If you just can't get your ideal sound out of it through a range of amps and settings – or something close to it, at least – it is probably worth moving on to another guitar.

Ultimately, remember that this will be your guitar. Others might offer all kinds of reasons why a particular make and model will be "perfect for you", but if it just doesn't feel or sound right in the end, go with your gut feeling. Even if you think you don't know enough about the instrument yet to make an informed decision, you should instinctively know what you want to hold and hear. At the end of the day, it's your money.

CARING FOR YOUR GUITAR

The steps required to take good care of your guitar fall broadly into two categories: cleaning and maintenance. The latter should include periodic adjustments – what guitarists and guitar techs refer to as set-ups – to keep the instrument in good playing condition, while the former, far from merely a cosmetic consideration, is important for keeping gunk and grime from building up on the wood and any moving hardware and electrical parts – and potentially impeding their function.

Cleaning

Above and beyond simply helping your guitar to look its best, proper and regular cleaning will also help to preserve its finish, help your strings last longer, and to keep the neck smooth and gunk-free, which will in turn make it easier to play. For the most part, a basic wipe-down of your guitar's strings, body and neck with a soft, clean, dry cloth after each playing session is all that's required (and it's a good idea to keep a cloth handy for a mid-session wipe down if it's a long rehearsal, or if you're a particularly sweaty player).

If you prevent the grime that builds up from sweat, dust and day-to-day handling from building up in the first place, you might never need anything more than a good lint-free rag in your cleaning kit. (Tip: An old, hundred per cent cotton T-shirt makes an ideal dust rag for guitar cleaning. Don't throw them out – save them and cut them up!)

Occasionally, though, your guitar might need closer attention; some players sweat more than others, or just neglect the daily wipe down, so a more vigorous cleaning session might sometimes be required. Acquire a good proprietary guitar polish, and follow the instructions on the bottle. If you have built up stubborn grime on the body that a standard spray-bottle polish won't tackle, a cream polish or light buffing compound as used to clean fine furniture will often do the trick.

Avoid cleaning products used to shine and restore your car's finish, however, as these are too harsh for most guitar finishes. Whatever you use, be careful not to get any cleaning products into your electric guitar's pickups, controls or switches, as these will almost surely destroy electronic components over time – if not immediately.

Routine maintenance & set-up

There are plenty of minor maintenance jobs that you can perform yourself, with a little instruction. A good set-up is crucial to achieving not only optimum playability, but maximum tone, too. By set-up, we usually mean a combination of things that all work towards keeping your guitar in good condition, like the full tune-up you occasionally give your car.

On a guitar, a full set-up generally includes adjusting neck relief, string height and intonation, and sometimes adjusting pickup height relative to the strings. It might also include conditioning the volume and tone controls (potentiometers), selector switches and jack with a squirt of contact cleaner/lubricant, and lightly sanding ("stoning") the frets to remove slight divots and uneven spots that have emerged with heavy playing – although the latter is best left to an experienced repairman.

More can be done to set up most electric guitars at home, while there are fewer adjustments to be made on acoustic guitars, which usually have fixed bridge saddles, and sometimes less accessible truss rods, too. Most new electric guitars should come with owner's manuals that explain suggested maintenance and set-up, although many manufacturers carry this information in their online support pages these days.

It's best to set up your guitar when you are ready to put on a fresh set of strings, and I would recommend doing so as two back-to-back set-ups, as it were: a quick-hit adjustment with the old strings in place, then a fine-tuning with the new ones on. While old, dead strings might not give you accurate intonation readings, extreme bridge – saddle adjustments can put severe kinks into new strings, thereby distorting their performance and shortening their life.

Make the broad adjustments with the old strings in place, put the new ones on (as per the instructions in Chapter 1), and check and readjust as necessary for optimum accuracy with the fresh set of strings. Let's break down the standard set-up into three steps: neck relief; saddle height; and intonation. It's best to perform these steps in this order, since either of the first two can alter the accuracy of the third.

Checking & adjusting neck relief

While a guitar's neck, in principle, should be as straight as possible, some do benefit from having just a little relief, or forward bow, which allows the strings to vibrate fully without buzzing against the frets. No amount of back bow is ever desirable, however. The component used to counteract the force of the strings' tension on the neck is the "truss rod", a steel rod installed in a channel inside the neck of most electric guitars. If too much or too little bow is in evidence, the truss rod can be tightened or loosened to correct this. (Many acoustic guitars also have truss rods, although some have fixed reinforcing rods that cannot be adjusted.)

There are many different types of truss rods, some of which are adjusted from the body end of the neck, some from the headstock, and different tools are required to adjust different types. Your guitar's manufacturer's instructions should always supersede any advice given here, but this will give you a basic grounding in the approach to this task.

To check neck relief, put a capo on at the first fret (meaning position it on the nut side of that fret), and hold the guitar on your lap in playing position. With a finger on your strumming hand, hold the low E string down at the last fret, and use your free hand to depress the same string around the 7th fret to check the space there. This gap shows you how much relief the neck is set up with. If there's enough room to just slide in a thin business card, it's probably in the right ballpark. If the gap is so big that a card slips right through, there is too much relief, and if the string is right down on the neck without you having to press it there, there might be too little. (Note that some players like a totally straight neck, and if the guitar plays fine all the way up and down the neck with no neck relief at all, with no buzzing frets and a good, ringing tone, you might choose to keep it that way. This is a judgement call, and often comes down to a matter of feel and taste.)

Detune your strings slightly before making a truss rod adjustment, then, to produce more neck relief (more bow), loosen the truss rod adjusting nut (that is, turn it anti-clockwise); to reduce relief and straighten the neck, tighten the nut. Do this a quarter turn at a time, retune the guitar, and check the relief again as above before proceeding with more. If a truss-rod adjustment nut requires more than a full turn or so to produce the desired amount of relief, or is too tight to turn easily (or, on the other hand, so loose that it rotates on the threads with little effort and no effect on the neck relief) it is a good idea to take your guitar to a professional for adjustment.

Note that on some guitars with truss-rod adjustment points at the body end of the neck you might be required to remove the pickguard or even loosen the neck in order to access the nut; again, refer to your manufacturer's instructions to ascertain the proper approach in all cases.

Adjusting saddle height

Setting bridge-saddle height essentially equates to setting string height, and this is a big part of creating the right playing feel for each individual player. The majority of acoustic guitars have fixed, one-piece bridge saddles that need to be sanded down (or built up, or replaced) to achieve a string height adjustment, and that is a job for a professional. Most electric guitars have had some form of saddle and/or bridge-height adjustment, whether it involves raising and lowering individual saddles independently, or adjusting each end of an entire bridge (such as a Gibson-style wraparound bridge) to achieve an overall adjustment.

String height, or what many players call action, is largely a matter of taste, but from a practical perspective you don't want the strings so low that they buzz against the frets, or so high that they are difficult to hold down on the fingerboard. Where you set them within that range is up to you, although most beginner and intermediate players will want their strings on the low side so they are easier to fret. Adjust your saddles or bridge by first detuning the string, then making small turns of the proper adjustment tool – perhaps an eighth to a quarter of a turn at a time – and checking the results on all strings up and down the fingerboard as you go. By doing it this way, if you go too far in one direction it's easy to backtrack a fraction of a turn to achieve the ideal height.

Checking & setting intonation

To check and adjust your electric guitar's intonation, you'll need an electric tuner and the correct tool to move the string saddles back and forth. (Note that the intonation on most acoustic guitars cannot easily be adjusted by the player.) Start with the low E string and proceed one string at a time.

First, tune the open string, then check its tuning at the 12th fret harmonic by very gently touching your fingertip to the string precisely above the fret. This harmonic should be in tune with the open string, but now, in order to check the string's intonation, fret the string at the 12th fret, and observe the tuner reading once again. If the fretted note is also accurately in tune, your intonation for that string is good to go. If the note is flat, you need to move the saddle forward slightly to shorten the string; if it is sharp, move the saddle back to lengthen it. Detune the string slightly to reduce the pressure on the saddle, make the adjustment – again, trying just short adjustments at a time – then tune up and check again. Continue to tune, check, adjust and tune again until the fretted note is in tune with the harmonic, then proceed to intonate all strings in the same manner.

This process usually flows without a hitch on any guitar with individually-adjustable bridge saddles, such as a Fender Stratocaster, a Gibson Les Paul or SG Standard or any other that bases its bridge on these designs. Guitars with Gibson-style wraparound bridges, or with solid bar bridges or floating archtop-style bridges with no independent saddles will obviously have to be given a gentle overall adjustment that yields the best compromise for decent intonation of all strings together.

Guitars carrying vintage Fender Telecaster-style three-saddle bridges also require a somewhat compromised approach to intonation. These saddles carry two strings each, and require some back-and-forth comparison between each string in the pair to determine which adjustment point will work best for both. Rarely can you get both strings in a pair precisely intonated with these vintage bridges, but you can usually find a halfway point that works well enough, one that's "good enough for rock'n'roll", anyway, as the old techs are fond of saying. A number of parts manufacturers now also offer angled, compensated saddles to make it easier to intonate vintage-style Telecasters.

Exceptions to the rules for straightforward set-ups are sometimes found with guitars that carry vibrato bridges. The classic Fender Strat, PRS, Floyd Rose designs and others like them use springs mounted in a cavity in the back of the guitar to counterbalance the string tension and to pull things back into tune when your whammy action ceases. Any slight adjustment of string height, or saddle or string tension in general will change the balance between strings and springs, so more radical set-ups and readjustments on guitars with such bridges also frequently require an adjustment of string tension in the back of the guitar. For full details on this, it's usually best to consult any instructions provided by the manufacturers of these guitars or the vibrato bridges they carry.

Pickup height

Any adjustment of string height in the set-up process might dictate a slight adjustment of pickup height, too, in order to maintain – or achieve – the correct output balance between pickups, and from the guitar as a whole. Most pickups on the market today can easily be adjusted by turning the mounting bolts at either end that hold them in position in the pickguard or mounting ring (on many humbucking pickups, don't confuse the adjustment screws with the four smaller screws that hold the mounting ring to the body). P-90 "soapbar" pickups and Gretsch Filter'Tron pickups differ in that they have two mounting/adjustment screws running right through the cover and body of the pickup, while "dogear" style P-90s and Gretsch DynaSonic (DeArmond Model 200) pickups have no means of overall height adjustment, although they can sometimes be raised or lowered by adding or removing a plastic shim-ring between pickup cover and guitar body.

The proximity of your electric guitar's pickups to the strings has a direct correlation to its output, but there are other factors to consider beyond merely "getting them as close as you can" to maximize volume. Obviously you don't want your pickups so close that the strings buzz against them when you fret notes high up the neck, but even beyond this there's another invisible force that dictates a little more consideration in pickup height adjustment. When a pickup is moved close to the strings, even short of touching them, the magnetic field that is a big part of its function can start to pull on those vibrating lengths of steel, impeding their performance and even pulling them slightly out of tune, at extremes.

Fender-style pickups or Gretsch Dynasonic/DeArmond pickups that use actual magnets as pole pieces will exert more force on the strings than Gibson-style humbuckers or P-90 pickups, which have steel pole pieces with magnets mounted underneath, but neither variety should be raised too close to the strings, and all will affect their vibration if you do so. Neck pickups tend to affect strings more than bridge pickups, because the strings' vibration describes a wider arc at this position, so this unit is usually adjusted a little further down into the body than the bridge pickup. This yields a double bonus of sorts, because, given any two pickups of a similar output, one mounted in the neck position will produce a greater output than the other mounted at the same height in the bridge position, as the result – once again – of that broader vibrational arc from the strings at the neck position. Setting the neck pickup a little lower than the bridge pickup therefore helps to balance their volume levels, too. And remember, you have to consider pickup height adjustments with the strings fretted at the highest fret you are going to play, because the gap between pickup and strings changes dramatically when you push the string down to the fingerboard.

By way of providing a rule of thumb for pickup height adjustment, try adjusting a single-coil (Fender-style) pickup in the bridge position to a height of 3/32" (2.4mm) on the treble side and 4/32" (3.6mm) on the bass side, as measured from the top of the pole piece to the bottom of the low and high E strings when pushed down at the highest fret. On a Stratocaster-style guitar, you might then want to adjust the middle and neck pickups a further 1/32" lower respectively. A Gibson-style humbucker or P-90 can be adjusted to more like 2/32" (1.6mm) on both the bass and treble side in the bridge position, and around 3/32" or 4/32" in the neck position. Some experienced players find that setting the pickups even a little further than this from the strings helps to aid resonance, sustain and warmth, and, even at the expense of a little volume, they prefer the overall tone they achieve by doing so. In any case, most pickups are fairly simple to adjust, so you can experiment and determine what works best for you.

Note that, while many pickups feature adjustable pole pieces, these are not usually provided as a means of overall height adjustment, but are intended to enable the player to balance the string-to-string output levels of the pickup. Raising an individual pole piece closer to its string will make that string slightly louder, and vice versa. Once an ideal pickup height has been established, pole pieces can be raised or lowered to produce an equal output level from each string (often such adjustment has been made at the factory, and doesn't need to be altered by the player).

FROM MOD TO HOTROD: UPGRADES & MODIFICATIONS

An entire industry has developed around the many ways of modifying and improving your guitar long after it has left the factory. Given the number and variety of components on even simple electric guitars, these instruments are more often candidates for upgrades, although there are a few things you can do to improve many acoustic guitars, too.

Electric players commonly change pickups to improve their tone, or simply to achieve a different tone than the one offered by the original pickups. This might be done to switch from a clean sound to a heavier sound, for example, or vice versa, or to achieve a more vintage-like tone, greater sustain, hum-free performance, meatier lows, punchier mids, sweeter highs... the sky's the limit. This is such a popular modification, in fact, that many guitarists acquire a soldering iron and learn to do the job themselves, perhaps going through several sets of replacement pickups in an effort to perfect just one guitar. Given the range of pickups discussed above, you can already see that there are few limits on what can be achieved.

Provided the new pickup fits the mounting and body route of your current guitar, the swap is usually just a matter of changing a few wire connections, and can be done by a professional for a nominal fee if you don't have experience with a soldering iron. One of the difficulties with pickup swapping, though, is that you never know how the new unit will sound once you get it into your guitar, and however detailed and accurate the manufacturer's description is, there's no easy way to quantify the sound of any pickup in all the different guitars it might possibly be mounted in. That said, you assess the descriptions, choose the one that seems most likely to do what you are seeking and hope for the best. Many pickup manufacturers allow you to swap one type for another if you try it and decide you need something a little different, provided you don't clip the hook-up wires in the process, and this offers at least a little insurance that you won't get stuck with a replacement pickup that doesn't live up to its promises on paper (to your ears, at least).

Many acoustic guitars come with factory-installed pickups, but a pickup can often be added to one that doesn't. A wide range of soundhole-mounted pickups is available, and these usually just need to be slotted into the edges of the guitar's soundhole, a job most players can do themselves. More permanent types take the form of a long, thin piezo-electric pickup strip mounted beneath the bridge saddle, or some other form of transducer mounted elsewhere under the top. These require more delicate work, and are usually partnered with an output jack that is installed in place of the end-block strap button, and sometimes a battery-powered, onboard preamp as well, so adding a pickup of this type is a job for a professional.

Other hardware alterations to electric guitars are undertaken as improvements of both tone and performance. Players will sometimes upgrade their tuners to higher-quality units, which is really just a step to improve the mechanical efficiency of these parts. Replacement bridges are popular with players of many types of guitars too, though, and these are often installed in a bid to improve both tone and tuning or intonation stability.

Saddles made of different types of metal offer different tonal responses, while some replacement bridge units themselves might promise improved stability and a better coupling between string and body. Where these fit the mountings and footprint of the existing hardware, they can often be installed successfully by the end user, provided you also know how to set up and re-intonate the instrument once you're done (this chapter gives the basic guidelines). Up at the other end of the neck, though, a replacement nut – which is occasionally desirable, once again, to improve both resonance and tuning stability and accuracy – is another job for an experienced repair man.

Nuts and bridge saddles often come under scrutiny from players of guitars with vibrato bridges, where a swap from traditional metal hardware to "slicker" graphite or Teflon-impregnated parts, or a bridge with roller-saddles, might improve a guitar's ability to return to pitch accurately after vibrato use. Tuners, nuts and bridge saddles offer some of the more likely upgrades for acoustic guitars, too, but given the delicacy of these instruments, guitarists are more likely to seek professional help for such work.

Players can, and do, replace literally every single individual part of a guitar, and some indulge in this form of tone-tweaking to the point of obsession, seeking plastic ware, pickguards and even mounting screws of the exact make and proportions of, for example, a specific model of vintage guitar that they seek to emulate. Such a variety of replacement parts is available that it's possible, and not uncommon, to make an entire electric guitar out of individual pieces, bodies and necks included.

This presents a lot of temptation, but before undertaking any modification, consider the overall cost, the real value of your guitar and whether it would make more financial sense to simply sell what you've got (or part-exchange it) and purchase a different guitar that offers right from the start what you're seeking to achieve. Sometimes this is a quicker, easier, less expensive and more assured means of getting what you're after in terms of sound and playability – and at least you can compare and contrast your current guitar with any new contenders before putting up your cash.

learning
TO PLAY

By now, you're bound to be itching to dive in and learn how to actually play the guitar (or to build on skills that you might have already developed elsewhere). This chapter presents a solid foundation in everything needed to take your new-found abilities out into the world and develop your playing further in the style of your choice. Before you can play satisfactorily, you need to get your guitar in tune and in good playing condition. We'll start there, then move onto the correct hand positions before getting to open chords, barre chords, power chords and single-note playing in several styles.

In short, consider this a springboard into playing. You'll enter a dabbler with a general interest in the guitar, and exit on the other side a player, ready to explore your craft through the wealth of further tutorial material available in a range of styles. (Note that all information given pertains to right-handed guitarists; left-handers should simply reverse the instructions.)

Rather than bogging you down with lots of stodgy music theory the way plenty of guitar-tutor books do, the *Rough Guide to Guitar* gives you a quick, easily accessible dip into several playing styles and techniques, through a series of exercises that are progressively more challenging. Note that I will take some liberties with standard notation and tab formats in this chapter and the next, in order to simplify many of the exercises and make them more accessible. The object is to get you playing the guitar, rather than worrying about the particulars of the traditional teaching techniques. To that end I use various forms of shorthand where it is advantageous to do so to make the exercises more concise and easily digestible.

One of the keys to successfully learning to play the guitar – or virtually any musical instrument – lies in playing music that engages you and captures your interest, once you have gathered a basic grounding in playing. No one book can guess at styles that will appeal to all readers. Our approach here, therefore, is to give you that basic grounding and get you playing some tunes that every learning guitarist can tackle enthusiastically. Once again, the important thing to remember, once you've learned basic chord structures, some simple scales and the technique behind a few styles of single-note playing, is to pursue *music that interests you*. That's what it's all about, after all, and you'll go much further with your efforts if you are truly engaged in the music you're making.

STRINGING & TUNING

Hopefully any new or second-hand guitar you acquire will have decent, serviceable strings on it to begin with. At some point, however, you'll need to change those, and if they're rusty, corroded or just sound dead, it's worth putting on a fresh set right from the start. Learning to string your guitar correctly from the start will save you a lot of time and aggravation down the road. Even experienced players continue to string and tune their guitars in ways that are inefficient at best and, at worst, impede their playing. There is such a wide variety of bridge and tuner types out there that not all guitars will necessarily want to be strung up in exactly the same way. But the following method applies to most instruments you'll encounter.

THE LOCKING WIND

The technique described here is known as a locking wind and it helps the strings lock themselves to the tuner post. This keeps them in tune with fewer winds around it – the more winds around the post, the greater the potential for any string to slacken and slip and create tuning problems.

1 Change strings one at a time, starting with the low E string. This makes it easier to maintain tension on the neck, which in turn makes it easier to get the guitar back into tune. If you're tuning an electric with a Fender-style vibrato tailpiece (or similar) this goes double: keeping the vibrato's spring close to its standard tension will help the new strings settle into place and stay in tune quicker when you are finished.

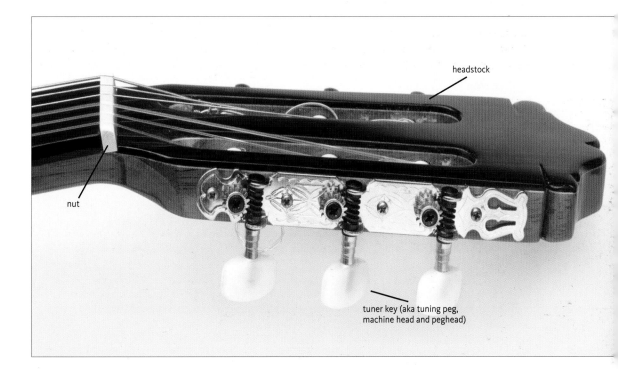

headstock

nut

tuner key (aka tuning peg, machine head and peghead)

2 After removing the old string, load the new one from the bridge end first.

3 Turn the post of the empty tuner so that its hole (or slot) is at right angles to the side of the headstock. On Gibson-style electric guitars and most acoustics (those with three tuners per side) pull the new string tight to a distance that's about a tuner and a half past the tuner post you are going to string it onto. Pinch the string tightly at that point between the thumb and index finger of your right hand, feed the string end through the post-hole from the inside side of the headstock heading outward, and stop when your fingers bump against the post. (See overleaf for a variation of this used for vintage Fender-style slot-post tuners.) With all guitars, avoid twisting or rotating the string as you pull it from bridge toward tuner or you could create distortions in its wind that can both impede its sound and create tuning problems down the road.

A string-winder is an easy way to turn the tuner keys of a guitar.

4 With your left hand, pull the string end coming out the other side of the post around the post clockwise for half a turn for the three bottom strings – or anti-clockwise for the three treble-side tuners – pass it under the string where it enters the hole, and pull it back tightly over itself to form a sideways "V" that hooks the string in place at the post-hole.

5 Turn the tuner key with your left hand so that the post rotates anti-clockwise when tuning the bottom three strings and clockwise for the three top ones – a string-winder makes this quicker and easier – and keep the speaking length of the string taut with your right hand as it winds onto the post. The "speaking length" of the string (the majority of it, from the guitar's bridge down to the nut) should pass under the wrap that is already on the post, and as the string pulls tighter that "V lock" you created will keep it from slipping. When it's all wound on, pull the string end down tight and cut it a few centimetres from the V with a small wire-clipper. For reasons of both safety and sound, it's best not to leave your long string ends loose and flapping.

6 With the low E string you should end up with approximately two turns around the tuner post, and each successive string, being thinner, will go a little further: two to three turns for the A string, three or three and a half for the D, and so on. Experience will help you get used to how much string you need to pass through the post to get the appropriate wind, but what you want to avoid is multiple wraps that wind their way down the post and present a lot of excess for potential slippage. Or, conversely, too few wraps, so the string doesn't have enough contact with the tuning post to hold on – a condition that will likewise lead to slippage.

7 Once the strings are loaded and brought up to pitch, grasp them between the thumb and second knuckle of the index finger at different points along their length and pull them vigorously away from the guitar to stretch them and help them better settle into tune. Stretch,

stretch, re-tune, stretch some more, tune again. As the strings finally get close to staying in tune with considerable stretching, they are ready to play, and should stay in tune much better than strings that have just been wound on, tuned up and played, without being pre-stretched. If your guitar has locking tuners, follow the manufacturer's instructions for loading and locking these. In most cases, you don't need to wind further wraps of the string onto the tuner post, as the pin or bolt of the locking tuner will hold it firmly in place on its own.

For vintage Fender-style slot-post tuners, follow steps 1–3, then do the following before stretching the strings as above:

8 After loading the string in the bridge, pull it through the nut slot and two tuners' length past the post you are going to load it into. Bend it downward at a right angle there, and cut the string about a 1/2" past the bend.

9 Poke the bent end of the string down into the hole in the slot that goes down into the post. Pull the rest of the string tightly down toward the neck, and wind it on.

10 You only need two to three wraps around the post for each string, although on vintage Fender-style guitars with all six tuners on the top of the headstock and only one string tree for the B and high E strings, it is often useful to leave the G string a little longer in order to put a few more turns around its tuner post, which will improve string tension over the nut and help to avoid the common "pinging" G string found on some Telecasters and Stratocasters.

Electronic tuners

Tuning used to be a more hit-and-miss affair than it is today. If you had a keyboard player in the band, or a piano somewhere in the house, great: you could ask them to give you an A and go from there, using the relative-tuning technique described below. If you were all on your own with no reference tone, however, or in a group of other string players, you had to pray someone was still close to standard pitch and just hope for the best.

The availability of accurate, affordable electronic chromatic tuners has put all that behind us, and made tuning a breeze for anyone capable of remembering what the strings are called. Models such as Korg's CA-30 and Boss's TU-12 have built-in microphones to sense the note played on an acoustic guitar, as well as inputs to receive an electric guitar for tuning. If you're at all serious about playing the guitar, you really should pick up one of these, or something similar, and treat yourself, and anyone else in the room, to accurate, in-tune playing at all times. Electronic tuners are extremely easy to use. An acoustic guitar will produce more than enough volume to register accurately from a few feet away, and while you might want to plug in an electric guitar to feed the tuner a clean signal, even a quiet electric played unplugged should register accurately as long as the tuner's placed fairly close to it. If you're starting from the very beginning, you need to know that the notes of the six strings on a guitar in standard tuning are E-A-D-G-B-E (from low to high).

Simply switch on your tuner, ensure it's in standard mode, and pluck the low E string cleanly to produce a full, crisp note. The tuner should register the actual note played, and the needle on its meter and/or its LED indicators will show you whether the guitar is sharp or flat of the right pitch. If you're tuning your low E string, for example, and the guitar is in fact flat to the extent that the meter reads a D (or so sharp as to register an F), you first need to bring the note into the E ballpark – so the tuner registers it as an E – then fine-tune it using the sharp/flat indicators as guides to bring it into true pitch. Once the low E string is in tune, proceed to the A string, tune it in the same manner, and work your way up until all strings are in tune.

Relative tuning

In the good old days, guitar players would carry a pitch pipe in their case and use that to tune by ear, or they'd simply find one accurate note – from a tuning fork, a piano, or some other instrument – to bring one string up to pitch, then use a method known as "relative tuning" to tune the others from this. Simply put, relative tuning is achieved by fretting a string known to be in tune at the correct fret to give the pitch of the next higher string (for example, fretting an in-tune A string at the 5th fret to yield a D), then tuning that string up to meet the pitch, using your ear to judge the accuracy of the note. In turn, fretting that string (the D, in our example) at the correct fret gives the pitch for the next string, and so on.

Relative tuning is simple enough, but it does have a few drawbacks that make the use of an electronic tuner preferable when accurate tuning is required. Firstly, and most obviously, you are using your own ear to judge the pitch, and if that ear is relatively untrained, you might have trouble matching the string-to-string pitch accurately. Secondly, the fret positions on the guitar are imperfect systems really, and involve a compromise that brings each string close, but not precisely, to a pitch that yields acceptable notes at all positions, so minor inaccuracies encountered at each fret position along the way toward tuning an entire guitar using relative tuning can be amplified to result in a high E string that really isn't quite in tune with the low E string that you started with.

Tuning tips

As simple as the process is, a few techniques will help you achieve accurate tuning more easily. When tuning your guitar, hold it so its face is vertical to the ground, that is, so that the plane of the guitar's top is at a ninety-degree angle to the plane of the floor, and avoid putting any artificial tension (from gravity, your hand or any other source) on its neck other than that supplied by the strings themselves. Tuning up with the guitar's back flat in your lap will shift the tension on the neck and in turn alter the tension at which the strings reach true pitch. This in turn will put the guitar back *out* of tune when you shift it into correct playing position.

The phrase "tune up" should remind you of the best way to proceed: when a note registers sharp on your electronic tuner, rather than merely turning the tuning key to lower it to the precise pitch, take it down below the pitch so that it is slightly flat, then turn the key the opposite direction to bring it up to pitch. Approaching the correct pitch in this way, from flat of the note rather than from sharp, pulls the string tightly around the tuning post and is therefore likely to keep it in tune longer. Also, if all six strings are so off their mark when you begin tuning as to register entirely different notes to standard tuning, you might find it helps to bring one string up to pitch with your electronic tuner, perhaps the low E or A string, then to bring the rest approximately in tune using the relative tuning technique described below. Once they are all in the right ballpark it is easier to fine-tune them using the electronic tuner, and you're less likely to accidentally tune a string to an entirely wrong note by watching the tuner's sharp/flat indicators while inadvertently ignoring the actual pitch it is registering.

When using an electronic tuner, pluck the string and tune it so the attack of that note is in tune, rather than its decay (that is, the first "peak" of the note that leaps out when you pluck it). Hopefully both the attack and the decay will be in tune (or very close), although some guitars, especially those with shorter scales or lighter gauge strings, vary considerably. The attack of the note, however, is what our ears detect first, and that's what tells us whether a sound is in or out of tune, so favour tuning toward the attack.

These considerations aside, used correctly, relative tuning is still likely to get you close enough to being in tune to play the guitar without any extremely adverse results.

Tuning to a piano

Of course, if you have a piano or keyboard handy, you can tune the entire guitar to it, rather than just tuning one string and using relative tuning from there. You will still be tuning by ear, but if it's an electric keyboard, or if the piano has recently been tuned, this should yield even better results than relative tuning.

GUITAR SET-UP

If your guitar seems to be difficult to tune or if the individual notes in chords don't sound entirely in tune with themselves (despite being in tune according to an electronic tuner) the guitar is very likely in need of a proper set-up. Accurate tuning depends upon a guitar's intonation and its neck relief, both of which interact with each other to create the optimum length for each string, producing a "speaking length" for the string. This ensures it will register the correct pitch when tuned to its designated open note, and will play in tune at each fret up the neck.

Intonation of each string can be corrected fairly easily on many makes of electric guitar by adjusting the bridge saddles. Neck relief (the amount of bow in the neck) can be corrected by

The first diagram (bottom right) shows how to tune your A string by fretting an A on the 5th fret of the low E string (assuming your low E is in tune to start with). The second (bottom left) shows how to tune your D string by fretting a D on the 5th fret of the A string. The third (middle right) shows how to tune your G. The fourth (middle left) shows how to tune your B, and the last (top right) shows how to tune the top E.

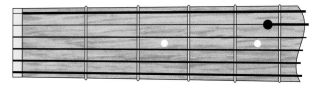

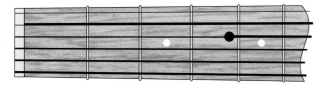

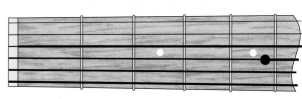

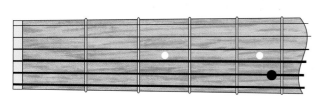

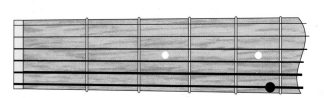

adjusting the truss rod that runs down the guitar's neck. This is a fairly simple operation in most guitars, but one to approach more cautiously in order to avoid over-adjustment, which could damage the neck.

It's also fairly simple on most acoustic guitars, although correcting faulty intonation is usually a job for a professional, since the bridge saddles on acoustics are generally fixed. Either way, these jobs often go hand in hand: a guitar with its strings' lengths adjusted for correct intonation will still most likely play out of tune at several positions on the fretboard if there is too much relief (bow) in the neck, since pressing the string down the extra distance to meet the frets will very likely pull it slightly out of pitch. Get your guitar set up correctly in terms of intonation, action and playing feel, then get it truly in tune, and you are ready to enjoy playing.

The truss rod's screw can be seen nestling within the little hole at the join of the neck and the headstock. Use an allen key to tighten or loosen it in order to adjust a guitar's neck relief and intonation.

How low can you go?

There are two schools of thought on how high or low you should let your guitar hang: looking cool and playing coolly. The punk, metal and indie ethos says that hanging your guitar as low as you can, while still just being able to reach your playing positions (think Johnny Ramone), looks far cooler than having the instrument up high on your chest.

Check out the players with really serious chops, though – many jazz players, country pickers and blues legends among them – and you'll notice that these guys frequently wear their guitars rather high, hovering somewhere between chest and belly, which affords the optimum angles and playing positions for both hands. As ever, some compromise between style and function will probably serve you best.

Green Day's Billie Joe Armstrong: a firm believer that no guitar can be slung too low.

THE ERGONOMICS OF PLAYING

Having a comfortable hand position, arm position and general posture helps you play with ease, and without undue fatigue. Physical ailments such as RSI (repetitive strain injury) in the hands, wrists and elbows, and aches and pains in the lower back are very real hazards of playing with poor posture or hand positioning.

Many experienced musicians who don't pay attention to this early in their guitar playing find themselves locked into bad habits, and end up doing themselves damage in very real ways as a result. But first and foremost, it is just easier to play if everything is in the right place. Getting it right now will make it easier to play more challenging riffs and chords further down the road.

HOLDING THE GUITAR

When playing seated, it's best to use a firm, armless chair with a comfortable but fairly upright back – one that's high enough that you can plant your feet on the floor, with your thighs at right angles to it (rather than tucked under you), but not so high that you are dangling above the floor.

Try to remember the posture they taught you in primary school, and keep your back straight with just a slight concave arch in the lower back. Avoid slumping or slouching. Most sofas do not make great seats for playing, because their backs tend to be too far from the front edge of the seat cushions for you to comfortably sit upright with good support. If you don't have a chair that fits these requirements, you might need to bolster one up with a cushion or two to provide the right kind of support for your lower back. If you have the discipline to maintain good posture on your own, a stool can also make a good seat for playing the guitar, provided you're not the kind of sitter who tends to slump down or slouch forward after a prolonged time, either of which are sure-fire guarantees of a deep back ache.

Rest the curved "waist" of the instrument over your right thigh and hold its back parallel to, and just slightly against, your belly. Extend your right arm across the front of the guitar, with the underside of your forearm resting slightly on the upper rearward edge of the body (the bass-side lower bout). Your hand should reach the strings in a position approximately halfway between the bridge and the end of the fingerboard (which will usually be right over the soundhole of an acoustic guitar). You don't want to squeeze the guitar body between your elbow and your ribcage, but merely to rest your arm gently on the body edge, which should help keep you comfortable, and prevent the right arm from tiring too easily. Your left arm should extend comfortably to the neck so that the forearm is approximately at a right angle both with the neck itself, and with your upper arm.

When playing while standing, you'll need a good strap that will hold the guitar safely and not slip off the strap buttons if you move around. Strap locks – which clip the straps to the strap buttons on the guitar to hold them securely – are often worth investing in, for electric guitars in particular (many types won't fit acoustic guitars). Strap length and guitar positioning are largely matters of taste, although you'll want to adjust the strap so the guitar sits at a point that lets your left and right hand comfortably reach all required playing positions without strain or discomfort.

Hand positions

The discipline of classical guitar has very rigorous notions of correct hand positioning. But we're not going to be quite as strict as that. Most rock, pop and blues players will find a slightly more flexible approach works just as well, and is perhaps even preferable.

The left hand

Proper classical left-hand positioning dictates that you brace your thumb behind, and just slightly towards, the upper side of the neck, with your hand extended under the neck almost at a right angle to the fingerboard (not cradling the underside of the neck, but with a gap between palm and neck), and curl your fingers inward to meet the strings at the fingerboard. Most players find it more comfortable to relax this a bit by bracing the thumb up just a bit higher on the back of the neck, and rotating the wrist slightly clockwise (i.e. rotating the thumb away from the headstock a little).

Teachers will often tell you that you shouldn't hook your thumb over the top edge of the neck and fingerboard, but even this isn't a real problem if you avoid other pitfalls while doing so, and plenty of outstanding players position their left hand this way sometimes. If you have big hands, and are playing a guitar with a fairly narrow neck, this might be the only way for you to brace your thumb while maintaining adequate, comfortable support at the back of the neck – especially for bending strings. Hooking your thumb over the top of the neck like this does, however, make it more difficult to use the little finger of your left hand to fret notes, which is something else you will want to incorporate in your playing eventually. Ultimately you will want to balance between positions that afford you the best blend of finger-reach and thumb support. In truth, many experienced players shift their hand position slightly according to what they're playing at the moment, so left-hand positioning needn't be considered a rigid art anyway.

What is really important is to avoid squeezing the neck while you play. You need to support the hand with the thumb at the back of the neck, but that support should be gentle and mobile. Squeezing the neck will lead to hand fatigue, and very likely, a greater instance of RSI, and will also often find you squeezing the strings, too, which will send your chords slightly out of tune.

The right hand

In addition to being in the correct position to play, the right hand also needs to properly grip the pick (or plectrum). Pinch the pick between thumb and forefinger so that the point of the pick extends approximately 1/4" from the point at which you are holding it, and forms something close to a right angle with your thumbnail. You need to grip the pick tight enough that you won't drop it, but not so tight that you feel any muscle strain. Let the right hand hang in a position that allows you to pick each string easily, or to strum all of them together, with just a slight motion from the wrist. Most players also like to brace the right hand by resting the tip of the little finger or both the little and ring fingers on the top of the guitar below the E string. Even the slightest bracing in this manner helps the right hand keep going without tiring out so easily.

To pick single notes and to strum most chords, you will usually rotate your hand from the wrist, with your forearm remaining fairly stationary. Vigorous strumming for hard-rock or punk styles might find you pivoting at the elbow, using your entire forearm, but this should be the exception rather than the rule. Picking a string enough to produce entirely adequate volume really doesn't require a vigorous motion, and you don't need to dig the pick in too deeply either. Use just the edge of the pick's point, and only a slight motion, to pick the string firmly and smoothly, and it will ring out just fine.

Use a slightly broader rotation of the wrist, brushing the pick along the tops of the strings as it passes, and you have strummed a chord. Whether you're picking single notes or strumming entire chords, you will want to become fluid in both directions, which is to say you need to be equally accomplished at picking and strumming with both up- and down-strokes. Some playing styles might occasionally specify down-strokes in order to create a certain rhythmic effect, but you will usually develop the most speed and fluidity by alternating down- and up-strokes.

None of this advice on posture and hand positioning is intended to dictate that you need to be stiff and uptight while playing – quite the opposite, really. Overall, you should find playing positions, both sitting and standing, that are both comfortable to you and which give you an easy range of motion, but if you find yourself slipping into positions that are also likely to lead to backache or joint and tendon troubles in the long run, it's best to correct yourself now.

PICKING & STRUMMING EXERCISES

Alternate single-note picking

There will be more about single-note playing later in this chapter, but we're going to start with two simple single-note picking exercises to help you practise pick technique and build fluidity of motion.

Exercise 1. Note the down- and up-stroke instructions beneath the tab.

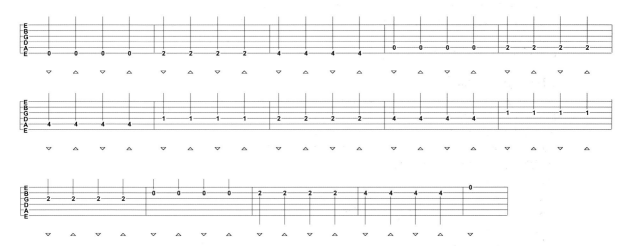

This picking exercise takes you across all six strings, from low E to high E, alternating between down- and up-strokes with every other stroke. In the course of doing so, it takes us through two full octaves of the E major scale, one note at a time, picking each note four times except for the final high E.

Look back to the guide to notation, tablature and chord boxes at the end of Chapter 1, if necessary, to refresh yourself on how to read tab. Take it slowly at first, concentrating on making steady, even strokes. Ideally, you would use all four fingers on your left hand to fret the notes, selecting the finger to use according to the fret position beneath it. Many beginners, however, need to build up strength and agility with the little finger before it can hold down a string adequately – use just your index, middle and ring fingers, if that makes it easier. This is a good exercise to perform on a regular basis as part of your practice warm-up routine, and it will help you gain the strength and flexibility needed to play successfully.

Exercise 2

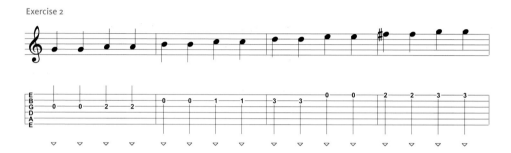

Single-note picking, all down-strokes

Some playing styles, namely those that require a forceful, driving rhythm, work better when you pick in steady down-strokes. Try this exercise, which takes you up the G major scale on the highest four strings (G-B-E).

Chord strumming

Now we'll move onto some simple chord-strumming exercises, all in the key of G. Chords for each of these will pull from the first-position G, C and D chords that you learned in Chapter 1's twenty-minute guitar tutor, the diagrams for which are repeated here for convenience, with a new chord, E minor, added to them for the third exercise.

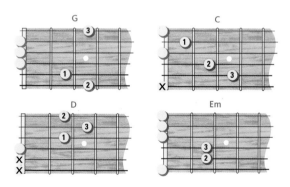

Strum & hold

To begin our exploration of strumming full chords, let's strum through just the G and C chords, giving each a smooth, steady down-stroke and letting the chord ring for a full measure (four beats) before moving on to strum the next. One of the biggest challenges for any beginner is the effort of moving between chords – shaping the C after having made the effort of shaping the G, for example – and this strum-and-hold exercise gives you a little more time to prepare yourself for the move.

Ideally, though, you still want to let each chord ring for the full measure before moving to the next. Practise moving back and forth between the chord shapes, without even strumming the strings, to get your hand familiar with the required positions.

Beginners tend to favour using their first three fingers (index, middle, ring) in shaping chords, but if you learn to use your little finger early in the process – and perhaps shift some chord shapes to the middle, ring

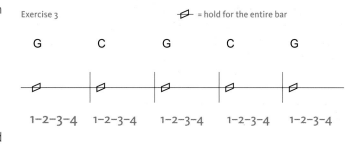

and little fingers – it can actually make it easier to move between certain chords. For example, try playing the G chord with your middle finger on the A string at the 2nd fret, ring finger on the low E at the 3rd fret, and little finger on the high E at the 3rd fret. This should leave your index finger hovering in approximately the right position to hit the high C (B string, 1st fret) when you change to the C chord, while your middle and ring fingers simply shift up to a higher string on the fret where each is already positioned (middle finger to the D string 2nd fret, ring finger to the A string 3rd fret).

Steady down-strokes

This exercise increases the challenge factor slightly, with four steady down-strokes per measure. Start slowly at first, so you can comfortably complete the final stroke of each chord before moving on to the next, then build up speed as your left hand becomes familiar with changing between shapes.

Exercise 4. Strum each chord four times each bar, ending on one final G chord.

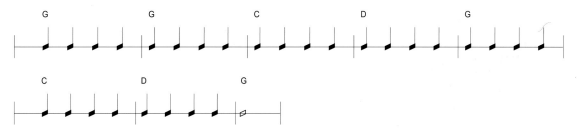

Alternating strokes

Most music that is played entirely with strummed chords (usually referred to as rhythm guitar), will use alternating up- and down-strokes for variety. Occasionally these will fall into a steady, repetitive down-up-down-up pattern (like that of our exercise for alternate single-note picking) but this can sound rather monotonous when strumming chords. More often than not the pattern will be mixed up for variety, and frequently it is played with more emphasis on the down-strokes, as in this exercise. We are now introducing eighth notes, too, which have half the rhythmic value of the quarter notes we have used so far. When one quarter note is split into two equal eighth notes, these will be "tied" with a bar that joins them together, as seen here (individual eighth notes that are not joined to their partner do not have a tie, but an incomplete stem instead).

In Exercise 5, the two up-strokes per measure fall on the second eighth notes of the third and fourth beat. This is sometimes referred to as the "and" in this kind of rhythm, as in "one, two, three-and four-and; one, two, three-and four-and", where equal weight is given to the "one, two, three, four" while the two "ands" are given only half of their rhythmic value. As such, each measure is played by strumming two quarter note down-strokes, then strumming two down-up-strokes in the same space of time for the second half of each measure.

Exercise 5: note the eighth notes (half the value of the quarter notes in the previous exercise).

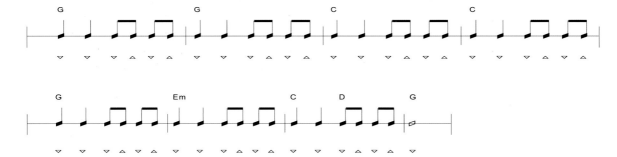

OPEN CHORDS

You already have the first-position G, C and D major chords at your command, commonly known as open chords, and you have just added E minor for variety. Now we will introduce several others, and practise using them in a handful of simple tunes. All but one of these chords contain at least one open string and are played within the first few frets of the neck; they are usually easier to shape than the barre chords that will follow later in this chapter.

There are actually fewer open chords on the guitar than you might think, because many other keys with root notes further up the fingerboard require you to play barre chords. For example, there is no conventional open variation of the B major chord. We will, however, give you an open F here – a chord usually played as a barre chord. Other, more unusual open chords *can* be formed, but they are more difficult for beginners' hands than many conventional barre chords. (You could,

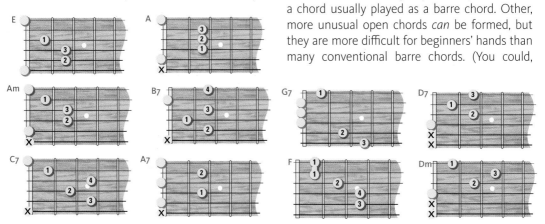

arguably, call this variation of F a barre chord because it contains no open strings, and is best played with the index finger fretting both the high E and B strings at the 1st fret. But the *proper* first-position F chord involves barring *all six strings* at the 1st fret with the index finger and fretting the others with your remaining three fingers, a more difficult proposition.)

Note that when no indication is given other than the letter of the chord, that chord will be major. Minor chords are indicated by a lower-case "m", which tells you that the third note of the scale is played a half-step down from the third note in a major scale to give it a minor sound. Chords that include the seventh note of the scale are indicated with a "7".

With all of these chords, the bold bar at the top of the chord box represents the nut at the end of the neck, so all of these positions occur within the first four frets. Remember, a circle above the nut means you play that string open, while an x means you don't play the string beneath it. Playing strings excluded from the chord will make the chord sound wrong. Note also that in each of these cases, the lowest note in the chord has the same name as the chord you are playing.

OPEN-CHORD EXERCISES

Exercise 6

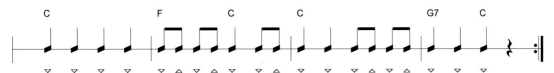

Now let's try a range of short strumming exercises, using different combinations of chords from the selection above, applying them to a variety of rhythmic patterns. Note the repeat symbol in Exercise 6: the double-bar at the end of the exercise with two dots in front of it. This tells you to go back to the start and play it all again.

Exercise 7 gets a little more challenging rhythmically – for the right feel, think 1950s rock'n'roll à la Buddy Holly. Take a close look at the strumming pattern, and the new eighth note strums and rests introduced here, and work on it slowly before taking it up to speed.

Exercise 7

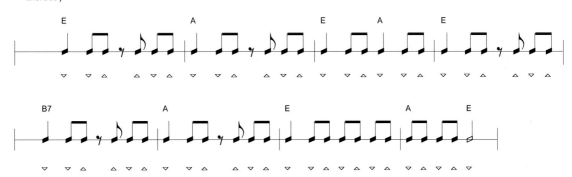

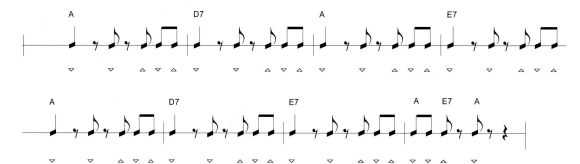

Exercise 8 is another progression that's at home in classic rock'n'roll (with just a little bit of a Latin feel, perhaps). At the same time it isn't too far from something that might sit easily in 1990s Britpop, either.

I-IV-V progressions

Did you notice anything about the sound and feel of the previous three exercises? Although they are in different keys, they all use chords from similar parts of the scale: the I chord, the IV chord and the V chord – named after the positions of their root notes in the scale (first, fourth and fifth), even if they use them in a slightly different order. (Note that when you count up the scale, you *start* with the root note as one, and work up from there.)

Usually designated with Roman numerals, these chords form a common chord group called a I-IV-V progression. It has a very natural feel because it moves up the scale, then resolves itself back on the I chord – a short trip away before returning home. The great thing about understanding these progressions is that once you're able to find the chords relative to the scale you're in, you can play a surprising number of different songs.

Say, for example, you know a I-IV-V song in the key of G (meaning it uses the G, C and D chords). Your friend, however, wants you to play it in the key of C, which is better for his or her vocal range. All you need to do is figure out which are the I-IV-V chords in C (namely C, F and G) and you have transposed that song to the new key. Even when you're trying to learn an entirely different song on the fly, if it uses some variation of the I-IV-V progression all you need to know is the relative chords of the scale you want to play it in, and what order that progression falls in. And you're there.

Plenty of great music has been written around nothing more than these three chords, and you can go a long way by knowing the I-IV-V chords in several keys (which becomes even easier once you master barre chords, discussed further along in this chapter). Hell, a lot of great music has even been written around a mere two chords. Bob Dylan has plenty of classic two-chord songs, while Johnny Cash's "Cocaine Blues" and Dwight Yoakam's "Guitars, Cadillacs" were both major country music hits that only used two chords throughout.

A little variety: dominant seventh & minor chords

I-IV-V progressions can be played with or without dominant seventh chords (usually known just as seventh chords, for short) – there's no hard or fast rule to say where they should or should not be used – and they simply help to set the melodic feel of the tune. We used them in exercises 6, 7 and 8, although each can be played with a standard major chord in place of the seventh in the progression – they're the ones created by adding a flattened seventh of the scale to what would otherwise be a major chord. They are particularly heard in poppy rock'n'roll songs of the 1950s and 60s, and in folk and blues songs, but they can add a certain feel that's right for many different kinds of music. That said, countless great artists go their entire careers without writing a song that contains a major seventh chord.

Minor chords, on the other hand, are essentials of the repertoire if you want to take your progressions beyond the predictable I-IV-V. Look back to Exercise 5: adding the E minor to the I-IV-V progression in G major adds depth and poignancy to the music, taking it somewhere you just can't go with three major chords. Note that adding a minor chord doesn't make this one a minor progression on the whole, because the piece is still based around the G major scale. To be minor, it would have to be based around a minor scale, with a minor chord as its "home base", or root. Potentially confusing, however, is the fact that a progression in a minor scale doesn't need to contain exclusively minor chords: often only the root chord is minor.

Let's bring a number of minor chords into play, both as elements of major-scale chord progressions, and as root chords of minor-scale progressions. Exercise 9 introduces an Am chord as part of a I-IV-V progression in C major. It also introduces us to 3/4 time, otherwise known as waltz time, which we touched upon in Chapter 1. In 3/4 time the quarter note still takes the beat, but there are only three quarter notes to each measure, rather than four. These can still be further divided into eighth notes (six per measure), and so on. Until now, I have not shown the time signature in these pieces to avoid cluttering the page and, potentially, confusing you – they have all been four beats to a bar – but you will now see the "3/4" at the left end of the first line of the exercise, telling you this is in waltz

Exercise 9

Exercise 10

time. Both standard music notation and tab frequently (but not always) leave out the time signature when a piece is in 4/4: if no time signature is given, then there are four beats to a bar. Exercise 10 is in the key of E minor, and should be played using only down-strokes for the first four measures, which gives it a rockier feel, and then a little variation in measures five and six. Try playing this one two different ways: firstly with the full chord ringing out with each stroke and then, to help tighten up the sound, try muting the strings slightly by resting the edge of your hand (the left edge of your right hand, when the palm is facing you) ever so gently against the strings just in front of the bridge.

This is also a great technique for dampening unwanted strings and keeping certain notes from ringing out when you want to favour others in the chord. Note that this one uses the chords from the I-IV-V progression in G major, which is the relative major scale to E minor. That's to say these two scales employ the same notes, but differ according to the root note on which each starts, the E in the case of E minor, the G in the case of G major.

Open sus chords

Sus chords are a standard part of any experienced player's repertoire. "Sus" is short for suspended, and these chords are also referred to with added numbers, referring to the note of the scale that they raise. So "sus4" is a standard major chord altered by raising the third of the scale to a fourth. These chords sound like they're dying to be resolved, a transition that comes when you go from the sus to its standard major chord, a change that can add great motion to the feel of a piece of music.

A classic example of a sus chord is Pete Townshend's guitar riff for The Who's "Pinball Wizard", which goes back and forth between the sus and the straight major chord. Sus chords are occasionally used on their own, but they are often played as a bridge to and from the major chord that they are based upon. Once you get the hang of

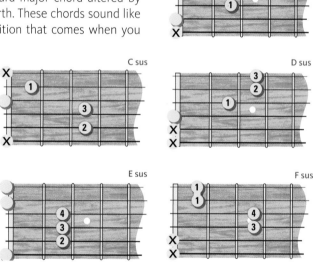

them, and have mastered the barre chords that are covered later in this chapter, it's easy to create the sus version of just about any major chord, without significantly shifting your left-hand position.

Exercise 11 takes us back and forth between Fsus and F, and Csus and C, to hear how these chords work together. I find the result sounds very like something from a Bruce Springsteen song – or indeed several of them. Note that the open form of the Csus as shown above can be a bit awkward to play because, properly speaking, you need to mute the open high E string in order to keep the third of the chord from sounding, otherwise you have both a third and a fourth in the same song. In some circumstances, however, letting that high E ring right out adds a certain complexity that actually works in some contexts. Try it both ways.

Exercise 12 uses the Dsus chord in a sweet little I-IV-V progression in D major with an indie jangle-pop feel that calls to mind bands such as Teenage Fanclub.

Exercise 11

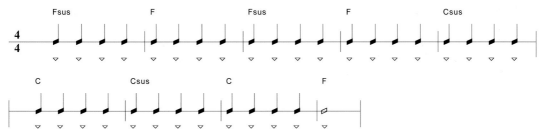

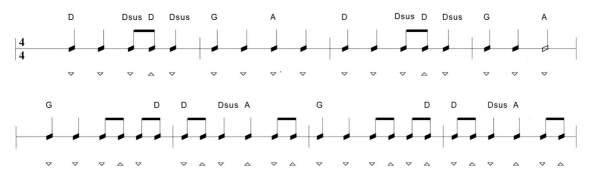

Exercise 12

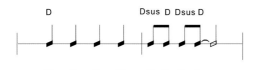

Open minor seventh chords

Minor seventh chords offer another flavour that can be useful in our playing, and often they help to give a poignant feel to tunes that employ them. These chords really are just·a mash-up of a dominant seventh and a minor chord, and contain both a flattened third and a flattened seventh (the seventh of the minor scale). Note that two variations for the open Em7 are given, which puts these elements in different parts of the chord.

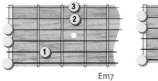

Em7

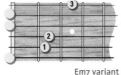

Em7 variant

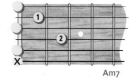

Am7

Exercise 13 runs us through a couple of these chords in a moody progression in 3/4 time; use the second version of Em7 to start the piece off, because it offers a more dramatic transition to the G major chord, then close with the first variation of Em7.

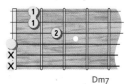

Dm7

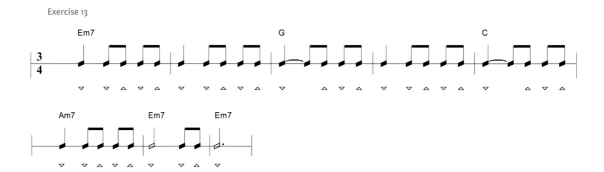

BARRE CHORDS

Master a range of barre chords and you are on your way to being able to play a little of just about anything on the guitar. Once your fingers have become familiar with their shapes it's easy to do, thanks to their uniformity and moveability. Barre chords are named for the fact that the index finger of your left hand forms a bar across all played strings at the 1st fret of the chord position, while the remaining fingers fret other notes on higher strings. This means they can be a bit tricky at first, and they require building both strength and flexibility in the hand and fingers in order to hold down so many strings without any buzzes. Once you've got the mechanics down, however, they open up a movable feast of new chord positions.

Beyond the sheer physical effort of playing them (which will lessen considerably with practice), barre chords are a simple and powerful tool because they require learning just two basic shapes for major chords, two basic shapes for minor chords and the same for all the various seventh, minor seventh, sus chords and variations of them. The two major shapes are much like the E and A chords you have already learned, but are moved further up the neck with your index finger holding down the strings one fret behind them to take the place of the nut in the E and A.

To get the hang of them, let's look at two common barre chords, G and C, both of which begin at the 3rd fret. G is formed by pressing your index finger down across all six strings at the 3rd fret and forming the open E shape beyond it at the 4th and 5th frets (middle finger on the G string, 4th fret; little finger on D, 5th fret; and ring finger on A, 5th fret). Before forming the entire chord, work on getting your index-finger positioning correct so that you can strum all six strings with no buzzing, then apply the rest of the fingers and work on strumming the whole chord smoothly.

The C chord is formed by pressing the five higher strings to the 3rd fret with your index finger (leaving the low E string unplayed), then forming the shape of an open A chord at the 5th fret with your remaining fingers. In many cases, this shape is played like a double barre, with your index finger forming the first (wider) bar, and your ring finger barring the D, G and B strings at the 5th fret. You can also play it by using all of your remaining fingers to fret those strings individually if that works best for you, but I think the double-barre technique is easier in the long run, once your fingers have gained the strength and flexibility to achieve it, and also lets you move and form this chord more quickly. Technically, the high G created by fretting the high E string at the 3rd fret (the bottom of your index-finger barre) is included in this chord, but even experienced players often have difficulty getting this high note to ring true, without accidentally muting it with the finger(s) forming the other notes. No problem – the four notes created by cleanly playing the middle four strings are enough to sound this chord anyway.

Take your time learning the shapes of these chords. Once you have got them down, practise by taking your hand away then placing it back in position to form the chord again, until you develop fluidity and speed in the movement. Note that when barre chords beyond the first two frets are indicated, the chord diagram will include a fret number to the left of the first fret used in forming the chord. In playing these two chords, note that the root of the G chord is found at the G note created by fretting the low E string at the 3rd fret, and the root of the C is found at the C created by fretting the A string at the 3rd fret. Part of the beauty of barre chords is that once you have learned these two shapes, you can find major chords all up and down the neck of the guitar.

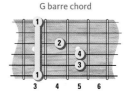

G barre chord

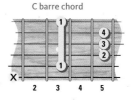

C barre chord

The neck diagram below indicates various root notes, which you can use to form E-shape and A-shape barre chords anywhere on the neck. Take your movable A-shape barre chord (as used to play the C major above) to any root note on the A string and that gives you the name of the chord. Similarly, transport your E shape to any E-string-based root note, and you instantly know what chord you're playing. Try both chord shapes all the way up the neck to become familiar with their locations and the relationships between these two positions.

Even if you keep playing mostly in the lower-fret positions, your new-found ability to play barre

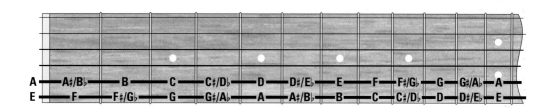

chords gives you access to chords that were missing from our compendium of open chords, above, such as B, B♭, and their variations and the full versions of F and F♯/G♭. Use these two barre-chord shapes, and the barre chord location diagram above, to help you with the following challenges and questions. (You'll find the answers on the following page, upside-down.)

1 Play an A major barre chord in two positions.

2 Name the E-shape barre chord found at the 8th fret.

3 Name the A-shape barre chord at the 7th fret.

4 Play a B♭ barre chord in two positions.

5 How many frets up do you have to travel from a chord with its root on the low E string to find the same chord with its root on the A string?

6 On which frets are the barre chords found that let you play a I-IV-V progression in G?

Minor barre chords

The beauty of barre chords continues. As with major chords, we only need two basic shapes to play minor chords all over the neck. Each of these begins with the shapes you just mastered above, and alters it slightly by flatting the third of the scale to make the chord minor. Essentially, you are once again taking the open Em and open Am shapes and moving them up the neck, using your index finger to take the role formerly played by the fret by barring all strings behind them.

This time, for the root-on-the-A-string shape you don't form a double barre, but use the individual fingers on your left hand to fret each remaining note, a technique that many players actually find easier than that used to form the major variation of this chord shape. With this minor chord, it's also easier to sound the note fretted on the high E string. The roots and locations remain exactly the same as they are for all the major barre chords you have already explored, so finding these minors is a breeze.

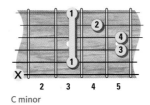

C minor

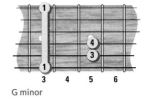

G minor

Dominant seventh, minor seventh & sus barre chords

Yep, you guessed it – here are further slight variations in chord shapes, and the same positions on the fingerboard get you the barre-chord voicings, too. Get these down, and you should be feeling pretty proud of yourself: by learning just ten chord shapes (which are really just variations on two basic major shapes) and memorizing the chromatic scales created by two strings as they head up the neck, you have added a whole plethora of new chords to your vocabulary.

Note that there are two variations of the E7-shape barre chord, played here as G7 at the 3rd fret. The second, which adds a second flattened seventh higher up the scale, is often used in blues, jazz and country playing in particular, and is heard a lot in rockabilly guitar styles, too. Also, be aware that playing sus barre chords is a little trickier than playing most open sus chords, because you need to have the fingers free, and in the right position, to fret all those strings. For this reason, the variations of

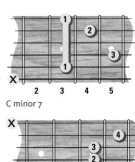

C minor 7

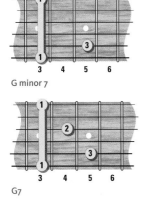

G minor 7

C7

Csus

G7

G7 (variation)

Gsus

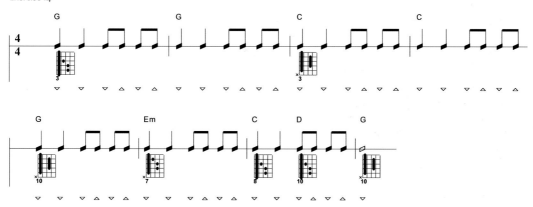

these given here are partial barre chords, which don't attempt to play all strings at once.

Now let's play a series of exercises to work out your barre-chord chops. To illustrate how easily you can find handy chord positions all over the neck using these shapes, Exercise 14 is a repeat of Exercise 5, but uses all barre chords, in several different positions that minimize extreme jumps up and down the neck. The exercise demonstrates another guitar-music commonplace: chord boxes placed within the notation. Examine these chord boxes before proceeding, to see how the progession moves smoothly from two chords on the 3rd fret to one on the 7th, then the 8th, then two at the 10th. See if you can transpose this I-IV-V progression with an added minor chord into the key of A major. (Hint: you simply need to move all chord shapes up by two frets.)

For the rest of these, you should be able to find the chords on your own – after all, you already know the shapes and locations – but there are a few hints regarding fret numbers now and then. (You can always find all the chord shapes in the diagram section (in the Resources chapter) of this book. Exercise 15 has a lively rock'n'roll feel with a little Latin swing mixed in, and sounds just slightly like numerous hits from over the years. For fun, the use of major and dominant seventh chords has been mixed up so you can hear the different feel that each of these give it.

Exercise 15

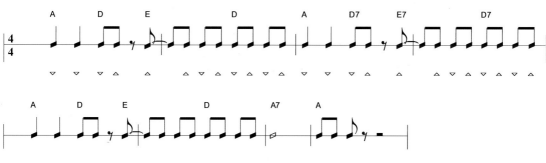

Try playing it in three different ways: using the E and A barre shapes on the 5th and 7th frets; by shifting them to the 12th and 10th frets; and then try it with our good old open chords down at the bottom of the neck. Notice how the piece sounds a little different in each position. For one thing, the versions played with barre chords make it easier to mute unwanted strings that ring out from

Playing barre chords is tough on your fingers at first, but your fingers will soon get used to it with practice.

previous chords when you're playing in the open-chord positions.

Now try driving Exercise 16 all the way home for a sound right out of the indie-rock camp (which can easily lean toward grunge if you're playing it on electric guitar with a little overdrive or distortion dialed in).

This is a good one for just making your barre shapes and moving them up and down the neck. Start with an open E, then push that shape up to the barre chord at the 5th fret (A) and work that shape back down the neck, then for the D that follows the E, jump back to the 5th fret again, and work your way back down (transposing it to other positions makes a great way to extend the exercise, too). Use pumping down-strokes for this one.

Exercise 17 is a slightly melancholy progression in D minor, which also introduces us to 6/4 time. This is another waltz-time signature, but it has a broader swing to it, with more space to breathe, given that there are now sixquarter notes to each measure. You can play this one in a number of ways, but the exercise works best if you use it to get better at moving up and down the neck.

Begin with the Dm barre chord at the 5th fret, move up one fret from there to the B♭ (now the open E chord shape), then move two frets higher to complete the first cycle. Return to your Dm at the 5th fret, then move down this time to the C and G at the 3rd fret, before working back up the neck to end the piece.

Single-note playing

You have already had a taste of single-note playing in the picking exercises earlier in this chapter, but now we'll dig a little deeper with a few scales and techniques. They will give you a good grounding for scales and soloing, and there are plenty of resources available to help you further develop your abilities. One of the beauties of the guitar is that you can find the same note in several places on the fingerboard, which makes it easy – once you learn your way around the neck – to find melodies in positions that are convenient for the chords you are using at the time. Let's begin our exploration of single-note playing by looking at a series of major scales, shown in positions both lower down and higher up the neck. There is not the space here to give you all possible scales

E major scale

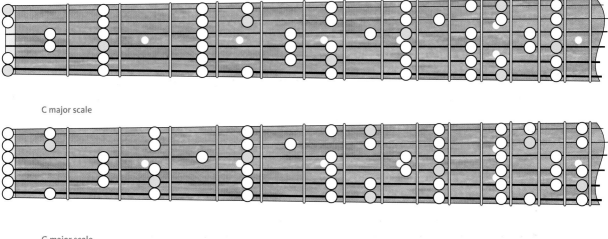

C major scale

G major scale

in all positions at which they could be played, but these will give you a springboard into single-note playing that should enable you to unearth plenty more on your own. The intervals between the notes in the major scale run like so: whole step; whole step; half step; whole step; whole step; whole step; half step. Which, thanks to the linear nature of the fingerboard, corresponds directly to two-fret and one-fret intervals. In other words, the fret jump required to play the E major scale, starting on the open low E string, is 0-2-2-1-2-2-2-1.

To illustrate this, the following scale diagrams will take you up a string in the given key, while also working across the strings to show the scale in a couple of fixed positions. Look for the shaded green root notes as your milestones along each scale (the thickest string pictured in the diagram is the low E string, as you might expect). These fixed positions are often referred to as "boxes": note how the E major scale occurs in two distinct places that could be "boxed off": the section that runs across all six strings at the first four frets of the neck, and the section that runs in the region of the 6th to 10th frets, from the E played on the A string at the 7th fret, with an extension to the 11th and 12th frets, which takes it up another octave.

When playing these scales within a "box" position, try to use all four fingers, with one assigned to each fret (with the occasional slide up or down to reach notes out of the box, if you want to take it further). For example, in the E major scale diagram, to play within the higher box, begin with your middle finger on the A string at the 7th fret, then sound the 9th fret with your little finger; move to the D string and play the 6th fret (index), the 7th (middle) and the 9th (little finger); move to the G string and play the 6th fret (index), 8th fret (ring) and 9th fret (little finger) for the octave E.

Try playing all three of the scales shown working from several different positions illustrated in the diagrams, using either all down-strokes or alternating strokes (or a combination of each) to get your right-hand fluency working. Although we aren't concentrating on music theory too much in this chapter, note that the musical staves in the following exercises will now include the key signatures of the scales or songs. You don't need to understand everything about key signatures. But you need to be aware that any note shown on the stave – the five-line musical notation above the tab – that carries a sharp or flat sign, must be played accordingly sharp or flat, unless it is preceded by a "natural" sign. (That applies to all instances of that note – whether or not it's an octave or two up or down.) Songs in the key of G major, for example, will have a sharp sign on the top line, F, because the F of the G major scale is sharpened. The C major scale has no sharps or flats, so its key signature has no symbols in it. (E major has four sharps, but these symbols were deliberately left off the notation in exercises 1 and 2 in favour of the actual sharps of the scale on the lines where they occur.) The tab is untroubled by such symbols: simply fret the indicated string at the fret given.

The G major scale is a handy one to know, at the very least in its first position, because all the open strings fit into it. This makes it a great key for picking out simple melodies on the lower frets. Note

Two octaves of the G major scale, in notation and tab form

that the finger pattern for the E major scale (described in the last paragraph above) works to play the higher-scale box of this G major scale, but it begins on the 10th fret rather than the 7th. (For now, play the notes in the neck diagram beginning at the low G – E string, 3rd fret – and ignore the notes below it indicated by the square "dots".) Like the G major scale, the C major scale is another handy one to memorize for lower-position playing, because it also incorporates all open strings.

TWO SIMPLE TUNES

Happy now? You should be – you're on your way to playing a little of just about anything. Well, at least you will be once you extend these scales to all the keys, their minors, various modes and so on. You're far enough along to play some tunes at least, so let's dive into two songs with appropriately celebratory themes, using each of the scales we have just learned. Each is shown with both the chords and melody line together (the latter in both tab and standard notation). Try playing each both ways, in whichever order you prefer, and if you have a guitar-playing friend, divide up the parts and take turns playing one and then the other. Feel free to use open chords to give both of them a nice, ringing sound, or try out your barre chords if you want to practise those positions.

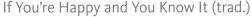

If You're Happy and You Know It (trad.)

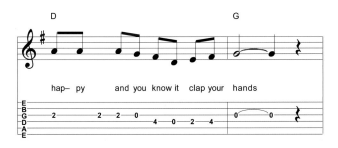

Ode To Joy (Ludwig van Beethoven)

Minor scales

We have already discussed minor chords, and learned how they are created by flattening specific notes in the major scale. As you can probably guess, minor scales employ these same flattened notes, which is what gives them their poignant sound. Have you noticed how well the E minor chord fits in with some of the chord progressions in G major that we have used it in already? That's because the key of G major and the key of E minor are relatives of each other: E minor is the relative minor of G major, and G major is the relative major of E minor. These two scales, major and minor, use the exact same notes; the different sound and feel between them is produced by the relationship created between the intervals by the starting note, or root note, of each scale: G major starts on the G, and E minor starts on the E.

"How about an E minor scale diagram then!" you ask? Well, you already have one. Turn back to the G major scale neck diagram and exercise, and simply start the scale at the bottom open E string (instead of the G). You are now playing the E minor scale instead of the G major scale, two octaves of which end on the high E string. Because these two scales are relatives of each other, they both use the same key signature, too: a single sharp symbol on the top (F) line.

PUTTING IT ALL TOGETHER:
A SONG IN E MINOR

Now strum your open Em chord and play the scale again. See how well it all hangs together? Let's use E minor to play both the melody and chord progression to one of the most famous tunes of all time, "Scarborough Fair". The tune's perhaps best known in the version by Simon and Garfunkel on their 1966 album *Parsley, Sage, Rosemary and Thyme*, but the traditional English folk song that it came from is several hundred years old, and perhaps even dates to an older Scottish folk song that originated around 1670.

The chords provide an accompaniment to the melody. You can play either at a time, get a guitar-playing friend and take turns playing each or, on your own, strum the chord above each measure and play that part of the tune, to hear how it all fits together. Don't be thrown off guard by the C♯ in the eighth measure. It's not a note that's in the E minor scale, but whatever key a song might be in, composers can, and will, use other notes to make the tune work.

Scarborough Fair (trad.)

POPULAR GENRES

But enough of old English folk tunes, kids' songs and classical airs. Let's get rocking, wailing and twanging. To close this chapter, we'll go through some of the scales, licks and tools that make rock, blues and country guitar playing what it is. Broadly speaking, these are the most popular song-based genres in the Western hemisphere so there's a good chance that your enjoyment of one or the other of these is what brought you to the guitar in the first place.

ROCK

Whether you call it rock'n'roll, as it was known in the 1950s and early 60s, or just plain rock, as the harder, heavier genre came to be known, this sound represents one of the most radical and enduring revolutions that popular music has ever seen. As such, it has grown into an extremely broad style, too. It's a genre that just keeps expanding: from the rock'n'roll of Elvis Presley and Buddy Holly, via the hard rock of Led Zeppelin and Jimi Hendrix, to the heavy metal of Black Sabbath and Metallica. Not forgetting the indie-rock of The Smiths and R.E.M. and the grunge of Nirvana and Soundgarden. We can't cover it all here. But we can put together a few of the building blocks that helped to define the sound of rock guitar in the first place, both rhythmically and melodically.

The boogie rhythm

Derived from the shuffle rhythm used in a lot of blues and R&B, the boogie has a straighter eighth note feel, and is usually a little more driving and head-nodding. Think Chuck Berry, The Beach Boys, early Beatles tunes and just about anything Status Quo ever did. To play the pattern in Exercise 18 hold the D string down at the 2nd fret with your index finger and use your ring finger to get the "boogie note" on the 4th fret of the string, while playing the open A and fretted D string together with all down-strokes. The chords are given here, too, and they can be either open chords or barre chords. Full chords really aren't necessary to the feel of this kind of playing – the two-note pattern defines the rhythm and the melodic movement just fine – but it's something for a second guitar to do if you're playing together.

You can repeat this exercise ad infinitum or, to make it into a typical twelve-bar rock'n'roll progression, play four bars of the A pattern, two bars of D, two bars of A, two bars of E, then finish on two of A. (Or alternatively, finish with one bar of A and another bar of E, the "V" chord.) The end result should sound very familiar.

Exercise 18

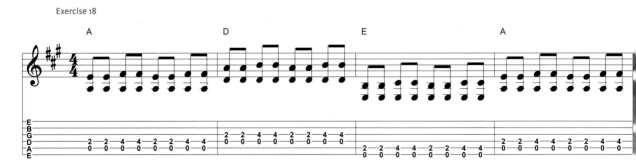

Chuck Berry: a master of pre-rock'n'roll styles, and a true boogie monster.

Exercises 19 and 19a offer two more variations of the boogie pattern, which extend it another half step, to produce another very familiar sound and feel. Exercise 19 drives straight up and back, while 19a gives it a little more movement by bouncing back and forth between the ascending note and the starting point. Of course, you can always transpose these variations to the chords in the full

pattern given in Exercise 18.

Look out for the natural symbol (♮)in this one, which occurs on the three Gs in the notation (on the D string at the 5th fret). This indicates that you do not play a G♯ here, even though the key signature for A major has a sharp in the G position (the space above the top line).

Lead guitar

Ready to play a little lead guitar? You know you are! Exercise 20 is an energetic little rock'n'roll lead part in the style of Chuck Berry. The three notes at the start act as a short introduction before the progression really kicks in, and the rest can be played over the boogie A chord, if you have a friend to play along. Alternatively, you could record yourself and play along – this sounds great with a little boogie-style rhythm guitar behind it. At the end of the four full bars given here, the progression would naturally move on to the D chord, as in the extended twelve-bar version of Exercise 18. If you're playing it unaccompanied, you can also simply play this four-and-three-eighths bars lead part as a solo, then pick up the boogie twelve-bar at the D chord. If you really want to be clever, transpose the first two full bars of this solo over the D barre chord found using the open E shape at the 10th fret (these solo licks are really pretty, simply because they largely just trace the shapes of these chords). Then, when the progression moves to E (the V in this I-IV-V), transpose the solo part over the E barre chord at the 12th fret, or the open E chord back down at the nut.

The lead guitarist's secret weapon: minor pentatonic scales

To take your 50s rock'n'roll playing forwards in time to the rock playing of 1970 and beyond, it's time you learned about the nifty little soloing tool known as the minor pentatonic scale. Pentatonic scales are made up of five notes, and in the minor pentatonic scale this handy five-note collection works perfectly for a surprisingly wide variety of solos, simply because – with the right kind of chord progression behind it – you really can't hit a wrong note. Although it's called *minor*

Power chords

As simple as they are, these chords are forceful both in name and in nature. Known technically as a "perfect fifth", a power chord is a two-note chord that includes a root note and a note that's a fifth away from it (remember, when you count intervals, to begin with "one" on the root, so the fifth from A is E, for example). Power chords occur in virtually all forms of rock, punk, heavy metal, grunge, new wave and pretty much every other sub-genre you can think of, simply because they work so well as a rhythm device, and are so extremely versatile.

What gives these measly two-note chords their power, when, for example, a full barre chord would seem to have more impact? For one thing, the tight, tidy perfect fifth plays extremely well with others: play it against a melody in a major or minor key and it's equally happy, because it contains no notes that will clash with either. That makes it easy to drive the power chord up and down the fingerboard as a chunky, pumping rhythm-guitar part, without having to reshape it to account for minor shifts, the arrival of a dominant seventh, or what have you. Another of its strengths lies in the fact that, when you want a big, tight, muscular sound in rock music, less is often more. Too much sonic information can sometimes clutter up the mix in the midst of a full band, especially when heavily distorted guitars are involved. The perfect-fifth interval behind the power chord creates no extraneous harmonics or dissonant tones when played with some overdrive pedal or amp filth, so it comes out sounding big, rather than flabby.

The real beauty of power chords, for beginners in particular, is that if you have already worked at your barre chord fingerings and locations, you already know where to find your power chords, and they're a whole lot easier to play, too. Find any major or minor barre chord you like, anywhere on the neck, and the lowest two strings give you the power chord. Play the open E-shaped G major at the 3rd fret, and the G and D on the low E and A strings give you the perfect fifth. *Voilà*, power chord! Shift to the open A shape at the same fret and the A string 3rd fret/D string 5th fret pairing gives you the C-G power chord and so on. It really couldn't be easier. If you want more emphasis on the root, you can even make these into three-string power chords with the fifth and the octave (G-D-G and C-G-C, for example), but two notes is usually plenty.

If there's anything tricky about power chords it's the way in which you play them, or more to the point, the way you need to mute other strings while just letting that two-note fifth ring out. The fingers that fret the notes (usually the index finger and ring finger, which have just the perfect spread to reach that interval with ease) can do the job for you by fretting only the notes to be played, while resting lightly on the unplayed strings. Sometimes you want to hear just the notes of your power chord and nothing else, but in some circumstances hearing a little of the tick-tick-tick-tick of the muted strings underneath adds some chunk and drive and a more aggressive feel to the entire rhythm guitar part. Power chords are also great tools for palm-muting, a technique where you dampen the played strings just a little with the edge of your hand, to firm up the entire sound and keep them from ringing too much and slopping up the rhythm.

Try the exercise on p.104 in several different ways, playing only the power chords and letting them ring, then muting them slightly, then muting the chords and adding a little tick-tick from the muted strings underneath them and so on. If you want more power chord practice, you can also go back to any of the rockier barre chord progressions that you have already played and find the power chords within those. If you're playing an electric guitar and have access to some form of overdrive, try putting a little hair on them to see how that sounds, too.

pentatonic, you don't have to play it to a progression in a minor key, and it fits in equally well with major, minor and dominant seventh progressions.

When exploring minor pentatonic scales, most players stick within a fairly restricted "scale box", or position, which makes mistakes unlikely. The fingerboard diagram below shows the most common boxes in which the E minor pentatonic, A minor pentatonic and D minor pentatonic

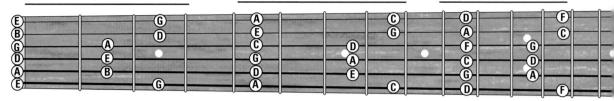

scales are located. The first of these is an extremely useful scale to know because it includes all the open strings. The second two are a little further up the neck, and are a good vehicle for blues-rock bends.

To see how well these simple scales work over major and minor progressions alike, go back to the music for "Scarborough Fair" and strum through the chord progressions without playing the melody. If you're able to record it to play along to, record this version of the chord progression – or, if not, have a friend play it for you – then play notes from the E minor pentatonic scale over the top of it, in any order you choose. You should be able to see (or rather, hear) how you really can't go too far wrong with these scales.

Exercise 21 takes you through a chord progression in A major with some simple rock soloing from the A minor pentatonic scale over the top of it (again, either record the chord progression, get a friend to play it or play one and then the other). The rhythm for the chord progression will be given in the stave this time, with the solo part in the tab only. Be aware that you have your first string bends coming up here in the fifth, sixth and final measures. As described in Chapter 1, a bend is indicated (here in the tab only) by an arched line connecting two notes, the first of which is the starting note, and the second of which is the note you want to reach by bending the string.

When indicated in tab in this way, you don't actually move your finger to the fret indicated by the number at the right side of the arched line, but you push the string upwards with your finger

Power chords exercise (see box on previous page)

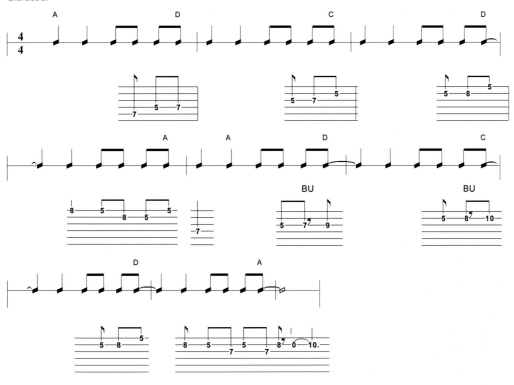

until it reaches the same tone indicated by that number. When you're just beginning to learn string bending, however, it might be a good idea to actually fret the higher note *first* to hear what you're aiming for, then go back to the starting point and push the string up to reach that pitch. The bend in the sixth measure is what we call a "unison bend": the proper way to play it is to fret the high E string at the 5th fret with your index finger, fret the B string at the 8th fret with your ring finger with your middle finger behind it for strength, then pick both strings together, letting the high E string ring while you bend the B string up to meet the note. If you're playing this on an electric guitar through an amplifier, you might want to try it with a little overdrive or distortion to make the bends really sing. Bending is a big part of rock lead guitar playing, but is perhaps even more characteristic of blues. For more detailed instructions on the art, see "Blues Bending" later in this chapter.

THE BLUES

Even if you don't count yourself a fan of the blues, it's worth learning to play a little of it on the guitar because it is one of the major building blocks of popular music of the past sixty years. Blues was certainly one of the parents of rock'n'roll, and its echoes continue to be heard in several sub-genres of rock to this day.

As much as anything, the blues is a *feel* thing: plenty of its greatest practitioners had very little technical prowess on the instrument, but could make a listener cry with the raw power and beauty of their playing. On the other hand, several other blues guitarists are among the most accomplished players out there in any genre, yet they can still move an audience with the pure emotion that just a handful of notes can convey. However simple or complex it might be, the blues usually distinguishes itself through a combination of rhythm and melodic sense, and you need to grasp a little of both to get this feel right.

Blues rhythm: the shuffle

Fail to grasp the blues shuffle, and many a great blues song becomes simply a rock'n'roll song, and feels all wrong in the process. Compared to the straight, steady, driving sound of the classic rock'n'roll rhythm, the blues shuffle has a bounce to it, a certain strut or swagger that gives it more swing, more groove. As with many rock songs, it's the eighth note that's the main rhythmic unit for most blues songs in 4/4 time. But to make this feel right for the blues, these eighth notes have a little space between them – quite literally. Rather than playing straight eighth notes – where eight beats in a measure all receive equal weight – a pair of blues eighth notes are played as if they were the first and last note of a triplet.

A triplet is a rhythmic figure used to squeeze three equally weighted beats into the space where two would normally exist. It doesn't convert the song into 3/4 time, but simply alters the rhythmic feel for the length of that triplet. Triplets occur in all kinds of music, but in the classic blues shuffle, eighth-note pairs throughout the piece are treated as triplets, although only the first and third beats of the three-beat figure are played. Looked at another way, if this is easier to grasp, you achieve the same rhythmic feel by approaching each pair of eighth notes as if the first is actually a quarter note, and the second is an eighth note. In other words, if counting out the beat for a blues shuffle, rather than counting straight eighth notes as discussed earlier in this chapter ("one-and 2-and 3-and 4-and"), count the blues rhythm out as "one-uh-and two-uh-and three-uh-and four-uh-and, but consider the "uh" silent, so it's "one-(uh)-and two-(uh)-and three-(uh)-and four-(uh)-and".

Throughout, the emphasis is on the first eighth note of each grouping, which creates the effect, once the beat gets rolling, of the second note of the grouping giving a little push to the first eighth note of the group that follows: "BAP-ba-BAP-ba-BAP-ba-BAP-ba". The best thing to do is to listen to a blues shuffle in action: check out Muddy Waters' "Hoochie Coochie Man" for a slow blues shuffle, or "Baby Please Don't Go" for something a little more mid-tempo, and you'll hear exactly what I'm talking about.

This rhythm can be applied to the basic strumming pattern of the rhythm guitar in a blues tune (as well as to the general feel and swing of any lead parts playing over it), or it can be played like the boogie rhythm that we investigated at the start of the Rock section above. Exercise 22 takes it both ways, so you can try two variations of this rhythm part: the stave gives you the rhythm pattern for playing this twelve-bar blues progression using seven chords (I like it best played using the D7 barre chord at the 10th fret, and the shortened variations of the G7 and A7 given in the chord boxes), while the tab gives you the fingering to play it boogie-shuffle style.

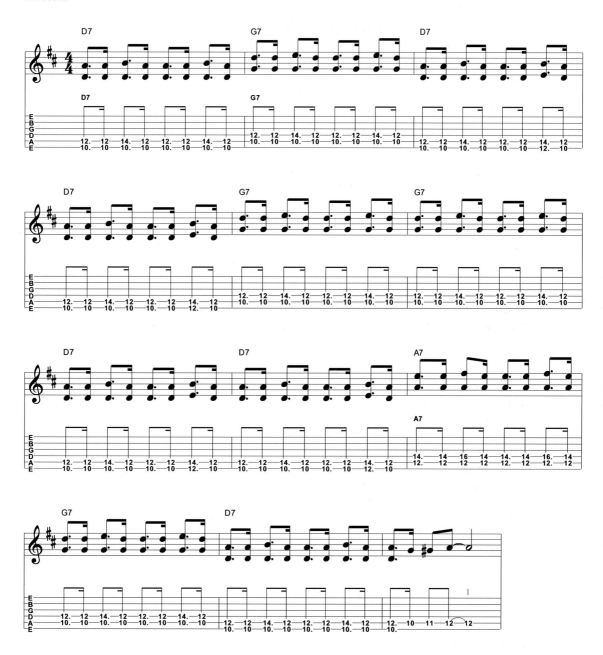

To play the latter, you fret the root note with your index finger, the fifth with your ring finger, and pump your little finger two frets up from there to hit the "boogie note" (be aware that often the blues version of this guitar boogie is played with the top note hit for one beat at a time, as it is in this case). If you have a friend to play with, or are able to record parts to play along to, two guitars can play one part each, and they fit extremely well together for a groovin', dual rhythm-

The Hoochie Coochie Man himself, Muddy Waters, was a master of the blues shuffle technique.

guitar blues progression. Otherwise, play it one way, then play it around again the other way. Note that the end of each part contains the same little three-note run-up, another little signature of the blues called a turnaround, countless variations of which are used to signal the end of a full cycle of the twelve-bar progression.

The blues scale

A whole lot of blues lead guitar can be played with the minor pentatonic scale discussed above in the Rock section, but one slight addition to this scale can make the entire affair a whole lot bluesier. And if you paid attention to that little turnaround in Exercise 22, you have already played it.

 The blues scale is simply the minor pentatonic scale with the addition of a flattened fifth, which gives you that chromatic run that we used in our turnaround: G, G♯, A which in the key of D is the four, flat five, and five of the scale. In a little turnaround like the one we just played, the run is fretted, but in a blues solo the flat five is often hit by bending up to it from the four, and back down again. This is only a semitone bend, but it really gives you the flavour of the blues.

Blues bends

Bending is a huge part of blues guitar, and is formative in creating that wailing, singing, moaning sound that this style of playing is known for. We have already encountered string bending, but it's worth putting a little more thought into the technique here, and few tips on the mechanics of this skill will be useful to beginners.

Somes blues bends will create mere trills that barely lift the note a semitone. Proper bending technique says that you usually ought to have a target pitch in mind before you push the string up, rather than just bending for all your worth – and possibly bending yourself right into a clunker. A good way to practise bending is to fret a note partway up the fingerboard on the G string – the D found at the 7th fret, say – pick it, then slide up two frets to pick the E found there. Now, take yourself back down to the D, and this time bend it up until you hit that same E note accurately.

The physical act of bending a string can be hard on your fingertips until you have built up some calluses, and it's always a lot easier on an electric guitar than on an acoustic, although you'll be able to do this too in time (light strings help considerably). To successfully achieve the bend just described, place your ring finger on the string just behind the 7th fret, then put your middle finger behind it – either in the same fret space, or behind the 6th fret, if you find that more comfortable – and use both fingers to push the string upwards along the fret, towards the top edge of the fingerboard.

Strings can also be bent by pulling down, and this technique suits certain playing situations well, but the pushed-up bend is more common. Practise this a while, and throw it into your playing when and where you can, and eventually you'll discover all kinds of sneaky ways to bend strings, and to use the sound in your music.

Look back at the minor pentatonic scales outlined on the neck diagram in the Rock section. Play each again, but this time add these notes:

◇ E minor pentatonic: A string, 1st fret; G string, 3rd fret

◇ A minor pentatonic: A string, 6th fret; G string, 8th fret

◇ D minor pentatonic: A string, 11th fret; G string 13th fret

Blue notes

Each of the following exercises displays riffs in E minor pentatonic that incorporate the "blue note" – the flattened five – either bent-up-to or fretted. (Note that although the scale you solo over is called the E minor pentatonic scale, these tunes would still be in the key of E major.)

Exercise 23

Exercise 23 is a classic solo lick that might come toward the start or middle of a solo, played against a boogie-shuffle rhythm (or alternately, a shuffle rhythm with dominant seventh chords). For this twelve-bar cycle, rather than the progression used above, which goes right to the IV chord in the second measure, we're using an alternative blues progression that stays on the I for the first four measures. So it goes: E–E–E–E–A–A–E–E–B–A–E–B.

Exercise 24

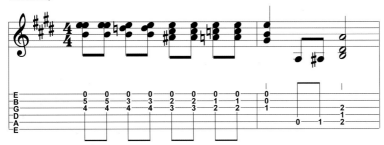

Exercise 24 is a typical turnaround riff that runs down chromatically, hitting that blue note on the way, then runs back up on the A string, hitting the flattened fifth again, and landing on the V chord (a B7 this time) to end the chorus. Note that the rendition in the tab includes a doubling of notes in the first eighth note pair that can't be shown in the notation, since you're playing an E both on the B string at the 5th fret and on the open high E string. This riff lets that high E ring throughout the entire first bar, which creates a counterpoint to the chromatic descent.

Exercise 25 runs down from the high E string to the low E string, using the blues rhythm and the E minor pentatonic blues scale to get there. Because the shuffle rhythm is based on a triplet with an absent middle note (otherwise indicated as a quarter note plus an eighth note), actual triplets also fit into blues leads extremely well.

There are three of them here, indicated by the bar with the "3" above the notation. For the blues bend in the second measure, you're not really playing the note at the 2nd fret before the bend, but hitting the note mid-bend to give the feel of bending into the target note, then bending back down out of it. You can play the accompanying rhythm part either as dominant seven chords or as a boogie-shuffle.

Exercise 25

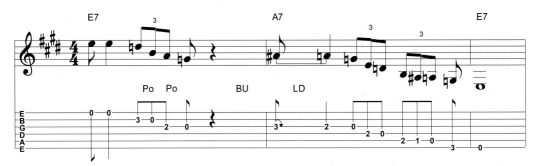

COUNTRY

Mention country music and many readers will think of big hats, tall boots and line-dancing. But in the twenty-first century, country has become a broad genre and, in the general sense, influences playing styles heard in plenty of sub-genres such as roots-rock, Americana, alt.country, rockabilly and plain old rock and pop too. Here we will cover a few of the distinctive elements of the country sound, so you can bring a touch of twang into your own playing in other genres (or, of course, pursue pure country playing further on your own).

The major pentatonic scale

While rock and – to some extent – blues soloing is based around the minor pentatonic scale, traditional country music, as influenced by bluegrass, is based around a more major pentatonic scale (often referred to without the "major" for short). You might describe this five-note sequence as having a jolly sound when compared to the minor pentatonic scale's slightly moody sound. Hot country pickers actually distinguish themselves by leaping around between these two scales, which lends a jazzy inflection to traditional country styles, but since we've already spent some time with the minor pentatonic, this is a good place to dig into the major pentatonic scale, which, when played with the right attitude, just screams country pickin', while it's also useful for lots of rock'n'roll and even some blues, with the proper inflections.

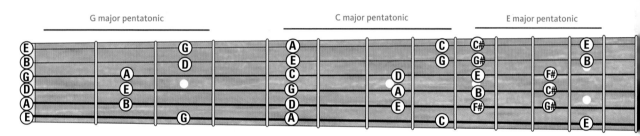

The best pentatonic scale for beginners is G major pentatonic, because it starts from the good old position of an open G chord and includes all the open strings on its way from low E to high E and beyond. Sound familiar? That's right – you already know this fingering as the E minor pentatonic scale. To play it as the G major pentatonic scale instead, start on the G found on the low E string, 3rd fret, instead of the open E.

Exercise 26

Play your way up the first octave of the G major pentatonic scale and you're already playing a classic country lick known as the G Run, which Exercise 26 (overleaf) gives you with the right feel and panache – an essential part of which involves the hammer-ons and hammer-off. To do the hammer-ons correctly, play, for example, the open A string then "hammer" your fingertip down just behind the 2nd fret to achieve the super-quick B note. For the next lick, play the open D string, then hammer on and off again at the 2nd fret with a steady rhythm. Hammer-ons and hammer-offs do take some practice, but you'll get the hang of it after a while, and they really help to increase your playing speed once you do.

While hammer-ons are a useful tool in rock and blues lead playing, they're also a big part of country rhythm playing, and a characteristic of bluegrass guitar in particular. Maybelle Carter is credited as one of the originators of this style of playing, which she first popularized with the Carter Family way back in the late 1920s, and she used hammer-ons amid simple open-chord structures to give movement and bounce to her rhythm guitar parts, as heard on songs such as "May the Circle Be Unbroken" and "Wildwood Flower".

The hand of Maybelle Carter, country legend, photographed by Alan Lomax as she showed him a few chords, during one of his many song-collecting expeditions.

Exercise 27 takes you across a couple of bars of chord changes in G major using hammer-ons in this way to propel you through the progression. To play this one, form your hands in the standard open G and open C chord shapes, and think of them as chords "played in pieces", built up of hammer-ons and hammer-offs, using the fingers already in position to achieve the desired notes.

Exercise 27

Doc Watson, genius of hot country flatpicking.

Country bends

String bends have long been a part of country guitar playing, and really define the "twang" that we think of when this style of music comes to mind. Such bends were first used to imitate the sound of a fiddle player sliding up the strings, and later, the extreme bends performed by the pedal-steel guitar. As such, country bends are often a little more precise-sounding than blues bends, and rather than pushing a string just a semitone up to the "blue note" (or similar), they tend to hit a target note more clinically and "mechanically", to achieve the desired pedal-steel guitar effect (certainly many blues players achieve wider bends than the semitone into the flattened fifth, and can be very precise too, but stick with me here...). To complete this sonic picture, country bends usually work against the backdrop of a second, un-bent note that stands in contrast, sometimes a unison note that the bend goes up to hit, but often a third interval, which harmonizes with the bent note.

Exercise 28 takes you through two classic country thirds bends in the key of G major. The notation for this can be a bit confusing – although the tab gives you the fingering you need to make it work.

Exercise 28

In short, you want to hold the high G on the high E string (3rd fret) with your little finger while using your ring finger (with the middle finger behind it for support) to bend the D on the B string (also 3rd fret) up to an E; next, hold the D on the B string (3rd fret) while bending the G string at the 2nd fret up to a B.

Although this is classic country guitar, you hear bends like these all over the place, and this is the kind of thing players whip out when they want to countrify a rock song. The second bend here, for

Keith Richards slipped plenty of country bends into Rolling Stones tracks such as "Honky Tonk Woman", and the country sound can be heard all over their *Beggars Banquet* album.

Using a capo

A capo is a movable clamp that attaches to the neck of the guitar to bar, or hold down, the strings at a desired fret, essentially shortening the playing length of all strings simultaneously. Players use capos for a variety of reasons. They are particularly useful for quickly changing the key of a song without having to transpose the chords that you might already be familiar with in a different key, if, for example, you're backing a singer who decides on the spur of the moment to change the key of a tune to better suit his or her vocal range.

A capo also provides an excellent means of achieving certain desirable open-string positions for riffs or chords that need to be played higher up the neck to fit a particular song. A capo is a handy tool for the beginner, making it possible to play a great many songs in a wide range of keys with knowledge of only a few basic chords, although plenty of experienced players use capos for a wide range of advanced techniques. Say you only know your first-position G, C, D and Em, but want to play a song along with other musicians who do it in the key of A major? No problem – slap on a capo at the second fret, use the same open-chord shapes, and away you go.

A wide variety of capos are available. The most affordable takes the form of an elastic strap that wraps around the neck and clips in place to keep a firm rubber pad with steel backing in place behind the fret. These do the job adequately, and might be fine for the occasional capo user, but they can be awkward to position and reposition. More elaborate models, made by companies such as Kyser and Shubb, are made out of steel or die-cast aluminium, with springs or thumb screws to provide the string-clamping tension. If you find a capo useful – and many players do – it's probably worth investing in one of a decent quality, because these are usually easier to put on and take off the guitar than the "elastic strap" variety, and frequently provide more balanced string tension and better tuning accuracy as well.

Once you've got your hands on a capo, you need to know how to use it. For most guitars, a capo works best when positioned fairly snugly up beside the fret at which you want to stop the strings (note, a capo is never placed right on top of the fret, but just behind it, on the nut-side of the desired fret). This positioning keeps the strings more secure on most guitars, and if your guitar was in tune before you positioned the capo – and its intonation is good – it should still be relatively in tune with the capo on.

If your fingerboard has the higher frets that are popular with some players today, you might need to take extra care in positioning the capo, and perhaps move it further back from the fret to avoid pulling the strings out of tune. Also, try to avoid tugging strings sideways or altering the spacing between each string when you position the capo, as this will both pull you out of tune, and create an awkward feel on the fingerboard. You can always re-tune once your capo is on, and sometimes this is necessary, but ideally you can clamp the thing on and off again with no need for readjustment, and with no interruption to the flow of your performance.

example, is very similar to the starting point of the Rolling Stones' "Honky Tonk Woman".

Between them, the exercises in rock, blues and country in this chapter will hopefully have given you some of the flavour of these popular genres, a taste of something you'll want to pursue further on your own. In the following chapter, I'll touch on some more advanced playing techniques, and explore a range of more alternative guitar styles and sounds that have contributed to creative music over the years.

advanced playing & TECHNIQUES

Plenty of guitarists go a long way simply by making the most of the "standard" playing styles we have already touched upon. Others go further, using more advanced techniques that push the envelope a little, and access some less conventional voices. In this chapter we'll explore several of these, from fingerstyle, alternate tunings and slide techniques on the playing side, to some radical amplifier and effects applications on the tone side. Even if you aren't drawn towards specializing in any of these, bringing a little of one or all of them into your everyday playing can certainly broaden your horizons, and challenge you as a musician as well.

As in the previous chapter, some liberties are taken with standard notation and tab formats here in an effort to simplify many of the exercises for readers who have little or no previous experience reading such exercises. Many conventions will still be followed, and these exercises will still be entirely legible to experienced players, but as rendered here they should also be more accessible to a wider range of players.

The object is to get you playing the guitar, rather than worrying about the particulars of the traditional teaching techniques. To that end various forms of shorthand have been used, in an effort to make the exercises more concise and easily digestible.

FINGERSTYLE

All guitar playing requires using your fingers in one way or another, sure, but the term fingerstyle guitar refers to a specific method. Instead of strumming, or picking with a plectrum, individual fingers of the right hand pluck strings independently of each other. It's a technique that can lead to increased speed and fluidity once mastered, and greatly ease the playing of certain figures such as arpeggios and cascades in particular.

Fingerstyle playing is big in several sub-genres of folk music, and is also used by many country players (who sometimes combine it with the use of a pick, a technique called hybrid picking). Some jazz artists use it too. It originates, of course, with classical guitar playing, which is *all* fingerstyle, and very strict in the way the art is approached.

The attitude to fingerstyle in this chapter won't be as rigid as the technique taught in classical guitar, but it will help to build up a set of skills that will help you make your own exploration of this versatile method. With all of the following exercises, begin slowly at first; the technique is likely to feel awkward the first time you try it, but your fingers will get used to it with practice. Keep your right hand and wrist loose and relaxed, and positioned much as they would be to strum the strings with a pick, but stationary in their position. Without a pick to grip, your thumb should extend slightly forwards of your index finger (that is, towards the neck of the guitar).

With your hand in position, you can get a feel for the technique, to begin with, by forming any open chord you like and simply plucking the low E string with your thumb, then plucking the G, B and high E strings in succession with your index, middle and ring fingers respectively. Work towards a fluid, easy motion with the thumb and fingers of the right hand – you don't need to grab the strings or pluck them too hard in order to achieve an adequate sound – and try to play to a steady, flowing rhythm. Practise this basic technique for a while, then move on to the following exercises.

PICKING PATTERNS

In the previous chapter the colloquial names of the fingers of the left hand were used – index, middle, ring and little finger – to instruct you on which was which when describing hand positions for chording. But for our purposes here, it will be easier to label them as: T (thumb), 1, 2 and 3. The little finger of the right hand is almost never used, other than by very advanced players to execute the occasional daring move.

Experienced fingerstyle guitarists use all kinds of picking patterns to play their music. The most basic is the straight T-1-2-3 pattern, but other patterns include a roll through these and back again (T-1-2-3-2-1), and patterns that skip back and forth across strings (such as T-2-1-3; or T-1-2-T-1-3; or T-2-1-T-3-2). Really, any conceivable finger order that gets the musical results you seek is entirely valid. We'll begin with some simple, steady and consistent picking patterns to help you build up your right-hand skills.

Exercise 1 takes you through the basic T-1-2-3 pattern over a simple I-IV-V chord change in C major. Your goal here is to maintain a steady rhythm with the fingers of the right hand and, once you feel you've got that down, you can try increasing your speed. Don't expect too much too soon: it's a tricky skill to master. As you progress through these chord changes, notice how the thumb takes the bass notes (the root note of each chord), while the fingers stay in position on the three

Exercise 1. Repeat the right-hand fingering given in the first bar throughout.

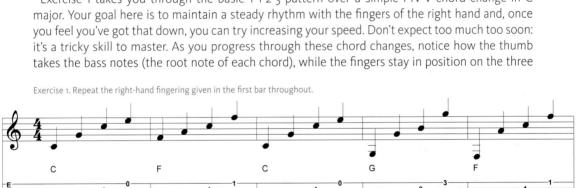

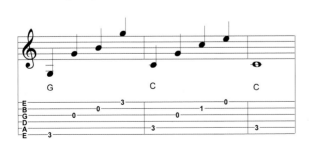

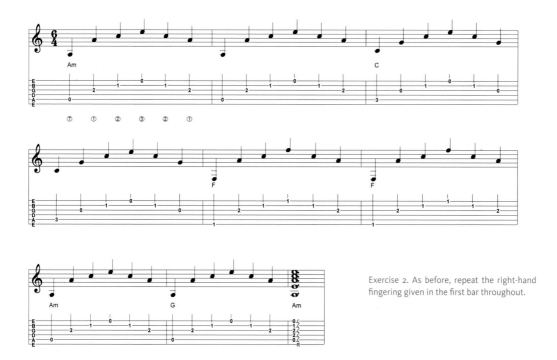

Exercise 2. As before, repeat the right-hand fingering given in the first bar throughout.

higher strings. This is one of the beauties of fingerstyle: even when playing a simple pattern such as this, it creates the effect of a self-accompaniment of sorts, with separate bass and melody parts.

Next, we'll get a little moodier, with a chord progression in A minor played in 6/4 time. This picking pattern takes us "out and back" through each measure: T-1-2-3-2-1. Exercise 2 is still a very simple piece, but playing it fingerstyle rather than just strumming the chords gives it a much more evocative sound. The wavy line with an arrow at the top after the final chord in the stave and tab indicates a "rake", meaning you strum smoothly through the chord, rather than *thrang* it all at once. Exercise 3 gets a little more complicated, because it requires you to skip back and forth through the order of fingers to achieve the T-2-1-3 pattern. It underlines another of the strengths of fingerstyle playing: note the way the pattern traces each chord, while also sounding like a sweet little melody in and of itself. It's simple, but extremely effective. Repeat the four-bar chord progression twice – or as often as you like – before ending on the raked G chord.

Things get a tad trickier in Exercise 4, which not only uses the T-1-2-T-1-3 pattern against a 6/4 time signature, but also has your thumb moving between strings even within the same chord to pick an alternating bass part. Work very slowly to begin with, and perhaps repeat the Em part several times until you get the hang of the right-hand technique before moving on through the piece.

Exercise 3

Also, note that the D chord is slightly different in the third and fourth bars, in that it first goes up to the open high E string on the sixth beat of the measure, then completes the D major chord by hitting the high D on the sixth beat of the following bar (high E string, 2nd fret). This is a

Exercise 4

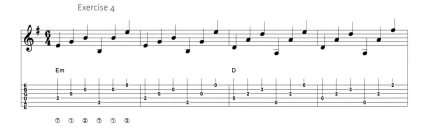

challenging one, but you'll get it if you let yourself build up gradually, and it has a lovely, plaintive sound when you finally nail it.

The House of the Rising Sun

Now that you've got a decent grounding in fingerstyle, let's turn you loose on a classic. "The House of the Rising Sun" is an American folk song (author unknown) that has been performed in many ways by many different artists, the best-known recording probably being the one that landed The Animals a number one hit in 1964. It lends itself beautifully to fingerstyle, particularly the "up and back" picking pattern we worked on in Exercise 2. As you work your way through it, be aware that the bass notes occasionally shift on chords that repeat: the first F, for example, hits its low root note on the D string, 3rd fret, while the next one goes down to the low E string, 1st fret, and the two E chords, back-to-back, do a similar trick.

Getting the feel of the fingerpicking right relies on setting a fairly quick, rolling pace, and keeping up with the swift progression – which usually changes chords every bar – but start out as slow as you need to get it going, and don't feel like you have to have the tune together all at once. Work on pieces one at a time, and simply strum through the chord changes first, if that helps

Ten great fingerstyle songs

1 **Don't Think Twice, It's Alright** Bob Dylan, *The Freewheelin' Bob Dylan*, 1963

2 **Going to California** Led Zeppelin (performed by Jimmy Page), *Led Zeppelin IV*, 1971

3 **Poor Boy Long Ways from Home** John Fahey, *Blind Joe Death, Vol 1*, 1963

4 **Landslide** Fleetwood Mac (performed by Lindsey Buckingham), *Fleetwood Mac*, 1975

5 **Carmine Street** Kaki King, *Everybody Loves You*, 2003

6 **One of These Things First** Nick Drake, *Bryter Layter*, 1970

7 **Peace Like a River** Paul Simon, *Paul Simon*, 1972

8 **Blackbird** The Beatles (performed by Paul McCartney), *The White Album*, 1968

9 **The Fisherman** Leo Kottke, *6- and 12-String Guitar*, 1971

10 **Angie** Bert Jansch, *Bert Jansch*, 1965

House of the Rising Sun (trad.)

you get the left hand down before worrying about the right. Build it up at your own pace. It's a fun song to play and sing, once you get there. Once you start getting into fingerstyle playing the technique can be addictive, and you'll also notice more and more great songs that are performed in this manner (see the playlist). If you find it's a style that you really enjoy, you might want to explore the work of some of the more adventurous players in this genre. Seek out the work of Leo Kottke, Bert Jansch, Michael Hedges, Adrian Legg, Kaki King, Laurence Juber, Pierre Bensusan or Will Ackerman to hear some astounding work on acoustic guitar – often in "alternate tunings" (which we will come to next in this chapter).

Plenty of big-name rock and folk singer-songwriters, such as Bob Dylan, Paul Simon and James Taylor, are actually very respectable fingerstyle players in their own right, having been inspired by blues and folk legends such as Robert Johnson, Leadbelly and Woody Guthrie, all of whom laid the groundwork for this style of playing.

OPEN & ALTERNATE TUNINGS

The traditional tuning of the six-string guitar – what we call standard tuning – has evolved as a compromise between playing easy chord shapes and accessing intervals from string to string for single-note playing. But players have long sought alternatives. Open and alternate tunings are used to achieve a wide variety of goals, whether to make certain scales more accessible on open strings for lead playing (regardless of the awkward chord shapes such retuning might throw up), or to create open and linear barre chords for slide playing. Several of the more adventurous instrumentalists named and listed toward the end of the Fingerstyle section use unusual tunings to achieve their desired sounds, and much of what they play would be extremely difficult to pull off in standard tuning.

Tunings other than standard (EADGBE, from low to high) fall into two camps – open and alternate – although there is occasionally some grey area between them. Put simply, open tunings are those that create a full chord when the strings are strummed as open notes (without pressing any fingers down).

Alternate tunings might not necessarily produce a desired chord when all strings are sounded, but simply retune the strings to make certain scales more accessible. To the uninitiated, these departures from standard tuning can be anywhere from slightly confusing to utterly baffling. It's easy to get into a mindset that says that standard tuning is "correct" and anything else is not quite right – it certainly might seem that way to your fingers and ears when you first venture into these uncharted waters. The fact is, however, that using an alternate tuning will actually make it a lot easier to play many styles of music, and chances are you'll feel at home with the changes a lot quicker than you might expect after just a short time of dedicated practice.

This is a lesson that is quickly learned by anybody who ever tries to master Jimmy Page's playing on Led Zeppelin's "Kashmir" in standard tuning, when they finally discover the secret of DADGAD. And one that will open new doors of creative freedom for the would-be bottleneck blues player when their more experienced friend finally tells them about open D or open G. After all, standard tuning is an accepted compromise: it sets up fingering positions on the six-string guitar that let us play a little of just about anything in any key relatively easily, but it doesn't by any means offer the easiest or most logical means of achieving other more specific stylistic ends... which is where alternate tunings rule the day.

Plenty of rock has been played on alternate and open tunings, too, so they aren't just the provinces of obscure blues artists and virtuoso fingerpickers. Keith Richards of the Rolling Stones often plays in open G (as heard in the signature riffs of "Honky Tonk Woman", "Brown Sugar" and "Start Me Up"), and Billy Gibbons of ZZ Top frequently uses it for his greasy Texas blues. Jimi Hendrix and Stevie Ray Vaughan both commonly played with their Strats tuned a half-step flat on all strings. Several rockers and country players alike keep their guitars in "dropped D", which is standard tuning other than dropping the low E string down to D.

Open and alternate tunings can be a lot of fun to play around with, particularly for the way they open up other melodic avenues, and they can freshen up your approach to the instrument when you're in a stylistic rut. The following section will introduce you to the tunings and scales associated with the most popular of these alternatives, and provide some chord diagrams and

Finger picks

While plenty of fingerstyle players use their bare fingertips and fingernails (sometimes one or the other, often a little of both), there's also a tradition of using finger picks for fingerstyle playing. Finger picks come to us from the banjo and Dobro (resonator guitar) worlds, where they have been in use for more than a century. They're not employed in classical guitar, where the softer nylon strings make them unnecessary. When discussed in the plural, a set of finger picks includes a thumb pick that fits over the thumb (something like a ring with a guitar pick extending from it) and three finger picks, which have bands to keep them in place on the tips of the index, middle, and ring fingers. All are traditionally made from steel, although plastic types exist today as well. Many players, country artists in particular, will use a thumb pick only for a hybrid picking style, and usually turn to a plastic pick for this application.

Finger picks offer several benefits to the steel-string fingerstyle player. In addition to increasing the volume of the instrument, the improve the clarity and definition of the picked notes, since they are harder and sharper than either flesh or fingernails. On top of their sonic benefits, finger picks will obviously help to preserve a player's fingertips, which can otherwise take a beating after hours of fingerstyle playing, especially on an instrument with heavy gauge strings.

They can take some getting used to, however, and many players find them ungainly and awkward upon first trying out a set. They do disconnect you from the direct feel of the strings, and that can sometimes be off putting, but for many playing styles the benefits make it worth persevering. For experienced players who use them, these appendages eventually become like a second skin. If you try some out, be aware that the finger picks are worn with the curved picking surface covering the curved, fleshy surface of the fingertip, rather than covering the fingernail.

exercises you can hone your skills on. Be aware that any open tuning can also be used to achieve easy positions in other keys, simply by placing a capo at the appropriate fret. For example, with your guitar tuned to open G, you can place a capo at the 5th fret to access open C, and so on.

Open G tuning

One of the main tunings of five-string banjo, open G is also popular with National and Dobro guitar players, but has proven itself surprisingly versatile in the rock world, too. It's a great tuning for bottleneck players (as we'll explore further below), opening up easy slide positions and accessible open-string runs, but is a great riffing tool as well, especially in the lower positions, where a handful of easy alternate chord shapes and a few hammer-on licks and bends can take you a long way. As Keith Richards would tell you.

Open G tuning (and an easy scale).

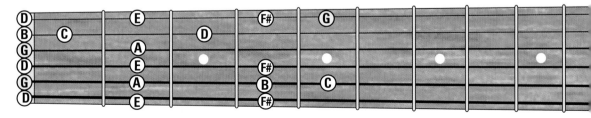

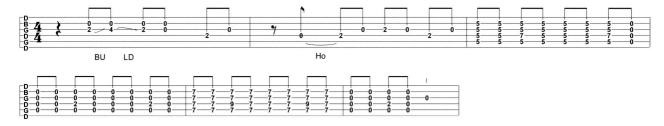

Open G requires changing just three strings down from standard tuning: the low E string drops down two tones to D, the A string drops down two tones to G and the high E string drops down two tones to D. You can use a chromatic tuner to get you there, but if you don't have one handy, and you're already relatively in tune with yourself, simply play the open D string and drop the low E down an octave below it by ear, play the open G string and drop the A string down to an octave below, then fret the B string at the 3rd fret and drop the high E down to match that pitch.

This tuning opens up a lot of easy single-note runs because every open string is part of a G major chord – and the scale runs along simple, (mostly) consistent patterns along the strings, as can be seen in the fretboard diagram opposite. The B string is the only deviant from the every-other-fret intervals – and even then, the B string works in your favour when you want to build up speed, because it lets you use the index finger to achieve the C at the 2nd fret, then hop right to the D on the open high string. To play a full two-octave G major scale, begin on the low open G string (formerly the A string) and work your way up to the high G at the 5th fret. The tuning also gives you three useful notes below the low root, but running down to the open D (on what used to be the low E string). Open G is popular because it really is a hybrid between an open tuning and an alternate tuning: it forms a full major chord across the six strings when strummed open, but it also sets up great intervals for single-note runs. Note that open G (and other open tunings that similarly form full open major chords) offers an easy I-IV-V progression for chord changes: all strings open gives you the I chord (G major); barring the 5th fret gives you the IV (C major); and barring the 7th fret gives you the V (D major).

Exercise 5 gives you a little of all of what open G is good at: a signature bend introduces a boogie-style rock'n'roll progression that makes use of these easy chord positions. Note that you really don't have to strum all six strings of the boogie chords to get the full effect, especially if you're playing this on electric guitar with a little overdrive on it, although you can try it both ways just to hear the difference. For these exercises in open and alternate tunings, we use tab only, since we're trying to get used to relative fretting positions on strings that have been altered to new pitches, rather than merely playing a piece of music as rendered in standard notation, which could be confusing. In some instances, the rhythmic values are given above the tab to help you get the sense of the timing of the exercise.

In Exercise 6, the melodic movement and chord progression aren't all that different, but this time we're playing it with a folkier feel and more emphasis on the single-note melody beneath the partial chords. You will also hit some open low strings that can be left ringing throughout each section, until the chord change brings in a new bass note. The right-hand fingering above the tab is only a suggestion, and after working through the piece you might find preferred fingerings of your own.

Also, be aware that the C chord in the fifth measure can be tricky to hit at first, since you're hitting a double hammer-on *and* forming a chord at the same time. The conventional way to do it is to use the

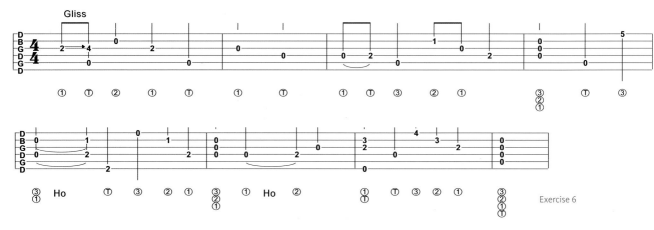

Exercise 6

index finger on the B string, the ring finger on the D string and the middle finger on that note on the low D string at the 2nd fret. But this is one of those occasions where you might like to cheat and wrap your thumb over the fingerboard to fret that low note, which makes it easier to fret the other strings with the index and middle fingers respectively. Try it both ways and see which works best for you. If you can't fret all those strings at once, however hard you try, feel free to break up the chord and just play part of it.

Open chords in open G

In Exercise 5 we saw how C and D major chords can be found by barring the 5th and 7th frets in open G and, of course, any other major chord can similarly be found on your way up the neck too. When playing melodic lines in lower positions, however, you will want some easy open chord shapes, and to master these you need to learn a handful of alternatives to the shapes you learned for standard tuning in the last chapter.

In Exercise 6 the C chord in the fifth measure was in fact an incomplete chord, because it didn't contain a low C note, the root of the chord. These are the kinds of compromises we sometimes

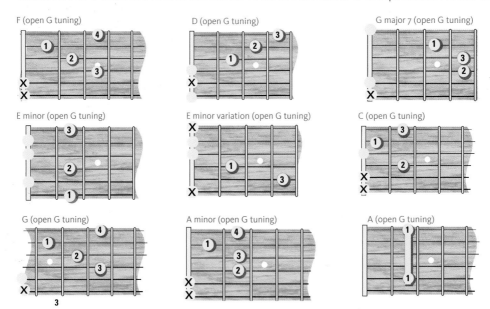

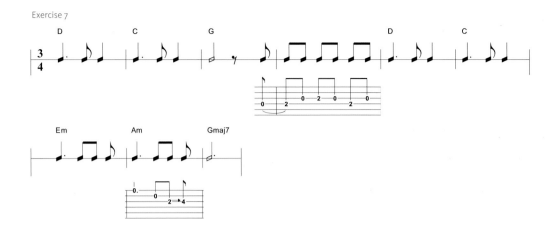

have to make to play easy chord shapes in open and alternate tunings, and the C and alternative Em offer similar shortcuts.

Let's use some of these new chords in combination with some simple single-note runs, to create exactly the kind of progression that works so well in open G. Exercise 7 once again emphasizes how simple it is to find little melodies within the scale intervals allowed by all those open strings.

For this one, the basic chord indications and the rhythm and strumming patterns are given, with the single-note tab for the little melody lines that link up the progression. You can decide for yourself which chord variations you prefer, although I find it works best with the open D and C from the chord boxes above, the alternative Em (with the low E on the G string [formerly A string]) at the 4th fret, and the first form of the Am.

Open D tuning

Open D (DADF♯AD) is very much an open-chord tuning – although it also creates some interesting intervals between strings that lend it to interesting melody lines, too. To get your head around open D, imagine forming an open E chord in standard tuning, then shifting the whole structure down by two frets. Doing this means dropping the low E down by two semitones, the G by one semitone and the B and high E another two semitones each.

To get to open D from standard tuning without using a chromatic tuner, drop the low E string an octave below the D string, fret the D string (fourth string) at the 4th fret and match the G string to it by dropping it a half step, fret the G string (now F♯) at the 3rd fret and match the B string to it, and fret this string at the 5th fret and drop the high E string down to that pitch.

Open D lends itself a little less to the combined chord/riff or boogie rock'n'roll progressions that

Open D tuning

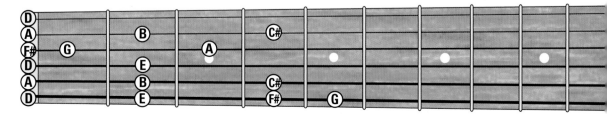

D minor pentatonic scale in open D tuning.

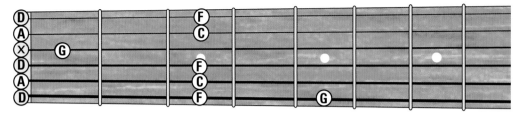

open G is so good for, because alternative chord shapes are a little harder to find in this tuning. You can find any major chord you like by simply barring the strings at the appropriate fret, of course – which is why it's another popular tuning for slide guitar – and that works fine for many purposes, but non-slide players who use open D tend to employ it as more of a riffing tuning, using it for the interesting intervals it sets up between the open strings and notes found on the lower frets.

It is often used for its easy access to the D minor pentatonic scale, popular with many blues and rock players. As the diagram above illustrates, this is an easy scale to find, since it uses every string open and fretted at the 3rd fret, except for the G string (tuned to F♯), which is fretted at the 1st fret, and the addition of the low D string/5th fret note, both of which yield a G, low and high.

Exercise 8

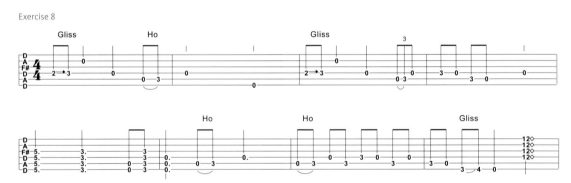

Exercise 8 shows us the kind of thing that open D excels at. This exercise has some evocative lower-string runs and a swampy, bluesy feel overall. You could play this as a single-note piece with a flat pick, but many Delta blues guitarists play similar things fingerstyle. Rather than a I-IV-V progression, this is a fragment from a I-III-V progression, as seen in the fifth measure where the bar chords run down from G to F to the open D. The liberal use of finger-slides (that is, not using a bottleneck slide, but sliding the finger from one fret up to the next) and hammer-ons helps to give it the bluesy attitude, and note that the entire piece ends on a harmonic chord.

Play this by laying your ring finger along the

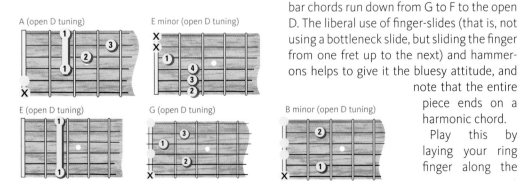

A (open D tuning)   E minor (open D tuning)

E (open D tuning)   G (open D tuning)   B minor (open D tuning)

Exercise 9

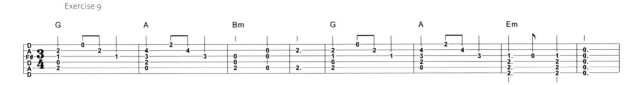

tops of the four highest strings right above the 12th fret – not pressing them down to the fret at all, but just touching them lightly as you strum, so that the octave-up harmonic notes come out. Right before that, there's a bluesy bend, where you pull that low string at the 3rd fret downward just slightly to give you a half-step bend before hitting the open low D, then the harmonics. Chords are a bit trickier to find in open D tuning than they are in open G, since more strings have changed from their familiar pitches in standard tuning. Here's a selection of useful open chords in this tuning, although many players who need anything more than this will usually turn to barre chords.

Exercise 9 takes us through a poignant progression in open D, which uses the IV and V chords and both minor chords from the box diagrams above, before finally landing on a full open D major chord.

DADGAD tuning

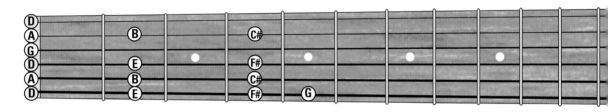

DADGAD by name, DADGAD by nature. This one is not an open tuning, because you get no obvious instant open chord out of this (unless you have a lot of use for a Dsus4). But it's an extremely expedient alternate tuning for fingerstyle players who seek a lot of easy, linear intervals on open strings and lower frets. Just one semitone different from open D, above, only with the G string "left alone" rather than dropped to F#, DADGAD nevertheless feels a world away.

Strum the open six strings, and while you don't get a chord as such, you do get a folky, almost Celtic sounding jangle of tones, and that impression only increases when you start running the scales. Also notice, while listening to those strummed strings ring, that this tuning doesn't lean predominantly toward a major or minor feel. It is very well balanced and lends itself

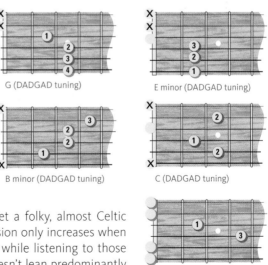

G (DADGAD tuning)

E minor (DADGAD tuning)

B minor (DADGAD tuning)

C (DADGAD tuning)

D (DADGAD tuning)

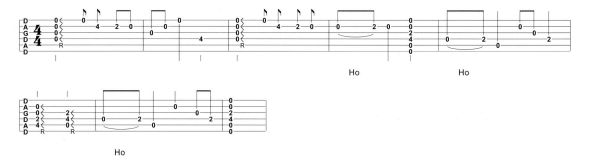

Kaki King is a formidable fingerstyle guitarist who has explored many different alternate tunings.

equally well to either, as well as to several other modes that DADGAD players like to access.

D major, however, might seem the most easily accessible DADGAD scale for the beginner, because it incorporates all the open strings of this alternate tuning. Notice the close intervals between the G and high A (formerly B) string, too. Being only a whole step apart, we don't even need to fret the G string to play this scale, so it contributes only one note to the effort, but this tight interval is useful in many other ways when playing in DADGAD. Follow the diagram below and play the scale from the lowest D to the highest D indicated, then back down again in reverse, and you will hear what an evocative, ringing, harp-like sound DADGAD has to offer.

Exercise 10 is a simple piece blending single-note melodic runs and partial chords to give you the

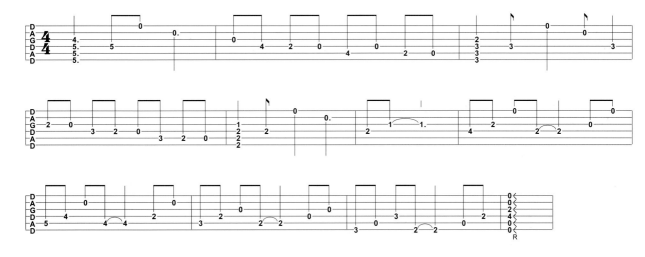

feel of this tuning. It works equally well at a slow or fast pace. For the rakes indicated alongside some of the chords, simply drag your pick or thumb smoothly and steadily across the strings, hitting one after another, evenly, so the notes ring into each other.

Several great DADGAD players, such as Martin Simpson, Laurence Juber and Pierre Bensusan use this tuning for its shape-shifting, modal feel, which allows an experienced player to run between scales and create complex-sounding melodic relationships with seeming ease. Exercise 11 gives us a taste of this. Note how it's actually rather difficult to tell what key it's in until the final chord sounds and pulls us back to D major. Be aware that, although those ascending three-note groupings in measures seven to ten look like triplets, other than in the first three, which have equal rhythmic weight, there's a little pause following the first of each of the three that follow.

Exercise 12

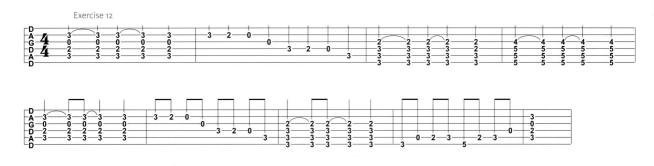

Just because DADGAD leans toward D scales, given all those open Ds, doesn't mean you have to play everything in D. We have just played G, F and E major chords in Exercise 11, along with D major. The DADGAD diagrams diagrams on p.131 give you the key shape for these (as G major) and a few others (for the tricky Bm, try barring the D and G-string notes at the 4th fret with your ring finger). Exercise 12 outlines a ringing little progression in C major, which still uses a lot of open strings and is easily accessed in first position.

Dropped D

Although plenty of players use it without thinking of it as such, the popular "dropped D" really is the simplest of the alternate tunings. It requires the alteration of just one string from standard tuning – dropping the low E down to D – and yields down-and-dirty voicings for rock and country playing alike. When playing in D major or minor, or for songs that use the D minor pentatonic scale, dropped D provides that low D note that rings through chord changes and higher melodic lines, and gives your playing a lot of impact in the lower register.

The Drive-By Truckers: greasy country-rock (with occasional use of dropped D).

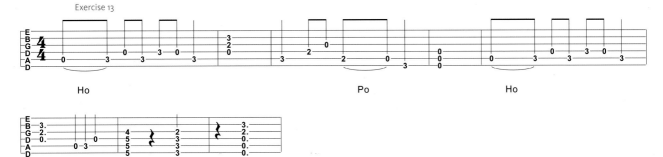

Ho   Po   Ho

Country players tend to utilize it for twangy bass runs in songs based around the open D chord, or to capo up to achieve the same relative positions in other keys. Rock players, on the other hand, often use dropped D to achieve mean-sounding barred power chords, or fierce bass runs beneath riffs and power chords higher up the neck. It's easy to see that you don't have to relearn a lot when using dropped D, although any chords from standard tuning that use what used to be your low E string need to be played two frets higher on what is now the low D string. For example, you'd play an Em by fretting all three bass strings at the 3rd fret, and power chords (in fifths) played on the two lower strings would now be fretted at the same fret.

Exercise 13 has that mean and evil country-rock sound that dropped D really excels at, with lots of menace in the lower register – the kind of thing you might hear from Steve Earle or the Drive-By Truckers. Take note of the rhythmic values given above the tab to get the feel of the low-string twang just right, observe the hammer-ons and hammer-offs, and note the chord shapes for the G and F major chords given in the penultimate measure. This kind of riff sounds equally good on acoustic and electric guitar, but if you're playing it on an electric, try using just a little dirt with it. It sounds outstanding with some tremolo, from an amp or FX pedal, too.

Injecting similar menace into a rock riff, Exercise 14 uses power chords for a chunky rhythm part. Play it with all down-strokes and observe the way the pauses give emphasis to the rhythm. If you're playing this on an electric through an amp or effects unit, a crunchy tone helps to give it that big, bad Soundgarden or Queens of the Stone Age feel it's looking for.

Exercise 14

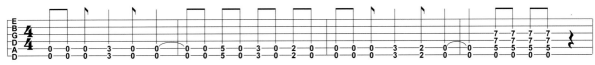

Other tunings

If you've enjoyed this exploration of open and alternate tunings, there's a lot more to be found out there in terms of books, DVDs and online tab for open G, open D, DADGAD or dropped D. If you want to broaden your repertoire even further, plenty of other tunings exist. Many guitarists use open E (like open D, but a whole step up on each string) or open A (a whole step up on the D, G and B strings), and adventurous players have devised countless original tunings to suit their

For Black Sabbath's Tony Iommi, if it wasn't detuned it just wasn't right.

Tony Iommi of Black Sabbath drops everything a step and a half down to C♯, and bluesman Albert King is known to have used his own closely guarded secret tuning, which is believed to drop the low E string down to C and which possibly ran CBEGBE or CFCFAD. And if you're in the mood for some Celtic fingerstyle guitar, you might want to try Orkney tuning, otherwise known as Gsus4, which runs CGDGCD low to high. In short, there are plenty of alternatives out there. While good old standard tuning does just fine for many of the world's best guitarists, there's plenty of mileage to be found off the beaten path.

SLIDE (BOTTLENECK) GUITAR

From the haunting National steel guitar of Son House and the wiry electric boogie of Johnny Winter, to the contemporary blues work of Derek Trucks, slide guitar has proven itself for decades to be one of the most evocative, atmospheric applications of the instrument. Also called bottleneck, after the source of many of the original tubular glass slides, slide is not the sole provenance of the blues guitarist, and is also popular in many walks of rock, pop and country, but it's hard to introduce a bottleneck solo into rock playing without giving the tune at least a little of a blues-rock or country-rock feel.

In Chapter 5, there's a discussion of several types of slides that are available, and you'll need to hunt down one of these simple devices if you want to check out this playing style. Even if you don't have a "genuine", store-bought slide, however, you can often get a feel for the sound of bottleneck guitar by trying it out with some found object from around the house that is smooth and hard enough to get a good note and adequate sustain out of your strings, and shaped to fit on a finger of your left hand. The slides used by many of the great original Delta blues players came from pretty unorthodox sources. A Coricidin medicine bottle (now out of production, though reproductions are available) was one common choice, and players have also used appropriately sized sockets from a socket-wrench (spanner) set, an 11/16" socket being the choice of slide master Lowell George of Little Feat.

In addition to selecting a slide to play with, the other question that novice slidesters have to wrestle with is "which finger?" There's no conclusive answer to this one, and great players have used any of the four. Placing the slide on your pinky (little finger) perhaps gives you the easiest access to standard, fretted chords when you're not playing slide, and also allows you to perform advanced techniques, like fretting strings behind the slide (while hitting slide chords) to create minor chords and other interesting effects. Plenty of outstanding slide artists also use the ring finger, and achieve similar results. As with your choice of material, slide placement is really a matter of experimentation for each individual player. Slip one on whichever digit feels most natural, slide it up the neck, and see if it works for you.

Son House made some of the most primal-sounding blues ever,, while playing a mean slide guitar.

The late Duane Allman, pictured playing his Les Paul with a medicine-bottle slide.

Slide technique

Whatever slide you use, you want it to feel snug enough that it doesn't flop around on the finger that's wearing it – with, often, a little supporting help from adjacent fingers – but not so tight that you feel constricted, or that it impedes your efforts to fret notes without the slide or to form other partial chords, as required in many playing circumstances. On occasions when I've wanted to use a slide that is too big for my finger of choice – my little finger, perhaps, because I like its sound for certain applications – I have inserted pieces of adhesive-backed weather stripping to produce a secure cushion for the finger.

To play a clear note, merely touch the slide to the strings directly above any given fret and perfectly parallel to it, but don't actually press it down onto the fret. Just to clarify, the slide touches the string but doesn't push the string to the fret. It hovers above it, making enough contact to produce a clean, clear note when you pick the string, but no more. With this in mind, slide playing is a bit easier on a guitar with an action that's a little higher (with the strings further away from the fingerboard) than you might prefer for ordinary playing, and most artists that dedicate themselves to slide playing keep their guitars set up this way – although you also need the strings to be frettable if you're mixing slide and standard playing, as many do.

Put your slide of choice on your desired finger, and try it out. Getting the hang of it can certainly be a bit tricky, and you'll often find there's a mere millimetre's difference between cleanly producing a note from the slide and actually pressing the string into the fret with the slide. It takes practice, certainly, but you'll get the hang of it in time. Start your adventures by playing the G string open, then with the slide at the 3rd fret, 5th fret and 7th fret – then repeat. Get this working cleanly for you, and you've already got a bluesy little I-III-IV-V riff going. Remember, to get an accurate pitch you position the slide directly above the fret, rather than slightly behind it, where you'd normally fret it with a finger.

Once you've got the notes coming out cleanly from the vibrating portion of the string, you might also be noticing some squeaks and buzzes from the part of the string behind the slide that is normally supposed to stay quiet. To mute these unwanted sounds slightly, lay your index and/or middle finger ever so slightly against the strings behind the slide – not enough to press them down at all, but just enough to dampen their vibrations. Once mastered, this behind-the-slide muting technique will clean up your playing immensely.

Sometimes, simply from the action of moving the slide, strings in front of the slide will vibrate when they're not supposed to be contributing to the sound. To minimize this, you can rest the edge of your right hand's palm against the bass strings, and, if you're using a pick between thumb and index finger, gently rest the tips of the remaining fingers against the unplayed strings. This right-hand muting technique usually takes a bit more practice to get right, but once you have it in your arsenal you'll be sliding like a pro.

When you get those single G-string notes working well, try getting a series of little three-string major chords out of the D, G and B strings. Plucked open, they give you a rudimentary G-major triad and, played with the slide at the 5th and 7th frets, they yield the C and D of a I-IV-V progression. Hear it? Hey, suddenly you're playing slide guitar! Now give those notes and chords just a little vibrato by gently but smoothly and rapidly moving back and forth across the fret, and you'll be sounding like a pro.

Slide guitar in standard tuning

Although slide guitar is known as a style that favours alternate tunings, you don't have to throw your guitar into an open tuning in order to dabble in the technique, and plenty of great slide guitarists use standard tuning throughout their playing, which gives them easy access to the traditional range of chords and lead scales when they're not doing slide work. Also, playing slide in standard tuning means there's no relearning of scales and positions, just find the single notes or multi-note groupings you need, and off you go.

The disadvantage to playing slide in standard tuning is that you don't have any big, open six-string chords to work with, but as we saw above there are plenty of three-note chords to be had, and often that's more than enough. Minor chords can be a bit trickier to find – as they will be in most open tunings, too – but you can often give the impression of a minor chord by playing the "minor note" (the flattened third) of a scale, then sliding into a two-note grouping of root and fifth (which is neither major nor minor – as with our power chords from Chapter 3) to complete your "chord". Standard tuning does throw out one handy minor triad all on its own, though: the Em found by playing the G, B and high E strings either open or with the slide at the 12th fret.

Another technique for accessing minor chords, both in standard tuning and some open or alternate tunings, is a little trickier, but easily achievable with practice. This involves behind-the-slide fretting, to achieve a note different from the notes of a chord that the slide itself is determining at any given fret.

For an example of this, return to our I-IV-V progression on the D, G and B strings open and at the 5th and 7th frets respectively. Position the slide at the 5th fret and pick all three strings for the C major chord, then, keeping the slide resting extremely gently against the D and G strings above the 5th fret, use your index finger to push the B string down behind the 4th fret. This should drop the B string below the edge of the slide, so its note is now produced at the 4th fret, while the D and G sound at the slide at the 5th fret – all resulting in a Cm chord. It's a tough one to master and, like slide playing in general, it's a lot easier on a guitar with a slightly high action (and nearly impossible on one with an extremely low action), but it's another tool for the toolbox when you get it right.

For clarity of instruction, we'll use only tab again for these slide-guitar exercises. When starting out with this technique, it's most important to focus on the fret positions needed to produce the desired notes, and after you get that down you can start thinking about what those notes actually are.

Exercise 15 is a boogie-blues slide riff with a shuffle feel to it. Use the slide to play everything on this one, except for the two open strings that each phrase ends on. A short diagonal line preceding any note, with the instruction "gliss" beneath it, indicates that you slide into these notes. Obviously we're playing all of these pieces with a slide, but where this instruction is given you want to reach those notes by hearing the slide into them from an unspecified lower note (or notes), which gives the sound and feel of genuine slide playings only much more exaggeratedly so. In this example, even though you are then also playing the descending progression with a slide, you are hitting these (the C and B♭ chords) more precisely, rather then slurring your way down into them.

Exercise 15

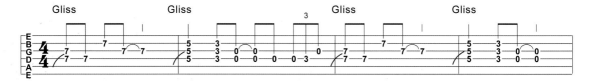

Sliding *down* into a note from an unspecified starting point rarely sounds as effective as sliding up into one, unless it is done as part of a complete phrase, returning to a note that you began from. Try playing the little turnaround lick in the second measure with your slide, by popping it down on the fretted note; if that's too tricky, you can just fret it with a spare finger for now.

Now we're going to mix up our standard playing and our slide playing, which is one of the benefits of standard tuning, with this simple but effective progression in C major.

Exercise 16 outlines the way you might go from a rootsy-feeling country-rock rhythm part to a slide solo that follows similar chord changes. Play the first four measures by fretting the C and G chords (and the hammer-ons that give them momentum) with your fingers, then bring the slide

Exercise 16

into the game for the next four measures, taking it up to outline the C chord at the 5th fret (with a little suspending thing for flavour), the G chord at the 12th fret and the high C at the 17th fret to end on.

Note the arched line in the sixth measure that connects the two notes at the 5th fret, with the 6th fret note between them: this indicates that you pick the first note and slide up to the second (at the 6th fret), then back to the original note, without picking again. If you're playing this on an acoustic guitar without a cutaway, it might be difficult to reach those final notes at the 17th fret. Instead, you can get a similar effect by playing the B and high E strings at the 8th fret instead, although of course you'll have to leave out the high E.

Slide in open G

Open G tuning (DGDGBD), which we have already explored via several standard playing techniques (and the tuning for which you can find in that section), lends itself extremely well to slide guitar. It gives you a bigger major chord at any given position, plus smaller chord fragments from other handy note groupings, and convenient intervals for single-note runs, too. This tuning works equally well for blues, country and rock'n'roll slide styles, and is easy to combine with several standard-fretted open chords, many of which we learned earlier in this chapter.

Let's start off with a classic boogie-blues slide riff, the kind of thing that might lay down the rhythm behind anything from ZZ Top – Billy Gibbons is a big fan of open G for his slide work – to

Exercise 17

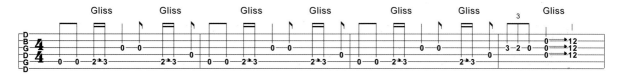

R.L. Burnside. To get Exercise 17 sounding and feeling just right, refresh yourself on our discussion of the blues shuffle from the previous chapter and get those eighth notes really swinging.

You should feel like there's a real bounce from that low G-string (formerly A-string) slide riff into the open G string/open D string exchange that propels the whole thing along. There's a repeat sign at the end of this simple four-bar phrase, because this one works well if you just keep playing it over and over again. If you're playing this on an acoustic guitar it will have more of a Delta blues feel, but on an electric with a little overdrive thrown in it will be pure Texas boogie.

Top's Billy Gibbons: a big fan of slide-guitar in open G tuning.

Exercise 18 has a Delta blues feel, a little like something you might hear in the playing of Son House or Blind Willie Johnson, with its run up the high string, its partial G-chord riff executed between the 10th and 12th frets, and its swampy concluding low-note run.

This one works either slow or fast and sounds great either way, so feel free to take it at your own pace, and give it that fat, greasy, mournful slide sound with plenty of vibrato where the rhythm gives you space to do so. Also, if you want to, you can shift this into more of a blues shuffle rhythm, and play it as a solo over the boogie figure in Example 17.

Open G tuning isn't only popular with blues players. It's also one of the most common tunings for country or bluegrass guitarists playing slide on a Dobro-style resonator guitar. Rather than using the minor pentatonic scale we have used for our two exercises so far, these players would often use a major pentatonic scale, as discussed in the country section of the previous chapter, although many will mix it up between major and minor pentatonic scales for a somewhat jazzier "hot country" feel.

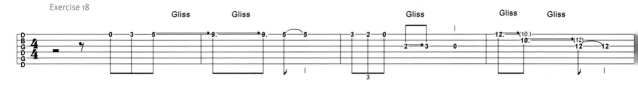

Exercise 19 gives you a slide run in this style, which works through a I-IV-V progression along the way. This kind of thing works extremely well on acoustic guitar, although you can certainly play it on electric, too.

Exercise 19

Open D tuning

Discussed in Chapter 3 in relation to standard left-hand fingering, open D tuning (DADF#AD) is also extremely popular with blues and rock slide players. Aside from, obviously, creating a different open chord to work with, and different major chords at the respective fret positions, open D gives you the root of the D scale on the lowest string, rather than three steps below the root (as in open G) – so there's a low growl for menacing blues or rock riffs.

Other than that, it's difficult to say why one player might prefer open D over open G – and both have their fans – other than to acknowledge that this tuning sets up different intervals across the strings and lower frets that just seem to work for certain types of playing styles. Many players will use both, depending upon the key they want to access, in order to set up a lot of handy open strings in the desired scale, and by using a capo with one or the other, you can extend the range of these tunings even further.

For a low'n'lonesome slide riff of the type that open D excels at, check out the phrase in Exercise 20 . This bluesy lick has a little introduction in a "pickup" measure that comes in on what would be the "three-and" of a normal first bar, and runs up and down each of the bass strings in the first one-and-three-eighths measures.

Note the downward gliss on the low D string in the second bar, and the hammer-on in the fourth bar, which

The playing of Blind Willie Johnson epitomizes the Delta blues feel you want in Exercise 18.

Exercise 20

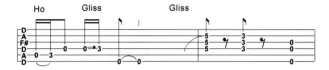

you can play by tapping the slide down on the low A string just above the 3rd fret. This piece works equally well on acoustic or electric, but with either it's often easier to play this kind of Delta-flavoured blues slide fingerstyle, or hybrid (with a flat pick and the middle and ring fingers of the picking hand), so you can mute unwanted strings with the right hand, while selecting only the strings you want to ring out with the picking fingers.

Another Delta blues legend, Bukka White, shows off his steel resonator guitar.

Resonator and lap-steel guitars

Many guitarists using traditional electric and acoustic six-strings employ the techniques for open and alternate tunings and slide guitar that we have explored in this chapter. But for a few variations of the instrument – such as lap-steel and resonator guitars – these are home territory. Prior to the inception of the electric guitar (and the amplifier that goes with it), guitarists had great difficulty being heard in a band setting, especially when competing against horns. One milestone in the quest for volume was the "resonator" guitar, originated by the National company in California in 1927.

These metal-bodied guitars had a built-in acoustic speaker of sorts in the form of a spun aluminium cone (or cones) that helped to amplify (entirely without electricity) the string vibrations transmitted to it through the bridge. Later made with wooden bodies too, more notably under the Dobro brand, these instruments are known for their brash, lively, metallic sound, and can be heard in the work of everyone from ancient blues originators such as Son House and Bukka White, to the bright chimes of much of Mark Knopfler's playing with Dire Straits. Although the resonator guitar's reign as king of the hill, volume-wise, was foreshortened by the electric guitar's rise to prominence in the late 1930s, its unique, haunting sound has helped it retain its status as a popular niche instrument, in the blues world in particular.

Resonator guitars can be played in the standard method, held vertically with their backs to the player's belly, or lap-style, with their backs laid flat in the player's lap. For either technique they are more often played with a slide, though the traditional position allows standard fingering, too. The electric instrument known as the lap-steel guitar, however, is played entirely lap-style, and made with an extremely high action for the purpose. Sometimes confused with the resonator because of their metal bodies, the "steel" in lap-steel actually refers to the metal slide bar with which the instruments are played. This type of instrument originated with Hawaiian music, originally as an acoustic guitar played in the lap, but it evolved into the electric lap-steel, again, as a means of making the instrument louder. Lap-steel guitars quickly became popular in country and in Western swing music in the 1930s, and in fact it was this breed of guitar that led the charge to amplification; it was the first solid-bodied electric guitar in mass production.

Both lap-steel and resonator guitars are usually played in open or alternate tunings. Open D and open G are popular for both, although several others are used (with prominent early players often devising their own), and the lap-steel in particular has been used through the years with a number of unusual tunings to provide the range of major, minor and dominant voices required by the music it has been used for.

It's a technique that helps you execute several elements in this style of playing, such as chords like the final D that's played on the open low D, middle D, F♯ and high A strings, without sounding the low A string.

Exercise 21 (overleaf) is a classic riff for open-tuned slide, where R&B meets seminal 1950s rock'n'roll in the style of Mr Bo Diddley, the man with the beat named after him. To play it just right you need to get that Bo Diddley beat into your blood, so let's check it out as a purely rhythmic exercise first. We'll break down the beat, then we'll put a slide riff over the top of it.

Feel-wise, the Bo Diddley beat plays like a measure of 3/4 played over the top of a measure of 2/4, with different beats from each measure emphasized. Blending it all into one two-measure line of 4/4 rhythm, with eighth notes, you can count it as "**one** and two **and** three and **four** and one and **two** and **three** and four and", where the beats in bold are those that are hit, while the others count the spaces between them. Say the count to yourself, and clap on the bold beats, and you'll start to get the hang of it. Or, for a more direct route, listen to a few songs by the man himself, such as

The Bo Diddley beat.

"Who Do You Love" or the eponymous "Bo Diddley".

The repeat sign is there because, yep, songs in this style often repeat the same rhythm throughout – or Bo's did, anyway. Note that the two pairs of eighth-note rests in the first measure could be written as a single quarter-note rest each, but I think seeing it as two rests per each of those beats helps you to get the hang of it a bit better.

Now let's put a slide part over the top. Really it's a rhythm part, too, rather than a lead or mixed rhythm/lead part of the kind we have mostly played so far. Lots of Bo Diddley's own songs thumped away on just a single chord throughout, with Mr Diddley himself alternating between muted open chords and sliding up to the 12th fret octave and back down again, often dragging out that downward slide on the lower strings to great effect. As applied by several other artists over the years – Buddy Holly, U2, Bruce Springsteen, the Rolling Stones – this rhythm can indeed survive a few chord changes, so we'll put that in, too.

Although it was said earlier in this section that you don't hear players use many downward glisses, this is one occasion where they are a big part of the style. After playing the phrase up at the 12th and 10th frets to the first part of the beat, you need to drag that slide down towards the nut at a steady eighth-note "chunka-chunka-chunka-chunka" (marked on the tab as "steady downward gliss") , mostly muting the strings with the edge of your picking hand as you go, but letting the two lowest strings ring out a little.

The Bo Diddley beat keeps bopping along behind you for the second section of the riff, even though you are chunking out a straighter rhythm on the guitar. Once you get the hang of it you can mix up the slide positions and the accent rhythms a little. If you have a drummer to play along with, or can set up a rhythm on a drum machine, this one's a lot of fun to groove to ad infinitum.

This concludes the advanced playing techniques section of this chapter. You've now had a taste of several different musical genres and playing styles. Next, we'll explore several advanced sonic techniques, to help you expand your tonal palette right alongside your playing skills, but if you want to further investigate any of the genres or styles we have already covered, there's a wealth of great tutorial books and DVD collections out there to help.

Exercise 21: the Bo Diddley beat with slide.

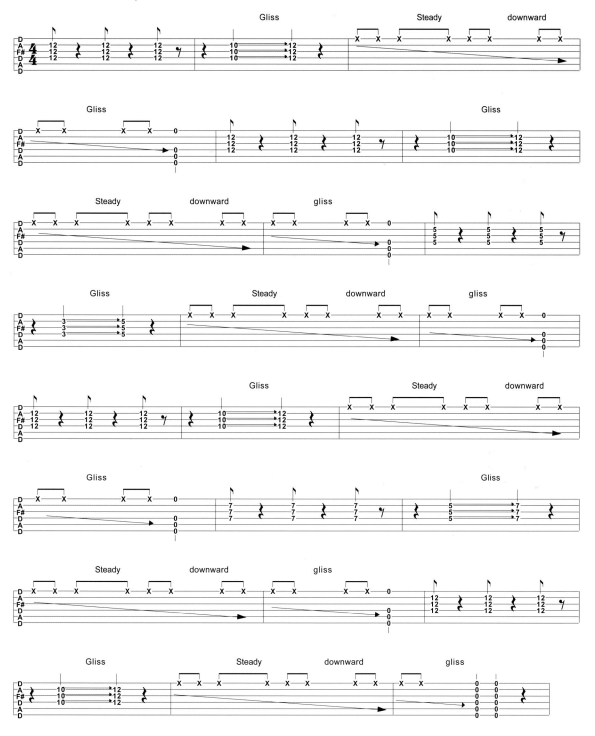

EXPERIMENTS IN SOUND

With a colourful palette of playing styles in your back pocket, you'll want some more adventurous ways in which to use them. More extreme and even experimental uses of effects, distortion, noise and feedback are most often found in music broadly termed as "rock", although some blues, jazz and fusion players can get fairly adventurous as well.

By and large, however, the following are techniques that you'll find at the fingertips of metal, hard rock, grunge, indie, alternative rock and more experimental "noise-art" genres. At the milder end of the spectrum, they can add a little colour and texture to your guitar sound; at the wilder end, they can influence your entire playing style, and be applied as a sound-sculpting tool in and of themselves.

USING EFFECTS

Enduring and timeless, the simple set-up of a good guitar played through a good tube amp can still provide some of the most compelling tones in popular music. But many players – and music genres – require something more in the sonic brew.

Effects pedals can add texture, dynamics, space and motion to an otherwise "2-D" sound, and have become part of every genre of electric-guitar-based music. There's an enormous range of sounds out there: the only way to choose what will work for you is to sample as many as you can lay your hands on and determine what's right for your music, your band and your playing style. Once you've done that, it pays to know a few things about connecting them between guitar and amp for optimum performance.

Pedal-connecting order

Wherever there are rules, of course, there are also outstanding ways to break them. Few things in this realm should be taken as hard and fast laws, but let's get a few rules down first, then look at the exceptions. The rule of thumb for connecting pedals between guitar and amp holds that you place any EQs or tone filters you wish to use *first* – that is, you plug your guitar lead directly into them. Gain-producing devices such as overdrive and distortion pedals come second, modulation devices, like chorus and flanger pedals, come third, and delay devices such as echo and reverb should go last (and in precisely that order, if you are using both).

A common variation on this – one that works best with certain types of pedals – is to swap the middle two of these four stages. Some modulation devices such as vintage-style analogue choruses and phasers – such as the Uni-Vibes and their clones – do their best work when placed before overdrive or fuzz pedals. This is mostly because their function and sound includes an element of filtering-type tone shifting that can sound great going into an overdrive pedal, but pretty gnarly when working its magic on a signal that is already distorted.

Wah-wah pedals can, for our purposes here, be considered as EQ or tone-filtering devices (which is, after all, ultimately what they are). For most applications, they work best when placed first in the chain, with your guitar going straight into them, and that's the way that everyone from Jimi Hendrix to Eric Johnson to Yngwie Malmsteen to J. Mascis has used them. Some others, however, do things a little differently: Carlos Santana sticks a Tube Screamer before his wah-wah, Brian May puts his treble booster first and Steve Vai has used wahs both before and after his Boss DS-1 Distortion pedal. The order in which you use such effects depends upon whether you want

J. Mascis, of grunge band Dinosaur Jr.

to distort the clean wah-wahed tone (i.e. wah first, overdrive second), or sweep the frequency of an already distorted tone (i.e. overdrive first, wah-wah second). The only way to decide for yourself is to try both.

Fuzz pedals provide another fly in the ointment here: most vintage-style fuzz pedals interact best with your guitar – in terms of dynamics, pick attack and volume control – when they are connected first in the chain. For many wah-wah applications, however, you want the wah before them. Convention says you should put the wah-wah first. But again, you'll need to decide this for yourself.

Delay: the final word-word-word-word...

Delay-based devices will usually go last in the chain because you want your fully overdriven and modulated tone to then be treated to the spatial effects of echo or reverb. Working in this order generally results in the highest fidelity and the greatest depth for each effect in the rig. Mixing it up, on the other hand, might create odd and unusual sounds that just happen to produce the sonic magic you were looking for, so don't be afraid to experiment. (Check your effects devices' manuals first to make sure you won't overload any given delay unit – digital units in particular – by running a hot gain/distortion device into it.)

Once again, the functions of certain components will also sometimes force you to change the conventional running order here. For example, if you get your overdrive sound from the lead channel in a channel-switching amp (rather than an overdrive or distortion pedal), and your reverb and/or echo sounds come from individual pedals or outboard units, then

The Edge, guitarist for U2, has perhaps the world's most famous delayed-guitar tone, heard all over his riffs for the band's 80s albums.

you're a little stuck. Many such amps have effects loops that you can run delay-based devices in – and that's exactly what they're intended for. (Again, you may need to read your manuals to make sure FX-loop levels won't overload such devices, and adjust your levels accordingly, where possible.) If your amp has no effects loop but you still want to get your lead sound from its high-gain channel, you'll just have to decide which compromise you'd prefer to make.

If you use more than one of each type of effects pedal, you will very likely have to compromise somewhere. Test, experiment and work with what you've got to create the best sound for your own music. It helps to know what the conventions are, but don't be bound by them if something a little out of the ordinary actually helps to better produce the tones in your head. Even Jimi Hendrix had to compromise, and he certainly broke plenty of rules too. His most legendary pedal set-up ran like this: guitar; Vox Wah-Wah; Fuzz Face; Octavia; and Uni-Vibe. In other words, that's filter/EQ, gain, filter and modulation. It worked alright for him.

Stereo pedals

Many delay and chorus pedals, and a few others, come with stereo outputs that enable you to make the most of the wide soundstage that these effects can produce – if you have two amps to run them through. With two amps and a single stereo pedal on the floor, you connect one amp to the left output and one to the right output. But sometimes it's not quite so simple. Effects chains with multiple pedals might throw up conflicts in connecting order: perhaps you have a stereo chorus or Uni-Vibe-style pedal that you prefer to use *before* your overdrive, but you also want to make use of the width of the stereo field.

Ideally, you would connect any stereo pedal *last* in the chain, but in the above scenario you would have to decide to either run the overdrive after only one of the stereo outputs and keep the other output clean, or compromise your sonic vision and put the overdrive before the stereo effect. That, or buy a second overdrive pedal and deal with the tap-dance of trying to switch on both simultaneously.

Other conflicts arise when you have two stereo pedals in your set-up. Sometimes more complex stereo delays and reverbs (rack-mounted units in particular) will have stereo inputs as well as outputs, and this makes it easy to (for example) connect a stereo chorus pedal before your delay to get the full stereo effect of both, one into the other. Otherwise, you will have to decide whether it's the sound of stereo chorus, stereo echo or stereo reverb that's most important to you. Try all the alternatives, and go with whatever feels like the least obtrusive compromise.

Split chains

Sometimes it's extremely useful to split your signal chain to achieve an asymmetrical, non-identical (i.e. non-stereo) sound from two amplifiers. For example, imagine your pedalboard runs: compressor; stereo vibe; overdrive; and echo. With two amps to play through, you could split the left output of the vibe pedal to the first amp, and send the right output to the rest of the effects chain, and ultimately to the second amp. Now, when you step on the overdrive, which is placed after the vibe pedal, you get crunch and lead tones in amp 2, while amp 1 stays crisp and clean to retain better definition. Or, you could set amp 1 to always be a little crunchy, to beef up your clean and rhythm tones, then you'll go into a thick, rich lead tone when you step on the overdrive, which will result in pedal-based clipping in amp 2, and milder amp-based clipping in amp 1. If you have two non-identical amps, or one big amp and one smaller amp, try using the smaller, less powerful of the two in the amp 1 position (with the split from earlier in the effects chain) and cranking it up to achieve some natural tube distortion. Often this blend works great with a larger, cleaner amp (which, again, can still be kicked into overdrive with the use of a pedal). Many artists have achieved their signature tones with a similarly mismatched amp set-up, notably Keith Richards of the Rolling Stones, who often paired a cranked-up Fender Champ and a cleaner Fender Twin in the studio.

Parallel paths

Multiple signal paths can also provide interesting results with just one amplifier, providing that amp has twochannels, or even two inputs. Say you want to maintain some definition and clarity in your tone, even when you're using overdrive for leads, and the dirty amp/clean amp blend described above appeals to you. With a two-channel amp (that is, an amp with two independent channels that can operate simultaneously, *not* a channel-switching amp), split your signal before your overdrive or distortion pedal, and run it to channel 1 with it set for clean, then send it on to the rest of the effects and out to channel 2. It's a technique that will preserve more of the unadulterated guitar tone in your overall sonic mix.

Even two channels in the same amp, each set to different gain and EQ levels, can yield a richer, more complex tone than just one channel. When doing this, ensure that the two channels are working in-phase of each other; if your sound is notably thin and hollow-sounding when you try both channels together, one is most likely out of phase.

Some effects pedals will reverse a signal's phase between input and output, so splitting the signal before that pedal could cause such a reversal. Many Fender "blackface" and "silverface" amps from the 1960s and 70s – named after the appearance of their faceplates – have two channels that are out of phase with each other. Splitting to different signal paths might cure this or retain it. You will have to experiment to see what works.

It's also worth noting that you can often use input 1 and input 2 in a single-channel amp that has two inputs to achieve some of the same results described above.

Effects-loop pedals

Effects-loop pedals are really just signal-chain-routing devices with footswitches: they allow you to select between a variety of FX loops that a player might have set up. They can be very useful if you have a lot of effects on your board, but don't want to run your signal through them at all times, thus potentially depleting its quality. If you use pedals that are notably noisy even when off, or pedals which result in a loss of highs, lows or general signal fidelity when they aren't switched on, then a looper is a great way of rectifying the situation. And you can use any number of pedals within even a single loop, to take them out of the signal path when not in use.

To use one of these, you run a patch cable from the loop pedal's "send" to the input of the first pedal in the loop and string the rest together as normal, concluding with a patch cable to the "return" of the loop pedal. Any pedals that you use frequently and which aren't problematic in terms of extraneous noise or tone-sucking – a good overdrive or compressor, for example – can still go before the loop pedal (i.e. between guitar and loop pedal).

If you have just one pedal in the loop, leave it on at all times, and let the loop footswitch take it in and out of the signal path. With more than one pedal in the loop, you'll need to switch any effects on at the start of the song that requires it (with the loop still off), and bring it in with the loop switch as needed, or use a looper with multiple loops to leave all the looped pedals on all the time.

True bypass versus buffering

There's a lot of talk about true-bypass pedals these days, and in many cases true bypass is a good feature. The term "true bypass" (also referred to as "hard-wired bypass") applies to an effects pedal that routes the signal directly from input to output when switched off. The feature is intended to preserve signal quality, which can sometimes be degraded when it is routed through a portion of the effects circuitry even when off, as some pedals do. Using a lot of true-bypass pedals in a row can still deplete your signal, however, even when they're all off (or, in fact, *particularly* when they're all off), because they still route it through a lot of extra wire. Also, the use of a long guitar cord both before and after a string of true-bypass pedals adds up to a long distance for that signal to travel, with the result of some inevitable loss of fidelity.

A quality buffer, either in the form of an individual unit or a buffer built within one of the pedals in your chain, can help to resolve this problem. Essentially a clean, unity gain (or low gain) preamp that is always on, a buffer enables your signal to travel through much greater lengths of wire without losing volume or tone. If you find your guitar sounds noticeably flatter and muddier when played through your chain of true-bypass pedals (when they are all switched off) than it does when plugged straight into the amp, a buffer might be the answer.

In the end, there are no fixed rules for the use of effects pedals: many, many variations in the "traditional" set-ups exist, and when rules do seem to exist, there are always exceptions. Experiment with whatever you can get your hands on, keep your mind open to the alternatives, and determine what works best for you and your music. Try some unconventional placement orders, crank up those knobs to settings that might seem extreme in traditional playing, and see what comes out. Many ground-breaking artists have discovered classic tones through just this kind of rule breaking, so a little renegade effects use might work for you, too.

Extreme distortion

Distorted guitar sounds – whether created by cranked-up amps, or overdrive, fuzz or distortion pedals – are a big part of much rock music. More extreme distortion, however, is often used to create, well, more extreme music – whether it's heavy metal, thrash, shred metal or wall-of-noise shoegaze. And, as the saying goes, with great power comes great responsibility: extreme distortion can be difficult to control and can easily run away with the inexperienced player, finding you not so much crafting a sound with noise, but making noise for noise's sake.

Put simply, a heavily distorted guitar can sound a lot bigger than a comparable clean guitar because heavy distortion adds a lot of extra harmonic content to each note. For this reason, you often want to trim down your chords when playing rhythm guitar with a lot of distortion applied. With all this extra harmonic content, you rarely need a full, six-string open or barre chord to make a big impact, and two or three strings will often do the job. Even one can sound pretty fat. For the basics on chords that work well with heavy distortion, see the "Power Chords" box in the previous chapter. But remember, these trimmed-down chords don't always stick to the pure fifths of power chords, and can use different intervals to imply different chord structures.

In addition to cutting back the size of your rhythm chords, it's often important to dampen (mute) strings more selectively when playing with extreme distortion in order to fend off unwanted feedback. The added gain and the saturated frequency content of distorted guitar tones – especially those played at high volumes – can lead to a lot of feedback squeal, and gently damping down strings with either the unused fingers of the fretting hand or the edge of the palm of the picking hand can help to avoid this. It'll also help tighten up your rhythmic chops at the same time.

Jimmy Page, ni his full-blown early-70s pomp. His guitars sounded huge on Led Zeppelin recordings (and he did like a big amp, as you can see), but often his loud, fat guitar sound isn't nearly as distorted as you might think.

Even more crucial than damping played strings is to mute those that aren't being played in any given chord or soloing sequence. Un-strummed strings that might not make a peep from an electric guitar played clean – the low E and A strings that are left out of a four-note open D chord for example – will start to vibrate all on their own when faced with high volumes and heavy distortion, and add unwanted note-content to the chord you're trying to play.

All of this might sound a little nebulous in theory. So if you have an electric guitar, amp and overdrive pedal at your disposal (or a headphone amp/effects unit capable of producing heavy distortion sounds), work on your playing technique with heavy distortion applied. Sounding good with such a set-up is often as much about what you *don't* play as what you do, and cleaning up that filth is just a matter of practice.

Be aware, too, that after a point that bigger-sounding guitar that distortion gives you can simply turn into mud if you don't keep it under control and use it correctly – which often means using it sparingly. In the same way that mixing too many colours from a palette of paints results in a dirty shade of brown rather than a rainbow, too much distortion can sometimes make your guitar sound flabby and indistinct. This will actually make it harder for you to be heard in a full-band setting than using a punchy clean guitar will at the same volume. Alternatively, you'll just mud-out the sound of the entire band... and they won't be happy with you.

It might seem contradictory, but in some cases cleaning up your overdrive tone a little can actually help you to sound bigger. Listen to several classic tracks from bands such as AC/DC and Led Zeppelin: the guitars sound huge, but they aren't really all that filthy-fuzzy all the time. If you've got a fat, juicy distortion tone going at a pretty high volume but still seem to have trouble being heard over your band's drummer, try cleaning it up a little. Doing so will often tighten up your low end, firm up your mids, and make your highs more cutting; this will frequently be just what you need.

Harmonic feedback

While feedback was universally reviled in the world of the electric guitar right up to the 1950s, several radical rockers of the 1960s soon discovered the power of this noise form, and adventurous guitarists have continued to bend it to their will ever since. The kind of feedback that we want to produce, in some circumstances at least, is known as "harmonic feedback". It's called that because it's usually heard as a hovering, sustained note which segues into a singing higher harmonic of its original self, even as the fundamental fades. In more recent years, bands such as Sonic Youth, the Pixies, Radiohead and the Flaming Lips have elevated feedback to an art form, and used right, it can provide an effective means of crafting anything from an atmospheric whale call to the landing of an alien invasion.

As much as howling feedback can be frustrating and hard to banish when you *don't* want it to be part of your music, desirable harmonic feedback can often be elusive and difficult to produce. The main ingredients in any effort to create harmonic feedback are gain and sustain. These are achieved with either a very loud amp, or one with a high-gain preamp channel, or an amp coupled with high-gain overdrive or distortion pedals, and a guitar with fairly hot pickups with good sustain. Humbucking pickups tend to excel at creating feedback, and they're a little quieter in the process, but single-coil pickups sometimes work well, too, and I've had excellent results from older Gibson P-90s, Fender Jazzmaster pickups and a variety of "fatter" sounding units.

To work on your feedback technique, get your amp up as loud as you (or others in your house, apartment, studio or rehearsal space) can tolerate it – use protective earplugs if this takes it up to uncomfortable volume levels – and either set an amp's lead channel for high-gain, or use a high-gain pedal at the amp's front end. Hit a note, or two (which often works better), and move closer to the amp – angling the guitar one way and the next as you do – until you hear the notes' decay hover into feedback. Now work with that feedback, and see if you can get it to last infinitely. Once you've got that happening for you, alter the angle of the guitar in relation to the amp a bit, or bend the strings slightly, to try to change the pitch of the feedback. Done correctly, this won't be perceived as a "bent note" but as a change in the pitch of the harmonic. The perfect-fifths of power chords often do a good job at inducing feedback, or you can try a root-fifth-octave chord to give

Thurston Moore, one half of Sonic Youth's guitar assault team, often uses waves of howling feedback in the band's music.

the amp a broader spectrum to chew on. When trying to induce feedback in a specific song, choose starting notes that are in the key of the tune you're playing, so their harmonics will sound complementary to the piece.

If this basic approach gets you nowhere, and you have more pedals at your disposal, try chaining two overdrive or distortion pedals in a row, or a compressor (set fairly high) or booster into an overdrive or fuzz pedal. Work with the gain and level controls of these, experiment with your positioning relative to the amp, and see if you can get there. It isn't always necessary to ram the front of the guitar right up against the speaker to produce good feedback, and often the most melodic response is found a little further back in the room. If it still isn't happening for you – or you need a quick feedback fix in a live situation, when you're unable to throw a couple more pedals into the set-up – try pressing the tip of your guitar's headstock against a vibrating edge of the amp's speaker cabinet, or against a solid part of the speaker baffle at the front (*not* into the soft grille cloth of the speaker cutout in front of the cone): directly coupling your amp's vibration with the guitar in this manner is usually a sure way of inducing a quick howl.

Harmonics

Harmonics, or "natural harmonics", to give them their full name, can lend an ethereal sound to your playing when used judiciously. I already threw a few into the playing exercises earlier and discussed the technique there, but it's worth covering in a little more depth here. You can play harmonics on both acoustic and electric guitars – on the latter they are produced more easily with the bridge pickup selected.

The easiest place to find harmonics is on any string just above the 12th fret; don't "fret" the string as such, but simply lay your fingertip gently on the string precisely above the fret, without pressing down at all, and pluck the string with your pick or fingers. You should hear a pure, ringing harmonic note that's an octave higher than the pitch of the open string. Harmonics in this position are easy to throw into songs in the key of E or G, major or minor, because you can find two-note groupings (diads) that sit effortlessly with those keys: the 12th fret harmonic of the B and high E strings, for example, or of the D and G strings in G minor, or the full triad of D, G and B in G major. Of course, you also have single notes you can throw into songs in A, D and B.

While the 12th fret harmonic is obvious, several others are less so. Use the same technique right above the 5th fret and, rather surprisingly, you also get a harmonic of the respective open string, but this time it's two octaves higher. Now try it above the 7th fret, and you'll hear a harmonic an octave higher than the fretted note in that position. Slightly more difficult to achieve, but sometimes effective on distorted electric guitar in particular (especially when you want to throw down some dissonant avant-garde sounds), are the harmonics found above the 9th fret, which, oddly enough, are pitched two octaves up from the third of the open string.

Why all the bizarre intervals? Well, when you pluck an open string on the guitar, these harmonics – and more – are all produced as part of what you hear as the "note" that the single string produces, although you hear the fundamental of the open string more than the harmonics themselves. Put them all together, and they account for the fact that a plucked guitar string sounds bigger and fatter than the pure note from a tuning fork, for instance. Placing your finger gently on the string at the fret positions indicated above (which are known as "harmonic nodes") dampens the fundamental note, and brings out the harmonic produced at that position. In truth, there are harmonics all up and down the length of the strings.

To hear a sequence of these together, lay a finger gently on the low E string at the 12th fret, as you would to play a harmonic there, and use a steady sweep of down-and-up picking to sound the string, while simultaneously moving your finger slowly down the string toward the nut (still touching the string gently, not pressing it down). Harmonics should jump out at you all along the way, particularly during the journey above the last three frets, where they're tightly packed.

What do you do if you're dying for some atmospheric harmonics to fit a chord or a key that doesn't easily mesh with those found on the more obvious frets? There are a few more advanced techniques you can use to achieve these, variously referred to as "slapped harmonics" "tapped harmonics", or "right-hand harmonics". All of these take quite a bit of practice to master, and can't easily be explained, but the principles are basically pretty simple, and not all that different from what has already been discussed.

Say you're fretting an A major barre chord at the 5th (thus fretting strings at the 5th, 6th and 7th frets) and would like to access some harmonics from this chord. Try gently "slapping" the strings with the edge of your right-hand index finger (obviously reverse all this if you're left-handed) just above the frets a full octave up from those where you're holding the chord. This should evoke some semblance of a ringing harmonic sound. To achieve individual notes, on the other hand, try "tapping" the strings individually – in a quick tap-and-release motion – against the fret an octave up from where you are holding it down with the left hand.

A little more difficult still, but useful when you want the harmonic note without the percussive tapping or slapping sound, is the right-hand harmonic technique. Still fretting your barre chord with the left hand, put down your pick (or tuck it in under your free fingers), and place the tip of your right-hand index finger gently on the string right above the fret where you want to achieve the harmonic, then use your thumb or thumbnail behind it to pluck the string. These are tricky to pull off at any speed, but you'd be amazed how swiftly some experienced guitarists can throw them into their playing.

Pinch harmonics

Working on the same principle as natural harmonics, but used quite differently, pinch (or pinched) harmonics are almost always heard on electric guitar, and usually one played with a degree of distortion applied via a pedal or the amp. Pinch harmonics are heard a lot in the soloing of Billy Gibbons with ZZ Top, and are also used by a wide range of rock and blues-rock players, such as Eddie Van Halen, Steve Vai, Zakk Wylde (with Ozzy Osbourne and Black Label Society), Dimebag Darrell of Pantera and Damage Plan, Leslie West of Mountain and David Gilmour of Pink Floyd (who perhaps most notably brings them out for the solo of "Comfortably Numb").

The technique is simple in principle, but can take a lot of practice to master. You can practise on an acoustic or an unplugged electric, too, but pinch harmonics will really sound their most effective on a distorted electric guitar. If you normally hold your pick so it protrudes a fair bit from the ends of your thumb and index finger, reposition it so its picking edge is closer to your fingertips – right between them, in fact, so it barely extends past the flesh. Now fret the G string at the 7th fret, and pick the string somewhere just behind the neck pickup of your electric guitar (or over the centre of the soundhole of an acoustic) so that the flesh of your thumb makes contact with the string gently but immediately after the pick itself makes contact. It should almost feel as if flesh and pick are plucking the string simultaneously. You need to experiment with different picking positions along the length of the string, because any given point will access a different harmonic node, some more obvious and more dramatic than others.

Do this correctly and the thumb should dampen the string at the node immediately after the pick attacks the fundamental, emitting a dramatic harmonic squeal. Also, because pinch harmonics often sound most effective going into bends, try bending that G string just as you pick it. In theory, you can get pinch harmonics out of any string, so work your way around the fingerboard and see what you can produce.

the
GEAR

hatever type of guitar you play, chances are you'll need a few bits and pieces to go with it. Whether it's just the simple accessories that many players use with acoustic guitars, such as a few picks (plectrums), an electric tuner and perhaps a capo, or an entire host of devices that can modify your electric guitar sound – effects pedals, outboard reverb and echo units, different amplifiers for different uses – you're likely to need to come to grips with at least a few gizmos in order to make your playing more enjoyable, and to extend the range of the instrument itself.

STRINGS'N'THINGS

ACOUSTIC STRINGS

Generally considered an accessory, and sold as such, strings are really in a category of their own since they are indispensable to any guitar's function. It's easy for the new player to come in with a "strings are strings" kind of attitude, and for a time, at least, you're likely to just play whatever strings arrive on the guitar you begin with. Different types of strings can make a big difference to the sound and feel of any guitar, however, and it's worth getting to know what's out there, and what works best for you. Strings vary widely both in gauge (thickness) and composition, and you need to understand the properties of both of these variables, and ideally try a few out for yourself, in order to decide what works for your own playing style.

The most common strings used on acoustic guitars (a term I will use to denote flat-top steel-string guitars, unless otherwise noted) are "phosphor bronze" strings, which refers to the composition with which the four wound strings are wrapped. The B and high E strings are made from plain steel wire, without any wrap around them, as are the cores of the G, D, A and low E strings around which this phosphor-bronze alloy is wrapped. These acoustic guitar strings are recognizable for their copper-brown colour, and they help to bring out the warmth and depth of the instrument, while giving it some brightness and clarity, too.

Many different manufacturers produce excellent phosphor-bronze strings, companies such as D'Addario, Martin, Gibson, GHS and Rotosound being notable among them, and all make their claims to distinction, and have won their devoted fans. Before you have had a chance to determine "your brand", any North American or European-made strings from a reputable manufacturer should give good results, although the grades of steel used in some of the cheaper Asian-made imports, and the lack of quality control applied to them, will be more likely to lead to disappointing tone and inferior longevity.

Coated strings

Some makers have made specific efforts to extend the longevity of even high-quality strings in recent years by coating them with a synthetic material that helps prevent sweat and grime from penetrating their wraps and corroding them, and dampening their ability to vibrate crisply. Elixir is one of the best-known brands of coated strings, and D'Addario also makes its own line, EXP.

Each uses a different process, but makes similar claims, adding the bonus of a smoother feel to promises of extended life. Other types of strings are popular with some acoustic players, too; folk players occasionally use strings with a silk core and copper-plated steel wrap wire for a smoother, mellower sound, while classical guitars notably use strings made from plain nylon or a nylon core with steel and copper or sometimes silver-plated copper wraps.

Acoustic string gauges

Given that your acoustic guitar carries strings of a decent quality, you are more likely to notice any difference in feel inspired by different string gauges than you are any great variance in tonal properties between strings (given that new strings of one brand are compared with new strings of another). The range of gauges across all six strings might vary slightly from maker to maker, but acoustic guitar string sets tend to run from a 0.010" high E to 0.047" low E in an "extra light" set to a 0.014" high E to 0.059" low E in a "heavy" set. The majority of players are likely to use a standard "light" set (0.012" to 0.053") or "medium" set (0.013" to 0.056"), and many manufacturers of guitars with light tops and/or braces even advise against using heavy strings, which can put more tension on the bridge and top of the guitar than it was designed to handle.

   While light or "custom light" (around 0.011" to 0.052") sets are likely to feel better to the fingers of new players, many guitars will benefit greatly from a set of mediums, with obvious improvements in volume and tone, thanks to the added vibration that these slightly heavier strings put into the top of the instrument. Beginners with soft fingertips, however, that are hurt by even the lightest traditional gauges for acoustic guitars, might want to start with some of the lighter gauges available to electric guitar, which can easily be found down to a 0.008" high E. They will give an inferior sound, and reduced volume, when used on an acoustic, but are fine for building up the calluses, and you can always switch to genuine acoustic strings when you start to get to grips with things.

ELECTRIC STRINGS

Electric guitar strings are available in somewhat greater variety than acoustic, and require a little more thought from the careful accessory shopper. Even plenty of experienced players, who give some consideration to the feel of their strings and select them mainly according to gauge, give little thought to what they are made from and how their composition affects their tone, aside from a simple awareness of the fact that new strings sound a little brighter than older strings.

   Since the early 70s strings wrapped with nickel-plated plain steel have been the standard, while guitarists have also been sold on the improved brightness, power and longevity available from stainless steel and chrome-wound strings. These certainly do accentuate highs, and their harder materials can help them to last longer, too. Plenty of more vintage-minded players, however, have sought a return to the tones of the 1950s and 60s and have gone in the opposite direction: toward softer strings, and warmer sounds. Prior to 1970, when the cost of nickel soared, strings were wound mostly in pure nickel wraps around a plain steel core. These pure nickel strings are a little softer to the touch than nickel-plated plain steel, chrome or stainless steel-wrapped strings, and their tone is slightly softer and a little richer as well. They wear better than nickel-plated strings, and are easier on frets than hard chromed or stainless steel strings, which are harder than most frets themselves (the majority of which, as we have seen, are made from an alloy containing nickel-silver).

   One trade-off is a slightly lower output from pure nickel strings, because their lower steel content offers less interaction with the pickup's magnetic field, but for many players this is just part of the magic, and they find tonal benefits in making up the gain at the amp anyway. Then again, many players find the increased highs and extra power of other string types really helps their sound to cut through, and for them the nickel-plated steel, stainless steel or chromed alternatives are the better choice. The important point here is to be aware of the alternatives, and to find the string that is best for your own style and sound. Strings are where it all starts, and changing to a different type of strings can be the fastest and cheapest way of altering your tone.

Electric string gauges

Electric guitars are able to produce adequate tone and volume from far lighter strings than are sufficient on acoustic guitars, because the steel in the strings interacts with the pickups' magnetic fields rather than having to move the top of the instrument to produce sound. With that being said, heavier strings do provide slightly greater volume even on electric guitars, and a slightly bigger overall tone along with it. The most popular gauges of electric strings are "extra lights" (0.009" – 0.042") and "lights" (0.010" – 0.046"), but they run from even lighter gauges, sometimes called "super lights", starting at a 0.008" high-E string, to "heavies", with a 0.012" or 0.013" high-E and 0.054" or 0.056" low-E strings.

Round-wound strings, which have round wire wrapped around the low strings, are far and away the most common type today, but flat-wound strings were prevalent in the early days of rock'n'roll, and are still used by some players today. These strings are wrapped with steel or nickel "tape" style wraps, with a square or rectangular cross section, to give strings a smoother feel, and a lightly mellower tone along with it. Flatwounds have long been popular (if not universal) with jazz players, but other players who seek authentic 1950s and early 60s rock'n'roll tones, or those who simply enjoy these strings' smooth feel, will use them too. Several makes of coated electric strings are also available, which claim to provide the benefits of coated acoustic strings, as described above.

PICKS

Generally given even less consideration than strings, the pick (aka plectrum, or flat pick) that you use to pluck the strings of any guitar is another formative component in setting the tone of every note you play. Players tend to select picks with a thickness that appeals to them, according to feel, while choosing a shape that is comfortable between thumb and forefinger. But somewhat like strings, picks of different sizes, shapes and thicknesses, and which are made of different materials, all exhibit different sounds.

As a basic rule of thumb, thinner and more flexible picks yield a lighter, softer sound, but one that can also be effectively percussive for rhythm playing. The heavier and more rigid a pick's material, the less it gives when attacking the string, and the more energy it transfers into the string rather than into itself as it bends. All of this, naturally, translates to a heavier sound and a more aggressive attack. Meanwhile, the shape of the attacking edge or corner of a pick also greatly affects

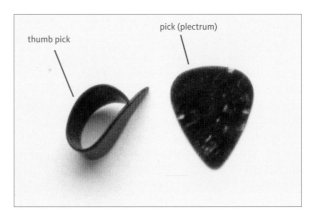

thumb pick

pick (plectrum)

the resultant sound. A triangular or pointed tip digs into the string sharply, inducing sparkling highs and good harmonic content thanks to its narrow but firm point of contact. A rounded edge blurs the attack slightly, yielding a warmer, "rounder" sound. (Blues artist Stevie Ray Vaughan, for one, commonly played using the rounded edge of the back of his picks to achieve a fatter tone.)

Old tortoiseshell picks are the epitome of the heavy pick: the rigid material has negligible give, and yields a firm attack with sparkling harmonics. Being made from an endangered material, they aren't available any more, but if you come across an old one give it a try; the difference between it and a synthetic pick will probably startle you (and is likely to feel a bit odd at first). Many man-made alternatives offer similar performance, and thick and thin picks alike come in a wide range of materials. Fortunately, picks are affordable little slivers of tonal goodness, and you can experiment easily without laying out too much cash. The best way to find what is right for you is to peruse the selection at any well-stocked guitar shop, choose a few shapes that offer alternative picking surfaces, and buy a light, medium and heavy version of each. Then, as ever, play, play, play. Chances are you'll quickly find a pick that you like most for everyday playing, but as any professional studio guitarist knows, it's worth keeping several alternatives on hand for when you need to generate different tones for different playing situations.

It's also worth mentioning fingerpicks here, which the absolute beginner isn't likely to want to try out in a hurry, but which you'll want to know something about if you eventually delve into fingerstyle playing in any kind of serious way. Fingerpicks are made to slip round the end of the thumb and the index, middle and ring fingers, to provide a rigid picking surface for fingerstyle guitar. They also come in a range of gauges (although most are firmer than the lighter flat picks available), and can be made from either steel or plastic. The types made for use on thumb and fingers are quite different, the former looking more like a pick attached to a looped ring, the latter almost like a prosthetic partial fingertip, and cannot be interchanged. Playing with fingerpicks is an art in itself and takes some getting used to, because they require a repositioning of the thumb and fingers' attack of the strings, and many players who want to try fingerstyle guitar will begin by using bare fingers – which provide another tone and feel alternative for advanced players, even so.

CAPOS

A capo is a movable clamp that attaches to the neck of the guitar to bar the strings at a desired fret, essentially shortening the playing length of all strings simultaneously. Players use capos for a variety of reasons. They are extremely useful for quickly changing the key of a song without having to transpose the chords that you might already be familiar with in a different key, or for achieving certain desirable open-string positions for riffs or chords that need to be played higher up the neck to fit a particular song. Plenty of

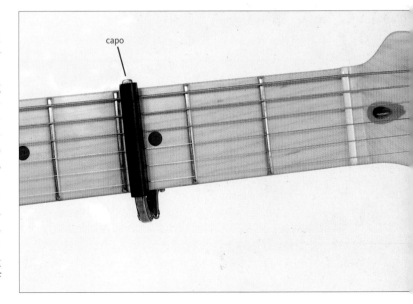

capo

experienced players use capos for a wide range of advanced techniques, but a capo is a handy tool for the beginner, too, and makes it possible to play a great many songs in a wide range of keys with knowledge of only a few basic chords (more instruction on using a capo is given in Chapter 4).

A wide variety of capos are available. The most affordable takes the form of an elastic strap that wraps around the neck and clips in place to keep a firm rubber pad with steel backing in place behind the fret. These do the job adequately, and might be fine for the occasional capo user, but they can be awkward to position and reposition. More elaborate models, made by companies such as Kyser and Shubb, are made out of steel or die-cast aluminium, with springs or thumb screws to provide the string-clamping tension. If you find a capo useful – and many players do – it's worth investing in one of a decent quality, because these are usually easier to put on and take off the guitar, and frequently provide more even string tension and better tuning accuracy as well.

ELECTRONIC TUNERS

Most beginners' guitar sets used to come with either a tuning fork or a pitch pipe to help you tune your guitar by ear, but accurate electronic tuners are so affordable these days that every player really should have one – we're talking £15–20 (even less in US dollars) for a simple unit. An electronic "chromatic tuner" will automatically detect the note played on the guitar and illuminate a series of sharp, flat or in-tune LEDs to indicate its status. Often such LEDs work in conjunction with a meter that will indicate how far off pitch any given note currently is. Many makes of compact chromatic tuners, such as Korg's CA-30 and Boss's TU-12, have a built-in microphone to sense the note played on an acoustic guitar, as well as an input where you can plug in an electric guitar for tuning.

Other floor-pedal types, intended for live use on stage during a performance, can detect a plugged in guitar only, and include a footswitch that mutes the output from the tuner while in tuning mode, so the audience isn't subjected to your tuning adventures. Among these types, the Boss TU-2 is a perennial favourite, and the newer Planet Waves CT04 and Peterson StroboStomp (a stroboscopic tuner) are winning many fans lately. A number of companies also make clip-on tuners that can be attached to the headstock of a guitar (more often an acoustic) and will sense the note automatically with a built-in piezo pickup. Whatever format works best for you, almost all are extremely accurate these days, and even a budget make is a worthwhile investment.

GUITAR LEADS (CORDS, CABLES)

Call it a lead, a cord or a cable, whatever, the sheathed, shielded wire that connects your electric guitar or electro-acoustic to its amplifier, PA or recording system is a vital link in the tone chain. However marvellous your guitar, and however rare and expensive your amplifier, none of it will sound very good with a cheap, poorly made cable carrying your signal from one to the other, and the quality of these long, thin accessories can vary dramatically. A good cable doesn't have to cost a whole lot of money, but the better ones often do cost a little more than the poor ones. It can be difficult to know exactly what you're getting before putting your money down, because these accessories are usually pre-packaged and pulled from the rack, and can't be opened and tested before you have paid and ripped into them. Buying a brand-name cable usually helps, and one with a guarantee ideally, and should result in at least a satisfactory performance.

Plenty of high-end "audiophile" cables are also available, and because of the quality of the signal wire, shield and connectors used in these they often do present a noticeable improvement in tone when compared to cheap or mediocre cables. When you're ready to invest in something beyond the run of the mill, explore cables made by companies such as Klotz, Mogami, Van Damme, Evidence Audio or Van Den Hul, or the even higher-end offerings from companies such as Vovox and Solid Cable. Some of the latter might be almost as expensive as an entry-level guitar, but they have plenty of fans among serious players.

Along with the pure quality of the cable you use, its length will also affect your tone. Any connecting cable will add some capacitance and inductive loading to your guitar's signal, and the longer the cable, the more that is added. A little won't often be audible, but a lot – the amount that can be introduced by cables of around twenty feet or more – can start to dull your tone slightly. Add to this length the factor of poor quality, and you will very likely hear some obvious loss of high end and muting of overall tone when comparing a long, cheap cable with a shorter one of a higher quality. In short, the cable market presents yet another minefield for the guitarist, but you can usually find satisfactory results without necessarily spending the big money that audiophile cable brands demand.

Try to compare several new cables when you have the opportunity, and note which one yields the clearer, fuller tone (we're talking fine points here, so listen closely!), and let your ears be the judge. Also steer clear of any microphonic cables, which will give themselves away by emitting an audible "thunk" through the amp when you tap them or whip them against the floor while plugged in. Likewise, some cables are better shielded against radio frequency (RF) interference than others, although this can be hard to detect if you happen to be testing a range of cables in a location with low RF interference in the first place. You'll know you bought the wrong cable when the local commercial rock station starts broadcasting AC/DC's "Hell's Bells" through your amp in the middle of your new band's first gig, so shop carefully and eliminate this nuisance in advance, if you can.

SLIDES

A slide is used to play a self-descriptive style of guitar known as slide, or "bottleneck", because many slides were once, and sometimes still are, made from the necks of glass bottles. Popular in blues, blues-rock and country guitar in particular, slide styles appear in virtually all types of music, from pop, to rock, to fusion, though perhaps they aren't especially popular in classical or jazz guitar. The slides used to play this style are made from a broad range of materials, and come in a wide variety of lengths and diameters, although the vast majority will be tubular in shape (to

The Rough Guide to Guitar | The Gear

165

The blues singer Cedell Davis had a novel attitude to playing slide guitar. Instead of a using a conventional slide, he raided the cutlery draw, and played using a knife.

fit comfortably on a finger of the player's choice), and from two to three inches long. Different materials offer different sounds as the slide glides across the strings, and notable players are fond of just about anything you can conceive of.

Among the most popular types are slides made from glass, steel and brass, but different types of clay and ceramics and even bone are not unheard of. If you decide to explore slide guitar for yourself, the only practical approach is to take your instrument to the nearest well-stocked guitar store to try a range of options for yourself. The decision-making process here, as with just about every other gear-selection decision, combines factors such as feel and tone, and is therefore particular to each individual player.

GUITAR AMPLIFIERS

Electric guitars aren't musical instruments in and of themselves. Sure, you can play music on them, but to fully convey the beauty and dynamics and emotion that great music can so wonderfully express, an electric guitar needs to be partnered with a good amplifier. Simply put, a guitar amplifier is an electronic device that makes a guitar louder.

For the most part, however, we don't just want these boxes full of circuits and tubes (valves) or transistors to make our guitar louder, we want them to make it sound good, too. To that end, let's think of a so-called guitar amplifier – or amp, for short – not only as a volume-increasing machine, but as a tone generator, too. You can plug an electric guitar into many different amplifying devices and make it louder, but if that increase in volume represents a sound that is clean, cold and sterile, it isn't going to make for an expressive, emotive instrument. To make any electric guitar "whole", you need to partner it with an amp that is inspiring both to hear and to play, one that makes the playing experience easier and more pleasurable, rather than merely louder.

The three main categories of amplifiers for electric guitar are divided according to the types of components that they use to shape and increase the guitar signal. Tube (valve) amps use a variety of the tubular, glass "lightbulb-like" components that are known as "vacuum tubes" in the US and "thermionic valves" in the UK. These are the oldest types of guitar amplifiers, and were introduced in the late 1920s and early 30s by manufacturers who adapted earlier existing circuits for radios and gramophones, but despite their archaic origins they remain the most popular breed of amp among professional players today. Solid-state, or transistorized, amplifiers are based on transistors, op-amps and other forms of solid-state (that is, non-tube) components. These emerged on the market in the mid and late 60s, and have remained with us ever since.

Solid-state technology covers everything from the small, affordable beginner's amp to several large, high-powered models that are popular on the jazz and heavy-metal scene in particular. The third, and newest, category of guitar amplifier is the digital amp, or "modelling" amp. These employ digital technology to shape and modify the guitar signal, often by modelling or emulating the tone of a popular vintage or modern tube amp, before feeding it to a solid-state output stage that increases the volume and sends it on its way to the speaker. Note that several models of solid-state and digital amplifiers also use one or more tubes, usually in their preamp or tone-processing stages, and this inclusion qualifies them as something usually referred to as a "hybrid" amp, though it doesn't make them a "tube amp" per se.

A fourth category of amplifier, one outside those I have mentioned so far, is the acoustic amp. Intended to amplify acoustic guitars with built-in or add-on pickups, an acoustic amp is really in principle more like a small, portable PA in a box, and seeks to accurately reproduce the sound of the guitar plugged into it, rather than to fatten it up with the artefacts of distortion (though many offer plenty of tone-shaping features, certainly). As such, some will also even carry microphone inputs, which can be used to blend in a mic aimed at your acoustic guitar, or to amplify a vocal for an all-in-one solo performance tool. Acoustic guitar amps are usually solid-state devices, although some do carry a tube stage in the preamp.

We'll dive in here by looking at tube amps in the greatest detail, since these remain the more consistent choice of professional players, and represent the technology with which the vast wealth of classic rock, blues, pop, country and jazz music has been produced since the dawn of the electric guitar. This "preferential treatment" doesn't mean to imply that solid-state amplifiers aren't complex devices – many carry a dizzying array of controls and features. Rather, I take this approach for two reasons: first, because the circuitry used to make solid-state amps is usually more "set in stone" than that of the wide range of tube amps available; second, because solid-state and digital amps largely seek to emulate the tube amps upon which their sounds are based, so it is logical to learn about these archaic-seeming beasts in more detail.

Put another way, with solid-state amps you pretty much get what you get: you can read the specs, study the features, play them and make your choice, but you don't need to know what tube goes where, and how the preamp feeds the output stage and so on. With tube amps, a broader knowledge of what goes on inside the sausage factory will also help you narrow down your choice in the first place.

TUBE (VALVE) GUITAR AMPS

Although tubes have been replaced in virtually every other type of electronic device and appliance, they remain the component of choice for the majority of tone-conscious guitarists, some eighty years after guitar first met amplifier. In the introduction to Amplifiers, above, I mentioned that guitar amps aren't just volume machines, they are tone generators, too, and that point of view is entirely apt as regards the humble old tube. The reason that so many serious players still turn to tube amps is because even the simplest tube amp does naturally what any good solid-state amp requires a lot of excess circuitry to achieve. In the process, this "simple" tube amp might be more expensive to produce, and to purchase, than even a fairly large, multi-featured solid-state amp, because the components used to build tube amps are both bulkier and costlier than the mass-manufactured components that can be found inside many solid-state amps, as well as DVD players, PCs, hi-fi amplifiers and so forth. Tube amps require heavy, complex power and output transformers, large filter capacitors and of course the tubes themselves, which are relatively more expensive today than when they were in more plentiful supply. Regardless, many, many guitarists are still willing to put up with the hassle and expense of tubes in order to reap the tonal goodness that tube amps offer.

Circuit stages

Players often perceive an amplifier as a single, self-contained unit: the signal goes in, it gets louder, it comes back out through the speaker. Just like any electric guitar, however, an amp contains several individual stages within it, each of which becomes its own link in the sound chain. Even the most basic "vintage" style tube amp – leaving out any onboard effects (which obviously change the sound in their own ways) – contains three major stages, with the further contribution of a fourth link, somewhat on the sidelines, in the form of the power rectification and filtering stage.

Thanks to the linearity of most tube amp circuits, it is easy to visualize the amp as a series of links in itself, once you lift the lid on the black box.

Tube (valve) distortion: what it is & why we love it

Vacuum tubes, or thermionic valves (tubes or valves for short), have enjoyed such longevity in the realm of guitar amplification not simply because they are capable of making an audio signal louder, but because of the way in which they make that signal louder. Most good electric guitar tones, and that includes virtually all of the legendary sounds recorded by myriad guitar heroes over the past six decades, rely to some extent on tube distortion to give them body and texture. Even amid guitar tones that we consider "clean", there's usually a modicum of natural tube distortion that adds thickness and increases the harmonic richness of each note. To hear an electric guitar played truly clean, plug into a very powerful amplifier such as a PA amp or a large hi-fi amp – preferably solid state – and play at a relatively low volume. That thin, clinical sound your beloved instrument produces is the sound of a truly clean electric guitar. In order to give it the punch, sweetness, juiciness and dynamics that we all love in great guitar tones, you need to process it with some distortion, and nothing distorts more sweetly, juicily and dynamically than tubes – and the beautiful part is, they do it naturally.

The reason we love tube distortion, whether used very lightly, moderately or slathered on like BBQ sauce at a Texas ribs joint, is because of the way these devices distort the audio signal when pushed into clipping. "Clipping" is a term used to describe how an amplifier responds when pushed beyond its ability to produce a clean signal. All clipping is a form of distortion, but the way in which different amplifiers clip defines the character, and thus the appeal (or lack thereof), of that distortion. When pushed past their limits, solid-state devices clip a signal suddenly, which results, in audio terms, in a harsh, jagged distortion, and one that is usually not very pleasant to the ear. Tubes, on the other hand, clip relatively smoothly and gradually when pushed further and further toward their operational limits. The result is a rounder, warmer, fuller-bodied distortion that is also smoother and more "musical" than that produced by a solid-state device. View two different sound waves on a scope, one from a solid-state amplifier and one from a tube amp, and you can actually see the "squareness" and "roundness" of the respective signals. Also, in the process of distorting, even when distorting just a little, a tube also adds harmonics to the fundamental note or notes in the signal, which gives the guitar tone added texture and dimension.

In order replicate the desirable characteristics of tube-amp distortion, solid-state guitar amps incorporate a lot of extra processing to shape, smooth, fur up, and round off the signal. Many of the good ones do an excellent job of it, too, but by and large they are still chasing a tone that tube amps produce simply and naturally, and usually with far fewer components.

Tubes: they might look like something from the controls of Dr Who's TARDIS, but they are the source of that lovely, warm sound inside your guitar amp.

Adjusting your tube gain: getting the distortion you want

Balancing gain and output levels to taste requires using the two controls in conjunction. To achieve a heavy overdrive sound at relatively low volumes, turn the preamp control (often labelled "drive" or "gain", but sometimes simply "volume") to a high setting, and turn the Master Volume to a lower setting. This gives you lots of preamp-tube sizzle while reining in the overall output level.

To get a cleaner sound with more headroom, turn both controls down to zero, then bring the master volume up high – to anywhere from three/four to the maximum – then slowly bring up the preamp control until you reach the sound and volume level you need. To get something in between – a semi-clean tone with just a little break-up when you play hard, for example – try starting with both controls up about halfway, and adjust each up or down from there.

Preamp stage

The first thing your guitar's signal hits after disappearing through that 1/4" jack in the amp's control panel is, in most cases, a single 68k resistor. Then it's a straight, short trip to the input of the first tube stage in the preamp. In actual fact, the preamp is generally considered to contain everything between the input and the phase inverter (explained below). This can include the first gain stage, any tone controls and sometimes a further gain make-up stage following the tone stack. To break it down, however, let's consider the first true point of amplification, known as the first gain stage.

As the name implies, the preamp is simply a small amplifier designed for the task of bringing an audio signal up to a level that the power amp can then boost to an even greater level, ready to be converted to audible airwaves pumped by a speaker. A guitar amplifier's preamp contains a gain stage that boosts the signal, a coupling capacitor that helps to determine the frequencies that are desirable to pass along to the next stage, and a volume control (a potentiometer, or "pot") to let the player determine how much signal to pass along.

Other capacitors and resistors take the jobs of conditioning the power supply and biasing the tube – that is, setting its operating level. But that's the gist of it, and many preamp stages are just as simple as that.

Even the preamps of many legendary vintage amps, such as the tweed Fender Bassman of the late 1950s or the Marshall JMP50 "Plexi" of the late 60s contain precisely these ingredients and no more, and these are considered by many to be the greatest rock and blues amps of all time. The first gain stage of most modern tube amps follows a similar, occasionally identical, formula.

Many contemporary tube amps with high-gain channels – often labelled "lead" or "drive" – add further gain stages to the single preamp stage found on vintage and old-school amps. These amps feed the signal from the first gain stage into a second gain stage, powered by half of another preamp tube. Sometimes they'll even have a third, a series often referred to as "cascading gain", because of the way that the audio signal flows over from one stage to the next. By chaining together several gain stages – each governed by its own level control (i.e. a knob labelled Gain, Drive, Level or Distortion) – and providing a Master Volume control at the end of the chain to determine final output levels, extreme quantities of preamp-tube distortion can be achieved while still playing at relatively low volume levels. Or, of course, at massive volume levels.

This format was pioneered mainly by Mesa/Boogie in the early 1970s, and has been taken up by most manufacturers. These days, most such high-gain amps also have channel-switching capabilities, to let you jump from clean (rhythm) to lead channels at the stomp of a footswitch, and many even offer a third "crunch" channel in between.

Tone-shaping stage

A tube amplifier's tone-shaping stages – known by amp techs as "tone stacks" because of their "stacked" appearance on many schematic diagrams – vary far more than those of the first gain stages in tube guitar amp preamps. Many early amps, smaller ones especially, had no tone controls at all (the tweed Fender Champ, for one). The signal went straight out of the Volume control and on to the output stage via a second coupling capacitor. Others, such as many smaller Voxes and Marshalls, tweed Fender Deluxes and its siblings, and many smaller contemporary amps, have just a single Tone control, while everything from the Bassman mentioned above to bigger Marshalls to most modern channel-switching amps have a three-part Bass, Middle, Treble tone stack, or at least a pair that includes Bass and Treble.

Other factors like the number of controls in a tone stage, the way they are configured, and the value of the capacitors they employ for frequency shelving will clearly affect the signal passing through them in different ways. More controls don't add more tone, they merely provide more fine-tuning of what's there. For example, adding a Middle control to an amp with just Bass and Treble controls doesn't give you more mid-range, it simply gives you more control over the mid-range frequencies that already exist. The two-control amp governs its mid-range content by the relative settings of the Bass, Treble and Volume controls. As with the preamp stage, the makeup of any components in this tone stack also plays a part in shaping the voice of this link in the chain.

In addition to these factors, the placement of the tone controls relative to the other stages in the amplifier can significantly affect how they perform. If the potentiometers follow the cathode of their own tube (known as a "cathode follower" tone stack), an amp will most likely feel and sound a little different than one in which they are placed between the anode of the first tube stage and the grid of the second. Many guitarists say the former gives a very dynamic, touch-sensitive playing feel, while the latter contributes to precise, well-defined response (a tweed Bassman versus a blackface Twin Reverb, for example).

Rather than merely shaping the amp's tonal response, many types of tone controls also help determine how hot the signal is that's passed along to the output stage, and thereby act in effect as a secondary level/distortion control. On a tweed Deluxe, for example, higher settings of the Tone control elicit a hotter output, even when you leave the Volume control alone.

Once the signal has cleared the tone stack, many amps pass it straight along to the output stage – often through a single coupling capacitor – although some send it first through further gain make-up stages, or reverb and/or tremolo circuits, in the case of amps with these effects onboard.

Output stage

A tube amp's output stage begins at the phase inverter tube (PI for short, or "driver"), which has the job of splitting the signal into two reverse-phase signals to feed the output tubes. The output stage ends at the other side of a transformer that converts these tubes' output into a signal that will power a speaker. Each of these sub-stages in the output section – PI, output tubes, output transformer – has a major impact on the voice of the amplifier, and the components that connect them play their part, too.

Different PI topologies have different sounds in themselves. Some types of PI circuits impart a little of their own distortion into the signal when pushed hard, and different PIs "drive" the output tubes in different ways – some yielding good headroom, others an earlier onset of distortion – so they play a part in how the output tubes themselves will sound. Players rave about vintage Fender tweed amps of the 1950s, but relatively few are aware that Leo and co went through at least three different evolutions of phase inverter designs in that decade alone, each of which exhibited very different characteristics regarding frequency range and distortion. Fender's final iteration, a phase inverter known as the "long-tailed pair", became the most-emulated PI topology of all time for large, high-output guitar amplifiers, and even the majority of smaller to medium-sized amps.

The PI sends the signal along to the output tubes, which do the bulk of the amplification work within the circuit. Output tubes also play a big part in determining the tone and distortion characteristics of your final guitar sound, and different types of tubes have their own sonic signatures. Today, British and European manufacturers select from the entire range of available tubes depending on what they intend to create, but traditionally makers of the 1950s, 60s and 70s relied on tube types that were manufactured closer to home, and were therefore more affordable, so it's still convenient to categorize these according to "British sound" and "American sound", to some extent at least.

◊ **Smaller output tubes (valves)** Amps rated at around 20 watts or less usually have a pair of EL84s or 6V6s. The EL84 is a tall, narrow, output tube of European origin that fits a nine-pin socket, and is best known for its appearance in classic Vox amps such as the AC15 and AC30 (the latter of which uses four of them). It is most often used in "class A" circuits, which seek to achieve a sweeter, more harmonically saturat-

Tube swapping

Any experienced guitarist who has owned a tube amp for several years, and has had to re-tube it every 12 or 24 months or so following periods of rigorous gigging, won't be surprised to hear that the output tubes are one of the most influential single links in the entire sound chain. Weak, badly mismatched or wrongly biased output tubes can seriously impede an amp's sound; even satisfactorily operational but poor quality tubes can choke its tone immensely.

Factors like the DC voltage level that the tubes run on and the way in which they are biased also greatly affect their tone and performance, not usually in a "more is better" fashion, but in a "matter of taste" manner that throws up further variables. In addition to having their own sonic characteristics according to type, different makes of the same types of output tubes will also sound slightly different.

Once you have nailed the right genre of tube amp for your style, it pays to experiment with a few different sets of quality output tubes to see which will work best for you. You'll be amazed to hear how simply swapping output tubes can take an amp, in some cases, from soft, fuzzy and bluesy to bold, punchy and twangy. As with all things tonal, there isn't necessarily any better or best here – whatever suits your sound is best for you.

ed sound at the expense of a little output efficiency (see box on p.176). The EL84 can still exhibit a pretty firm, chunky low end in the right amp, but is most known for its chimey, sparkling highs and a mid-range that is crunchy and aggressive when pushed.

Smaller and medium-sized American-made amps most often carried 6V6 tubes, eight-pin tubes that are known for their juicy, well-rounded tone and smooth, rich distortion, which occasionally exhibits an element of appealing grittiness that helps to make them great blues and rock'n'roll amps. The 6V6 is the tube of Fender's legendary tweed and blackface Deluxe amps as well as the Princeton and Champ, and was used by many other makers in amps such as the Gibson GA-40 Les Paul Amp, and several models from Ampeg, Danelectro, Valco and others. Like the EL84, the 6V6 is occasionally used in quartets to produce upwards of around 30 to 40 watts, as in Victoria's Double Deluxe and Budda's V-40.

◊ **Larger output tubes (valves)** Bigger American-made amps traditionally used the 6L6, the big brother to the 6V6. It has a bold, solid voice with firm lows and prominent highs, which can be strident in some loud, clean amps, or more silky and rounded in softer, "tweed" style amps. A pair of these will generate around 40 to 50 watts in an efficient class AB amp, and a quartet (with two pairs working in teams on each side of the phase-inverted signal) can put out up to 100 watts. This is the tube of anything from the Fender tweed Bassman and blackface Twin and Super Reverbs, to early Marshall JTM45 heads and "Bluesbreaker" combos (which were based on the late 1950s Bassman), to the Mesa/Boogie Mark Series and beyond. Amps designed for 6L6s can also use 5881 output tubes (originally a ruggedized version of the same tube), and the European KT66 is also swappable for either type, and is a little bolder, fatter and louder.

The EL34 was the big boy of British amplification from the mid-1960s onward. It can be driven to produce a little more output than the 6L6, and it sounds somewhat different, too, characterized by a fat and juicy but softer low end, sizzling highs and a mid-range that exhibits a classic crispy-crunchy tone when driven into distortion. This is the tube of post-1967 Marshalls like the JMP50 "plexi" and "metal" panel amps, the JCM800, and the majority of modern models; they also appear in the classic Hiwatt models, and plenty of modern amps seeking a big Brit-rock sound. (Note that some Marshalls distributed in the US years ago carried 6550 output tubes instead of EL34s. The 6550 is probably best described, in brief, as a "bolder, louder 6L6".)

Output transformers

From the output tubes the signal runs straight to the input of the output transformer (OT). The OT that you can see hanging from the underside of many an amp chassis (they are usually the smaller of two, or the middle-sized of three) plays a part that would outwardly seem purely functional, in that it transforms a high-impedance current from the tubes to a low-impedance current that will drive a speaker.

  Given that the entire product of our sound chain up to now passes through it, however, with only one link in the chain to follow, you can already guess that it is likely to have a major impact on the resultant sound. The OT's efficiency (or lack thereof), its physical size, the ratio at which it converts the current and many other factors all affect how it will sound, and the sum of these variables determines the way it will convert your signal into one capable of pumping a speaker, and therefore, of once again becoming sound waves in the air.

Roughly speaking, bigger transformers offer more headroom and better bass response, or simply put, a more accurate reproduction of the signal the tubes send them. On the other hand, some vintage types exhibit juicier distortion, while more efficient modern designs offer impressive clarity and definition. OTs can be designed to roll off low frequencies that might overload speakers, or to exhibit other frequency-related characteristics. As with virtually every component we have analysed so far, the choice isn't usually a matter of bad, good, better or best, but more a matter of being aware that different OTs contribute to different sounds. And sometimes contribute a lot.

Negative feedback loops

Although we have already sent the signal on to the speaker, there are some other parts of the output stage that we should double back upon, elements that we could call "side chains", that tend to determine the performance of an amp's output stage, and in fact all of its circuitry. One such ingredient, known as a "negative feedback loop", is often of the most sonic significance, and warrants a mention here.

In simple terms, this loop taps a portion of the signal at the output of the OT and feeds it back to the input point of the output stage, where it arrives as a sound wave that is the reverse (or negative image) of the one entering that stage. The result of combining these reverse-image signals is the suppression of part of the sound wave, heard in a dampening of resonant peaks and extremes in the frequency response, all of which can help to produce a tighter, firmer sound with more headroom, but a harsher onset of distortion when it finally comes. Removing the loop (or never installing one in the first place) yields an amp with a more raw, aggressive voice, usually with a pronounced mid-range response and a smoother onset of distortion, but with less headroom and a looser feel overall. Either has its uses, depending upon your sonic goals, and numerous classics have been made to either formula.

Power stage

The section of a tube amp that supplies the correct voltages to the tubes is a distinctly separate entity within the amp as a whole, and is not in the signal chain itself – which is to say, your guitar signal does not pass through it. The power stage does, however, provide the fuel that keeps the engine burning, and the amount of fuel it provides and the speed at which it can cough it up at times of high demand greatly affect the feel and, to some extent, sound of the amp. This stage consists of the power (or mains) transformer, the rectifier and the filtering stages that clean and condition the current that the tubes feed on.

The power transformer (PT) takes the power from your domestic wall socket, around 120VAC in the US and 240VAC in the UK, for example, and steps it up to the higher voltage required by the amplification duties of the tubes. As such, it's a purely functional device, but quality still counts. An under-rated PT that strains to meet demands from the tubes will ultimately affect your tone for the worse. In addition to ramping up AC voltages, the PT also taps off other lower-voltage feeds to run the tubes' AC-powered heaters (filaments), which warm up the tubes so they can function properly, and the filaments of the tube rectifier, if there is one. This latter component, the rectifier, is where we begin to encounter the variables within the power supply that the player is most likely to notice.

Rectifiers

If your amp has a tube rectifier it will look something like another large output tube, and will most likely have a designation of either GZ34, 5AR4, 5U4G, 5R4 or 5Y3, or, if it's a tall, narrow tube, possibly EZ81. If it has a solid-state rectifier it will be concealed within the chassis, and not externally visible. The rectifier converts the AC voltages that have been increased by the PT into even higher DC voltages required by the tubes' plates.

Solid-state rectifiers, the common alternative to tube rectifiers, are usually made up of twin strands of silicon diodes wired in series. These diodes supply this voltage very quickly on demand, with very little lag between 0V AC and, for example, the full requirement of 450V DC that some bigger amps might demand. Think of this as fuel injection within a car's engine, with a quick acceleration equating to a tight, firm, detailed attack and playing feel for the guitarist.

Tube rectifiers take a little longer to ramp up to full voltage when a note is hit hard and the tubes express their hunger for more voltage, and this slight delay results in a dip and swell in the amp's output response, referred to as "sag". Sag is a compression-like sensation that lends a softer edge and tactile feel to some tube amps, making them suitable, for example, for certain blues and classic rock styles, but perhaps less suitable for firm, heavy contemporary rock and metal or ultra-tight, clean work. Different tube rectifiers have different sag characteristics, which is to say, they convert AC to DC at different rates of efficiency, so the type that is in place in this position in your amp will have some impact on its playing feel (note that the list of types given at the start of this paragraph is in descending order, from more efficient to less so, with a GZ34 or 5AR4 giving the least sag, and a 5Y3 or EZ81 giving the most).

Once it has passed the rectifier, whether tube or solid state, this DC voltage is also subjected to the filtering of electrolytic capacitors and sometimes a choke (a small transformer with a single input and output), which serves to remove "ripple" in the current that would end up as unwanted noise and undesirable overtones. The extent and degree of this filtering also affects the amp's sound and performance. Lightly filtered amps tend to be a little grittier and sometimes more raw sounding, and often have a softer, looser bass response, while heavily filtered amps usually exhibit a little more definition, clarity and solidity.

Changing tubes

If your tube amp begins to sound dull, muddy and lifeless, the most likely culprit is a worn tube, and this will need to be changed. You can do this yourself for many tubes – consult your amp's manual for instructions, and to find out the correct replacement tube types. Determining which tube is failing will probably be a job for a professional, but if you have the correct replacement tubes on hand – and the time and patience to do it – you can try to find the culprit by the process of elimination. Before removing any tube, switch the amp off, unplug it from the mains power and let it cool for ten minutes or so, until the tubes are cool to the touch.

Position the amp in a way that yields a good view of the tube sockets, hold the tube in question by the top of the glass bottle and slowly wiggle it in a rotating pattern, pulling it gently outward, until you feel the pins loosen from the socket. Installing the new tube is a little trickier, since you will need to line up the pins to fit accurately into the socket.

Smaller nine-pin preamp tubes and EL84 output tubes have a gap between the ninth and first pin, so you can accurately align them in the socket. But their small, metal pins can sometimes bend slightly, too, making the job trickier than it might seem. Inspect the tube to ensure all pins are straight, position yourself with a good, clear view of the underside of the socket, and proceed carefully. If the tube doesn't slip into the socket with just a little gentle pressure something is probably amiss, and you have most likely either misaligned the tube or bent one of its pins. If a reassessment and another careful try doesn't get the job done, seek the help of a professional. Larger eight-pin output tubes have a ridged centre post that helps you align them correctly in the notched hole in the centre of the socket. Line them up correctly, push them gently and you should have few problems.

Class A: what is it?

Tube (valve) amplifiers, whether designed for guitar, hi-fi, PA systems or what have you, mainly fall into two categories, or "classes": class A, and class AB. These designations don't distinguish the quality of the amp, as they might imply, but the operating class of the output tubes. Many manufacturers today, however, are fond of advertising certain types of amps as "class A" as if to imply a certain superiority, but such a shallow use of the term can be misleading – particularly when, as the case often is, many such amps really are not operating in class A according to the strict definition of the term. Almost all amplifiers rated at eight to ten watts or more are using two or four output tubes in a "push-pull" configuration, meaning each tube (or pair of tubes, in a set of four) is working to amplify one side of the waveform after the signal is split at the phase inverter. The signal looks like a rolling wave, with peaks and troughs.

In a class-AB amplifier, each tube shuts down for a portion of the waveform, when hit with the troughs, while its partner is amplifying the peaks, thus the term "push-pull". In a class-A amp, two tubes still work in a push-pull fashion, but because of the way the tubes are biased (the manner in which their operating voltages are governed), neither shuts down at any part of the waveform—both are operating the entire time. The important caveat to all this is that these operating classes can only be measured at maximum volume before clipping (distortion). Once the amp begins to distort, such measurement is meaningless.

Manufacturers who advertise amps as being class A are rarely, if ever, measuring their amplifiers under these conditions, but are instead trying to tell you that the output stage of their product shares certain qualities with classic amps that have come to be thought of as "class-A amps", most famously Vox's AC15 and AC30. What really gives these amps their characteristic tone is the fact that their EL84 output tubes are cathode biased, and that there is no negative feedback loop around the output stage. These are characteristics that are also shared by other classic amps such as Fender's tweed Deluxe, most Gibson GA-series amps of the 1950s, and several others that were never advertised as "class-A amps". All of these do share the smooth onset of distortion and high harmonic saturation that we have come to think of as defining the class-A sound, but these are not, strictly speaking, factors that can be attributed to their actual operating class.

The category of class-AB amps includes such classics as Fender's tweed Bassman and blackface Deluxe Reverb and Twin Reverb, Marshall's Bluesbreaker combo and "Plexi" head and countless others. If a so-called class-A amp provides the kind of tone you seek, that's great, but don't let your amp-seeking decisions hang on potentially misrepresented class definitions.

The Vox AC-15: it's a classic for a reason.

SPEAKER & SPEAKER CABINET

In moving along to this stage, we are finally on our way back out of the kingdom of the electrical current and back into the realm of sound waves moving through air. In a very rough sense, a speaker works somewhat like a pickup in reverse: it receives an electrical signal, and translates it to electromagnetic impulses that drive a paper cone, which in turn pumps out sound waves into the air. Given that a speaker is an electromechanical device that produces sound by actually moving, its type, quality and construction have a big effect on our final tone, and one that is too often ignored by guitarists on a quest to tweak their sound.

Every manufacturer who has ever issued a classic amplifier design has paid a lot of attention to the speaker(s) they put into it. Speakers have the final say in every note we play, and hear, and arguably make the biggest single mark on our tone of any individual component all the way down the chain. In addition to shaping the sound of any new amplifier, a speaker change offers a way to fine-tune or freshen up an older amp, too. Players will chase that elusive "perfect tone" by making pickup swaps, changing bridges and hardware, upgrading nut, tuners and more. But one of the biggest sonic alterations achievable, short of getting an entirely new guitar or amp, can be had from changing out your speaker. It's usually even simpler than changing a pickup, costs around the same and arguably has a more immediate impact on your overall sound.

Vintage or modern?

Or, perhaps, British or American?

Guitar speakers (by which I mean the raw drivers, not the cabinets they are mounted in) come in an enormous range of styles, and you need to understand a little bit about the types available before you can begin to choose what might be right for you. Although few categories of anything apply universally in this post-modern age of tonal options, for the sake of attacking the subject at all we can generally divide speakers, in the sonic sense, into two categories – vintage and modern – and two more sub-categories – British and American. There is a lot of crossover these days, with plenty of great new designs that are uncategorizable, and many modern designs emulate vintage tones but exhibit advanced technical specifications. As a rule, however, these categories will help you hone in on what you might want in a speaker.

Vintage-style speakers

"Vintage" speakers, which, unless you've got a vintage amp with speakers that still function well, means new speakers designed to sound like those of the 1950s, 60s and early 70s, tend to have lower power-handling capabilities and exhibit a lot of interaction with the amp, and thereby the player. These are speakers rated anywhere between 15 watts and 35 watts. As a result of these characteristics, they tend to break up quicker than more modern (and/or higher rated) speakers, contributing an element of what we call "speaker distortion" to the amp's own distortion sound. The earliest of these usually have alnico magnets, which are highly prized for their slightly softer response and overall musicality. In the British camp they include primarily the Celestion Alnico Blue (Vox Blue) and, from the mid- and late 1960s respectively, the G12M Greenback and G12H-30, both ceramic-magnet speakers. All are still made in reproduction form by Celestion today, with some similar versions made in the US by Eminence, Weber, and others. Other lesser-seen British makes include Fane and Goodmans. In the American-flavoured camp notable drivers are the main Jensen alnico and ceramic models, such as the P10R and P10Q 10" speakers, and P12R, P12Q and P12N 12" speakers (all of which are alnico speakers, but are represented in the ceramic-magnet camp by siblings with

a "C" prefix). These, too, are made today by the current owner of the Jensen brand, Recoton in Italy, alongside similar drivers made in the US by Eminence, Weber and others.

Lower-powered, vintage-styled drivers tend to partner well with lower-powered tube amps, especially when you're looking for a lot of interaction from the speaker and a lively, juicy sound suitable for rock'n'roll, classic rock, blues, alt-country or garage rock or any of the more rough-and-ready genres.

You don't necessarily need to partner British-style speakers with British amps,

An amp that won't damage your health, your wallet or your next-door-neighbour's hearing: the Smokey Amp is made from used cigarette boxes (see p.170).

or vice-versa. British and American amps of the old days were born with British and American speakers respectively, but plenty of great tone tweaking can be achieved by mixing and matching the types available today.

Modern speakers

By contrast, "modern" speakers include the more advanced designs that appeared in the 1960s and beyond (the earliest types being from makers like JBL, Altec and Electro Voice) and were much more commonplace from the late 70s onward, when several of the "vintage" speaker makes got in on the modern design game, too. These speakers have higher power-handling capabilities of 50 watts or more, and are firmer and more robust overall, meaning they give way to less speaker distortion, and instead translate the sound of the amp itself with more fidelity. These speakers are very often made with ceramic magnets, which have the combined qualities of being much more affordable and somewhat more powerful so they can be used to really crank up the output, although some classic models like the early JBLs were made with alnico magnets. Modern drivers are more appropriate for big amps that you want to stay clean right up to the max, and also for modern high-gain amps where the majority of the distortion sound is to be generated by preamp distortion of one kind or another. Some players like to use them in vintage-style, non-master-volume amps, however, in order to get more fidelity from the amp and to drive that juicy, cranked-tube tone with a lot of punch and clarity, rather than softening it out with the speaker distortion generated by a vintage-styled driver.

Note that, while much of the above might imply that "ceramic" equals "modern", or at least "less vintage", the great vintage designs are not all alnico-magnet speakers by any means. Celestion's G12M Greenback and G12H-30, as mentioned above, both use ceramic magnets, and are among the most revered rock and blues-rock speakers of all time. Also, note that a speaker's efficiency should always be taken into consideration, which is to say the amount of volume it is capable of putting out for every watt put into it. This rating is usually somewhere between 95dB and

The Rig-In-A-Box

The digital revolution has brought guitarists several nifty practice and direct-recording tools, and these can be a great place for a learner to get started with the electric guitar. Products such as the Line 6 POD, Behringer V-Amp, DigiTech RP55 and Korg ToneWorks Pandora are all compact, self-contained amp and effects emulators that contain no power amp or speakers themselves, and must be patched into some further form of amp, powered monitor or PA system for live performance.

What they do all have, however, are manifold types of digitized amp sounds and effects, with outputs for stereo headphones that provide a great means of practising as loud as you like without bothering roommates and neighbours. They also have DI (direct injection) outputs for recording straight to your computer, using any digital recording package like GarageBand, Pro Tools, Cubase, Logic or any number of others.

If you're completely in the dark as to what type of amp you want, or if you suspect a very basic model is something you're likely to outgrow in the near future – or if you'll only be playing on your own anyway – this is certainly a direction to consider. The more affordable of these units can be had for between $50 and $100 (or slightly more in the UK), and even the cheapest offer a great deal of sounds to explore, while often containing bonuses like onboard electric tuners and sometimes even drum machines. If you become fond of the sounds in any of these but do eventually need a real amplifier for rehearsal or performance, you can still use the unit as a multi-FX pedal, patched between guitar and amp.

100dB (occasionally a little more or less) for current-manufacture drivers, and it indicates the decibel level the speaker will achieve at one meter with a one-watt input. A more efficient speaker can really pep up a low-powered amp, which might suddenly be loud enough to gig with where previously its low-efficiency speaker had trouble competing with your drummer. On the other hand, a less efficient speaker sometimes helps to achieve just the right sense of drive and attack without being too harsh – and of course louder isn't always better. Low and high efficiency don't necessarily correspond with vintage and modern designs, by the way, so you just need to check specs. Celestion's original G12, aka Alnico Blue, for example, a design with roots dating back to 1936, is rated at 100dB.

SOLID-STATE AMPLIFIERS

When introduced by several major manufacturers in the mid- to late 1960s, solid-state units were hailed as the future of guitar amplification. Makers such as Fender and Vox were big early players in the solid-stage field, and, despite having several very popular tube models still in the field, both made claims about the trouble-free performance of their modern new transistorized designs. Solid-state amps sold in pretty high quantities, but the response from experienced players was largely cold – as was the tone of the new products, according to the judgements of many guitarists. The majority of professionals returned to their trusty old tube amps, and have stayed with them ever since. Meanwhile, solid-state guitar amplifiers have improved immensely over the past forty years, and the technology now offers viable and good-sounding alternatives that will suit many players, especially those on a limited budget.

The very real trouble with the early generations of solid-state amps was that their designers generally just substituted transistor-based circuits for tube-based circuits, otherwise following largely similar formats, without rethinking the guitar amp from the ground up. As a result, these early efforts lacked many of the support systems that would later help to give solid-state amps more of the sound, feel and dynamics of tube amplifiers (see the box on p.169 for a discussion of this). In some cases, a lack of adequate retraining of employees who had previously been assembling tube amplifiers also led to high rates of equipment failure in the new solid-state amps that they suddenly found themselves building, an unfortunate development in an industry that was trying to sell a new technology on the fact that it was "more reliable and trouble-free".

But all this is behind us now, and solid-state amps offer a broad and entirely viable range of alternatives to the tube-amps that preceded them, catering to everything from the smallest and most affordable beginners' amps to monstrous double-stacks offering several hundred watts of power to heavy metal merchants seeking the Armageddon-sized crunch... along with plenty in between.

By the early 1970s many major manufacturers that still sold tube amps were also having success with solid-state amps, alongside several other manufacturers who specialized in the breed. Kustom amps have become somewhat collectible thanks to their groovy tuck'n'roll vinyl coverings in a range of bright, metallic covers. They also sounded pretty good for the day, too, but don't really compete with many more fully featured larger solid-state amps of today.

Polytone was launched in 1968 as an all-solid-state line, and by the early 1970s the company sold a handful of models, such as the Brute and Mini-Brute, that had established themselves as a favourite among jazz guitarists in particular. As if to attack that very market, Roland released the JC-120 Jazz Chorus in 1975, a large combo with two 12" speakers that actually became popular with a wide range of musicians.

The Jazz Chorus was one of the better-sounding solid-state amps to date, carried an impressive built-in stereo chorus effect and has stayed in production, with a few changes, for 35 years. Over the intervening years, models such as the Fender Backstage series, the Peavey Bandit and the Vox Pathfinder have proven popular as rehearsal and small-gig combos, while Marshall has carved out a big chunk of the solid-state market with its Valvestate line, a range of "hybrid" amps that include a single 12AX7 tube in the preamp to contribute to overdrive duties.

From the tiny Smokey Amps introduced in the early 1980s — housed in replica cigarette packs— to monstrous stacks like the 300-watt Randall Warhead (an amp endorsed by the late Dimebag Darrell), solid-state amps are going strong in the market, and seem to be encroaching upon the hallowed ground of the tube amp more and more every year.

In any case, for the past thirty years or more, the vast majority of beginners who pick up an electric guitar learn to play it through a solid-state amp, unless they've inherited a small Fender Champ or a Vox AC4 from a gracious uncle who was kind enough to pass along his little tube combo. The chances are good that this will remain the state of play for many years to come, although more and more often these small solid-state beginners' amps will carry a digital preamp, with all the sonic versatility these can offer.

DIGITAL AMPS

Digital technology has been prevalent in the musical instrument industry since the early 1980s. It was first widely used in delay and modulation effects (echo, reverb, chorus and flanging), and eventually made inroads into studio and home recording, too. Digital guitar amplifiers are a relatively late arrival to the party, and only really started to make an impact in the market in the late 1990s, when makers such as Johnson, Peavey, Crate and Line 6 all brought impressive designs to the table. Legendary tube-amp manufacturers have also gotten into the game with well-received models, such as Fender's Cyber Twin and Vox's Valvetronix range.

Much in the way that digital delay units create their echoes by modelling any guitar signal you feed into them and reproducing it in a digital form, digital amplifiers accomplish their versatile sound-shaping by modelling the sounds of numerous existing vintage and modern amps (along with new amps right out of their designers' imaginations) and storing them within a digital preamplifier, where they are applied to your raw guitar signal in real time when you play.

The Roland Jazz Chorus: solid state amps don't get much better.

As such, digital amps seek to be several classic amps in one box: dial up selections with evocative names such as "big tweed", "British stack", "rectifier" or "modern class A" from the selection menu, and you are rewarded with tonal emulations intended to represent, for example, a 1950s Fender Bassman, Marshall Super Lead, Mesa Triple Rectifier and Matchless DC30 respectively. Once you have selected an amp model to work with, the basic tone of the emulation can also be tweaked by the tone and gain controls on the digital amp itself, and most advanced models allow you to save your adjustments in the preamp's memory to call them up instantaneously at a later time, often via a footswitch for easy access in live performance. Digital amps also tend to host a wide range of onboard digital effects through which the sound of your amp model can run, such as echo, reverb, chorus, tremolo, phaser, flanger and so forth, as well as emulations of different speaker cabinets, so you can mix and match amp and speaker.

Most of the better digital amps available today sound extremely good. So good, in fact, that several professional players have taken to using them on tour. A far greater number still prefer to use tube amps, on the other hand, and the more outspoken of these are likely to tell you that, while digital amps get close to the sound of the tube amps they emulate, they still don't go all the way as far as tube amp tone and, notably, feel are concerned. It's hard to deny that digital amps are extremely convenient, however, and having so many sonic flavours at your fingertips is a lot of fun, and can get to be addictive, too.

Looked at another way, however, some guitarists worry that having all of these options is a distraction from the important business of just playing their guitars. Most of the world's greatest guitarists have made their music with just a few basic tones at their disposal, using the time-honoured tools of a pickup selector switch, the guitar and the amp's volume and tone controls.

WHAT AMP DO I NEED?

Back in the so-called good old days, beginners' amps didn't offer much more than a volume control and a couple of tone knobs, so a learner's choice was dictated more by what they could afford than by what kind of amp they really wanted to have. These days, you can buy starter amps from all major brands without hitting triple digits, and even these will often carry added features.

Nevertheless, choosing an amp today requires a little shopping around. It's mainly the style of music you want to play that will make your decision. If you want to play any form of rock music that requires a hot lead guitar tone, then built-in overdrive (indicated by the knob labelled Drive, Lead, or Gain in addition to a standard volume control) will be important to you. A learner player might find features such as an aux (auxiliary) input for CD or MP3 player useful – so you can play along with songs you are learning – or a headphone output so you can do it all without invoking the wrath of your housemates.

If you want to play clean or semi-clean pop, blues, jazz, country or other styles – or if you already have effects pedals or multi-effects units to generate your sounds – you might get better bang for your buck by steering clear of the extras. It's true that you get what you pay for, so if you're assessing two amps priced at $79 – one with built-in overdrive, reverb, aux inputs and headphone output; one with just volume and tone controls – the amp with all the features will be cutting corners somewhere in order to pay for them. And the amp without them might well contain better basic components. If you want or need the extra features, buy the amp that has them, but if you really don't need them, and aren't likely to use them, you will almost certainly get more for your money by purchasing the simpler amplifier.

As you move up the scale, and you want to buy an amp that you can do more with, and go public with in band rehearsals or gigs, the question gets tougher. Similar rules still apply, in that it's best to seek features that you really need, but not to pay for something you won't use (unless, of course, it's a real steal that you just can't pass up). If your preference is for clean or semi-clean unaffected tones, with maybe just a little reverb and a bit of old-school crunch when you crank up the Volume control, you should check out simple tube and solid-state amps that offer a good, rugged tonal platform with a propensity toward high-quality clean sounds for pop, blues, jazz or country.

For heavy rock, indie or punk, you'll want something with just a little more drive: almost certainly a Gain/Volume or Volume/Master Volume combination so you can turn up the preamp (and still keep levels down at the output, if you don't have the luxury of being able to play at full volume). For metal sounds, or any playing with a lot of soloing, look toward amps with footswitchable Rhythm/Lead or Clean/Overdrive channels, and perhaps more advanced EQ sections that will help you craft the appropriate tone.

Of course, you can crank up distortion tones from FX pedals, too, but many players like to have this feature available right on the amplifier. Some feel amp-based overdrive or distortion sounds and feels different than pedal-generated dirt, and the convenience of footswitchable channels offers further creative options to the rocker. There's nothing to stop you from using a distortion pedal and an amp's lead channel simultaneously, or alternately, to broaden your sonic palette. Listen to the bands that make the sounds you want to nail and, when shopping for that big amp, audition the makes and models that at least get you in the right vicinity without extra effects pedals and tone shapers. After that, it's all icing on the cake.

Basic care and maintenance of amplifiers

Amp servicing is generally best left to a qualified professional, given the high voltage levels those boxes have inside them. Even amplifiers that are switched off and unplugged can contain lethal voltage levels: the electrolytic capacitors that help them filter their electrical supply can store high charges for many days, a little like high-powered batteries, so there's no safe way to experiment or play around with your own amp maintenance. Unless you get a degree in electrical engineering, of course.

There are, however, several things you can do to help keep any amp solid, secure and rattle-free, without poking around inside the chassis where the dangerous voltages live. As with your guitar, the first step to caring for your amplifier is storing it correctly. Water and humidity are the enemies of all electronics devices, so don't keep your amp in a damp basement or cellar. The high moisture content in the air will corrode electrical contacts within the circuit, as well as making the speaker cone soggy and sloppy – although this might not be detectable to the touch, even a little water absorption by the paper speaker cone will impede its performance and make it sound dull and muddy.

This goes double for storing amps in sheds or garages where a leaking roof might bring on serious water damage, or where extremes of temperature might weaken components or connections. When transporting any amplifier – whether tube or solid state – prop it carefully in the car to prevent it from bouncing, tipping or sliding when you round corners and hit bumps. If you're carrying it in the boot, put a piece of carpet or a folded blanket under it to soften the ride, and wedge a cushion or a piece of foam against the side of it so it won't tumble from side to side.

Other items of home maintenance involve simply keeping major components tight within the amp's cabinet. The speaker's mounting bolts are likely to vibrate loose over time, and you should check these periodically to ensure that the speaker frame isn't rattling against the baffle (front panel). The object here is just to keep them tight enough to secure the speaker to the baffle, not so tight that you can't loosen them if you need to make a speaker swap, or so that you even bend or distort the speaker's frame, or crack the baffle. Turn the nut or bolt with your fingers until it is finger-tight (meaning you can't turn it any further), then use a tool of the appropriate size and tighten it between another half to a full turn.

Periodically check the amp chassis' mounting within the cabinet, and tighten its mounting bolts if it's loose or moves too much within the cab. While you're at it, check anything else mounted to the amp cabinet that might rattle when the amp is playing or, worse still, that could fall off and cause expensive damage.

The tubes in tube amps are particularly sensitive to jolts and bumps, but the electrical components in *all* amplifiers can be weakened, loosened or even broken by rough handling. Tube amps do require a little more consideration, however, and a few simple tips regarding care and handling will help you extend the life of the components that make them tick.

The suggestions below are just about all you can safely do yourself in terms of amp maintenance, and any other suspected trouble should be left to a qualified professional. Undesirable noises, improper control functions or a generally worn, tired tone doesn't have to mean the death of an amp, and might be cured by a basic cleaning or the replacement of a simple, inexpensive component. Find a good amp tech in your vicinity, and use them when necessary.

Warm up

All tube amps need to warm up before they will emit sound, because the tubes' "heaters" need to reach their operating temperature before the other components within the tube will do their job. If your tube amp has a standby switch, switch the power switch to the on position before bringing in the standby switch, and let the tubes warm up for a full minute before engaging standby. Amps without standby switches can simply be switched on, and the tubes will begin their own slow warm-up.

Cool down

When powering down a tube amp, switch off and let the tubes cool for a few minutes before moving the amp or packing it away. Tubes are at their most delicate when hot, and jostling them without allowing an adequate cooling-down is more likely to induce premature failure, and the need for replacement.

Ventilate!

Tubes need to stay as cool as reasonably possible while operating, or they will overheat and burn out. Never enclose your amp in a sealed box, trunk or small closet while running, and don't block the rear opening or the tube vents. And never position the amp hard up against a wall or other surface so that natural air flow is cut off. The manufacturer of any tube amp will have designed it to receive adequate ventilation to keep the tubes from overheating while in use. Impeding the flow of air will not only burn up expensive tubes prematurely, but will very likely take out other components within the amp if the tubes go pop mid-flight.

Biasing output tubes

Old preamp tubes can be swapped for new tubes of the same type without the need of any adjustment being made to the amp, but some amps need to have their bias levels reset when output tubes are changed. Your user's manual will tell you if and when this needs to be done – it's usually necessary with amps designated "class AB fixed bias". Cathode-biased amps, on the other hand – such as Vox AC15s and AC30s, tweed Fender Deluxes and others based on them – do not need to be rebiased. Biasing is a job for a professional, but it should only cost a nominal bench charge, although it will cost a little more if the technician has to remove your amp's chassis.

EFFECTS PEDALS & MULTI-FX UNITS

Chances are you're soon going to want to broaden your horizons with some add-on effects. You can get perfectly good straight-up tones with a good guitar and amp (and the knowledge and skill required to play them, of course). There are plenty of old-school garage rockers, bluesers and jazz players that still prefer the simplicity of this approach. Adding a few effects to your rig, though, will expand your sonic potential considerably, and are a hell of a lot of fun too. External effects (as opposed to what's built in to your amp) come in two main types: effects pedals (aka stompboxes), which usually contain a single, individual type of effect (although some might join two in one box) and multi-FX units, which contain several (usually digital) effects within one box.

An effects pedal carries a footswitch that will turn it on and off with a quick stomp, and is usually positioned at the player's feet for easy access. The guitar is plugged into the input of the pedal, and

Multi-FX units

Back in the day, these used to be large, rack-mounted devices. They'd often be routed through an amp's effects loop (and sometimes still are), via a send output and a return input on the back of the amp, rather than between the guitar and amp. Advances in digital technology have meant that, these days, dedicated guitar effects units are much smaller and most of them have stomp switches.

Even the larger of today's processors (often known as floorboards), such as the Vox ToneLab LE, Line 6 M13 Stompbox Modeler or TC Electronics Nova System, carry a number of built-in footswitches, just like their smaller, budget-friendly brethren such as the DeltaLab DGFX1 or the DigiTech RP55. Rack-mounted units persist, in the form of powerhouses such as the Boss GT-Pro or Digidesign Eleven, but have outputs for controller pedals and footswitches that the player can trigger in live performance.

Different multi-FX units might be noted for certain sounds and characteristics, to some extent – one excelling at reverbs, for example, another being praised for its vintage-style phaser or chorus sounds. But the nature of digital technology does make them all a little homogenous. Most units, from the affordable to the pricey, will let you alter preset sounds and save them as user sounds, and then access these instantly with the tap of a switch by your foot. Price, the number and combinations of effects available and the parameters used to select, alter and save them, tend to be the biggest selling factors.

Some units include both analogue and digital technology in the same box: providing the oft-preferred analogue overdrive stages in front of digital modulation and delay stages, for example. These might lure guitarists enamoured of old-school overdrive pedals, who are nevertheless drawn to the power and convenience of a multi-FX unit. Also, the proliferation of compact amp-simulators that also carry many effects has led to something of a grey area between multi-FX units and amp modellers. Is the Line 6 POD or Johnson J-Station a multi-FX or an amp sim? It's a bit of both and can be used as either.

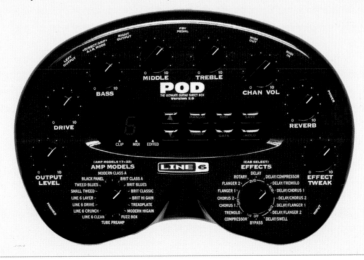

a cable is run from the pedal's output to the amp, or to the next pedal in a string of two or more that are chained together. Multi-FX units are in one sense more complicated, since they contain many options in the same unit, and have a menu-select system that usually needs to be studied a bit before you dive in. But they are also simpler in that the digital technology behind them makes them, in practice, less affected by other effects that you might chain before or after them.

Twenty years ago it seemed that the booming market in powerful multi-FX units would drive the humble, single effects pedal into extinction. But plenty of tone-conscious players gradually rediscovered that one well-rendered and individual-sounding analogue effect in a sturdy pedal – or several chained together – was often better than a handful of sometimes generic-sounding digital effects in a computerized box, lumped in with a lot of other features that they might never use. An effects-pedal renaissance began. Now there are more effects pedals on the market than ever before, and the range includes reproductions of virtually any worthwhile vintage effect you can think of, alongside all sorts of clever new designs.

What's best for you is a matter of taste and opinion, and might to some extent depend on the type of music you play (and, of course, your budget). Certainly many players, professional and amateur alike, use a combination of individual pedals and multi-FX units, while others use just one or the other. Some of the same thinking that applied to selecting an amplifier applies here too: if you only need one or two sounds from your effects units, investing in individual pedals will sometimes give you results of a better quality. If, on the other hand, you need to chain together four or five different effects to achieve your desired sound – say, compression, overdrive, chorus, echo and reverb – you might be better off with an all-in-one unit.

Let's take a broad look at multi-FX units first, then we'll examine each effect type more closely as they apply to individual sounds.

For our purposes, effects pedals basically fall into four categories: boost, compression, overdrive, distortion and fuzz; modulation; echo and delay; and filtering and EQ-based effects. Some manufacturers would categorize things differently – for example, modulation is a broad umbrella that covers different effects such as chorus, vibrato and phasing. But these headings are mainly a means of seeing what makes them tick. The leading multi-FX units on the market incorporate all or most of the following individual effects.

BOOSTER, COMPRESSION, OVERDRIVE, DISTORTION & FUZZ

This is easily the most popular category of effect, and sonically is the natural first step away from the thin sound of a straight, clean amplified guitar. If a player only owns one pedal, chances are it's a distortion, fuzz or booster box, and plenty of players have collections of several or even dozens of them. They might use two or three at a time on their pedalboards for different colours, textures and staggered levels of sonic sizzle.

Boosters

A booster pedal (essentially a transistorized preamp stage in a small box) is often billed as "linear", clean or distortion-free, and is intended to boost the guitar signal before it reaches the amplifier, without adding any artefacts like fuzz or distortion. The "linear" part of the name refers to the guitar's frequency range, and therefore its tone, which should remain unchanged as it passes through the booster. Only the signal level should be increased.

The resultant sound from most boosters is usually something other than totally clean, however. Many boosters do fatten up the tone of the guitar somewhat, while also hitting the amplifier harder – they tend to be used with tube amps, mainly – in order to produce some distortion at the amp itself. Plenty of players use them for a supposedly "clean" volume lift for undistorted lead lines, certainly, but this perceived clean tone is always thickened by a degree of distortion anyway. Back in the good old days, players such as Eric Clapton, Jimmy Page and Brian May all achieved ground-breaking lead tones by using simple transistor-based booster pedals to kick their tube amps into overdrive.

Compressors

These generally contain a boosting stage as well, but they are designed to be compact versions of the large studio compressors. Compressors are levelling devices, bringing down the loud peaks in music in order to bring up the quieter parts and make the whole thing louder as a whole. They can be set to work in many different ways as a mixing tool on recordings. But as a guitar effect they are used to create longer sustain, which they achieve by smoothing the attack and decay of a signal and simultaneously amplifying its tail.

Part of the compressor's original appeal to guitarists was its ability to replicate the natural compression, or "sag", of a tube amp being run at medium to high levels. Whether induced by a pedal or by the amp itself, compression is often as much a feel thing as a tonal element, making the guitar feel more tactile, touch-sensitive and playable. Though they are predominantly used as sustainers, some players also use them as booster pedals, by turning down the Compression or Sustain control and winding up the Gain or Volume. While all compressors have a squashing or sustaining effect, certain compressors have been attributed with magical tonal properties, especially the grey Ross Compressor, MXR's Dyna Comp and Dan Armstrong's little Orange Squeezer, and there are several copies of these around today.

In addition to their function as compressors, each of these units adds its own characteristic thickening of the tone, often with a little appealing grit thrown in as a bonus.

The compressor has long been considered an essential weapon in the Nashville session-player's arsenal. It helps to smooth out snappy chicken-pickin' runs or to thicken up otherwise thin, clean rhythm and lead parts. But the effect can be heard in the work of players from all genres, from LA session player Jay Graydon (guitar player on several Steely Dan records) and British Strat-picker Mark Knopfler to alt-rocker Trey Anastasio of Phish.

Joe Satriani gets heavily into a two-finger "tapping" style of super-fast lead guitar, a technique best attempted with plenty of compression and distortion.

Overdrives

Confusion sometimes revolves around the distinctions between overdrives, distortions and fuzzes, but in theory each should do approximately what it says on the box, even if one type also does a little of the others' jobs along the way. In the case of overdrive pedals, the intention is often twofold: either to provide a gain boost to "overdrive" a tube amp into distortion, or to approximate the mildly distorted sound of a slightly overdriven tube amp. In practice, most do a little of both.

Crank the average overdrive toward the max and it usually coughs up an element of self-generated distortion; generate enough of this distortion, and things can also sound a little fuzzy. Despite the grey areas, however, there are definitely distinctions between the types. It all makes some sense if you think in terms of the degree of clipping achieved by the pedal, with overdrives generally being soft-clipping devices and distortions being hard-clipping devices. Fuzzes simply generate, well, fuzz.

The Ibanez TS-808 Tube Screamer of the late 1970s and the TS9 which followed are considered the grandaddies of overdrive pedals, while other early units, such as the Boss SD-1 Super Over Drive and MXR Distortion+ (despite its misleading name) also helped to establish the template for this sound. Many newer pedals today aim at a "modified Tube Screamer" sound, while others seek to achieve entirely original overdrive tones.

Distortion pedals

By definition, distortion pedals are designed to adulterate the guitar's signal in and of themselves, rather than to provide a mild overdrive sound or boost in conjunction with the amp. These pedals unashamedly mess up your sound, making it – at maximum drive or distortion levels – as filthy as possible, while also slapping their own notion of the ideal heavy rock or metal EQ all over your tone's backside. But of course they will also boost the guitar signal as well (depending on the volume/output/level settings), and the sound we associate with them is still a partnership of pedal and amp (not to mention guitar).

In 1979, the ProCo Rat set the standard for heavy distortion sounds above and beyond the

Vintage effects: Copicats, Fuzz Faces, Cry Babies & Echoplexes

Guitar geeks love effects units from the very dawn of the technology – the 1950s and 60s – and interviews of major players in guitar magazines are often filled with the hallowed names of vintage effects that they have rediscovered and used in their recordings. There were indeed some great sounds made in the golden age of rock, and the tools used to make them often had less of a mass-produced sound, and feel, than much of what's on the market today.

Some attribute the supposed superiority of them to analogue technology, to the tubes used in some types, to the use of better-sounding components that were more readily available back in those days or the care taken with the design and assembly processes. Part of the continued appeal of vintage effects pedals, as with vintage guitars and amps, can also be attributed to pure nostalgia, and our desire to use the same gadgets our heroes from the 1960s and 70s might have used. There's a flip side to this, though. As great as many vintage effects might sound, they are often more expensive than newer units with similar functions. They can sometimes require expensive maintenance, which often involves obtaining hard-to-find replacement parts, and even when they're working can frequently be noisier than modern units. That said, they can be a lot of fun to explore, if you get the opportunity.

Some of the more prized vintage effects units were with us even before effects pedals as we know them today were invented. Many players still swear by the rich, juicy echo sounds produced by old units such as the US-made Maestro Echoplex, the UK-made Watkins/WEM Copicat and the Italian-made Binson Echorec. All of these were tube-powered echo units introduced in the late 1950s to early 60s, which used cycling tape loops to produce variable echo repeats.

Their scarcity means that good, working original examples are expensive today, and they'll often need regular servicing, too. Among contemporary makers seeking to capture this sound, Fulltone's Tube Tape Echo is particularly well regarded, but it is also quite an expensive unit. Early examples of the Univox Uni-Vibe of the late 1960s tend to be priced in the same region as some early tape echoes, but many players swear you can't get that thick, liquid, phasey sound from anything else, thanks to the vintage photoresistors used in the original units.

Much simpler and more compact than these, seminal fuzz boxes from the mid- to late 1960s are also highly prized, as are wah-wah pedals of the same era. Players gush over the germanium transistors used in the early Maestro Fuzz-Tone, Arbiter Fuzz Face and Sola Sound/Colorsound Tone Bender (and similar pedals), which were made legendary by Keith Richards, Jimi Hendrix and Jeff Beck respectively. The germanium transistors responsible for these lush fuzz sounds were also extremely inconsistent, however, and two vintage pedals rarely sound quite the same.

Contemporary makers doing the best job of creating germanium-based fuzzes do so by carefully selecting and matching the best transistors, a process undertaken by Roger Mayer, Fulltone, ZVex and a few others. In vintage wah-wahs, the little coil-like inductors that shape their sound are credited with these expressive pedals' magical tonal properties, and original Vox Wah-Wah and Thomas Organ Cry Baby pedals each have their followers according to the characteristic tones they produce.

Have fun with your vintage-effects explorations, but beware of laying down vast sums of cash for units that are untested and which might have been modified or poorly repaired over the years – they could be ready to break down at any moment. It's always wise to try a wide range of contemporary offerings available on the market, too, and to go in with your eyes wide open.

capabilities of the MXR Distortion+ and the Ibanez Tube Screamer, and all mass-market brands now offer at least one distortion pedal, and often many. Boss, for one, tries to cater to all possible tastes. Its DS-1 (not to be confused with the SD-1 overdrive mentioned above) is one of the workhorses of the breed, with some big-name players happy to stomp on its rectangular switch, including both

Steve Vai and Joe Satriani, and it also has several other flavours of distortion in other pedals, including the popular Metal Zone. Other popular units include Marshall's ShredMaster, DOD's Grunge and ZVex's Box of Rock.

Fuzzes

Fuzz boxes are the grandaddies of distortion pedals, and were among the first of the transistorized guitar effects being built back in the early 1960s – which is no surprise when you discover the simplicity of most of them. It's almost pointless to describe the sound of a vintage-style fuzz tone more than the name already does. They slather a slightly wooly, rounded, warm but sparkly distortion all over the guitar signal (see, you could just say "fuzzy") to give more meat, girth and sustain to the sound.

The more playable devices are known for retaining elements of your dynamics, touch, feel and core tonality, and for interacting well with your guitar and amp, while some other extreme units pump out a heavy "brick wall" style fuzz whatever you put into them.

Great originals of the fuzz box world are the Maestro Fuzz-Tone, Arbiter Fuzz Face and Sola Sound/Colorsound Tone Bender. Many contemporary makers offer renditions of both classic and contemporary styled fuzzes, with higher quality units coming from brands such as Fulltone, ZVex and Roger Mayer. The 1990s grunge band Mudhoney immortalized two classic fuzz pedals in the title of their debut EP, *Superfuzz Bigmuff* and their first few albums are a great example of just how fuzzy a few fuzz pedals can get.

MODULATION DEVICES

This group of effects includes phasing, flanging, chorus, vibrato and tremolo, rotary speaker effects, and octave dividers, the latter of which aren't really modulation devices, but they do affect your guitar's pitch. Later analogue versions of the first three of these – phasing, flanging and chorus – do, as a matter of fact, often use much of the same technology as echo and delay units, but it makes sense to include them here because of their sonic relationship to older units made from very different kinds of circuits.

Most modulation effects were developed in an effort to add depth, dimension and movement to the guitar's natural sound without necessarily distorting it. A few noteworthy types also developed from effects that were in use on the electronic organ before they were reconfigured as guitar pedals.

Phasers

These boxes were called "phase shifters" because they split the guitar signal, reverse the phase of one and shift the two against each other at a user-determinable speed, resulting in a warbling, tremulous, "swooshing" sound. The sound of good examples can run from gentle and watery at lower depth and speed settings to spacey and extreme when the knobs are maxed.

Many players use the effect very subtly, to add some dimension and motion to otherwise clean tones (think the Rolling Stones' "Shattered" from the album *Some Girls*, or The Clash's "Lost in the Supermarket" from *London Calling*), or to thicken up overdriven tones that aren't heard as outwardly "phasey" as such (Nirvana's "Come As You Are" from *Nevermind*), while they can also produce odd-sounding special effects when desired.

"No Quarter" by Led Zeppelin is a great example of a weird, "cold water"-sounding effect that phasing can conjure up. The Mu-Tron Bi-Phase, MXR Phase 45, Phase 90 and Phase 100, and Electro-Harmonix Small Stone are among the grandaddies of phaser pedals, and several manufacturers make outstanding units today.

Flangers

Usually considered something of a sonic big brother to the phaser, the flanger is indeed related in a sense, but achieves its heavier – some would say more oppressive – sonic results by imposing more control over its placement of the notches created by the phase relationship, rather than spacing them evenly as the phaser's sweep does. Achieving the more extreme sound of flanging requires more complex engineering, and more control over the split, phase-reversed and time-controlled signals within the box – complicated stuff that also usually makes good flangers a little more expensive than good phasers.

Having said that, the more extreme sound of flanging is less appealing to many players than the gentle, bubbly sound of phasing. As a result, it is heard used for many wild space-aged effects, but is at the heart of fewer subtler classic tones the way that phasing is. The first truly successful flanger, in terms of both sound and function, was probably A/DA's Flanger of 1977, which was followed by Electro-Harmonix's beloved Electric Mistress and MXR's popular grey Flanger.

Choruses

Made possible by the same types of technology that enabled makers to put phasers and flangers into relatively small boxes, chorus pedals came along in the mid-to-late 1970s, and by the 80s were among the most popular of all modulation devices.

Strictly speaking, modern chorus effects are a type of delay, but rather than using the delay technology to create echoes or reverb, chorus pedals use it to simulate the sound of several guitars playing at once. They do this by splitting the signal into several strands, all with slightly different pitch and spatial relationships, which results in the shimmering, slightly warbling sound of a chorus of guitar voices. Hence the name.

Andy Summers' guitar sound on The Police's big 1979 hit "Message in a Bottle" (produced with a Boss CE-1 Chorus Ensemble), is not only one of the earliest, but one of the best known examples of this sound, and several others followed through the 1980s. A generation later, Nirvana logged another classic example of great chorus usage (right alongside their classic phaser sounds on the same album) with Kurt Cobain's use of an Electro-Harmonix Small Clone on the massive hit "Smells Like Teen Spirit".

MXR, Boss, DOD, Ibanez and countless others have offered compact and good sounding chorus pedals. Used with the settings up high on clean guitars, a chorus pedal produces the thick but ethereal sounds heard on albums by the Cocteau Twins or Lush. Used with the dials turned a little less towards the right, a mildly distorted guitar and a few sparse minor chords, you can conjure up those moody early-1980s goth tones beloved of The Cure or Siouxsie & the Banshees.

Vibrato & tremolo

These two "old school" effects are often grouped together, and Fender even inaccurately labelled one as the other on many of its classic amplifiers for years. Strictly speaking, they are two different effects. Tremolo was the first effect commonly included on early guitar amps, and is now popular in pedal form too. Correctly defined, tremolo modulates a signal's volume up and down at a steady ready, at a speed determined by a Speed or Rate control and to a degree determined by the depth of an Intensity control. At extremes, some versions of the effect will cut the signal to (or near to) zero in its downward swing, creating a very choppy, staccato tremolo sound, while more subtle renditions – or lower depth settings – produce a gentler, bubbling effect.

Tremolo was popular in early rock'n'roll and has long been one of the staples of country guitar playing, but it has made a big comeback in several other genres of music in recent years. For an evocative use of this effect, check out the haunting soundtrack to David Lynch's *Twin Peaks* TV series of the late 1980s. A heavy, radical use of tremolo can be heard on "How Soon Is Now?" by The Smiths. In addition to Rate (speed) and Depth (intensity) controls, some tremolo pedals have controls or switches that let you alter the shape of the wave between a smooth, rounded up-and-down to a sharp square or triangular wave, and all of these give a slightly different feel to the sound of the effect.

Vibrato is similar to tremolo in that it creates a pulsing sensation at varying speeds and intensities, but true vibrato also modulates the pitch of the note, warbling it back and forth between a shade sharp and a shade flat in time with the pulsation of volume. Fender did make a few amps in the early 1960s that carried something close to true vibrato: something called "harmonic vibrato". Some pedals try to emulate this subtle yet atmospheric effect, while others offer a full-on, pitch-modulating vibrato.

Rotary speakers/Uni-Vibe emulators

Made popular by the large, heavy, but extremely cool sounding Leslie cabinets that were first used by Hammond organs, and later adopted by some guitar players, rotary speakers are heard on many classic 1960s recordings, such as The Beatles' "Lucy in the Sky With Diamonds", Led Zeppelin's "Black Dog" (on Jimmy Page's solo) and on Stevie Ray Vaughan's "Cold Shot".

The Univox Uni-Vibe pedal came about in the late 1960s to bring a simulation of that sound to a small, portable, effects unit, and quickly made itself known on ground-breaking recordings such as Jimi Hendrix's "Star Spangled Banner" and Robin Trower's "Bridge of Sighs". Today, effects pedal makers go both routes. Some aim to reproduce the whirling, three-dimensional Doppler effect of a rotating speaker, while others try to accurately nail the Uni-Vibe tone, which is actually slightly more akin to a deep phaser or vibrato sound.

Of the former, Hughes & Kettner's Rotosphere is among the more successful pedals, while Fulltone, Roger Mayer, Voodoovibe and others have made popular contemporary clones of the latter.

Octave dividers & ring modulators

This is a relatively simple effect, but also one of the freakiest when used correctly – and sometimes even more so when used incorrectly. Like a surprising number of classic sounds, this first came to the world's attention via Jimi Hendrix, from a custom-built Roger Mayer Octavia pedal – famously heard on "Purple Haze" and plenty of other Hendrix tracks besides – where the fat upper octave it adds to each note gives a freaky, almost robotic tone to the guitar. Octave effects are among the trickier pedals to use well, because the circuit only tracks well if a single, pure, cleanly played note is introduced – and honks into total freakout if it sees an interval. Also, the fewer harmonics the better, so firm picking on a neck pickup does it the most favours. Many players use octave dividers before fuzz pedals, to add some real girth to solos.

Ring modulators, on the other hand, come to us from the world of analogue synthesizers, and the ideas behind them have far more applications there, but they can be useful for the guitarist who needs some wild, whacked-out, totally anti-guitaral sonic obliteration every so often. Think in terms of the octave divider's percussive, synthesized octave-up sound, but with more jagged, atonal, random-interval performance. Ring modulators usually aren't particularly "musical" effects, but they can sure help to get your guitar parts noticed.

DELAY EFFECTS: ECHO & REVERB

We all know the sound of this effect: it replicates varying degrees of the sound your guitar might make being played in the gym showers, a cathedral or in mammoth cave. It has proved itself one of the most atmospheric aural adulterations available. Since none of those locations is entirely gig-friendly, however, those ever-handy techs bottled the flavour in a reliable, portable form. This category covers both echo and reverb effects, since they are versions of the same thing. The term echo was used more often in the early days, and is sometimes used today to refer to the distinct and distant repeats of a signal, while delay refers to anything from the same, to the short repeats heard as reverb, to the complex, long, manipulated repeats of an intricate digital delay line.

Reverb

The second effect to be included in amps themselves, following tremolo, reverb as used for guitar is usually quite different from reverb as used to add "room sound" to drums, vocals and other parts in a recording studio. Some of the more successful, and semi-compact, means of producing reverb in the mid- to late 1950s came in the form of a small amplifier driving one end of a set of long springs (rather than a speaker), with a pickup at the other end to capture the resultant watery, echoey sound, so this is the breed of reverb that found its way into the first amps that carried the feature.

Being first, it also became the classic, and the vast majority of guitarists looking for a reverb sound today still appreciate a good spring reverb. This is perenially popular as an effect built right into an amplifier, but separate tube-driven reverb units are available from companies like Fender, Dr Z and several others, although they are more the size of a large breadbox, and not a pedal as such. Digital technology has allowed designers to emulate spring reverb in much smaller pedals, and often, at the same time, to throw in some studio-style reverb options, such as emulations of the spatial sounds of medium rooms, concert halls and cathedrals. Models such as Electro-Harmonix's Holy Grail, Marshall's Reflector, Line 6's Verbzilla and Danelectro's affordable Corned Beef are all popular reverb pedals of recent years.

Analogue & digital delay (echo)

The transmogrification of bulky, fiddly tape echo units into transistorized analogue echo pedals in the late 1970s is arguably one of the greatest economies the delay-loving guitarist has ever experienced (physically more than financially). Players addicted to anything from slapback to the hypnotic sonic cloning of their Echoplexes, Copicats and Space Echoes breathed collective sighs of relief when Electro-Harmonix and MXR introduced relatively affordable analogue delay pedals, bringing short to medium echoes to the feet of players around the world. Soon there was barely a rocker going who stepped on stage without a delay pedal, and every major effects maker offered a model or two, and still does.

By the early 1980s, digital technology was sweeping the delay market, just as it was the chorus and flanger market, but many players eventually decided they preferred the warmth and texture of simpler analogue delays to the power and versatility of digital delays (which some considered a bit cold and sterile sounding). Today, you can get digital delay pedals that mimic warm, gritty sounding old tube tape echo units, while analogue echo pedals continue their resurgence right alongside them.

WAH-WAH, FILTERING & EQ

Some extremely emotive sounds can be produced simply by manipulating or filtering the frequency spectrum in which the guitar operates. We know this category best in the form of the wah-wah pedal, taken to an art form by guitarists from Jimi Hendrix and Eric Clapton to Slash and Zakk Wylde. Filtering also gives us voltage-controlled envelope follower auto-wah sounds. Down at the simpler end of the scale, plenty of guitarists seek the aid of an active tone control in the form of a graphic EQ.

Wah-Wah

A wah-wah pedal is often explained as being a tone control with a rocking pedal attached, but there's a lot more to it than that. In truth, the wah circuit is a sweepable peaking filter, that is, a bandpass filter that creates a peak in the frequency response that the player can manually sweep up and down the frequency spectrum. When that peak is swept through the portion of the spectrum that contains the notes we are playing, it emphasizes those frequencies and produces the "wah" sound we hear.

The differing amounts of resonance produced as this peak is swept also contributes to the characteristic sound of any given wah-wah pedal, and this is something that can vary considerably from model to model. Players use wah-wah pedals for everything from clean funk and disco rhythm-guitar parts, to wailing rock solo work in conjunction with heavy distortion or fuzz. The Vox Wah and CryBaby are the godparents of wah-wah, and both are still available today in reissue form, alongside many outstanding reproductions and some entirely new designs.

Auto-Wah

For foot-free wah sounds, turn to the "envelope follower", otherwise known as the voltage-controlled filter, or auto-wah. These effects contain a sweepable peaking filter much like that of the traditional wah-wah, but use the intensity of the incoming signal – in other words, the guitarist's pick attack – to generate the control voltage that sends the peak up and down the frequency spectrum.

With most such devices, pick lightly and the sound remains bassy and muted; hit the strings hard, and brighter wah-like frequencies leap out. Musitronics's Mu-Tron III, introduced in 1972, was the first widely available envelope follower, and remains one of the best-loved. Electro-Harmonix followed with a range of models such as the Doctor Q, Zipper, Bass Balls and Y Triggered Filter, and most major makers of the 1970s joined in.

While the treadle-pedal version is generally considered the rocker's wah (despite the disco-era's clichéd appropriation of the effect), the envelope follower auto-wah is the archetypal funk machine. Think Parliament-Funkadelic, just about anything from bassist Bootsy Collins, or Stevie Wonder's "Higher Ground" (a famous early use of a Clavinet through a Mu-Tron III).

Graphic EQ

The mini guitar-pedal-sized equalizer is not an effect as such, but an inline tone circuit in the form of a multi-band active tone control. It has sliders (rather than dials) for graph-style presentation of the equalization settings. The frequency bands assigned to the sliders are fixed, and tailored to be useful to the frequency spectrum in which the guitar operates, and the bands are logarithmically related to correspond to the way the human ear perceives frequencies. As such, they provide a simple, intuitive means of tweaking your tone settings, and can be useful when your guitar or amp's tone controls alone aren't enough to carve out the sound you hear in your head.

This covers the main categories of effects available, and the configurations in which you'll find them, although clever designers are coming up with new sonic tools every day. Advice on how to use effects, and on which ones will help you to emulate the sounds of artists whose playing you might admire, appear in the chapter on "Advanced Playing Techniques" later in the book.

BUYING GUIDE TO ELECTRONIC GEAR

Purchasing amps and effects in guitar shops can be even trickier than buying guitars. With the "feel" and "playability" elements less a part of the equation, what remains, in addition to any assessment of such gear's pure functionality, is their sound, and the sound of any piece of equipment will be slightly different in any room you play it in. If at all possible, take along your own guitar to test amps and effects units with, because all will sound and perform differently with any type of guitar you play through them.

If it isn't convenient to bring your own, at least pull a demo guitar off the shelf that is as close to the make and model that you play, rather than taking the opportunity to, for example, test drive an Epiphone Les Paul if you play a Squier Stratocaster. To extend this thinking, if you're trying out an effects pedal, endeavour also to run it through an amp that's similar to the one you'll be using it with (bringing your own amp into a shop for a test-play is usually less welcomed than bringing your own guitar, unless it's a particularly compact amp). Different amps react very differently to effects pedals – in extreme cases, some just don't seem to gibe very well with certain pedals, whereas others will take all comers – and overdrive pedals in particular will interact very differently with different amps, on some occasions at least.

When shopping for amplifiers, be sure the sales assistant walks you through all basic functions at some of the settings you are likely to use yourself, so you don't find any surprises or disappointments when you get home. Also, although some retailers might not like you to play too loud for too long, be sure to put it up to, or near to, top volume for a while, and ensure it performs without freaking out. Even if you're unlikely to play the amp at full volume in day-to-day use, it should be capable of going there for a while without lurching into its death throws. (Note: Playing at high volume can damage your ears, and those of anyone listening. When conducting such a test, move a reasonable distance from the speaker, and if it's a particularly large, powerful amp, consider putting in some approved ear plugs to prevent hearing loss.)

Plenty of guitar stores are staffed with hotshot guitarists who will happily run the gear through its paces for you, showing off both their own chops and the equipment's in the process, but don't let this be sufficient to sell you on anything. You need to know how any given piece of equipment will perform for your playing, and make no mistake: every player has a "sound", and guitars, amps and effects pedals will all sound different with different people playing them. Put any performance anxiety aside, and give it what you've got. You're the one putting the cash on the barrelhead, so you need to know whether this particular item works for you, too, and not just some flashy sales assistant.

New electronic gear should come with a warranty of some sort, and this should give you some piece of mind. More can go wrong with these items than with most guitars, so check what is covered, and for how long. Making a used-gear purchase, however, requires more thorough testing, and often something of a leap of faith. Let's look into things you want to check for when buying amps and effects secondhand, and you can also apply much of the following to assessing new equipment, if you want to be extra thorough.

USED EQUIPMENT

As with guitars, secondhand amps and effects units can sometimes be great bargains, and provide a means of acquiring more for your money than sticking strictly to the new gear market is likely to yield. That said, used electronics gear inherently presents more risks than used electric or acoustic guitars: first, there are generally more small parts that can fail and render a unit "dead" (or in need of significant repair, at best), and with amps in particular, the high voltages that allow them to function also mean there can be a very genuine physical hazard if a previous owner hasn't maintained the item correctly, or has performed an ill-advised modification. The old adage *caveat emptor* – "let the buyer beware" – applies to the purchase of any pre-owned musical equipment, but doubly so to gear that is electronic in nature.

Here's a list of tests and checks that can help you assess the viability of any used amps and effects you might be considering, whether in a retail outlet or for sale privately. Use any or all of them, as applicable, to help you secure a good purchase.

Visual check

Given that there is a very real safety issue with any secondhand equipment that is plugged into a wall outlet, or is connected to something that is, you should inspect any such gear visually before even switching on and plugging into it. These checks apply more strictly to amplifiers, but you can extrapolate some helpful hints for checking effects pedals from these, too.

◊ Is the amp reasonably clean, or does it appear to have been neglected? If the latter, does it look like it will clean up okay, or is this deep-down gunge?

◊ Do the tubes look old (is the lettering faded and discoloured from excessive heat?), or do they appear to be fairly fresh, even if they are NOS (new old stock) types? It's cool to find an old amp with its original tubes, or very old replacements, if they are still in decent playable condition. An amp that carries old, burnt-out (or nearly so) tubes, however, just indicates gear that has been neglected.

◊ Are the tubes reasonably tight in their sockets? Any tubes that are loose enough to fall out from carrying, or simple playing vibration, could signal trouble.

◊ Does the speaker look sound, tightly mounted and in good condition, even if it's an old one? Or is it dusty, discoloured, have a brittle cone, tears in the cone or loose mounting bolts/screws/nuts?

◊ Are the cabinet's edges and corners tight and solid?

Your assessment of all of the above will give you a general idea of the amp's condition before you have even plugged it in. An amp that is old and a little dusty and grimy, but basically in decent condition underneath, is possibly one that was cared for well, but just stored for years and left untouched. An amp that was cared for poorly or not serviced at all, or serviced poorly while in use for many years, is a riskier proposition.

◊ **Grounded AC cable** Has the seller properly installed a safe, grounded, three-prong AC cable (cord)? If not, don't touch any other electrical equipment while testing, and ask them if they will have one correctly installed (if it's a guitar store) before selling the amp. If not, they should consider making a concession on the price so that you can do so. If you buy it as-is, have a three-prong cord properly and professionally installed asap. This is a safety issue, and it won't be safe to gig or record with the amp – in short, to touch any other electrical equipment, such as a microphone plugged into a PA system or a guitar plugged into a friend's amp – until you have done so.

◊ **Power up** Turn the amp's volume controls down to zero, switch the power on and let it warm up. Does the pilot light work? Are the tubes glowing as normal? Switch the standby on if it has one, and/or turn up the volume controls slightly. You should hear a slight – but not excessive – hum through the speaker. If there are any loud hums, squeals or oscillations in the amp at any stage in this process, switch off immediately and unplug from the AC receptacle.

◊ **Play it** If all is well so far, plug in and play. Start at a lower volume, try all the other control knobs for function and scratchiness. If you get a little static-like scratchy sound when you turn any of the potentiometers but they still function much as they should, this isn't a big deal. A tech can clean these with a squirt of contact cleaner for a minimum charge, and sometimes this noise will disappear on its own with use. If you get any major volume jumps or dead spots, that might mean the pot needs replacing. Still not too big a deal if the price is right and it's an amp you are really interested in, but it means a slightly larger investment in repairs.

◊ **Play it louder** Turn up, and play louder. If the seller insists that you test it at quiet volumes only, explain that you need to at least play it briefly at or near full volume, or the deal is off. You don't have to crank it for hours, and it's unreasonable to expect others to tolerate that, but play it at a fairly advanced volume for thirty seconds or a minute or so at least, and listen to how the whole amp, and the speaker in particular, reacts to the wattage you're putting through it. Note: playing at high volume can damage your ears, and those of anyone listening. When conducting such a test, move a reasonable distance from the speaker, and if it's a particularly large, powerful amp, consider putting in some approved ear plugs to prevent hearing loss.

◊ **Noise assessment** If you get "ringing" or "pinging" sounds (known as microphonics) at medium or higher volumes, this could be the sign of a bad tube (as well as a number of other things that are more difficult to suspect). You can sometimes check this by, carefully, gently tapping each tube in succession with a pen or pencil – with the volume at around ten o'clock (that is, around four on a scale of ten) – while listening for the one that reacts excessively (note that you will get a little sound out of almost any good tube by doing this). If there are any particularly noisy tubes, ask the seller if they have a good replacement tube you can try in that position. Switch off the amp, let it cool down for a few minutes and make the swap, using a dust cloth or other protection to remove the suspect tube if it's still hot. If the tubes are old and worn anyway, as mentioned at the top of this check list, you'll need to figure a replacement set into the purchase price.

◊ **Speaker assessment** If the amp sounds intermittently fine, but emits odd rasping, scratching or vibrating sounds from time to time, it might have a faulty speaker, or some loose piece of hardware that is rattling against the cab. If you suspect the speaker at all, ask the seller if you can patch the amplifier's output – if it's possible – into another cabinet of a similar impedance rating, with a speaker that is known to be good, to test it further. If all is well in the new cab, you have a speaker issue to consider, and need to figure a replacement cost into the purchase price.

◊ **Make your decision** Does all seem well and good? You like the tone? You might have a groovy new amp, if the price is right. Even so, it's still a very good idea to have a professional amp tech check and service any used amp you acquire, especially if it's old and looks at all worn or neglected.

finding your SOUND

If you're going to get very far with guitar playing, it's important to have your own sound, one that listeners will recognize and instantly identify as being distinctively "you". One of the best ways to get there, paradoxically, is to study the sounds of great players who have gone before you: to find out what gear makes up their sound chains, learn what you can tweak this way or that to mould tones to your own liking, and incorporate this into your music-making. To that end, this chapter will check out the rigs used by several guitar heroes, past and present (in roughly chronological order), investigating the guitar-effects-amplifier set-ups that make them sound like *them*.

While some major artists stick with the same (or similar) gear throughout their careers, many are changing it around all the time. Also, artists will often use different equipment live and in the studio, so it's rarely possible to know *precisely* what any great guitarist played on any given track. In the studio in particular, a recording artist will grab hold of whatever might help to make a given part stand out, and they aren't always making lists to remind guitar journalists at a later date what amp was used for song X and what guitar was used for song Y.

Some players with distinctive sounds are notorious for misleading interviewers and fans too, offering apocryphal details of their secret weapons just to further spin their own myths... or simply to have a little fun with doting journalists. Interviews with Eddy Van Halen and Billy F. Gibbons of ZZ Top, to name but two, have been full of red herrings over the years. But the deeper your knowledge of the wide variety of guitars, effects and amplifiers that have been used to create legendary music, the better you'll be able to craft specific tones for your own use.

SUPERSTAR SET-UPS

Before diving into the world of great guitarists' gear, it's worth remembering that many, many great artists have made ground-breaking sounds with ordinary, workaday guitars and amplifiers. The now-expensive vintage guitars that so many guitarists used to make classic recordings in the 1950s, 60s and early 70s weren't vintage at the time, they were just current production models or, often, affordable used instruments.

So don't let any of the detail contained here persuade you that you must go out and spend a small fortune to obtain serviceable gear: many manufacturers produce guitars, amps and effects today that are sonically and visually similar to those of forty to sixty years ago, at a fraction of the cost of the original.

Scotty Moore
Elvis's guitar guy

We might think of the solidbody electric guitar as having given birth to rock'n'roll, but the majority of the formative players of the 1950s plied their trade on big hollowbody archtop electric guitars that had been known primarily as "jazz boxes" just a few years before. One such player was Scotty Moore, Elvis Presley's lead guitarist through the early, peak years of his career.

Ironically, Moore's first good electric was a Fender Esquire (the single-pickup version of the Telecaster), which he played before hitching up with Elvis, in a country band known as the Starlite Wranglers. Shortly before joining forces with the King of Rock'n'Roll, however, Moore went

Scotty Moore shows Elvis his "jazz box": a Gibson archtop. Scotty's guitar playing on the early Elvis songs changed rock'n'roll – and rock music – forever.

upmarket to a big, gold-finished Gibson ES-295, and he was all about Gibson archtop electric guitars after that.

After laying down several classic Elvis tracks for Sun Records such as "That's All Right" and "Good Rockin' Tonight" in 1954, and "Milkcow Blues Boogie" and "Baby Let's Play House" in 1955 (among others), Moore traded his ES-295 for a new L-5CES on 7 July 1955, taking another step up the guitar ladder. The ES-295 was a guitar made with a laminated maple top that was pressed into an arch, much in the style of the better-known ES-175, while the L-5CES was a more elaborately constructed carved-arch guitar with a solid spruce top. Amplified in the middle of a smokin' rock'n'roll band, both would sound rather similar, however, with a warm, full voice, but plenty of bite from the P-90 pickups on the ES-295 and the Alnico V pickups (aka "staple" pickups) on the L-5CES, both of which were single-coil units.

In October of 1956 Moore moved up the ladder once again when he signed an endorsement deal with Gibson, for which the company supplied him with a new blond Super 400CESN, another instrument that was really designed for professional jazz artists, with a carved, solid-spruce top. As influential on Moore's sound as any of these guitars, however – and hence on the classic "rocka-billy" sound that his playing with Elvis helped to inspire – was an amplifier that he used throughout the mid- to late 1950s.

Custom-made by electrical designer Ray Butts (who also built versions for Chet Atkins and Carl Perkins), Moore's EchoSonic amp had a built-in tape-delay unit in the back that provided the short "slap-back" echo that characterizes so much rock'n'roll and rockabilly playing. Although he only ever made a limited number of EchoSonics himself, Butts' concept for the tape echo would be emulated by a number of other popular products. An external tape echo unit called the Echoplex was built first by Market Electronics in Cleveland, Ohio, in the late 50s, then by Harris-Teller of Chicago. The latter was marketed by Gibson's sibling company, Maestro, and is the best-known version of the early tube-powered EchoPlex. (In Europe, other firms were simultaneously manufacturing similar-sounding units.)

Actual tube-powered tape echo units are rare and rather expensive today, although the effects manufacturer Fulltone does produce a highly regarded device named the Tube Tape Echo (which remains nevertheless quite expensive). Later, solid-state Echoplexes and Roland's Space Echo are a little more affordable, but many players seeking that classic rock'n'roll/rockabilly slap-back tone achieve it with a simpler analogue or digital delay pedal set for a very short echo, into a vintage-style tube amp. For the real thing, though, check out several of Scotty Moore's early recordings with Elvis – notably "Mystery Train" and their rendition of Carl Perkins' "Blue Suede Shoes" – and dig that boppin' slap-back bounce. While Moore was riffing on an electric, Elvis was still solidly in charge of rhythm-guitar duties in the early days, which he pulled off with an aggressive, driving style and a heavy hand that, by all accounts, led to plenty of broken strings. He exclusively played acoustic guitars in the 1950s: first a Martin 000-18 concert-bodied flat-top, then D-18 and D-28 dreadnoughts.

In 1956, Elvis moved up to a big Gibson J-200, at the same time that Moore acquired his Super 400CESN. Previously a badge of honour for several country and cowboy singers, the J-200 would also come to define the image of the rock'n'roll front man in Elvis's hands, particularly after the star had it upgraded with several customized touches, including an "Elvis Presley" inlay along the fingerboard.

Duane Eddy
Fuzzy king of "twang"

In addition to Scotty Moore, several other rock'n'roll guitarists of the 1950s are notable for their seminal sounds. Carl Perkins, Eddie Cochran, Cliff Gallup (with Gene Vincent and the Blue Caps) and Buddy Holly perhaps deserve special mention. Duane Eddy makes a fitting emissary for the lot of them, though, particularly for his adoption of big Gretsch archtop-electrics, guitars that were prime movers in the rock'n'roll revolution. As one of the top-selling instrumental artists of his day, with fifteen top forty singles in the first five years of his career, Eddy established that big, biting "twang" sound on a guitar that was originally designed for country and jazz players.

Gretsch's 6120 Chet Atkins Hollow Body model was developed in 1954 and officially released in 1955, with the name of one of Nashville's hottest picking aces attached to give it an instant promotional boost. While it did appeal to some country players, it caught fire in an even bigger way with burgeoning rock'n'rollers. The young Duane Eddy was in the midst of a similar transition from country to rock'n'roll in the mid-1950s, and he very deliberately sought out a Gretsch 6120 when looking for a new guitar in 1957, partly in admiration of Atkins' sound,

and partly because he wanted an instrument with a Bigsby vibrato tailpiece (which he traded his hard-tail Gibson Les Paul to acquire).

Eddy put the Gretsch, in particular its Bigsby, to excellent use, and in 1958 he released the first of a string of hits, "Rebel Rouser", which set the tone for an entire breed of raw, meaty, riff-inspired rock'n'roll instrumentals.

In addition to Eddy's judicious use of the Bigsby to produce anything from gentle warbles to dramatic dives, the Gretsch's single-coil DeArmond 200 (aka Gretsch DynaSonic) pickups were a big part of that infectious sound, providing the clarity and high-end shimmer necessary to help the tone of that big-bodied archtop cut through. Another major ingredient of the studio recordings, at least, came not from Eddy's guitar, but from the big, empty water tank behind the Arizona recording studio which producer Lee Hazlewood used to produce the new star's distinctive reverb sound. By placing Eddy's guitar amp at one end of the tank and a microphone at the other, Hazlewood captured an effective, genuine ambient reverb sound long before compact analogue or digital reverb effects units were

This man produced the fuzziest, twangiest, dirtiest guitar of the 1950s and 60s, inspiring legions of rockabillies and even future heavy metallers.

available, and helped to create one of the legendary tones of rock'n'roll. For other examples of that big, twangy reverb tone and Eddy's characteristic low-string riffing, dip into "Cannonball", "Forty Miles of Bad Road" and "Peter Gunn".

In later years Eddy moved on to play signature models made first by Guild and later by Gibson, occasionally returning to Gretsch in between, but the 6120 Chet Atkins Hollowbody that first launched him to fame remains the guitar best associated with his sound.

Hank Marvin

Clean mean Strat machine

As impressive as Duane Eddy's stats looked for an instrumental artist, over in the UK Hank Marvin would soon be racking up astounding numbers with The Shadows as an instrumental act, as well as scoring numerous hits backing singer Cliff Richard. In these two incarnations, Marvin would be at the forefront of a total of 69 British top forty chart singles, including a whopping 12 number one hits. The best known of these, the classic "Apache" among them, were recorded with Marvin's 1959 Fender Stratocaster, famous for being the first Stratocaster brought into the UK. Cliff had it couriered by hand to the UK following a trip to the US, before Fenders were officially being imported into the UK. The Strat was sought after by a young Marvin who wanted a Fender electric guitar "like James Burton played". Unbeknownst to either Marvin or Richard, Burton played a Telecaster (with Ricky Nelson and others), but as it happened the Strat suited the up-and-coming British guitar star just fine.

Marvin played a European-made Antoria guitar in the early days of The Shadows (originally named The Drifters) in 1958, but it's difficult today to think of Marvin playing anything other than a Strat (his early 60s dalliance with a Burns signature model aside). In contrast to Duane Eddy's meaty, bass-heavy tone, Marvin's sound was bright and lean, yet still biting and rich. The Strat's vibrato bridge became a major part of Marvin's playing style, and he frequently used it to bend up into target notes (by depressing the arm before picking the string), as well as to add shimmer and motion to his playing in general. His amplifiers of choice, initially a Vox AC15, then an AC30 when more volume was required, also accentuated the brightness of the Strat, while adding a punchy mid-range element that gave his overall tone a mildly aggressive edge.

Like Eddy – and Scotty Moore and several other early rock'n'rollers, for that matter – Marvin also made good use of delay in his playing. He adopted an echo effect after being shown an early

He may have been Cliff Richard's right-hand man, but don't be fooled: Hank Marvin's surf-rock pickin' (far left) was clean, relentless and formidable.

Italian-made Meazzi Echomatic by fellow British pop star Joe Brown, and later used other echo units such as a drum-based Binson Echorec and a Vox CopyCat tape echo (moving on to more modern devices in later years). Rather than sticking with the short slap-back echoes that so many American rockers of the mid-to-late 50s were using, however, Marvin's sound often made use of a longer delay, with atmospheric repeats falling further from the initial attack of the note.

With his signature tone firmly established a full fifty years ago, Hank Marvin has held on to a sizeable and devoted following for half a century, spawning a cult of players intent on mimicking his playing. The ingredients in the recipe have often been updated over the years (although the Stratocaster usually remains a constant), but the resultant sound itself has stayed the same.

George Harrison & John Lennon
The Fab Four's six-stringers

The Beatles' evolved their sound throughout the 1960s (building on rock'n'roll roots they first planted in the late 50s), and they rarely sounded entirely the same, nor used the same equipment, for more than a couple of records in a row. In any discussion of "The Beatles' guitar sound", however, most fans will look to their early to mid-60s tones as archetypal. In their early days, in their pre-Beatles incarnation as The Quarrymen, both George Harrison and John Lennon played European-made electrics (a Hofner Club 40 and Selmer Futurama among them) but while gigging in Hamburg in 1960 Lennon acquired the first American-made guitar owned by a Beatle, a Rickenbacker 325. A year later and back in Liverpool, Harrison purchased another American guitar, a used 1957 Gretsch Duo Jet that a sailor had brought back to the UK. Between them, these two guitars – both snappy, gritty and a little raw sounding – defined the sound of the band for the first four years of its existence, and on several early hits.

Lennon's Rickenbacker 325 was a short-scale guitar, with a scale length of 20.75" (compared to the 24.75" of most Gibsons and 25.5" of most Fenders). The shorter scale made for less string tension, and a slightly more "rubbery", indistinct tonal definition as a result, although the Rick's single-coil "toaster-top" pickups contributed plenty of clarity and sparkle to the overall brew. Listen to Lennon's electric rhythm playing from his Rickenbacker era, and you hear a chunky, slightly gnarly tone that really drives these simpler, more rock'n'roll-influenced tunes from the band's early years.

Harrison's Gretsch, on the other hand, was closer to the Gibson standard at around 24.6", and offered a little more bite and sizzle, too, thanks to its slightly hotter DeArmond single-coils. If you ever find yourself surprised that the Fab Four's poppy, minimalist hits of 1962–64 could inspire such a fanatical following, take another listen to "Love Me Do", "Please Please Me", "She Loves You" and "I Want to Hold Your Hand", and hear how compelling the guitars alone are, let alone the harmonies and the melodies that drive it all.

Having used older Fender and Selmer amps in their Hamburg days, The Beatles became poster children for Vox amplifiers once the hits started rolling out. Lennon and Harrison started with AC30s, but soon needed more volume. Vox owner Tom Jennings and designer Dick Denney created the bigger AC50 and AC100 amps largely so The Beatles could be heard over the hoards of screaming girls that populated their live shows, but even these 50- and 100-watters – monsters for their day – couldn't do the trick, let down in part by the under-powered PA systems that accompanied them in their day.

The guitar-playing Beatles graduated to other guitars and amps in the mid-1960s, becoming real gear hounds in the process, going from Gretsch, to Epiphone, to Fender, to Gibson through the course of the decade. But there's one of Harrison's acquisitions in particular that's notable as quintessentially Beatles. In February 1964, The Beatles travelled to New York for three concerts

George and John rehearse in a hotel room while on tour in Stockholm, Sweden, in 1963.

and two appearances on the popular *Ed Sullivan Show*, and Rickenbacker seized the opportunity to have George Harrison try out their new 360/12 electric twelve-string guitar. Harrison, it seems, bonded with the thing from the start, and soon after used it to record "You Can't Do That", "I Should Have Known Better" and several songs on *A Hard Day's Night* (where it's probably best known for producing the chiming kerrang of the opening chord to the title track). As such, the Rickenbacker 360/12 would prove another enduring tone of the British Invasion, which Roger McGuinn of The Byrds would take in a different direction, establishing the California jangle-pop sound.

Pete Townshend
The Who's windmilling wonder

Another artist who has used a plethora of guitars and amps over the years, Pete Townshend of The Who has, in later years, often been seen playing modified Gibson Les Paul Deluxes and Fender Strats and Teles (or custom-made equivalents of these). When we think classic Townshend, however, we tend to think of two specific early eras in the evolution of his rig.

Townshend was already playing a Rickenbacker when the band formed in 1964, and he primarily played two-pickup Rick 1997 and three-pickup 1998 six-string models, and similar twelve-string models, throughout the early years of the band. These were the export equivalents of domestic US335 and 345 models, with a few modifications at the request of British importers Rose-Morris, including the use of more traditional F-holes in place of the usual "slash" soundholes and, often, simple dot position markers in place of the larger blocks of the US-market models. Cosmetics aside, these guitars still carried the bright, jangly single-coil toaster-top pickups that early Ricks are known for, and which gave these guitars their characteristically bright, clangy, percussion tone. Played with severe aggression through a cranked early 60s Fender Bassman or Vox AC-100 (his amps of choice in those days), these Ricks with rather low-output pickups give you the driving, edgy tones heard on Who classics such as "I Can't Explain", "My Generation" and "Anyway, Anyhow, Anywhere" (the first and last of which also benefited from his use of a Rickenbacker electric twelve-string, the export equivalent of George Harrison's guitar).

In the late 60s Townshend moved to Gibson SG Special guitars and custom-made Hiwatt amplifiers and speaker cabs, the rig that was captured for posterity in 1970 on the *Live at Leeds* album. It showcases The Who approaching its *Guinness Book of World Records* "Loudest Band in the World" status, and the volume Townshend produced from two 100-plus-watts Hiwatt heads into a 4x12 cab each (on top of two more unused "dummy" cabs) had a near-tangible mass to it. Rather than the fuzzy, ultra-filthy overdrive tone of many guitarists in heavy rock bands of the

Guitars frequently took a battering at the hands of Pete Townshend. The technically minded will notice Townshend's ingenious use of what guitar experts call "Sellotape" on the bottom of his Rickenbacker.

era, Townshend's tone with The Who was mainly big – enormous – while still fairly clear, punchy and well-defined. All these were attributes the P-90 single coils on his late 60s SG Specials helped to maintain.

Keeping it all simple, Townshend removed the Maestro vibrato units from these SG Specials, and still got plenty of vibrato in his sound by just giving the guitar's neck a good shake when desired, the high neck/body joints on these designs allowing more motion than a single-cutaway Gibson, such as a Les Paul.

The "big gig" sound

Guitar-playing fans are obsessed with the gear used by their heroes. But it's important to realize that the sound heard at larger gigs – those in big venues, concert halls and sports arenas – has something of a disconnect from the sound of the guitars, pedals and amps that you see on stage. The large, professional PA ("public address") systems used today are extremely powerful and incredibly complex, and provide an exponential increase in the volume of any guitar amp that is miked up and fed into them. In "the old days" – mainly the late 50s and early to mid-60s – PA systems were largely just for vocals, and guitarists playing larger and larger halls (which was the way things progressed as rock'n'roll began to boom) needed bigger and bigger amps in order to be heard. When live sound engineers began miking up amps – placing microphones in front of the guitar amplifiers and running them through the PA – it was initially just to supplement the sound of the big double-stacks, several of them at times, that players were having to play through on stage.

As sound-support technology improved, however, a guitarist's need for multiple large amp-stacks decreased. Of course, plenty of rockers held onto them, and still do, since such stacks became the sound – and look – of heavy rock music. With the quality of PA systems today, however, a touring guitarist can play through an amp as small as he or she likes, really, and have it ramped up to usable volume by the PA system. Can't hear your small amp on the big stage? No problem, as, in tandem with the part of the sound-support system that feeds the band's performance to the "mains", or house, speakers, there's a monitor, or fold back, system to provide a mix for the performers to hear on stage.

At larger shows, this monitor sound is produced by its own engineer, and has a dedicated mix that's independent of the house sound, often using a system that can provide individually tailored mixes to each of several performers in the band, giving one a little more vocals, the other a little less drums, yet another more lead guitar and less keyboard, and so on and so forth. Many of the slicker professional acts these days even receive these mixes through in-ear monitors (not unlike deluxe versions of your iPod's earbuds), as part of a system that seeks to keep on-stage volumes at a minimum.

In theory, such large sound-support systems should provide an accurate rendition of what is coming out of a performer's amplifier, only much, much louder. The fact is, however, that there's often a lot of post-mic processing applied to the sound. For big shows, there is very likely to be some EQ and compression after the amp, and many players will have effects such as reverb and delay added at the mix, too, so they don't have to deal with these pre-amplifier or in an effects loop. Also, plenty of professional guitarists use a lot of further processing that the concertgoer isn't aware of, in the form of rack-mounted units that are tucked out of sight at the back of the stage. These aren't as visible as the guitar, pedalboard and amp that form any such players, more obvious sound chain, but play a big part in shaping their tone, nonetheless. The short lesson from all this is that, where big-concert sound is concerned, there is usually a lot more going on than meets the eye, and any attempt to emulate a guitar hero's sound based on a replication of what they *seem* to be using on stage can often lead to frustration. Add to that, as stated elsewhere in this book, the fact that many professional guitarists use entirely different sets of equipment live and in the studio, and such tone cloning really becomes a tough nut to crack.

While these (and the instruments mentioned above) are the guitars he was usually seen with live, from around late 1970 onwardd Townshend habitually employed a handful of "secret weapons" in the studio. Big amps in particular, like the Hiwatts, are an engineer's nightmare: they make almost every aspect of capturing a winning guitar track more difficult, and can even destroy some sensitive studio mics – the kinds of mics that will deliver stunning depth and harmonic clarity when placed in front of just the right amp. So, achieving three minutes of magic on tape required something entirely different.

Townshend's secret ingredients locked into place in one fell swoop when American guitarist Joe Walsh reciprocated Townshend's earlier gift of an Arp synthesizer by giving The Who guitarist a fully formed studio rig, consisting of a 1959 Gretsch 6120 Chet Atkins Hollow Body electric guitar and a late 1950s Fender narrow-panel tweed Bandmaster 3x10" combo. Unlikely as it might sound – this was a rig seemingly more suited to vintage rockabilly – the set-up gave Townshend the gargantuan blast he was seeking, as revealed throughout 1971's *Who's Next*, 1973's *Quadrophenia* and a little of everything else he recorded in the studio from then on, solo or with the band. Between them, this guitar-to-amp combination offers enough clarity to present a broad, shimmering soundstage at clean settings, while remaining capable of breaking up early enough to provide chunky tube overdrive at volume levels that won't send most delicate condenser and ribbon mics into meltdown. Working together, the hollowbody Gretsch with FilterTron humbucking pickups made it easy for Townshend to achieve the hovering feedback he has always been so fond of. Together, they created "a sound from paradise", as Townshend told *Guitar Player* magazine in 1993, having just used the rig once again to record parts of the latter-day Who album *Psychoderelict*.

Eric Clapton
Blues-rock god

Over the course of the past thirty years or so, Gibson Les Paul Standards from 1958–60 have become the most desirable, and expensive, electric guitars on the vintage market, a trend that had its beginnings another decade and a half before that, thanks largely to one man: Eric Clapton. Massively underappreciated in its day, the original model of the Les Paul came into its own half a decade after its demise in 1960 to be the first truly effective tool of heavy rock lead guitar.

At the time, however, the purveyor of said electric revolution thought he was playing the blues. Yep, with a Les Paul, Marshall Model 1962 combo amp, a head full of delta blues licks and enough youthful drive and desire to push the entire brew right over the top, Clapton forged a tone for all time way back in 1965, while recording *Blues Breakers With Eric Clapton* with John Mayall (a disc often referred to as "The Beano Album" after the comic Clapton is reading in its cover photo), and rock guitar has never looked back.

Sure, this was a collection of Brits trying to be a blues band, but the resultant "blues rock" sound that achieved its alchemical perfection in a London studio also laid the bedrock for one of the most sought-after rock tones of all time. Clapton worshipped the American blues masters, just like all the rest of the collective of British musicians like John Mayall and Alexis Korner, but rather than replicate what Robert Johnson, Muddy Waters or B.B. King had done, he was looking to push it into another dimension. Clapton's tone has become a universal among guitar players, often cited and endlessly documented. Listen to that sweet, fat, juicy humbucker-driven blues-rock tone on any of several tracks from the Beano album – such as "Hideaway", "All Your Love", "Steppin' Out" and "Key to Love" – and you can quickly hear why.

Several ingredients went into making the Les Paul magic that Clapton tapped for his *Blues Breakers* sound. The combination of a solid mahogany body with a hard maple cap gives the

Eric Clapton has played a number of guitars over his long career: here he's making blues-rock magic using a Gibson SG.

guitar a warm, round tone that nevertheless achieves good cut, snap and clarity. Gibson's 24 3/4" scale length also contributes to a slightly plumper, thicker tonality than the 25 1/2" scale that Fender has traditionally used, while also making the Les Paul a more bend-friendly instrument (a characteristic the wider frets used from 1959 onwards also contributed to).

An enormous vein of these guitars' gold load, however, is considered to lie in their pickups. The humbuckers of the original run of Les Pauls, known as PAFs because of the "Patent Applied For" stickers found on their undersides, are widely considered to be the first pickups with the power to really rock. In fact, electronically, PAFs aren't especially hot pickups, but their broad, thick tone sends a meatier spread of frequencies to the amp, which more easily drives it into distortion than the average single coil. The result is a fatter signal, which often can behave as if it's more powerful than its actual resistance reading would suggest. In a good original PAF, an impressive amount of clarity and definition helps create an irresistible tonal combination.

Alongside the Les Paul, the fledgling Marshall company's foray into guitar amplification was rapidly setting the standards for big rock tones. The Model 1962 combo that Clapton selected for the Beano sessions was the 2x12" combo version of the 45-watt JTM45 head that was normally partnered with a closed-back 4x12" cabinet. (Note that although many Marshall model numbers look like years of manufacture, they actually have nothing to do with when the amps were issued; the 1962, for example, was introduced in the year 1964.) Putting the same powerhouse in an open-backed combo with just two 12" Celestion Greenbacks really drove the speakers to some serious wailing when this amp was cranked up, and that's exactly what Clapton was looking for.

Like that of many great tone masters, Clapton's rig didn't sit static for long, although he continued to be Clapton whatever he played. His Les Paul was stolen in the summer of 1966 during the rehearsals for the first Cream tour and it has never resurfaced. After that, he went on to use a Gibson SG, ES-335 and a Firebird with that supergroup, though he began to use larger Marshall 100-watt stacks, with a Vox Wah-Wah pedal added into the chain to provide his emotive, wailing sound, and a Dallas Rangemaster Treble Booster to help kick the amps into overdrive. In the early 70s, he made a broader sideways move to Fender guitars, adopting the Stratocaster for his work with Derek and the Dominoes, Delaney & Bonnie and most of his solo ventures after that. Notable among these are "Brownie", the sunburst 1956 Strat with which he recorded "Layla" and several other tunes, and "Blackie", a "parts-guitar" that Clapton assembled from the best pieces of a handful of late 50s Strats. In recent years, Clapton has played Fender's Eric Clapton Signature Stratocasters, through tweed 50s Fender Twin amps, or reproductions of them.

Jimi Hendrix
Best guitarist ever?

Given his status as one of rock's most ground-breaking, and most revered, electric guitar artists, Jimi Hendrix's gear has always garnered a lot of attention from fans, and the guitar world at large. Just about anything he touched in the course of his music making has attained mythical status over the years. There's also a lot of speculation in online chat rooms and guitar magazines about Hendrix's left-handed playing of right-handed Fender Stratocasters upside down, and the sonic and performance variables that this flip-flopping might induce. Given the man's talent, however, and his agile playing style, any variation this might present when compared with the sound of a straight old Strat played right-way-up has got to be minimal, and dwelling on such details is only likely to sidetrack us.

Maybe everyone should play their Strats upside-down. It worked for Jimi.

Early in his rise to fame Hendrix played pre-CBS or "transition era" early CBS Strats from the mid-1960s with small headstocks and, usually, rosewood fingerboards. At the time, however, these weren't the prized vintage pieces that they are today, but simply "used guitars", and after smashing or burning a few of these he was more often seen with late-60s Strats with wide headstocks and fatter, modern-era Fender logos. The single-coil pickups on these guitars might be considered thin, bright and underpowered for the major noise he created with them, but by retaining a clear, tight, dynamic signal from the guitar, Hendrix retained outstanding dynamics and a broad, rich voice at his amplifiers, where the Marshall JMP100 stacks he most often preferred were capable of making him sound as huge as could be desired. Hendrix also made dramatic use of the Strat's vibrato tailpiece, becoming the first real master of this creative piece of hardware. From deep dives, to soaring up-bends, to subtle wobbles and shimmers that would segue into searing feedback, the "whammy bar" became a big part of his playing style, and sound.

When a more extreme sonic assault was needed than even Strat-with-Marshall could provide, Hendrix stomped on a Dallas-Arbiter Fuzz Face, an early germanium-transistor fuzz pedal known for its sweet, thick, creamy distortion tones. In fact, he often used this very dynamic-sounding pedal with his guitar volume wound down to clean up the tones while retaining some of the fuzz's added texture.

The only other two effects used regularly in the early Hendrix rig were a Vox Wah-Wah pedal, placed in front of the fuzz, and occasionally a Roger Mayer Octavia pedal, a pedal that sent the guitar signal an octave up, of which only half a dozen or so were originally built. From 1969, a Univox Uni-Vibe became the other essential in the Hendrix effects line-up. Taken as a whole, these are pretty simple ingredients compared to the complex and convoluted pedalboards and rack systems that many professional players employ today, but Hendrix sure could whip up a maelstrom of sound with them. That said, it's important to once again acknowledge that an unparalleled touch and a rare musical vision also had a lot to do with it.

Like others, Jimi Hendrix had his studio secrets, too. Although he most often played the Strats live, an arsenal he later fortified with the occasional Gibson Flying V and SG, he purportedly used a Fender Telecaster to record the solo to "Purple Haze" and possibly "Fire", and he often partnered – or replaced – his Marshalls with smaller amps from Fender, Valco (Supro) and other makers. Also, Hendrix, like others, often ran "parallel paths" in the studio, meaning he would split the guitar signal to two or more amps (or to an amp and a direct input to the recording desk, via various effects) in order to have a range of sonic options in the final mix. The main point to take away from this, and all of these profiles, is that while we rarely know exactly what a particular player used on any given recording session, the fact that they managed to sound like themselves regardless, and to forge distinctive tones in the process, is what really matters.

Jimmy Page
Led Zep's fretboard fiend

Start a debate about late 60s and early 70s British blues-rock guitar tone, and Jimmy Page's name will be one of the first mentioned every time. From huge and gutsy to atmospheric and mellow, from an ominous rhythm-guitar crunch tone to soaring, wailing lead, Page's sonic palette was every bit as wide as his flares. We usually think of Page as using a Gibson Les Paul, an EDS-1275 Double Neck and a Marshall stack, and the mammoth tone on tracks such as "Dazed and Confused", "Communication Breakdown", "Ramble On", and "Whole Lotta Love" would seem to bear this out.

Once again, however, there was more in his arsenal than it seemed. His number one Les Paul is believed to be a 1958 model, although the serial number was removed during severe modifications to the neck, which also left it with an ultra-slim neck profile, similar to that of a 1960 Les Paul. His number two Les Paul, used mainly as a back-up guitar with Led Zeppelin, is a 1959 model.

It's well documented that Page also frequently played a Fender Telecaster. He is seen in live photos playing a couple of different Teles on stage, and it's often quoted that he used one to record the famous guitar solo to "Stairway to Heaven", along with a lot of his earlier work. For slide guitar, Page often used a slightly modified Danelectro with lipstick-tube pickups, both live and in the studio. While spinning their latest Led Zeppelin record, the average kid in the 1970s was no doubt picturing Page wailing and shredding on a Les Paul. The diversity of these guitars just goes to show what a difference the other links in the chain can make, from the starting point to the end point, in the studio. Plug a Telecaster into a cranked amp, for example, and its bright yet meaty bridge pickup can sound searing and hot – not unlike, in fact, that of a Les Paul. Plug the Les Paul in right after it, though, and it would undoubtedly sound quite different, with a fatter, thicker, slightly looser voice.

More shrouded in mystery, however, are Page's recording amps, and debates

Jimmy Page shows why the Les Paul is the most "rock" guitar there will ever be.

about which model was used on what continue to rage to this day. The star has mentioned in interviews that he owned many small amps, and often turned to these for recording duties. Valco-made Supro amps were apparently among his recording favourites, and it was long thought that Page's "studio secret" was a mid-60s Thunderbolt, which had a 15" speaker, two 6L6GC output tubes and about 35 watts of power. It seems (and sounds) very likely, however, that he frequently used a slightly smaller, lower-powered Supro 1x12" combo with a pair of more unusual 6973 output tubes. Although these tubes look something like the EL84s that Vox and others used, and fit the same nine-pin sockets, they sound quite different. They're more like fat, crunchy junior 6L6s, in fact, which manage a thick, juicy distortion more easily and at lower volumes. The fact is, Jimmy Page very likely used a wide range of amps in the studio, grabbing whatever might help him produce those fleeting seconds of magic on any occasion. And he probably didn't take notes, either.

Page also used several effects in the studio to help him get the job done, and brought many of these out on tour, too. Among his favourite fuzz pedals were units designed and modified by Roger Mayer (who also built pedals for Jimi Hendrix), and Page also used a CryBaby Wah-Wah pedal, a Maestro EP-3 Echoplex (for the sound of its solid-state preamp as well as its echo) and, later, an MXR Phase 90 phaser pedal, among others.

Eddie Van Halen
Guitar bricoleur & tapper *extraordinaire*

For one of the greatest contrasts between "pedigree of instrument used" and "impact made by performer" you need look no further than Edward Van Halen. His repainted, hacked and heavily modified Strat copy is a certified mutt of a guitar if there ever was one, but his playing on this beast launched a revolution in rock guitar. Van Halen's guitar style is all about sustain, drama, dynamics and power, although there's plenty of nuance in his playing, too, and he set about creating a guitar that would give him the qualities he needed, even if it came out looking like a botched DIY project.

Van Halen's "tapping" technique required gain and sustain from the guitar, so rewinding a vintage Gibson humbucking pickup to make it a little hotter made perfect sense. His soaring-and-diving whammy technique, however, really demanded the kind of vibrato unit found on a Stratocaster, however, and a modified one at that. Put these two major requirements together, and, bam: Eddie's Frankenstrat! Naming names, Van Halen's guitar comprised a body and neck purchased from parts supplier Charvel, said rewound Gibson pickup (purportedly taken from an ES-335) and, originally, a

Eddie Van Halen, tapping furiously on his Frankensteinian assemblage.

vintage Strat vibrato bridge (later replaced by a "double-locking" Floyd Rose vibrato system). Eddie decorated the instrument by painting the body black, then wrapping it somewhat randomly with tape, and painting it again in white, revealing a striped effect once the tape was removed (he later added a red coat to this after further wrappings of tape). It can be heard all over the band's mega-selling eponymous 1978 release.

Just as important to his sonic assault was Van Halen's adulterated amp set-up. For his early recordings in particular, he used a 100-watt 1960s Marshall head and Marshall speaker cabinets, with a Variac – a device capable of varying AC voltage between wall outlet and amplifier – to reduce the operating voltage of the Marshall. In doing so, he was able to more easily achieve a dirty, singing, overdriven "brown" sound from the amp, to further enhance his sustaining tone.

He also used a Boss SD-1 Super Overdrive pedal, and to add motion to the sound, he often employed an MXR Phase 90 phaser pedal. These were the main ingredients used on early tracks such as "Eruption", "Runnin' With the Devil", "Janey's Cryin'", and Van Halen's cover of The Kinks' "You Really Got Me". In more recent years, Eddie has turned to signature model guitars made by Ernie Ball/Music Man and Peavey, plugging into Peavey 5150 and Fender 5150 III amplifiers.

Peter Buck
R.E.M.'s master of clarity and shimmer

Having used a great many different guitars through the course of R.E.M.'s long and varied career, Peter Buck is still best known as a proponent of the indie jangle sound, a style he propagated over the band's first four albums in particular. Buck's sound has often been considered something of a 1980s update of the 60s jangle of players such as George Harrison of The Beatles and Roger McGuinn of The Byrds – and he did his thing on similar equipment, too. Buck has played a Rickenbacker since the very early days of R.E.M., mainly a 1970s 360 model with the slightly hotter "button-top" (aka Hi-Gain) single-coil pickups that the company introduced in 1969. He has also played a number of Rick electric twelve-strings, and several back-up six-strings.

Having used Fender amps in the early days of the band, Buck soon moved over to Vox AC30s, and

Peter Buck, REM's guitarist, coaxes a whole world of Byrds-style jangle and sparkle out of his Rickenbacker.

these have been a big part of his sound ever since. With these class-A tube combos set to a clean tone that's just on the edge of crunch, Buck's Ricks with button-top pickups induce a chiming, ringing tone that still has plenty of bite and attack amid all the bright jangle, much like the sound of songs such as "Pretty Persuasion", "So. Central Rain (I'm Sorry)", "Driver eight" and "Auctioneer (Another Engine)".

Buck frequently turned to a Gibson Les Paul, among other guitars, for some of the heavier sounds of the *Document* and *Green* albums (and later, *Monster* and *New Adventures in Hi-Fi*), and in later years began to select among a wide range of instruments that are taken out on the road. Usually among them are a couple each of Rickenbacker six-string and twelve-string electrics, Fender Telecasters, a Les Paul and occasionally a Gretsch Country Gentleman that he has owned and often played for many years.

Stevie Ray Vaughan
The 80s bad boy bluesman

In addition to being a major proponent of the blues revival of the early 1980s, Stevie Ray Vaughan has remained a major figure in fans' "what gear did they use?" discussions, even a full two decades after his death in a helicopter crash in 1990. Always a Fender Stratocaster player first and foremost, Vaughan was rarely happy with stock instruments, and modified every guitar that he used regularly – some slightly, some severely.

His main guitar, which he referred to as "Number One", was a 1962 sunburst Strat with 1959 pickups, notable for the large reflective "SRV" stickers he added to its replacement pickguard, and the "Custom" sticker affixed behind the bridge. Either because he wanted to emulate the vibrato action of one of his heroes, left-hander Jimi Hendrix, or because it was the only repair part available at a time of necessity, Vaughan replaced Number One's original right-handed vibrato bridge with a left-handed unit in the early 1980s, positioning the vibrato arm at the top of the bridge block rather than the bottom. Among a number of back-up Strats, the most notable was another early 60s model known as "Lenny", in honour of his ex-wife Lenora, who had arranged for its purchase from a Texas pawnshop in 1980 as a surprise birthday gift. Refinished in brown and adorned with decorative inlays before Vaughan's ownership of it, Lenny also later received a new maple neck at Vaughan's hands.

Vaughan had the necks of his Strats refretted with jumbo frets, preferring both the feel and the supposedly fatter sound of this wider wire, and also used extremely heavy strings, upwards of .013 on the high E string, two factors that helped him wrangle such a big tone out of the bright, clear pickups on these guitars. Vaughan dabbled with a range of overdrive pedals to help pump up the grind, too. His mainstays were Ibanez Tube Screamers (he graduated from the original TS-808 to TS9 and TS10 models as they came out), though he used these more for a clean boost rather than heavy overdrive, and for more dirt he stomped on a Dallas-Arbiter Fuzz Face or, later, a Cesar Diaz remake of the Fuzz Face circuit. The majority of the depth of Vaughan's tone, post-guitar, can be credited to his amp – or rather amps.

In the early days, Vaughan played mostly 60s or early 70s Fender tube amps, usually two at a time, and rotated between Vibroverbs, Twin Reverbs and Super Reverbs. At some point he also acquired a 100-watt Marshall Town & Country 2x12 combo and often subbed that into the pair. You can already hear a big sound brewing, but however you mix and match the amplifier contingent he always sounded like Stevie Ray Vaughan. His legendary amp excesses set in during the recording of *In Step*, when – according to amp tech Cesar Diaz – as many as 32 amps were up and running around the studio, used in varying combinations on different tracks. Among these, in addition

The late Stevie Ray Vaughn, who brought back the blues in the 1980s, might just possibly be having a bad hair day.

to those already listed, were a 150-watt Dumble Steel String Singer, a vintage 1959 Fender tweed Bassman and a pair of massive 200-watt Marshall Major stacks.

Fans have gone to great lengths to obtain that huge and driven – yet perplexingly clear – Stevie amp tone. But before you set off down the long road to nailing that *In Step* tone for yourself, consider the possible permutations of those 32 amps... and the fact that no one really knows which ones, or how many, were used on which tracks. Bear in mind, too, that there are plenty of reports of Vaughan being invited up on stage with other players and just using their guitar and single amp – and totally ripping up, while sounding exactly like SRV in the process.

While he was no slouch onstage, in the studio Johnny Marr overdubbed his guitars into six-string orchestras.

Johnny Marr
Artisan Smith

Almost as a British parallel to what Peter Buck was doing in the States with R.E.M., Johnny Marr dressed The Smiths' recordings of the early to mid-1980s in layers of chiming, blooming, cascading guitars while so many other chart bands were swamping their music either in synthesizers or arena-rock guitar distortion. Listen to great examples of his work such as "William, It Was Really Nothing" or "Cemetery Gates", and there's a fresh, dreamy quality that few other guitarists of the era were able to muster so successfully.

Marr is largely known for playing a Gibson ES-335 or ES-355 and a Rickenbacker 360/twelve-string, although a greater proportion of the band's eponymous first album, 1984's *The Smiths*, was recorded with producer John Porter's 1954 Fender Telecaster, with some Gibson Les Paul thrown in for good measure, and he tended to turn to these instruments, along with a Gretsch 6120, up until the band's final studio release, 1987's *Strangeways, Here We Come*. Later Marr also became fond of Fender Stratocasters, and has even used a shorter-scale Fender Jaguar in his recent stint with Modest Mouse. Marr's two main acoustic guitars have long been a Martin D-28 and D-45.

More than the result of any single guitar, though, Marr's Smiths sound often owed a lot to clever multi-tracking, a process during which the guitarist would layer up one part after another, often using alternate chord positions to add depth and texture to the overall sound, rather than merely creating a solid wall of sound. A versatile and creative musician, Marr also used open and alternative tunings and slide playing to thicken the stew. The extremes to which he was willing to go to capture a sound are epitomized, perhaps, by the introduction to "How Soon is Now", where a thumping rhythm-guitar part using guitar-amp tremolo is contrasted with a haunting slide lead-guitar line. To obtain the mammoth tremolo sound in the studio, Marr and Porter (producer of the session) used four Fender Twin Reverb amps, with each man triggering two amps simultaneously, time and again, until all four throbbed in sync for the take. The majority of The Smiths' debut album was recorded through the studio's solid-state Roland Jazz Chorus 120 combo, but Marr more often used Fender amps after those sessions.

James Hetfield & Kirk Hammett

Metallican maestros

Like that of many contemporary metal players, the guitar tones of James Hetfield and Kirk Hammett with Metallica rely mainly on girth and aggression. The specific instruments used don't influence the final outcome entirely, provided they – and the amps they're played through – are capable of producing a thumping, scooped mid-range, mammoth lows and plenty of saturated distortion when required. Hetfield and Hammett do employ tools that easily get the job done, though, and plenty of them, each having accrued an extensive gear list over the course of the band's career.

Both guitarists have developed arsenals primarily populated by ESP Explorer and Flying V style guitars, although Hammett has also used a Gibson Les Paul and a Jackson Randy Rhodes model, while Hetfield used an Epiphone Flying V around the time of *Kill 'Em All*, and has also played a number of contemporary Gibson Explorers. One common denominator of the mainstays, though, is their EMG 81 humbucking pickups, units that have become standard with several leading metal players. These active pickups (which require an onboard battery to power their built-in circuitry) offer extremely high fidelity and low noise, along with a crisp, well-defined tone amid their high output, a combination that works superbly toward pushing large amps into overdrive.

As ever, their amplifiers play a big part in the equation. Both often used Marshall stacks early on, but in recent years Hammett has taken to playing through a combination of Mesa/Boogie amps, including a Tremoverb 2x12" combo, a Triaxis Preamp through a Strategy 400 Stereo Power amp and a Dual Rectifier, through assorted Mesa speaker cabs.

Hetfiled uses a similar range of Mesa/Boogies, his Mk IV being a notable substitution for Hammett's Tremoverb, although the singer also frequently supplements these with a solid-state Roland Jazz Chorus 120. Chain it all together, and it's more than enough to give you the grind of "Enter Sandman" or "Master of Puppets" any day of the week.

Hetfield and Hammett unleash a two-pronged assault of Flying V guitars.

Kurt Cobain
Godfather of grunge

Hailed by many critics as the saviours of guitar rock in the early 1990s, Nirvana really were a very simple, straightforward band, gear-wise – for all the noise they were capable of making. Guitarist Kurt Cobain embodied a punk ethos that had long declared that it just wasn't cool to care too much about your guitars. But he definitely had his favourites, and cherished certain styles of electric guitars over the course of his tragically short career.

While most players looking to create mammoth, visceral, crunching guitar tones seek heavyweight instruments like Gibson Les Pauls, SGs, Flying Vs and Explorers, Cobain preferred Fender's "student model" guitars, which were brighter and lighter, both physically and sonically. His all-time favourite was a 1969 "Competition Series" Fender Mustang, finished in "sonic blue" with a diagonal racing stripe – an all-factory original. Mustangs have covered single-coil pickups that provide a similar output to those of single-coil Stratocaster pickups, so they're not prone to lots of crunch and sustain without a bit of help. They are also shorter guitars, with a 24" scale length and slightly narrower, thinner necks than the average Strat or Tele. That Cobain used a guitar like this to make some of the most powerful music of the past two decades is a real testament to his skill and vision, and less a comment on what a Fender Mustang would usually sound like. For a little more power directly from the guitar, however, he also used several others – frequently Fender Jaguars, Stratocasters or Jazzmasters – with added humbucking pickups for increased output.

Cobain played through a number of different amplifiers, usually using what was available in any given studio, and selecting different rigs for live work. Among the former were a Mesa/Boogie Studio .22, Fender Twin Reverb, Vox AC30 and Fender Bassman, as well as an assortment of others.

The late Nirvana frontman generally played Fender electrics and liked to keep things simple pedal-wise.

Some of these were also used live, although he frequently ran a Mesa/Boogie preamp into a Crown or Crest PA-style power amp with Marshall speaker cabs. A big part of Cobain's ominous crunch tone came from a simple selection of distortion pedals: early on, and purportedly for much of the recording of *Nevermind*, Cobain used a ProCo Rat pedal, while his later touring preferences were a Boss DS-1 Distortion or DS-2 Turbo Distortion, later supplementing them with a Tech 21 Sans Amp Classic amp simulator. He achieved the legendary watery guitar tones on "Come As You Are" and "Smells Like Teen Spirit" with an Electro-Harmonix Small Clone chorus pedal. Other pedals occasionally found their way into – and back out of – the line-up, but these were by and large the main ingredients of the Cobain sound. A far more minimalist rig than that used by the majority of rock artists today.

Thom Yorke, Jonny Greenwood & Ed O'Brien
Radiohead's art-rock rigs

The three-guitar assault known as Radiohead has shown us, ever since the release of their first hit, "Creep", in 1992, what creative noises can be made with a varied collection of otherwise standard, workaday gear. Thom Yorke, Jonny Greenwood and Ed O'Brien have some decent guitars, amps and effects, certainly, but little of it is out of the ordinary – no high-end "custom shop" models or expensive vintage pieces far out of reach of the average musician.

Radiohead's Jonny Greenwood uses a wealth of effects pedals, including the Shred Master distortion pedal – responsible for the "Creep Crunch".

Ed O'Brien's beloved Rickenbacker 360 and 360/12 are perhaps the most desirable guitars of the Radiohead collection, while Thom Yorke's 1970s Fender Telecaster Deluxes and Customs (in addition to other customized Teles and a Fender Jazzmaster) might turn some other players on. Greenwood's extreme sonic sculpting, however, has often been performed with one of a couple of Fender Telecaster Plus models, products of the late 80s and early 90s that never really caught fire with the public at large. These have active Lace-Sensor pickups, which are both low-noise and high-output, with a single unit at the neck and two at the bridge wired as a humbucker (with coil-splitting capabilities), and a contemporary six-saddle bridge, as well as several modifications on Greenwood's own guitars.

More crucial to Radiohead's tone-crafting, however, are their odd, esoteric pedal rigs. Take Jonny Greenwood's pedal collection, for instance. A Marshall Shred Master distortion pedal has long been considered the "Creep" pedal, for its part in creating the enormous crunch that heralds the chorus of that song. Chained to this are a ProCo Rat, Boss SD-1 Super Distortion, a DigiTech WH-1 Whammy, a DIY tremolo pedal, a DOD Envelope Filter, an Electro-Harmonix Small Stone phase shifter, a Roland Space Echo and a Mutronics Mutator (a stereo analogue filter and envelope follower used to make space-age sounds, such as those on the closing solo in "Paranoid Android"). Following all of these are a fairly straightforward pair of amps: a Vox AC30 tube amp, and a Fender Deluxe 85, a generally unloved "red-knob" solid state amp from the mid-1980s.

O'Brien is also known for his radical effects usage, and strings together an impressive array of units, in addition to a rack-mounted Korg A-2 multi-FX unit which is in itself capable of generating a plethora of sounds. Like Greenwood, O'Brien often uses a Marshall Shred Master for distortion, along with the Whammy-Wah version of the DigiTech pedal. In addition to these, he has frequently tapped into a ProCo Rat distortion pedal; Lovetone Meatball envelope filter pedal, Big Cheese fuzz and Ring Stinger ring modulater; a Jim Dulop Tremolo; an Electro-Harmonix Small Stone phaser and Electric Mistress flanger; an MXR Micro Amp preamp; and a Boss TR2 Tremolo/Pan. Ed's delay effects come from a number of units, including a Roland Space Echo, an AMS Digital Delay, a Line 6 Delay Modeler, a Boss DD5 Digital Delay and an Akai Headrush echo unit. These run through various parallel paths to a pair of Mesa/Boogie combos, and a Vox AC30. Much more straightforward than Greenwood and O'Brien, Yorke generally uses just a pair of ProCo Rat distortion pedals and a Boss DD3 Digital Delay for a little echo, into a single Fender Twin Reverb amplifier.

While you can see the potential of all these effects chains, the art is clearly in how Greenwood and O'Brien use them. Attacked randomly, such rigs would usher in muddy mayhem. Tweaked and nudged to perfection, however, and played with great skill and finesse, they conjure up anything from haunting deep-space soundscapes to near-orchestral guitar figures.

Jack White
Stripey "Airline" pilot

Few players have done more to elevate the status of a funky, C-list vintage guitar than Jack White of the White Stripes. Thanks to the meaty, fuzzed out riffs of "Seven Nation Army", "Fell in Love With a Girl" and "Icky Thump", a red 1960s Airline Res-O-Glas guitar (like White's) is now hard to come by for any money, having formerly been on the secondhand market for lowish three-figure sums. They sound that good? Well, in White's hands they certainly make an impact, that's for sure.

Occasionally referred to as the "J.B. Hutto" model due to their use by the 60s bluesman, the Airline guitar was a model manufactured by Valco in Chicago, and marketed by catalogue company Montgomery Ward. The body of White's guitars, and some similar Valco-made instruments branded with the Supro and National names, was moulded from a type of fibreglass which the company called "Res-O-Glas", and its pickups, while appearing to be wide humbuckers, are in fact single-coils. The hardware on these guitars, too, is somewhat below the standard of components found on the instruments of major makers such as Gibson, Fender, Gretsch and Rickenbacker, but add it all up, and the red Airline makes a sound that is likely to get an artist noticed, with plenty of honk and grit in its voice, and an aggressive, lively tone overall. In addition to his trademark Airline, White has also used thinline acoustic electrics from Harmony and Crestline (both also red), and a full-bodied archtop from Kay with a single pickup in the neck position, which he often plays live for slide work.

White frequently uses a pair of Fender Twin Reverbs for amplification. His other main amp of choice, a 1960s Silvertone 1485 100-watt head with 6x10" speaker cabinet, falls more in line with the pawnshop prizes in his guitar line-up, and he has also used a vintage Selmer Zodiac 30 tube amp to record much of *Elephant*. As is the case with many players using heavily fuzzed or overdriven

Jack and Meg – The White Stripes – in the red and white uniforms that were their early trademark.

sounds, however, a handful of pedals play a big part in shaping White's sound. An MXR Micro Amp preamp provides clean boost, a DigiTech Whammy offers way-out pitch shifting effects, an Electro-Harmonix Big Muff helps him achieve the saturated distortion sound he is known for and an Electro-Harmonix POG Polyphonic Octave Generator is occasionally tapped for more extreme effects, such as the thudding tones of "Icky Thump".

Alex Turner & Jamie Cook
Arctic Monkeys keep things simple
In accordance with their early DIY ethic, singer/guitarist Alex Turner and lead guitarist Jamie Cook of Arctic Monkeys tended to favour relatively simple rigs, using minimal accoutrements on their early tours, in support of 2006's mammoth album *Whatever People Say I Am, That's What I'm Not*. At the time, Turner fired up his contemporary Fender Stratocaster through a pair of ProCo Rat 2 distortion pedals and an Orange AD30 tube combo, while Cook's reissue 1960s Telecaster was chained to a 50-watt Hiwatt Custom 2x12 combo via two or three overdrives, including an Electro-Harmonix Big Muff, a T-Rex Dr Swamp and an MXR Distortion+. Given the four-on-the-floor energy and straight-up drive of the band's style, and frenetic guitar work that propels it, this was really all the pair needed to get the job done. As their studio adventure indulged in a little more sonic manipulation, though, they began taking more adventurous pedals out on the road.

Arctic Monkeys Alex Turner and Jamie Cook.

Their pedalboards in particular have been expanding, however. Recently, Turner has tended to employ a Dunlop Uni-Vibe (to imitate the whirling sound of a Leslie speaker) and an Ibanez TS-808 Tube Screamer for overdrive. He's used a Boss DM-1 Analogue Delay for echo, and an Electro-Harmonix Memory Man delay unit before that. While moving up in the world pedal-wise, Turner moved downmarket in his guitar of choice, replacing the Strat with a short-scale 1970s Fender Bronco, a single-pickup "student" model. More recently, however, he has played a sunburst Fender Jazzmaster, long a popular choice with indie and alternative players. A similarly powered Vox AC30 has taken the place of the Orange AD30.

Jamie Cook's Hiwatt combo and MXR Distortion+ seem to remain constant, but it's been all-change with just about everything else in the rig from the time of 2007's *Favourite Worst Nightmare*. He has more often been seen playing a Gibson ES-335, with further sonic wrangling supplied by a Big Muff fuzz pedal, HOG polyphonic guitar synth, Pulsar tremolo and Deluxe Memory Man delay, all made by Electro-Harmonix.

forming a BAND

Once you've got going, and grown confident in your playing, you'll probably want to play with other musicians and get a band together. As rewarding as playing the guitar on your own can be, playing with others takes it to an entirely different level. Hearing your guitar parts played with drums, bass and vocals behind them is a thrill that's hard to beat. And unless you intend to be a solo singer-songwriter, it'll be difficult to fulfil any ambitions as a performing musician if you can't learn to play well with others, and to gel with a group of like-minded musicians as a band.

You don't have to be a guitar genius before you start playing with others. Playing in a band, or even jamming as a duo or trio, presents challenges and develops your skills in ways that playing alone cannot. Even if you have no immediate desire to record or to perform live, playing with other people and other instruments is a very big part of the learning process. Keeping a steady rhythm, meshing with others harmonically and melodically, learning when to hold back and back up a voice and when to come forward and solo – these are all skills an adept team-player guitarist needs. They make you a better musician, even if you learn no new scales or progressions in the process.

In this chapter there's a wealth of tips and advice that will help you get a band together and to tackle your first performance and recording situations with confidence.

GETTING GOING

No one can tell you what kind of band to be. If you are pulling your first band together from a pool of friends, your mission statement might simply be "we want to play some music together". If that means doing a couple of Beatles tunes that the bassist brings in, a Foo Fighters cover that the drummer is desperate to play, a blues progression the keyboard player wants to work on, and an original punk tune that you just wrote on guitar, it's still a way of getting going, however unlikely the mix is. If you want to turn it into a gigging unit, though, you'll probably need to settle on some kind of style and direction.

Do you want to be a covers band or an originals band? Will you learn and perform versions of other artists' songs, or will you write your own? Plenty of bands begin by learning covers – a great way of discovering how songs are structured and performed – and then progress to writing their own tunes. It's a useful approach, provided all band members are on the same page. More often, however, musicians

Unless you're an Elvis impersonator determined to perform the songs of Led Zeppelin in a reggae style, the way LA band Dread Zeppelin do, you really ought to have a consensus on the style of music you play.

are driven by the desire to get their songs out, even if their playing hasn't got much further than three-chord I-IV-V songs. There's nothing wrong with this – see the playlist in this book's introduction for some of the classics that have been written with only a handful of chords – and aiming to create fantastic original music right from the band's start is a great attitude to take. Plenty of bands created compelling original music out of what some considered to be meagre amounts of musicianship. Members of The Ramones, Talking Heads, The Sex Pistols, U2, Arctic Monkeys and many others were in exactly that position when their now-famous bands first formed.

If you all have different musical backgrounds, it's important to have a consensus about what you're going to play together. It's okay to play a little metal, a little country and a little chart pop if you're just messing around for the sake of playing some

Johnny Ramone on stage in 1977. The Ramones proved that you don't need to know a lot of chords to be a great band.

music with other people now and then. Or, of course, if you aim to form the world's most successful country-metal-pop outfit. But if you have big ambitions for the band, and have a direction and style in mind, it's a good idea to lay that out right from the start.

Quite apart from anything, it will save you frustration and personnel issues down the road – and avoid the need to replace that bassist who leaves in anger at your efforts to play original indie guitar-pop because he thought you had agreed to do authentic Led Zeppelin covers.

Are you taking this thing seriously, or is it a casual venture? You need to know right from the start if all band members are on the same page commitment and expectations-wise; you don't want to get to a critical turning point and discover that someone isn't entirely on board, or is expecting more than the rest of you have signed up for. It needn't be deadly serious: just sit down together to talk music, motivation and expectations, and make sure everyone is in a situation that's likely to suit them now and two years from now, when the band is beginning to make its mark (hopefully).

If you are planning to play original tunes, who will be the songwriter? Will it be a communal effort, with all band members writing together, or will individual members – or just one member – bring in compositions they have completed on their own? The one-songwriter approach does help create a cohesive and identifiable style and direction – especially if you have one member who seems to be more gifted and prolific than the others. But it can also generate bad feelings among bandmates who had hoped to make more of their own creative contribution, so it's best to come to an understanding earlier rather than later.

Address these issues and, with any luck, you'll find yourself amongst a crew of like-minded musicians. That way it's a lot easier to build a lasting foundation, and keep all bandmates happy at the same time.

REHEARSING

Bands need places to play, too, and finding that space can often be more difficult than it sounds. There are thousands of professional rehearsal studios rented out by bands with deals or serious aspirations – some of which offer catered sushi and a full bar, others of which smell like old socks and rumble with every train that passes overhead.

I have rehearsed over the years in a kitchen, a shed, the empty swimming pool of a closed-down health spa, a pub's billiards room after hours and countless bedrooms, basements and garages. Your own efforts to find places in which to play are likely to go a similar way: just about anywhere you're allowed to make a noise without threat of arrest can be considered a good rehearsal space for your band.

The most obvious resource for young musicians is domestic space. The garage gave birth to an entire sub-genre of rock in the US in the 1960s and 70s. Plenty of bands that eventually made a pretty big splash would have gotten nowhere without the use of their parents' two-car facility with power and overhead door in their teen years. The basement has proved another popular venue for launching musical careers, as has the attic rec room.

In the UK, where space is often tighter and garages and basements are fewer and further between, the domestic rehearsal space is more of a problem for an up-and-coming band. And even with a spacious garage, basement or rec-room available, noise can remain an issue. Sound often escapes from rooms with frustrating ease, and unless neighbours are happy to lose their peace and quiet, you can still find yourselves shut down.

Examine this checklist of rehearsal-space requirements. If the room ticks enough boxes, you might just have yourselves a base from which to launch your assault on the world of music. A satisfactory rehearsal space needs to be:

◊ Large enough to house all members and instruments without guitar headstocks clanging into cymbals or singers tripping over amplifiers.

◊ Safely wired for grounded (earthed) AC electrical power.

◊ Insulated and heated (if winter rehearsals in colder climates are even remotely expected).

◊ Dry: free from rising damp or leaky roof tiles.

◊ Secure and lockable, if you intend to store gear there.

◊ Fairly noise-proof, or located amidst neighbours who won't object to a loud band learning their chops.

◊ Properly ventilated. Things will get pretty musty with four or five guys and girls in a basement for three or four hours straight. You'll need to be able to open a door or a couple of windows during break times (and to close them when you start up again, to prevent even more sound from escaping). If there's no obvious source of ventilation, at least bring an electric fan or two to move the air around.

Rehearsal PAs

Plenty of bands get started by working on their instrumental arrangements alone, and you can do that with the gear you already possess. If you plan on introducing vocals into the brew, though, you'll obviously need some form of PA system. This needn't be a rig that suitable to gigging, but if you plan to play venues that require you to bring your own PA, and your budget can stretch to it, it does sometimes help to kill two birds with one stone.

That said, most venues have their own house PAs, so it might not pay to invest too much in your own equipment until you find out what you'll be requiring when you finally take the act out of the garage and into the clubs. Research the scene a bit. Find out what sort of stuff the bands that are playing the kinds of places you hope to play in a year or so are using. And invest accordingly.

Small rehearsal-ready systems are easy to come by these days, and relatively affordable. All-in-one systems such as Fender's Passport 150 and PD-250, Yamaha's Stagepas and Kustom's Profile 1A include a pair of small PA speakers and a powered multi-channel mixer that, in some cases, clip together into a portable package. Each makes a great rehearsal system – if you don't get too carried away with your amp and drum volumes – and can even cut it at an acoustic gig, or low-volume electric gig, in a small club.

If you'd prefer to try to piece something together out of separates, there are also plenty of options available. A range of powered PA cabs make a good place to start, from Behringer's affordable Eurolive range to Mackie's more robust SRM series, and you can use just one unit to begin with, if it will cover your vocal needs for rehearsal and that's all your budget will stretch to. These active speaker units (which carry their own built-in power amps) need to be used with an external mixer, but smaller and more basic examples of these are also fairly affordable. The potential advantage to piecing together your own system is that you can later add larger powered speakers if you require greater volume, and convert your smaller original units to monitor duties for gig sound.

The Kingsmen released "Louie Louie" in 1963 – a three-chord wonder of a song that became a garage rock classic, up there with "Wild Thing" by The Troggs as one of the easiest songs for a beginner guitarist to play.

John Spenser, of the John Spenser Blues Explosion, loved his cheap Sennheiser SM58 mic so much, he wrote a song about it.

In addition, you're obviously going to need at least one microphone and stand for each singer in the band, and it's worth investing in something that will last you a while. An industry standard from a company such as Shure, AKG or Audio-Technica is usually worthwhile. A good SM58, for example, should last the lifetime of the band if treated right, and can do double duty for some home-recording applications, too.

Rehearsal studios

Professional rehearsal facilities address all of the above issues in one fell swoop, and are the best option for bands who don't mind chipping in some cash to pay for rehearsal space (which is also their biggest drawback). They'll have (relatively) decent PA systems in place, often offer guitar and bass amps and even drums (either as part of the room fee, or for an extra per-item charge), and sometimes have lock-up equipment storage services available.

The better rehearsal studios in several of the world's larger music centres – London, New York, Nashville, LA – will have stages and gear equal to that in the large venues that a name band might be performing in. They tend to be booked out in blocks of weeks at a time by signed artists who are getting their sets together pre-tour, with on-site catering and other niceties available. More affordable rehearsal spaces are more likely to have a Coke machine down the hall, and somewhat road-weary but serviceable PAs in a handful of musty rooms – perfectly adequate for most purposes, since the main thing you're paying for is a place to play music without the potential hassle and interruption of perturbed neighbours or housemates.

In between the paid-for studio and the parents' basement is a range of other potential rehearsal spaces that can sometimes be rooted out with a little creative thinking. Arts centres, crafts studios, community centres and even workshops or storage spaces (with proper, safe electrical power) might all offer options that get the noise out of the house.

You'll need to ensure that the owner or manager and other tenants will be okay with the noise – and that they understand what such noise levels are likely to be (underselling your volume doesn't do you any favours in the long run). And you will probably need to bring along your own PA, too. But these kinds of places have worked out well for countless bands over the years, and might do the job for you, too.

Playing together and sounding right

Beyond these practical considerations to rehearsing, it helps enormously to understand a little bit about how different instruments – or even two or three of the same instrument, in the case of the guitar – can work together, or against, each other to create a complementary sonic blend.

The quartet is a classic rock format: guitar, bass, drums and vocals. The power trio is another – it's the same mix of instruments, only with the singer being one of the musicians. They have been enduringly successful over the years partly because they provide a sonic spectrum in which each instrument naturally occupies its own space, and avoids stepping on the toes of the others. For this reason, this format is also an easy one to get sounding good if you're just starting out playing together.

Often, however, you'll want two guitars in order to better fill out the sound, and to adequately cover the parts in the songs you want to play. Once you get two of the same of any kind of instrument playing in a rock band, you need to put some thought into differentiating the parts that each performs, in order to avoid battering away in the same portions of the frequency range. The combination of two guitars, bass and drums can make a lot of noise, which is why it has been such a mainstay of rock'n'roll for more than fifty years now. But two six-string guitars can also really get in each other's way if the musicians behind them aren't working together and approaching the arrangements as a team – rather than as competitors, each trying to outshine the other.

When two guitars are playing together in one band, they usually divide their duties into the traditional roles of rhythm and lead, the former strumming the chords that underpin the melody, and the latter playing the hooks, riffs, fills and solos that add dynamics and spice to the arrangement. Often when bands form from a group of beginner or novice players, it's the more advanced guitarist who'll take the lead-guitar role, but this doesn't have to be the case.

Keeping it hush-hush

Since noise is often the biggest factor in rehearsing a band – otherwise the living room would be fine – an alternative is to construct or obtain a headphone-based rehearsal system. Some such "jam stations" are available from a range of manufacturers these days. But you could piece together your own by using a range of guitar and bass FX units or digital amp emulators running through a multi-channel mixer alongside your vocal mic, and output that mix to an affordable multi-channel headphone amplifier such as Nady's HPA-4, Rolls' HA43 or Behringer's AMP800.

The drummer would need to use an electronic practice kit, which would be the biggest investment of all, but the convenience of a low-volume rehearsal facility might make it all worthwhile. That said, you're likely to want to rehearse at full volume, through a genuine PA system and your full-size guitar amps, at least a few times before your first gig, because the reaction of your vocals and instruments in an in-ear system and in the room will be quite different, and there is likely to be a readjustment period between the two. Futhermore, you must always remember that listening to loud music on headphones for long periods will permanently damage your hearing.

Songwriting tips

Songwriting is clearly an art form, one that requires a lot of study, practice and plenty of work. If you're just getting started with writing original songs, these simple pointers might help you to get the juices flowing.

Begin by copying other people. If you are eager to write original songs but haven't a clue where to begin, get the ball rolling by copying songs by artists you admire. I'm not talking about learning cover versions (though that's a good way to practice pre-songwriting), but about mimicking their style and chord progressions, and putting your own lyrics and instrumental twists to the results. You might want to move away from direct copying before you let the public hear your creations. But when you start by emulating the sounds and styles of your favourite bands, then modify them to suit your own tastes and abilities, you can often, surprisingly, find yourself sounding more like you than like them after just a short while. Many great bands have begun in this way, and eventually landed upon a unique and instantly recognizable style of their own in the effort.

Break out of the box. You might write a song or two that works well with a straight-ahead I-IV-V chord progression, but too many of these will leave you sounding tired and predictable. Shake up the changes, experiment with chord progressions that might outwardly seem to break the rules, and you will stumble on some ear-catching sounds in due course. Learn some alternative scales and modes and experiment with time signatures other than 4/4. In short, shake it up a little, and you'll sound more original in no time.

Write what you know. Trying to channel Bob Dylan, Kurt Cobain or Marilyn Manson will probably just come off sounding fake, but if you pull your lyrical inspiration from your own life, thoughts and dreams, you're bound to at least sound authentic, and your songs will probably be much more original as a result. Countless creative writing teachers tell their students to "write what they know", and the same applies to songwriting.

Don't be too precious. If a song just doesn't seem to work for your band, don't be afraid to change it up in a major way, or to rearrange parts to suit the players. Sometimes a song that sounds great in the isolation of your bedroom just doesn't pan out with the musicians you hope will play it. Also, be ready to change keys if necessary. If you or a bandmate has written a great song that is proving difficult for your singer's vocal range, then it's the key that needs to change. Capo up if necessary, and put that tune in your lead singer's ballpark. A strong, confident vocal is, for the listener, the most prominent feature of any song. So that's where your priorities lie.

Rhythm guitar is equally important – it keeps the song chugging along – and often the rhythm player will be a good guitarist who is also a singer, as it's generally easier to sing while playing chords than lead. If two guitarists are of roughly similar abilities, and both have a lot of varied musical ideas, it's a good idea to share lead and rhythm roles – playing a little of both is also the best way to develop your chops. There are no set rules for this, and the lead/rhythm roles can swap within the same song – perhaps even in the same verse.

However, the aforementioned hooks, riffs, fills and solos won't be required throughout all sections of a given song, and so two guitars will both strum the rhythm chords. For these passages, you want to craft parts that avoid having you play the exact same chords in the exact same positions, which, however accurately you do it, can come out sounding like a sonic mess that overcrowds the mix. Consider having one guitar play first-position or "open" chords low down on the neck, while the other plays partial barre chords higher up. Or have one player strum rhythmically while the other plays "jangle" style arpeggios in a different position. There are a lot of ways to differentiate your parts.

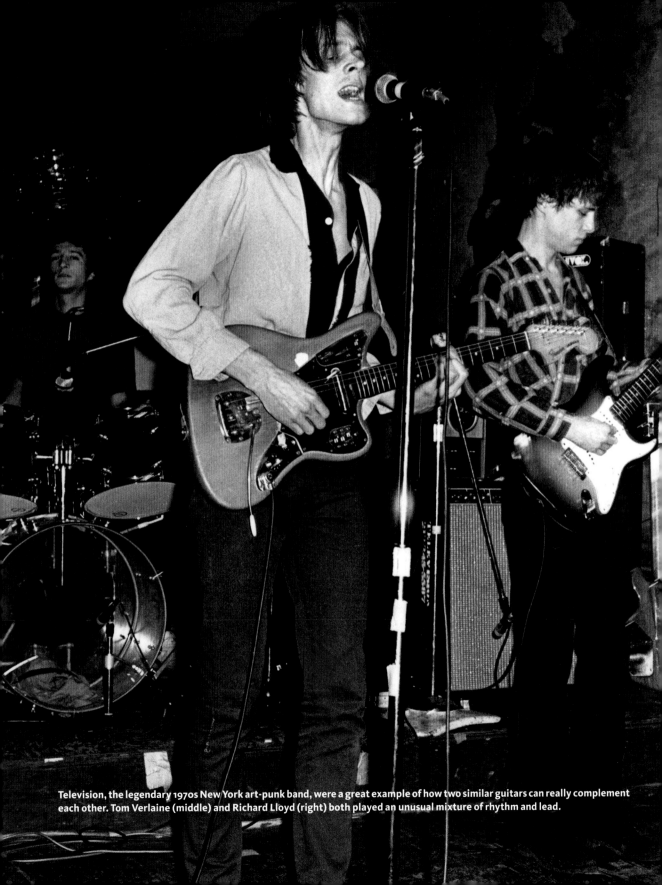

Television, the legendary 1970s New York art-punk band, were a great example of how two similar guitars can really complement each other. Tom Verlaine (middle) and Richard Lloyd (right) both played an unusual mixture of rhythm and lead.

Another important means of creating two distinctive and complementary guitar parts lies in crafting different tones. Even with slightly different parts, if they are played on the same guitars, with the same pickup settings, through the same effects and the same amplifiers, they'll end up sounding opaque and muddy.

With two very different guitar tones working together – for example, one warm and crunchy, the other bright and chimey – even two fairly similar parts will remain distinctive to the listener's ear. Listen to any professional two-guitar band, and you'll usually hear two considerably different tones going on on stage or on the recording. You'll also notice that such players often use different but complementary gear, too: perhaps a Gibson Les Paul and a Fender Stratocaster through Marshall and Vox amps respectively, for example.

Even if you're already stuck with two similar guitar and amp rigs, you can differentiate your tones by setting your pickup selections and amp EQs differently – work with it until your own ears can easily pick out each instrument, even when you're playing the exact same thing. My own band recently played on a bill with a great surf/instrumental-style band that had three guitarists in the line-up, and at one point in the set the guitarists had two twelve-string guitars and one six-string all playing together, plus bass. Thirty-four strings in all. A muddy mess? No, because they all crafted distinctive tones and played distinctive parts, with a lot of skill and finesse.

Get your different tones and your different parts working in harmony, and you can really start to make some music. Consider the dual-rhythm attack of one clean, jangly guitar strumming full, open chords, while another slightly dirty guitar chunks away at power chords. Or mix one electric and one acoustic. This blend has driven many a hit song very successfully; either one of these guitars can break into riffs, fills and solos and still stand out in the mix. Get your guitars working *together*, rather than against each other, and you will be a good way down the road to sounding like a real band.

Constructive rehearsals

If you have all agreed that rehearsals are an excuse to hang out, chat, share a few laughs and maybe play a little music in between, that's fine –it's a perfectly valid way to socialize with your friends now and then. If, on the other hand, you really hope to get something done musically and to progress as a band, you will need to establish a work ethic, with some agreed-upon standards for rehearsals.

This is another matter about which you all need to be on the same page from the start. But for many people time is precious, and rehearsing is hard work even before they have strapped on their guitar. You need to secure and equip the space, block out some free time, drag your gear there and be ready to play. And with all this effort expended on the notion of learning to play as a band, it's pretty frustrating if you mainly just end up standing around and yacking for hours on end. Establish in advance what you hope to get done, make lists of songs and song structures in advance, and prepare ahead of time any charts or cheat sheets required by you or by other band members who might be less familiar with songs you already know.

It's often good to warm up by playing a song or two that you already know pretty well, or by jamming to something casual, but be prepared to take your efforts seriously, and to look for progress in the band's absorption of the material at hand. During all this hard work, be sure to take regular breaks, too: get some fresh air, something to drink, rejuvenate yourself for ten minutes and you'll get more out of the rest of the session.

Give some thought to the physical arrangement of the band during rehearsal, too. Right before an important gig you might want to set up in gig formation – strung out in a line, as if on stage, with the drums approximately in the middle – but for weekly rehearsals it really isn't necessary to pretend you're in front of a crowd, and might even be detrimental. Often, setting up in a circle, with all band members facing each other, makes communication and mid-song visual cues much easier, and helps the learning flow better in general.

When using this arrangement you'll need to give some thought to equipment placement, so all members can hear each other adequately. Your PA set-up might need particular attention, since you want everyone to hear the vocals, but you don't want any microphones pointing into monitor speakers (to avoid howling feedback). Work with it, though, and you'll find a set-up that works, while also proving constructive to the rehearsal process.

GETTING THE GIG

So you've rehearsed your hearts out, got your set down tight, and you're ready to take it out of the rehearsal room. What now? You need to land your first gig. But that can sometimes be a little harder than it seems. The best way to figure what kind of club is suitable for your band, and how to approach them, is to familiarize yourself with the music scene in your city, town or region. Check out the live music clubs where local bands that you admire, and which play the same kind of music you play, perform on a regular basis. If you play covers, check out the venues where covers bands play. Also, if you can do it without getting in their way, introduce yourself casually to the sound guy, or the club's booker or manager, if you know who they are. But don't push your band on them just yet. Keep it cool, and simply introduce yourself as any friendly patron might.

When you have some form of demo material available, find the venue's website and see if they offer links to any information about submitting your band's material. If they do, follow their instructions to the "T": if they say "email us with links to your bio and music", get yourself some web presence (on MySpace or Facebook at the very least) and do exactly that. If they say "mail us your CD", then do so; and if they say "don't call us, we'll call you", you need to respect that too.

If there are no online instructions, email a request for booking guidelines, or if there's no email address provided, call the venue in the early evening (when things are likely to be quiet, but when a manager or knowledgeable employee is likely to be on hand) and briefly and politely ask about their booking policy. Bookers are notorious at failing to reply to email queries so don't be afraid to follow up after a couple of weeks. But you'll also want to gauge the mood and not annoy a booker that you may need a favour from further down the road. If the venue's booking guidelines tell you it often takes three to four weeks to respond to queries, don't email after two weeks. It can be frustrating, but you need to give it time.

Another good way to land early gigs is to hook up with slightly better-known bands in your area and offer to open for them at upcoming shows where they might need another act on the bill. If you don't know any of the members personally and don't have the opportunity to bump into them in person – before or after one of their own shows, perhaps – send them a message on MySpace, Facebook or whatever other personal network they might use. Explain your situation, offer a link to samples of your music, and ask if they might consider having you open at an upcoming gig.

If you can confidently rally twenty, thirty or forty friends and fans to attend and help boost the door takings, mention that. And if it means playing for no money to land that first gig – irrespective of how many friends you can get to come along – then do so. The important thing is to get that gig, and you can't expect to get rich right from the start. Perhaps, if it goes well, you could arrange a "gig swap", whereby said band might open for you for nothing at a future date when you get rolling on your own steam.

Promoting it

Musicians climbing the ladder today are in the golden age of self-promotion. In the good old days – in fact, right up until the last five years or so – the most a local, unsigned band could do was contact the local press and radio (and hope they paid at least enough attention to them to put the gig in the calendar listings, at least) and post a handful of fliers around town (and hope they stayed put long enough to be noticed before the next band tacked their own flier over the top). These are still viable avenues for promotion, but thanks to the online revolution there are several other means of plugging your gig in the virtual world that are often even less effort, and are becoming more and more the accepted ways of getting noticed.

Successful online promotion begins with establishing a web presence for your band, then using it to create as broad a social network as you can. An official website with your band's name as the domain still looks good (such as www.mygreatband.com), and if you can use an email address with that domain name for contacting bookers, the press and fans, that adds a professional sheen to things, too. You have to pay hosting fees for a domain, though, and if you don't have the ability to design and maintain yourself, you'll also need to fork out for those services. So it isn't always a cheap proposition.

Established online social networks such as MySpace and Facebook provide a free and easy way to go, and in many ways they also provide more of an instant communications base for a new band than a nifty looking personal domain. Friends and fans can at least easily find your band's page on an established network, and make instant use of the communications facilities built into it to get in touch with you – as can you to contact them – while they might have to make more effort to stumble onto your official site.

Also, the "instant message" and "personal message" facilities that these networks provide, and their ability to invite all friends in your address book to an upcoming event in one go, are hard to beat. Set yourself up on MySpace or Facebook at the very least – ideally both, and any other network that has boomed since this book went to print. Make the pages look as professional as possible, while also making them fun and creative to attract new fans, and hit their messaging services hard when gig time approaches. Try to strike a balance between having an interesting page and an annoyingly busy one that takes forever for all the pictures and YouTube links to appear.

That said, the old-school promotional outlets of local press and radio – and even local or regional cable TV and public-access stations – are still invaluable, and should remain a big part of your promo strategy. Compose a brief but effective band bio, offer up all your relevant facts, provide all pertinent details of the upcoming event, and have some professional-looking high-resolution band photos taken that you can send along – or at least have them available upon request. Work to establish good relations with your local press and broadcast journalists. If you can get yourself "in" with the local newspaper or arts and entertainment magazine, a feature in print still carries a lot of weight, even if (sadly), fewer and fewer people are likely to see it these days.

Get your gear gig-ready

Sure, being able to put on a show is a big part of the battle, but it also helps to have a list of all the little things that can help the gig go smoothly – so you don't spoil a potentially great performance with some small, avoidable glitch. Have both your gear and your attitude in the right condition to pull off that first gig, and every one after it, like a pro. This should be obvious, but far too many guitarists still turn up for their gigs with gear that could fail at any time, spoiling their own playing enjoyment along with the listening enjoyment of the audience while they take a forced pause to remedy the situation. If you can't deal with the following tasks yourself, have a pro take care of them for you, well before you're headed up the stairs to the stage.

On your guitar

◊ Strings are reasonably fresh and hold their tuning.

◊ The bridge, tailpiece, tuners and nut are in good condition, and don't rattle or slip.

◊ Pots (dials) and switches are functional, clean (not scratchy) and operate smoothly.

◊ Pickups are adjusted for optimum tone and are free from excessive noise.

◊ Knobs are secure (not waiting to fall off mid-solo).

◊ The jack is both clean and tight enough to hold the cord's jack-plug securely.

◊ Your strap doesn't slip off your strap buttons when you start getting into it. Install strap locks if it does.

◊ General intonation, set-up and action are optimum for you to give your best performance.

On your amp

◊ Tubes are in good condition, firmly secured in their sockets and biased correctly (if applicable).

◊ Pots and switches are clean (not scratchy) and functional.

◊ Any channel-switching, effects-switching or boost-switching controls work correctly, and you have the appropriate footswitch.

◊ Speaker is mounted securely inside the cab, and doesn't rattle or buzz when you play at gig volume.

◊ Speaker is connected to the amp output with the correct speaker cable, and correct impedance match between the two.

◊ If it's an older amp, ensure a grounded three-prong AC power cord and plug have been installed by a professional (this is a major safety issue when you start playing with a PA and other plugged-in instruments).

Effects and accessories

◊ All pedals should have fresh batteries or, if you're using an AC/DC adaptor, check that it's connected and working correctly.

◊ All guitar cords (leads) and effects pedals patch-cords should be in good condition and short-free.

In addition to having all of the working components of your rig in good playing condition, you will want to carry plenty of spares in your gig bag (not the gig bag your guitar rides in, but a weekend bag that holds all your accessories and extras). You can't necessarily be prepared for every single thing that might go wrong with your equipment at a gig, but as a good rule of thumb you should try to carry spares of everything that might be considered consumables, along with a few other handy items. These include: strings, picks, cables (cords), batteries, amp fuses, amp tubes (a known-good spare for every tube position), slide (bottleneck) and capo if you use one, spare AC extension cable with power strip and duck tape/gaffer tape.

It's really worth having a spare guitar if at all possible, so you can grab it on the fly if you break a string, or if your main instrument develops some fatal flaw. Tune it before the set, right before tuning your main guitar, and set it on a stand within easy reach. If you can't afford a functional spare, and you're in a two-guitar band, see if you can at least acquire or borrow one spare to share between you (hopefully you won't break strings at the same time), or ask a sympathetic guitarist in a band on the same bill if he or she doesn't mind having one available just in case.

Behaviour & attitude

Just as important as having all the gear working is the need to have your head in the right place for the gig. More than just being positive and ready to play, this means adhering to any time-slots and ground rules that the venue's owner or manager has established, and being polite and cooperative with everyone involved in helping the gig come off smoothly.

Show up on time, or even a little early – but not so early that you'll just annoy the club owner/bar staff/sound tech. Introduce yourself to the stage manager or sound tech the first time you have a chance to do so without bugging or interrupting him or her. Ask where to stow your gear before going on stage, when to put it on stage, where you might put any cases to keep them out of the way while playing or during other bands' sets. You should have been given a time for sound check in advance – if you weren't, remember for next time to call or email to ask for one – but confirm this with the sound guy now.

If there isn't time for a full sound check – which is often the case with multi-band bills at smaller clubs – don't moan and complain. You should at least have time for a quick line check, which is a level check of all mics and instruments. Get on with this quickly and efficiently when asked to do so. Observe the sound person's requests regarding volume level. If you feel you need to be cranked up to hit your tonal sweet spot, make sure in advance that you aren't bringing an amp that's too loud for the venue. If the sound guy asks you to turn it down, do so, and continue to do so until he or she is satisfied. It isn't their fault if you can't hit your sweet spot at a volume appropriate to the venue – it's yours for bringing an inappropriate amp.

If you really must play that monster of an amp in a small room, or it's just all you've got, try to get an attenuator to lower the level at the output stage. Over-baked guitar volume levels are a surefire show spoiler, and a sign of an unprofessional player, and won't win you many new fans, either. When you have finished your sound check or line check, clear away any gear that will be in the way of any band checking after you, or performing before your set time.

Leave your gear as performance-ready as it can be without being in anyone's way, then quit the stage. But be on hand in plenty of time to begin your set promptly. When performing, stick to your allotted set time – running over can be a sure way of not getting asked back – and at the end, it never hurts to thank the audience for coming and either the venue or one of the other bands "for having us".

Honour thy sound tech

By now, you'll have a good idea of the first rule of the smooth gig: honour the sound engineer, for they are gods of the gig. They might act like they own the place, and some of them have pretty big chips on their shoulders, but they have usually earned them from having to deal with too many uncooperative and unpleasant bands in the past. Ultimately they know a lot more about smoothly running the live sound – and the entire gig – than you do.

Even if you feel the guy needs an attitude adjustment, listen, obey, cooperate and avoid getting on his nerves: he literally has his finger on the buttons that can make you suck or succeed and it isn't worth picking a fight with him. Work with him, even if it feels like you're giving in, and you can grumble about him all you like when you're headed home in the van after a great show.

Johnny Rotten props up the sound desk in a rare moment of calm on the disastrous, riotous Sex Pistols tour of the southern US in 1978, which ultimately led to the band splitting up.

RECORDING AS A BAND

Once you get a band really humming, and you've started writing some original tunes – or even if you need to demo a covers set for promotional use to land gigs, you are going to need to do some recording. If you haven't got the gear, or the space, to record in a home studio, you'll need to make use of a professional-quality studio.

Even if it's a small demo studio, or a friend's project studio, a first venture into a recording facility can be a daunting proposition. The red-light fever that sets in when you're trying to get that one great take under pressure can sometimes be worse than the nerves that hit you before going on stage. A few tips about preparation for the studio – regarding gear, performance and attitude – can go a long way toward calming anxieties, and helping to make you ready to get the best and most efficient performance out of yourself, and your bandmates.

Get your gear into shape

Under the sonic microscope of a good studio microphone, your gear's flaws will reveal themselves alarmingly quickly. The basic rule of thumb here is to get everything shipshape before you get into the studio, to avoid any essential maintenance work while the clock is ticking.

Your guitar

Make sure your intonation is accurate and the guitar stays in tune well. There should be no unwanted rattles or buzzes or any noises in any of the controls that will be used in the course of playing. You should put a new set of strings on before you go to record, but not at the very last minute – give yourself time to stretch them in and let them settle so they're ready to stay in tune.

Amp and speaker(s)

If you have any noisy or – even worse – dying tubes replace them now. Check that everything functions as it should, and play the amp long enough (before entering the studio) to ensure that nothing will fail or grow noisy with prolonged use. Check your speaker and speaker cab thoroughly and eliminate any rattles by tightening the speaker mounting bolts, back panels, handles and whatever else might start to vibrate when played at volume. Perhaps you don't notice these when cranked up on stage or in rehearsal, but a studio mic will slather that annoying buzz all over your precious solo.

Effects & accessories

Test all cables (cords) that you plan to use, and clean the tips with a squirt of electrical contact cleaner and a little muscular rubbing with a soft cloth. Put fresh batteries in any pedals that use them, and check the AC/DC converters (aka wall-warts) that you use with any others to ensure they aren't faulty or noisy.

Have your performance ready to roll

Major-label artists with unlimited studio budgets, or anyone with the luxury of a good home studio and all the time in the world, can afford to improvise and compose in the studio with the proverbial tape rolling. The rest of us need to make the most of that time we're paying for, and you need to have your performance down before you cross the hallowed studio threshold.

Make extra time for the band to rehearse ahead of your studio date, and put in some additional woodshedding on your own parts at home. Ensure that any bandmates who are unsure of their parts or song arrangements in general are brought up to speed. Make any charts, notes and cheat-sheets you might need to help things go smoothly – you're not on stage here, so there's no shame in following a chart if it helps you get things right – and have them ready to go for the big day.

And after all that... take a few deep breaths, loosen up and try to bring a little life and spontaneity into your playing. In one sense you can never be too well rehearsed; in another, you can't afford to let yourself start feeling bored with your playing.

Romy Croft, guitarist of The xx, who recorded their atmospheric debut album in a garage (albeit a garage that had been recently converted into a small recording studio).

Once you get an acceptable take or takes, if there's enough time, don't be afraid to change it up and try something different. It might just be the one.

Attitude, dude

If you've never recorded in a professional studio before, the first thing you want to get into your head is the fact that the best stage sound and the best studio sound are usually two very different things. The recording engineer's job is to help you get the latter. So don't be offended if he or she makes suggestions about altering your approach, such as asking you to change your guitar settings, trying different amps or effects pedals or even suggesting you play your part slightly differently.

Any good engineer should take account of the gear you would prefer to use, and of your own playing style in the light of the kind of music you're trying to make. But if they suggest any major changes, it's worth trying them out. Engineers have no agenda other than getting the best results for you and your band, and if they work in that same studio day after day, with different bands, they will know what is likely to get the job done. They're trying to work with you, not against you, so take any advice in the spirit in which it is intended, and see what you can make with it.

On the other hand, they are also working for you, since you're paying them. If you think an engineer's methods or suggestions are actually wrong, for artistic reasons – if you are convinced you have an off-the-wall approach that really will work, and perhaps they don't entirely understand what you are trying to achieve – you need to explain yourself (politely). In the end, a successful studio experience usually requires a dash of give and take and a pinch of compromise, so polish up your diplomacy badge and be prepared to pin it on.

Most importantly of all – have some fun in there. This is your time, your money and your music. Sure, you're likely to be a little nervous, but you got into this thing in the first place because you love it. You want to enjoy yourself in the studio, savour the experience and come away with results that you can live with at the very least, and that you are over the moon with ideally. Take all of these practical considerations to heart, but don't let them get in the way of achieving these goals, and your day in the studio will have been a worthwhile venture.

RECORDING

he quality of home recording systems has improved unrecognizably over the last decade. This is great news. But it also means that, these days, being able to play an instrument well isn't enough. A musician is expected to produce increasingly professional-sounding recordings too. Recording is something that, in the past, you really didn't have to worry much about until you were on the verge of landing a record deal. And even then, there would usually be a pro sound engineer on hand to deal with the technicalities. Not so today. The affordability of high-quality digital recording systems that run on any decent Mac or PC, and the explosion of budget-level mics, preamps and effects, has led to a boom in home-recording studios.

The vast improvement in equipment has blurred the lines between "home recording" and "studio recording": many bands and solo artists maintain "project studios" in which they get results that aren't discernibly different from pro recordings made in big studios. And even complete beginners can learn to use cheap equipment to make perfectly adequate demo recordings, which will at the very least help them land gigs and get a little attention via all the music-hosting websites out there.

But while even the cheapest digital audio workstations (DAWs) and interfaces can make higher-than-CD-quality recordings, there's still a lot more to a professional-sounding recording than hitting Record and counting in your tune. Recording is still an art form and new technology will only get you so far. To get results you can be proud of, you'll need to know about microphone types, miking techniques (for both acoustic and electric guitars – as well as vocals and other instruments in the band), outboard processing, mixing and mastering.

Fear not: this chapter is here to cover precisely these topics, with a wealth of pro studio tips and tricks thrown in. Whether you want to make a demo or a full broadcast-quality recording for release and distribution, the skills discussed in this chapter will get you there.

THE HOME STUDIO

A home studio can comprise anything from the simplest portable recorder with built-in microphone to a fully featured set-up that could rival many smaller professional studios. Here is an overview of a few of the more important pieces of equipment that you'll need to acquire for a range of music-production tasks. You could get by with much less, at a pinch, while many home studios these days have a fair bit more. But the basic requirements, covered in detail later, are:

◊ **A recording system** These days, this will probably be a digital interface and software-based workstation for your computer. Alternatively, a standalone digital or analogue recorder.

◊ **Microphones** While some basic recorders have mics built in, external mics of any decent quality will usually do a better job and provide more flexibility. A small collection of several types will help you cover different applications.

◊ **Monitor speakers and headphones** Ideally you'd have both, and something to plug them into, to hear what you're recording and mixing, both privately and in the room.

◊ **Processors and plug-ins** The majority of digital systems have built-in effects and processors (known as plug-ins), and these are often enough to get you started. You can download extra ones, or buy external hardware (outboard) processors to broaden your sound-crafting palette.

◊ **Microphone preamps** Many digital interfaces have surprisingly good mic preamps built in. As with outboard processors, external mic preamps will increase your recording capabilities, and often, the overall quality of your recorded sounds.

◊ **Extras and hardware** A selection of microphone and instrument cables (1/4" and XLR), mic stands and pop filters, and other bits and pieces is always useful for any home studio.

DIGITAL RECORDING SYSTEMS

Computer-based digital recording systems come in two parts:

◊ **The digital audio interface**

◊ **The digital audio workstation (DAW)**

The interface connects analogue instruments and microphones to your computer (Mac or PC), converting their analogue signal to a digital signal that can be stored on the computer. The DAW, on the other hand, is the software package that enables you to handle and manipulate these digital files – a virtual mixing desk, or in many cases an entire virtual studio. The two work hand in hand to capture audio, and to let you reconfigure it into the form you want it to take before you export it to MP3 or burn it to a CD.

While the interface handles the critical job of converting analogue audio signals to digital audio, once you've got it configured (and have set the levels on any of its built-in preamps) it pretty much just sits there. The DAW, on the other hand, connects you to the world of digital recording: not for nothing is its full name "digital audio workstation".

A wide range of both interfaces and DAWs are available at very cheap prices, and many packages bundle the two together. Prominent among these are products such as Digidesign's M-Box range of compact interfaces (which come bundled with Digidesign's popular Pro Tools LE software – a starter version of the Pro Tools that many professional studios use); MOTU's UltraLite and Traveler, which include the company's proprietary Audio Desk software (a starter version of their professional Digital Performer DAW); and PreSonus's FireBox and FireStudio, with the Studio One Artists DAW software. Mac users have also long had access to Apple's popular and extremely simple GarageBand, which comes bundled free with Mac computers, and which is compatible with most interfaces.

Given this boom in the entry level of the digital recording market – the products listed above are just the tip of the iceberg – the most important thing is to know what you should expect from basic systems, and what use they will be to your recording efforts. All of the above units include at least a pair of analogue inputs, and some have as many as eight, in a combination of Mic and Line level inputs. Mic inputs are routed via an interface's built-in mic pres, a component which is essential for bringing the low signal of a microphone up to the level required for a recording.

Line inputs are for signals or instruments that have already been boosted to an adequate level (known industry-wide as "line level") – such as a guitar through a processing unit or DI system, an electronic keyboard with line-level outs, an outboard drum machine or a microphone routed through an external preamp or mixing desk, where it has been boosted to line level before reaching the interface.

Let's take a look at some of the important points to consider when shopping for an interface and a DAW.

The interface

Number of inputs

If you're a singer-songwriter, you might need only two inputs to satisfy your requirements. But if you want to record a full band with live instruments (rather than MIDI, samples or software instruments), you will need more inputs, or you'll have to use an external mixer and group tracks for a stereo mix to the interface, which will compromise your options later.

Mic preamps

The built-in mic pres on many interfaces are pretty good these days, but of inherently limited quality given the space allowed for their components, and the total cost of entry-level interfaces. These pres usually do an adequate job for demo purposes and some other uses in a pinch, but more professional results can often be had from dedicated outboard mic pres.

Bitrate & sample rate

Although most interfaces are capable of recording at a higher quality rate than you are likely to use, these two are factors worth checking. Check the analogue-to-digital conversion rates as well, and make sure the unit has a high enough sample resolution to supply the quality you are hoping to achieve. If your songs will be burned to CD, your files will be compressed down to 16 bits at a sample rate of 44.1kHz anyway, but machines with resolutions of up to 24 bits at 192kHz (with lesser rates selectable) offer the audio equivalent of High Definition TV, letting you capture high-resolution recordings for use with even higher-spec formats in the future.

Conversion quality

The quality of an interface's analogue-to-digital converters will play a big part in determining the sound quality of your final recording, regardless of the bitrate and sample rate used. There's no easy specification that will tell you how good any given unit's converters are, but industry and user reviews in print and online should point you toward the better products in this department.

Connectivity

Contemporary interfaces commonly use either FireWire or USB connections between the unit and your computer. Each has its fans, although your choice mainly needs to correspond with your budget, and what your computer and DAW are capable of working with (some systems, such as MOTU's UltraLite, will work with both). On most applications FireWire is faster, while USB is usually cheaper.

Number of outputs

The FireWire or USB connection of an interface will carry individual outputs for each mic or instrument at an input of the interface, but other analogue outputs might be useful for side-chain or bus connections, which are sometimes used for external effects processing, or external mixes for monitoring.

A typical layout in the popular DAW Logic.

Analogue versus digital

The debate about the overall sound quality of analogue audio as compared to digital audio still rages, with many purists falling on the side of analogue. About fifteen years ago, there was good reason for that. But digital audio has progressed leaps and bounds as regards its resolution capabilities (sound quality). And it's now hard to argue with its convenience.

When digital audio first hit the market in the form of the compact disc (CD), it was billed as being quieter and better sounding than existing vinyl LPs – the first part was often true, but music fans with high-end hi-fi systems quickly discovered that the new digital medium was lacking something that the analogue forms had always offered. Literally. CDs are described as having a bitrate of 16 and a sampling rate of 44.1kHz, specs that are best examined in reverse. The 44.1kHz sample rate tells us that the recording has taken a little snapshot of the audio source – "sampled" it – 44,100 times per second. The 16-bit bitrate tells us the length of each sample, which governs its overall precision and quality. To reproduce sound, a CD player strings together these 44,100 little recordings per second to paint the overall picture of what we hear. And while that might sound like a lot of pieces of data (in other words, a very high resolution), it is still only lots of chunks of a limited size strung together, not continuous audio data. Unlike analogue audio.

Old-school analogue audio, as heard on a vinyl LP or a cassette or reel-to-reel tape, captures and reproduces sound in a physical manner, one which never departs from the realm in which the sound came from, and where it ends up again. In short, many purists found those little bits of the picture that were missing between the 44,100 samples per second led to a colder, flatter sound when compared to analogue reproduction. In describing the sound of analogue recordings, these same purists often use terms such as "warmer", "richer", "deeper" and other cosy-sounding adjectives.

Digital recording has, however, come a long way since the early 1980s, and higher bit and sample rates have improved resolution considerably. Even most basic home studios are now capable of recording at 24 bits and 88.2 or 96kHz (which is dithered down to 16 bits and 44.1kHz for burning to CD), and there have been major improvements in analogue-to-digital converters, too. The main point for most home recordists, however, is that newer digital systems just can't be beaten for ease of use, affordability and overall convenience. This is not to discount some of the sundry glories of analogue audio (and I have always been a big fan of it myself), but the features and flexibility provided by a $500 digital interface/DAW bundle is difficult to match with analogue equipment costing four times that amount. It's also harder and harder to come by these days, too, should you decide to go the old-school route.

In the end, for most musicians who have to pay for, and operate, their own production equipment, the breeze of recording and mixing with plug-ins, linear editing, near-limitless tracks and multiple takes, and all the rest of digital's conveniences just wins the day, hands down.

Features of the DAW

Linear editing

This feature yields far more powerful control of your audio tracks than was ever available in the days of multi-track tape recording. It allows you to visually edit audio tracks with your mouse, to cut-and-paste one part over another or in a different place, graphically edit volume levels and fades, create loops (sections where a given number of bars of a performance repeat for a desired number of measures), and so forth.

Virtual mixing desk

Like a giant, fully functional studio mixing desk compacted onto the size of your computer screen, this lets you use your mouse to control the faders (volume controls), pan, EQ, effects sends and returns, and many other parameters of each individual track you have recorded. Most systems today should provide automated mixing facilities, allowing you to tweak your mix either in real time or in an editing window, and to save different mixes of each composition for different applications.

Virtual instruments

Many DAWs also include several virtual instruments, that let you build drum tracks, bass lines, keyboard parts and more right from the software behind the DAW itself, rather than having to record everything from actual instruments. This is a great facility for guitarists working to build up entire compositions on their own. Some critics feel, however, that certain DAWs that provide a wealth of virtual instruments aren't necessarily the same ones that are best at recording live instruments, so check the reviews before you jump one way or the other.

Control of interface functions

Any DAW that is fully compatible with your interface (and certainly one that was included with it) should be able to control several functions of the interface itself, giving you access to parameters of the interface without lifting your hand from your mouse. They should work together to give you control over record functions, input levels, output levels and a whole lot more, right from your computer screen.

Plug-ins

These are digital effects which can be applied to the sounds in your DAW: they provide very real alterations to the noises and instruments in your tracks. Plug-ins get their name from the fact that they're often third-party products that you plug in to the system you are using – although any decent DAW system provides quite a few of its own. These digital effects and processors manipulate sound much in the way that stand-alone digital effects units do, except of course they exist as software only, with no hardware to contain them. They are applied as inserts in individual channels or master or auxiliary channels in your virtual mixer.

Any self-respecting DAW supplied these days should include at least reverb, delay/echo, compression, limiting, gating, EQ and probably some guitar-dedicated effects, too. More powerful plug-ins can be purchased separately and loaded into most DAWs, provided the systems are compatible, enabling you to expand the roster of virtual processors in your system. (Sometimes virtual instruments, such as all the many software synthesizers out there, are referred to as plug-ins too.)

Compatibility and conversion options

Most newer systems should be compatible with a wide range of sound files – WAV, AIFF and SDII being the most common these days. You'd have to try hard to find a DAW that couldn't convert your final product to one format or the other for sharing with musicians using systems with different preferences.

How do you choose?

Your DAW and interface are the heart of your recording studio, so quality counts. After the instruments you play and the computer that records them, this pair will be your next biggest financial outlay. And that's the key point, really: buy the best system that your budget allows (keeping in mind that you might need to hold back some money for outboard gear like mics and hardware), and it is likely to pay off in the long run.

The same truth that applies to guitar amplifiers and effects units applies equally to the affordable end of DAW interfaces. The systems that seem to carry a plethora of features will inevitably be compromising somewhere when compared to simple but more expensive systems. The extra knobs and effects and options are likely to come at the expense of the basic quality of such units' analogue-to-digital conversion capabilities, or the overall robustness of their build.

Also, some systems are known for being great handlers of MIDI and virtual-instrument audio for totally "in the box" music production, while others excel at recording live audio (that is, real instruments), but are perhaps less adept at handling virtual and MIDI instruments. Once again, it's worth reading both professional and user reviews of any such products, in terms of their quality and functions, and weighing up the verdicts according to what you need from your package.

Additional software

A variety of other software packages can help you expand your recording, mixing and mastering capabilities beyond those of your core system. As mentioned above, there are a variety of plug-ins out there – software-based effects, processors and instruments that can be loaded into your DAW.

The plug-ins available today cover every possible type of sound effect a studio might require, and include many accurate digital emulations of much-loved analogue processors, from Roland's Space Echo tape delay and big Fairchild compressors to Neve's highly respected preamps and limiters. There are plenty of plug-ins that you can download for free, while other plug-ins – some of which are surprisingly expensive – can be had for a trial period (commonly from a week to thirty days) while you decide whether you want to buy them. Some high-end systems, such as those by Universal Audio and TC Electronics, create "powered plug-ins" – software that needs to be coupled with their own hardware-based driver system (in the form of an external box, or a card to install in your computer) – which makes them both more expensive and more powerful.

A number of powerful plug-ins known as mastering suites are also available. These are used not for recording or mixing, but for the last, crucial part of the process: mastering your own final mixes – and tend to be expensive. Mastering is the stage that recorded music goes through after all the parts have been recorded and mixed into a single stereo file. It's when you make the tweaks of overall EQ, compression and limiting.

Sometimes various other processors that give a finished product a little extra sparkle and punch are used. In short, mastering is the process of making a track the best it can be for pressing to CD, broadcast on the radio or hosted online. We'll come back to mastering again later, but suffice to say, for now, mastering plug-ins are probably not something you'll need to invest time or money in until you've properly got to grips with recording and mixing your tracks.

THE HARDWARE

If you're recording live music – and that's what we're here for, after all, given that this is a book about playing the guitar – you will need a bit more equipment than just a DAW and interface to get the sounds outside the box into the box. You can make perfectly good recordings with just the bare minimum, but gradually building up a small selection of specific pieces of gear will enable you to capture more flavours, and will always be useful to help you out of a creative rut.

Microphones

Unless you're just making very, very rough demos you'll need something more than the built-in mic that's in your laptop, desktop or portable digital recorder. (Though those mics are very handy for jotting down quick ideas for songs.) The DAW/interface packages discussed above all require the use of external microphones.

There are several different types of mic, and they excel at different uses. A quality mic used to be an expensive proposition, and even decent basic dynamic microphones – the kind you usually see an artist singing into at a live show – cost easily $100 (or £100) or more. These days, however, a wave of affordable Asian imports that emulate the performance of more expensive mics, only with cheaper parts (and probably lower labour costs) has opened the field for novice recordists to sample a much wider range of microphone flavours.

There are three basic types of mics that you're likely to encounter: dynamic, condenser (aka capacitor) and ribbon. Each is constructed quite differently, and while there is some crossover in their applications, each tends to excel at different aspects of recording.

The dynamic mic can take a lot of punishment – far more than a condenser or ribbon. That's handy to know when you're the lead singer of Gallows.

Dynamic mics

We usually see these atop microphone stands with a singer behind them. They are the most robust of the three types, and can usually take high sound pressure levels (SPLs), so they are popular for live sound reproduction, where they're used for everything from vocals and guitar amps, to miking drums. The most famous dynamic mics are probably the Shure SM58 (a vocal mic) and SM57 (an instrument mic), but many, many others exist. Dynamic mics are passive, meaning they need no power supply to operate.

Essentially, they work like a speaker but in reverse. They incorporate a suspended diaphragm and a coil of wire within a magnetic field; when sound waves cause the diaphragm to move, the coil's corresponding movement within that magnetic field creates an electronic signal, which is transmitted down the mic cable to the PA mixer or recording unit. Dynamic mics excel at close-miking of guitar amplifiers, and are adequate for any applications producing lower SPLs, although they often don't have quite the sensitivity or fidelity of other mics when used for subtler sound sources such as vocals, acoustic guitars, acoustic pianos and so forth.

Condenser mics

These are better known as the larger units seen more often in photos of artists in the studio (although some very small condensers do exist, too), or occasionally on the desks of talk-show hosts. They are also sometimes seen miking guitar amps or drums at larger professional concerts.

Condensers require a power source to function, most commonly applied in the form of "phantom power" from a mixer or preamp, although sometimes by an external power supply or internal battery. The condenser mic is similar to the dynamic in that it also uses a diaphragm that is moved by sound waves, but all similarities end there. In the condenser, the diaphragm is mounted close to a back plate, and the changing distance between these components (both of which are electrically charged) creates the signal that carries the sound. Better condenser mics are extremely sensitive, and they tend to produce a more detailed, high-fidelity sound than the average dynamic mic.

Their sensitivity means that they can often overload and distort when faced with sound sources producing high SPLs, so they are more often placed further back from loud voices or instruments than dynamic mics, although some are constructed to be used close in, or can be partnered with "pads" that reduce the signal from the mic to the mixer or preamp, to help prevent distortion. Condensers are the first choice of many engineers for vocals, acoustic guitars, drum overheads (where they capture the shimmer of cymbals particularly well), acoustic pianos and other applications where a lot of sensitivity and added detail and sparkle is desired.

Some of the most famous condenser mics are made by Neumann and AKG, and the better of these can cost well into the four (and even five) figures – although much more affordable imported condensers costing in the low two and three figures now bring some of this breed's performance to the basic home studio.

Ribbon mics

These are related to dynamic mics, and were the popular high-end option even before better condenser mics became available. Having almost dropped from the scene several years back – as far as most home and project studios were concerned, at least – ribbon mics have made a major comeback in recent years. As the name implies, ribbon mics function by means of a very thin metallic ribbon (in the range of 0.001") that is suspended between the poles of a magnet. When a sound source causes that thin ribbon to move, its movement within the magnetic field produces a signal. Ribbons are also passive, but the accidental application of phantom power can fatally damage many types of ribbon mic (although there are a few newer makes that can use phantom power to bump up their signal strength and sensitivity).

Ribbons are inherently more sensitive than standard dynamic mics, but they require a lot of clean gain from a mixer or mic preamp to bring their signals up to acceptable levels. So they can be trickier to use on some subtle sound sources where condenser mics traditionally excel. The sensitivity of that thin ribbon also means that these mics have to be used very carefully, and many types can't be placed close to loud sources such as kick drums, high-wattage guitar amps or loud singers without risk of blowing their ribbons. (Again, there are others made specifically to handle

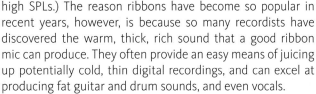

The Coles 4038 ribbon mic: "dark" sounding but an absolute classic, and used on albums by both The Beatles and Pink Floyd.

high SPLs.) The reason ribbons have become so popular in recent years, however, is because so many recordists have discovered the warm, thick, rich sound that a good ribbon mic can produce. They often provide an easy means of juicing up potentially cold, thin digital recordings, and can excel at producing fat guitar and drum sounds, and even vocals.

Highly desirable vintage ribbon mics include those made by RCA, Coles/STC and Beyerdynamic, and like the better US and European-made condensers these can be expensive propositions for the home studio. Also, like the newer Asian-made condensers, recent imported offerings have brought the ribbon mic to the entry-level project studio and considerably broadened your miking options.

Equipping your mic cupboard

So many options, so little cash. What should your priority in microphone acquisition be? The answer really depends on what you want to do with it. If you can only afford one decent microphone to begin with, and will need to mic any loud sound sources, a good dynamic mic is often a sensible first purchase purchase.

Countless singer-songwriters have made great recordings of voice and acoustic guitar on a single Shure SM58, too – you can use a mic like this to do just about anything, even applications that aren't quite its traditional rock band forte.

If you are only doing acoustic guitar and vocals, however, an affordable condenser mic will give you more detailed results. It will capture a bigger, more high-fidelity soundscape than most affordable dynamics, while having the benefit – thanks to its increased sensitivity – of allowing you to use it at a further distance from the guitar or the singer, without producing such noticeable shifts in signal strength or sound if you move slightly during performance.

The current hipness, and affordability, of ribbon mics makes one of these a tempting first purchase, too, but you'll need a very quiet mic preamp with a lot of gain on it to successfully record subtler sound sources (like acoustic guitar or vocals) with most ribbon mics. They require careful handling and some technical know-how, too; they're not an obvious first mic.

If you have covered your expenses for a good interface and DAW and have something in the region of $300 to $500 (£250 to £400) remaining for microphones, you can put together quite a useful little selection of these beasties. If you're likely to be recording a range of sound sources – both acoustic and electric guitars, vocals, drums and occasionally a few other things – one decent entry-level example of each of these mic types will get you started.

Working a pair of either condensers or ribbons into the mix will give you the added bonus of stereo miking for drums and acoustic guitars in particular, while a pair of dynamic mics instead will allow you to close-mike both the kick and snare of a drum set, if you plan on recording live drums. Searching a range of online outlets in the US at the time of writing, I'm able to find:

◊ Shure SM57 or Blue enCORE 100 dynamic for $99 (for close-miking guitar amps, and kick or snare drum).

◊ A pair of Nady CM90 or CAD CM217 small-diaphragm "pencil" condenser mics for $50 each (for stereo drum overheads or acoustic guitar).

◊ An MXL 992 or Audio-Technica AT2020 large diaphragm condenser mic for $99 (for vocals, mono drum overheads or front-of-kit, acoustic guitar, guitar amp at a distance or general room miking).

◊ A Nady RSM-5 or MXL 990 ribbon mic for $79-$99 (for guitar-amp miking, drum overhead or front-of-kit, or retro-sounding vocals).

These are just examples, and plenty of other makes and models are available at similar prices. Even with this much to spend, you're unlikely to get your hands on enough suitable mics to make your best possible recording of an entire band all at once. But you could mike up the drums well and DI some scratch (rough) guitar, vocal and bass takes, before overdubbing better takes afterwards by repositioning your best mics as desired.

With three or four decent mics placed correctly, you can at least get a representative, rough-and-ready and slightly lo-fi sounding recording of an entire band in the room, and possibly – with a little extra care – produce something that sounds surprisingly good. As with everything in the home studio, though, it's important to remain aware of the necessity for compromise, and unless you can afford a limitless supply of mics, this is one area where you have to make some choices early in the recording process.

Microphone preamps

Most budget interfaces have one or two inputs that accept microphones directly, with XLR sockets and built-in preamps to boost the mic's signal. If you want to either improve on the quality of these, or add other mics to your recording array to simultaneously track more instruments (or mic positions) than the one or two mic inputs your machine offers, you will need to use an external mic pre. These units increase the gain of a signal to a line level that can be handled by a standard 1/4" line input, and, in addition to a basic gain (level, volume) control, sometimes offer features such as phantom power for condenser mics, some EQ and occasionally frequency shelving and padding, too.

Basic mic pres costing well under $100 will at least broaden your options and allow you to work with multi-mic set-ups, although they won't usually offer much of an increase in sound quality over built-in mic channels supplied with an affordable interface. (In fact, they may even end up introducing a bit of low-level hiss to your signal.) Also, while tubes and valves remain hot buzz words in tone circles, any such glowing bottles included in units at these low prices are likely to be there for show more than for legitimate reasons of sound reproduction. Such units might sound just fine for your purposes, but don't necessarily be swayed by the inclusion of a tube/valve, when comparing products with and without.

Spending upwards of $250 to $300 or more on a single or dual-channel mic pre is likely to attain results that are somewhat superior to those of a built-in mic input, while pushing your budget up into four digits can find you approaching professional-grade preamps (which, make no mistake, can also sell for many thousands). While this might sound like a lot of money for a device that just makes your microphone louder, a mic pre is an important link in any signal chain, and should at least be of a comparable quality to your instruments, amps, microphones and recording devices, otherwise it might be letting you down.

External effects & processors

The proliferation of excellent-sounding plug-ins means that many home recordists today are able to work entirely "inside the box" once the live sound has been captured – recording mic or instrument signals via an interface (and perhaps an outboard preamp for improved quality), but achieving all dynamics and effects processing from computer software programs running within the DAW. Some, however, still make use of the sounds and features of external processors. While these are a long way from being essential these days with a digital package with plenty of good effects bundles included, they do broaden your options.

For instance, software programs related to dynamics – such as compressors or limiters – can be extremely powerful and easy to use, but plenty of musicians still like to record certain instruments with a little outboard compression in the chain, even if they're likely to apply even more compression, via a plug-in, during mixing. Recording your live electric guitar, bass or drum tracks through some outboard compression (which would be placed after the mic pre, or in an insert – a loop – from the interface) can sometimes help to fatten up the sounds of these instruments, and to give the final results a more glued together feel. Musicians enamoured of old-school analogue delay, chorus or reverb effects, or even good sounding digital rack units, might also access these while mixing via sends from the interface, bringing out-of-the-box sounds back into the box to be part of the final picture. (Your individual interface and DAW should explain whether this can be done, and how.)

Taking a signal back out of the box in this way, and thereby converting it from digital to analogue and back to digital again, via lengths of patch cable, can introduce a little unwanted noise to the track, but often this – if less than extreme – isn't noticed much within the context of an entire mix. In any case, tapping into a lush tone that you wouldn't otherwise be able to access might make it all worthwhile. There are certainly advantages to staying inside the box, however, in that you will maintain higher fidelity and a lower noise floor by keeping your digital tracks digital. Often the plug-in processing available to you these days is so powerful and versatile that there are few sounds that can't be replicated. Unless, of course, you're fortunate enough to have access to some extremely precious and esoteric analogue equipment.

Monitor speakers & headphones

If you're recording music, you will need something to hear it played back on, too. Plenty of home recordists make do with a decent pair of headphones, which can be plugged straight into most interfaces or computers without need of further preamp. You'll most likely need headphones for monitoring your performance while tracking (recording tracks), too, or for following backing tracks while recording overdubs. Useable headphones can be found on a pretty tight budget these days, but better quality comes at a price.

Either way, for use in the studio you will want enclosed headphones with some padding that totally encircles the ear, keeping sound in as well as out. In addition to hearing what you're playing, you don't want the sound of backing tracks in the headphones to bleed into any mics positioned to capture the overdubs you're recording (vocals are a particular culprit for bleed, since your headphones will be relatively close to a sensitive mic).

If you want to go further than making basic recordings for home use and the occasional rough demo, you will need a pair of monitor speakers of passable quality. The sound of a mix in the headphones and from a pair of speakers can be very different, and it's often hard to get an accurate balance of certain frequencies – lows in particular – when mixing purely in the cans (headphones). If you have a decent home hi-fi system, you can connect your interface or computer audio output

There are a number of affordable monitoring systems for mixing in your home studio: the Adam A5 (above) or the Yamaha NS10s (opposite) are two good choices.

to that and use it for monitoring, but most lower to mid-level home stereo set-ups aren't optimized for studio monitoring: this can only ever be a workaround to get you started.

The easiest solution available today for home studio monitoring lies in powered monitors, which have amplifiers built right into the speaker cabinets. These eliminate the need for a separate power amplifier (though they will need to be plugged into a power socket). They can be connected directly to your interface or computer audio output, and their volume controlled from the DAW, the interface or your computer.

Monitor speakers are an arena where you really do get what you pay for. Although you can buy a functional pair of powered, compact monitors for as little as $150 a pair, you can't expect pro-studio-quality results from them. You want a flat response from your monitors – as accurate and neutral a sound as possible, with no hyped (heightened) bass or treble, to give your songs the best chance of sounding good on any system. If at all possible, it's worth budgeting both for a set of enclosed headphones, and for as good a pair of monitor speakers as you can reasonably afford.

Bits & pieces

When working out a budget to equip a home recording studio it's easy to forget some of the essential bits and pieces. You need several of these less glamorous items in order to function, and the cost of them can add up to the price of a good microphone. That said, quality hardware will make your life easier, and all of these things can last a long time if you take care of them.

Mic cables

If you have invested in a decent recording system, it's worth getting quality mic cables to use with it. You'll want one good cable for each mic you own, plus a spare for the time when one of these shorts out in the middle of an important session. Make sure they are all long enough to reach any corner of your recording space that you might want to put a mic in, but no longer than you think necessary, either.

Mic stands and clips

Sure, you can make do by gaffer-taping mics to coat stands and guitar stands for a while, but eventually it just gets frustrating. Ideally, you'll want a decent quality boom stand and clip (if one hasn't been provided) for each microphone you own, and it's also generally useful to have a shorter desktop stand or two – they save space and don't get in the way when miking amp cabs and kick drums.

Pop shield (pop screen)

The old standby of a pair of tights wrapped around a wire coat-hanger bent into a circle and taped to the mic stand might do at a stretch, but a good, factory-made pop shield – which goes in front of a vocal mic to reduce the effect of plosives (hard "P"s) and breath sounds – should be both more sonically transparent, and more effective. Besides, your singer might not relish the idea of having their mouth quite so close to someone's cast-off undergarment.

Sound-absorbing foam

Although you should buy the best pair of studio monitors you can afford, you should remember that even the best monitors in the world won't sound accurate if they're in an untreated box-shaped room with symmetrical walls. The low-end, mid-range and top-end frequencies will be skewed. Proper acoustic foam (also known as acoustic treatment) for studio use is the answer. It can be surprisingly expensive, but just a few squares and a corner baffle or two will help to deaden reflections from large bare walls and unfriendly corners (where low frequencies can be unduly amplified or distorted), and thus make your room more acoustically neutral. This in turn will mean you can hear your recordings more accurately, and as a result, produce better mixes.

If you can't afford tailor-made acoustic foam, such as that made by Auralex, you can usually make do with sheets of more bog-standard packing foam or foam carpet underlay. It may not be designed to offer the same absorption properties as proper studio foam, but will nonetheless help to deaden walls and corners somewhat.

External hard drive

High-resolution recording is hungry stuff, and it eats up a lot of computer memory. If you're going to get into a lot of home recording, you will probably want to invest in an external hard drive with several tens of gigabytes worth of storage area to which you can offload (or at the very least, back up) your files.

FireWire drives tend to be preferred by many for their speed and efficiency, but a good USB drive should also do the trick, if this works better with your system. The good news is that these are getting more affordable all the time, and you'll feel much more secure having that extra storage space once you start nailing down recordings that you're proud of, and want to keep secure.

HOME-STUDIO LAYOUT

The layout of your home studio is likely to be dictated by the space and equipment available to you, rather than the space and equipment you'd ideally like to have. But a few tips can help you get the most out of what you've got. There really should be two main goals to laying out your studio space: organizing the equipment logically, so it's in the right place when you need it, and creating a listening environment that's as neutral as possible, so what you think you are hearing is close to what you are actually recording and mixing. The second of these is the most important, and if you are tracking (recording) parts in the same room that you'll be mixing in – as most of us in home studios are – this will affect your perception of the sounds you're recording and the sounds you are mixing.

The central point of most home studios is the workstation (a physical workstation, in this instance, rather than the virtual workstation of the DAW), which usually means a desk. If your recording system is computer-based and you mix in the box, using your DAW, that computer should take centre stage.

If you're using another form of digital (or even analogue) recording system, the mixer attached to that unit should be fairly central. From here, you obviously want to place other equipment within reach, ranked by frequency of use of any piece of gear or instrument. If you've got rack-mounted outboard equipment that you use a lot in tracking, have that under either side of the desk (if it's big enough), or to your immediate left or right. If you have a stand-alone mic pre or compressor that you also turn to frequently, stack those within arm's reach on either side of the desk. If you're recording a lot of singer-songwriter material, or demoing your songs in rough takes, you'll probably want to have a desktop mic stand handy, too, and to have your guitar on a stand within easy reach of your control position.

The most important placement consideration of all, though, involves where you put the monitors – and to that end, where you put the desk itself. Inevitably, given the space most of us have to work with, your workstation will be up against a wall, but ideally you don't want your monitors backed up right against that wall themselves, or placed in corners either. Close proximity to walls and corners will accentuate (or at very least distort) your perception of low frequencies in particular, and make it difficult to get the right amount of bass in your mixes, and in your recorded sounds in general.

The problem here is mainly that you won't know you're not hearing the troublesome frequencies accurately: if, for example, your room is accentuating bass through unwanted reflections, you'll mix your bass (and other low frequencies) down so it doesn't sound overwhelming in your room. When you burn this mix to play on another system, in a different room, you'll experience a sudden "where'd my bass go?" sensation. This sort of inaccuracy is what you're trying to avoid.

If possible, set up your workstation so your monitor speakers are slightly out from the wall at least, and space them at equal heights and equally left and right of you – ideally getting them about as far apart from each other as you are from them, like a triangle with sides of equal length. Raise them to a position where the tweeters are aimed approximately at your own ears while

John Lennon during the recording of *Imagine*, at his "home studio", built in his mansion at Tittenhurst.

you are seated in your control/mixing position, angle them in toward the listener slightly, and listen to several commercial recordings that you're familiar with – adjusting monitor positions as required – until you feel you're hearing a good balance of lows and highs and an accurate stereo spectrum. You're not likely to perfect this: professional studios spend thousands of dollars on acoustic analysis and design of their control room, and still occasionally end up with less-than-ideal results. But if you can get something that's close to neutral, you're doing pretty well.

To increase your chances of avoiding any unwanted frequencies in your studio room, you will most likely need to make use of some of that acoustic foam. A few strategically placed squares of foam on the wall in front of your working position (in other words, behind the monitors) should help to absorb some unwanted reflections from those positions. Larger, wedge-shaped corner traps in all unadorned corners will help further, and some treatment behind and to the side of you will assist the quest, too. Most of us won't be paying an acoustical consultant to analyse our rooms, so such treatment will necessarily be rather hit-and-miss. But a judicial use of some sound-deadening material should at least improve the situation.

Be aware that this studio foam does nothing to soundproof a room; it only helps to cut down on unwanted reflections and, therefore, to minimize problematic frequencies. True soundproofing requires multiple layers for walls, doors and windows, and a lot of extra effort and expense – it's beyond the scope of any basic home studio. If you can't spring for proper studio treatments, thick blankets and curtains can help absorb some sound at least. If you've got a spare mattress in the guest room that has become your home studio, prop it up against a wall or in a corner where you feel you might be experiencing pesky reflections, or hang a quilt over a large window or a bare wall. Use your imagination, and a little creative dampening can usually at least improve matters in a less-than-ideal recording environment.

RECORDING TECHNIQUES

Advances in the quality and affordability of digital recording systems have led to a strange situation. There are thousands of musicians out there who are labouring away at "better than CD quality" recordings – as promised by the specs of these DAWs and interfaces – while consistently failing to achieve anything that sounds remotely like the pro recordings they admire.

It's no easy task to get an entirely convincing big-studio sound in a home studio equipped on a tight budget, but you can get satisfying, usable results at the very least – and ones that are fine for broadcast and distribution. And a fantastic studio full of great gear can't make up for a lack of technique: it's in the application of recording technique that so many home recordists fall down. We've covered the gear end, so let's look at the skills that will help you get your sounds into those boxes, and end up with the most professional results possible.

MICROPHONES: WHERE TO PUT THEM & WHY

The use and placement of microphones – mic technique – remains the cornerstone skill of the recording engineer. Capturing the best possible sound in the first place makes the rest of the job easier – often eliminating, or at least minimizing, any need for excessive EQ or dynamics treatment further down the road. The lack of good mic usage can't ever entirely be made up for in the mix, or with any kind of plug-in or hardware gizmo.

Plenty of sounds are recorded direct into the mixer, preamp or interface these days. But the best, most natural sounds of many instruments are still achieved using microphones, and the majority of professional guitarists you admire still mike up their amps and acoustic guitars. To that end, we'll cover several standard and more creative techniques for miking all kinds of guitars, offering a sonic palette that should give you a solution for just about any recording situation.

Miking guitar amps

It doesn't get much more basic than putting the right mic in the right place, and while this might seem a simple and obvious process it really is an art in itself, one which can often separate the men from the boys even among professional recording engineers. That said, the rule of law in mic placement is that there are no rules – what sounds best, works. The real trick is in taking the time to find the placement that really does sound best, and not just sticking the mic randomly in front of the speaker and hitting Record. Great guitar recordings have been made with one, two, three and even more microphones, but let's start with some ways of finding the correct positioning for a single-mic recording.

The type of microphone you use will partially determine where you place it. Here we'll discuss three basic mic types: dynamic, ribbon and condenser. Rugged (and relatively affordable) dynamic mics like the classic Shure SM57 or Beyer M201 are typically used for close miking, which – just as it sounds – means you put them very close to a guitar amp's speaker: as close to the grille cloth as you can get without touching. Ribbon microphones are both very delicate (other than a few designs that are able to withstand high sound pressure levels) and mostly pretty expensive, and most of them sound best and are most safely used at a distance of a foot or so away from the speaker.

Condenser mics, which have become much more affordable in recent years, are very sensitive and are generally used at even further distances, or as a second mic to blend in some ambient sound with that of a close mic. Many condensers can handle the SPLs produced by close miking, but will distort too easily up close and give you a harsh, crackly sound.

You'd think close miking with, for example, a Shure SM57 would be the most straightforward process of all, but changes in position of even half an inch to the left or right, and up or down across the cone of the speaker, will produce noticeably different tones. Many home recordists routinely place a dynamic mic right in front of the centre of the speaker cone and start playing, but in many instances this captures the harshest sound from the speaker. Moving the mic to the edge of the speaker cone often yields a warmer, edgier sound, and you will hear something a little different from just about every position in between. Even turning the mic at a slight angle to the front of the speaker cabinet picks up a slightly different tone. Switch your recording system to "input monitor", and listen – ideally from a different room – to the sound produced through the monitors or a good set of headphones when you move the mic around to a number of different positions. To do this right, you will need a friend or band member to move the mic while you listen and play, or, if you're working alone, record a little of the same playing passage with the mic in different places, note which is which, and select the one that sounds best on playback. Pick the sound that works best for you... but don't stop there. Listen to how that sound works in the mix with the tune you're recording. All too often the best solo guitar sound doesn't prove the most effective – the punchiest, most powerful or most attention grabbing – when you hear it with the rest of the band.

Condenser mics can be placed following a similar process, but because you start by extending your miking distance at least a couple feet from the amp (unless you're recording a very small amp, or one set to extremely low volumes) that means you've got a much bigger field to play with. One great technique for placing a condenser mic to record a guitar amp was told to me a few years ago by John Paul Jones himself (not only the bassist for Led Zeppelin, but an outstanding engineer and producer in his own right). It's simple enough: use your own ear like a mic, and stick the mic at the position in the room where the guitar tone sounds the best to you. This is ideally done with another person playing the guitar. Cover one ear, and walk around the room listening to the sound in different positions. When you hear a sound that really nails what you're trying to capture, set up the mic right there. Done.

Ribbon microphones, which are becoming more and more popular these days (and, in some cases, more affordable), are often placed by combining these two techniques. Certain models, such as high-end designs by Royer and more affordable designs by Nady and CAD, can take high SPLs. Others, such as classics like the Coles 4038 or an old RCA 44, might go "poof" in front of a raging 50-watter. In most cases, ribbons will sound best at least a few inches back from the speaker anyway, and sometimes will capture the most lifelike sound two or three feet away. Many ribbon mics also exhibit something known as "proximity effect", which increases their low-end response incrementally – thus making them sound boomier – the closer you get them to the sound source. Again, experiment with positioning, and be sure to check what works in the track.

Frequently a single mic will capture all the amp tone you need. Using a single mic also has the benefit of minimizing phase cancellation issues, although it won't necessarily eliminate them entirely. Phase cancellation can hamper an amp tone when signals from two different mics cancel some frequencies or create unpleasant dissonances, which are caused by the "out of phase" relationship of sound from two different positions (see box overleaf for some tips on dealing

Phased and confused

When using two mics on a single amp you will almost always encounter some phase cancellation issues; whether they are bad enough to cause a problem, or even to be heard, depends on the situation. First, ensure it isn't an entirely reverse-phase mix by flipping the phase of one of the two channels and listening again (many DAWs include "reverse phase" channel functions, occasionally found on a "trim" plug-in, that you can use right on your virtual mixer). If your two-mic sound goes from hollow and bottomless sounding to fat and full, you have isolated a reverse-phase issue. Once you know that both mics are at least in phase with each other, you can try moving around the position of one until the phasing issues are less obtrusive, which is simply determined by finding a pair of positions that are really smoking, tone-wise. Alternatively, you can often fix phase issues in the digital realm. Record your two-mic signal on two separate tracks, then zoom in on the sound waves (soundbites) in each of the two channels in your DAW's editing window, and drag or nudge the soundbite of the ambient mic forward a few milliseconds at a time until the soundwaves line up perfectly. Listen again, and you should hear a very different blend. Phase issues can also be fixed by some phase-alignment tools available as plug-ins, such as UAD's

You can even experience phase cancellation issues with one mic, which are usually caused when a lot of reflected sound – sound waves bounced off a hard surface in the room – is picked up by the mic simultaneous with the direct sound. Sometimes reflected sound contributes to a great recorded sound, providing air, depth and ambience. Other times, however, the time delay of its reflection creates detrimental phase issues. To minimize detrimental reflected sound, observe any hard, reflective surfaces in your recording space such as wooden floors or hard walls, large uncovered glass windows and so forth, and dampen them down with some acoustic foam or even, temporarily, a heavy blanket. Listen again, and tweak accordingly.

with these issues). With that caveat, the perfect guitar sound for your track will sometimes be best captured by using two microphones in different positions around the room. Here are some advanced techniques to try out.

Close & room (ambient) miking

Far and away the most common form of multi-mic placements, this is intended to simultaneously capture the punchy, in-your-face sound of a close mic positioned an inch or less from the speaker cloth and the airy, spacious, slightly reverberant sound of the amp in the room. The room mic is the "ambient" mic, and is usually a condenser, while the close mic is usually a dynamic mic, but you can try whatever works for you. Ribbon mics can work well in either or both positions too, provided you have one that takes high SPLs and has minimal proximity effect for close miking.

As a starting point, try placing the dynamic mic slightly off-centre on the speaker, about half an inch away, and the ambient mic six feet back, and six feet off the ground. Move them around. You'll find the distant mic will have a lot of options, and you might move it further, or closer, up or down – and tweak the mix accordingly. You can either mix down the two mic signals to one signal that you send into your interface, or record each on an individual track to process and mix later, if you have enough available channels in the system. For the best possible blend of a close/ambient mic pair, try getting the best individual sound from each first, as explained above, then putting the two together.

Multi-miking

To capture two speakers in a multi-speaker cab, or to record a bigger sound that delivers the response of two different mics in similar positions on one speaker, you can try using two mics in a close or semi-close placement. If you're using two different mics on a single speaker, place the receiving end of each (known as the capsule) as close together as possible, without touching, in order to minimize phase cancellation. This technique might seem redundant, but can often yield outstanding results, allowing you to blend the characteristics of two different microphones to capture one amp sound, a bright, detailed condenser and a punchy, mid-range-heavy dynamic, for example.

On guitar cabs carrying two or more different speakers, try miking each speaker separately, placing each of two mics – of the same type, or different – at the same distance away. Some amp makers use two different types of speakers in 2x12 cabs to fatten up the tone, and this miking technique will make the most of those. Even two different speakers of exactly the same type, however, will often sound slightly different, and blending them might yield great results, giving you more of the "big-cab sound" that the amp produces live.

Front-and-back miking

Interesting sounds can often be captured by miking the back of an open-backed speaker cab, too. You can use your single-mic techniques on the back of the cab by placing the mic close to, or even into, the opening in the back of a combo or extension cab. The back-of-cab sound is usually a little more raw, fat and warm than the front-of-cab sound. Or use two mics to close-mike the front of the cab and the back of the cab. Be aware that you will need to reverse the phase of one channel when using this technique, since the sound produced by the back of any speaker is always 180 degrees out of phase with the sound produced by the front of the speaker.

However hard you try, and however elaborate your multi-mic set-up, a two-mic set-up just might not sound as good as one mic on its own. This might be curable with some attention to phase cancellation issues, but it might just be the way the sound is working for you that day. In that case, there's no shame in going with the one-mic sound. Do whatever sounds best in the track. There are no fixed rules here, other than the sin of not experimenting at all. Play around with your mic placement, have fun with it, and you'll discover some powerful new recording techniques all on your own. You may even stumble upon some clever mic set-ups that work great for you time and time again.

Miking acoustic guitars

Condenser mics have traditionally been the most popular mics for recording acoustics because of their sensitivity and broad frequency range, which usually includes more prominent and shimmery highs than the other two types of mics we have discussed, something many artists like to hear in their acoustic sound.

Thankfully, decent condensers are a lot more affordable than they were just a few years ago. The renewed popularity of some ribbon mics has led many recordists to use them on acoustics, too, the Beyerdynamic M160 being a perennial favourite for guitars and other stringed instruments too. Standard dynamic mics such as the seminal Shure SM57 and SM58 and mics based on those formats tend to be less flattering than condensers, but if that's all you've got handy you can still get perfectly good results from them with careful use. In some cases, when you want to capture a thumping, mid-rangey rhythm part without intrusive highs that might get in the way of cymbals or other instruments, a dynamic might be your best bet anyway. Whichever type you have available to you for recording acoustics, keep the following basic pointers in mind.

As with miking guitar amps, the best way to find the right place to put your acoustic guitar mic is to listen to the sound your guitar produces from a number of different "ear positions", record a little of it with a mic placed there, and listen back. One important tip at this point, however, and perhaps

Recording bass

This is the *Rough Guide to Guitar* of course. But if this recording lark starts to really appeal to you, you'll want to record the rest of your band, and bass is one that is handled a little differently than six-string guitar. While relatively few notable guitar tones on classic records have been achieved with DI'd ("direct injection" –see p.267) electric guitars, bass guitars are DI'd far more frequently. Since the bass's role is often to provide a solid, full, low end, the same degree of amp tone (which is to say, distortion) just isn't required. DI'ing a pure bass signal straight in preserves the full frequency range of the instrument to boot. As such, great bass tones often don't even require the effects processors and/or amp simulators that help home recordists capture more realistic guitar tones. A simple old passive DI box straight into a mic/instrument input (with preamp) on your digital interface will often do the trick, and applying a little compression on the way, or as a plug-in afterward in the DAW, is usually icing on the cake.

That said, miking a bass amp the good old-fashioned way can still yield very satisfying results, especially if you're going for a more raw sound in the final mix. If your mic cupboard is limited, a basic, sturdy dynamic mic such as a Shure SM57 or a Beyer M201 will do a decent enough job at close-miking a bass amp, the technique you most often want to use. But several bass-specific mics are available, and most excel both at capturing the low frequencies from bass guitars as well as from kick drums, so you can usually get dual-purpose use out of these, provided you're not trying to track both instruments simultaneously. Classics of the type are the AKG D112 and Shure Beta 52, while going up-market takes you to the Electrovoice RE20, and down-market options include the affordable CAD KBM412 or Nady DM-90 and others of their ilk.

Unless you're going for a real punk or grunge tone, you probably want to retain some tightness in your bass amp sound, because you can't get back any low-end thump and definition that you lose at this stage. For the same reason, it is usually simplest and most effective to close-mike a bass amp, too, to avoid any washed-out room sounds or overtones that might deplete the weight of the track. Alternatively, if you have enough inputs and/or channels available, use a parallel-path method as described above for recording guitars: split one pure bass guitar signal into one input, and send the other to an amp that you mic up. When doing this, you don't necessarily even have to use a bass amp, and it's less important to keep the amp path clean and full. You can mike up a smaller guitar amp that's cranked up to get some hair (provided its speaker will handle the low frequencies produced by the bass guitar without suffering any damage), and blend in the DI'd signal to tighten up the final result.

the most important thing to get down from the start, is that you should not place the microphone pointing straight into the soundhole. Do this, and you capture a woofy, muddy, booming sound that is pretty loud, certainly, but not really representative of your full acoustic guitar tone in any other way. For beginning recordists this can take some getting used to, because of course whenever you take your guitar out to an un-amped acoustic gig the sound engineer points an SM57 right into the soundhole. Even in live performance this doesn't capture the most flattering acoustic tone, but it does tend to capture the most volume from an acoustic in a live situation, and that's a compromise that we are often willing to live with in a small club or coffeehouse gig.

To record an acoustic guitar well, however, it's important to understand that its sound isn't produced from the soundhole alone, and in fact that is really just the point where sound reflected from the underside of the top and the inside of the back of the guitar escapes the guitar's body. A lot of the more flattering tone of any acoustic guitar is produced in the area around the bridge and the broad portions of the lower-bout section of the top, while other frequencies are produced in the region of the upper bout where the fingerboard joins the body. The sound coming off the back of the guitar has its own tone, too. Usually you will want to use a technique that captures a blend of a few or all of these sounds.

One of the most popular traditional studio techniques for recording mono acoustic guitar involves placing a microphone at around the 12th fret, a few inches away from the fingerboard, and aimed back toward the end of the fingerboard (at the body end), but not into the soundhole. This captures a bright, lively acoustic tone with a good, rounded body and some crispy string tone for added jangle.

Another position that captures a full, woody and somewhat less jangly tone is found by pointing a mic at the guitar's top in the region of the lower bout just below and behind the bridge. Moving the mic further down and away from the lower end of the guitar and aiming it at the edge of the body, where the top meets the side of the guitar, can produce another interesting tone, one which is usually heard as being a little more edgy, hard and cutting.

As with recording guitar amps, you can often achieve a broader, more multi-dimensional sound from an acoustic by carefully positioning more than one microphone. Be aware, however, that two mics are not always better than one: in some cases you might want the straightforward, less harmonically saturated (less frequency-range dominating, if you will) sound of just a single microphone, when you want to have a driving acoustic rhythm guitar part in a busy mix where other sounds are more prominent, for example. With that in mind, if you want to coax the richest, deepest, most in-the-room acoustic guitar sounds onto your recording, you will often turn to two mics to do it. Here are some techniques to try out:

Spaced stereo pair

This sounds pretty obvious, but there are some pretty huge variables depending upon what tones your acoustic guitar generates from different vantage points, sonically speaking, just as with the single-mic techniques discussed above. For this technique you use two of the same mics (or at least very similar, if that's all you've got) positioned about a foot back from the guitar, and three feet apart. Placing them in this three-to-one relationship, i.e. three times as far from each other as they are from the sound source, helps to minimize phase cancellation between the mics. This technique can yield a broad and fairly realistic stereo image, although it can sometimes result in the feeling of there being a "hole" in the middle of the sonic picture, depending how wide you pan them in the mix. Our next technique tries to eliminate that.

XY pair

Also called "coincident pair", this technique involves placing two identical microphones – usually cardioid mics – with their capsules (their sound-receiving ends) as close together as possible without touching, but at right angles, so that the mic on the left is aiming across toward the right of the sound source, and the right microphone is aiming toward the left side of the sound source. As such, the mics are positioned in a "Y" pattern (with the base of the "Y" pointing toward the sound source), and capture a sound source that crosses over to them in an "X" pattern. This might seem an odd configuration, but it can be very effective at creating a realistic stereo image that is very full and spatial, with no "hole" in the middle.

Mid-side pair

This is an interesting technique that can yield a broad, full stereo image. It requires either two microphones with figure-eight patterns (that is, which receive sound equally from in front and behind their capsules, though not from the sides), or one figure-eight as side mic and one cardioid as mid mic, along with some know-how regarding how you record and/or mix the signals. Although it uses two microphones, the M-S pair technique results in three signals, one from the mid mic, and two from the figure-eight side mic, split far left and far right, with one reverse-phase of the other to create a perfect stereo image. As such, the two reverse-phase sides of the figure-eight mic create the stereo image, while the mid mic fills in the hole. Place the side mic side-on to a sonically desirable point on the acoustic guitar, a slight distance away (try a foot and a half to begin with). Place the mid mic with the capsule as close to the first (side) mic as you can get it, without touching, but aiming straight at the sound source. Now, this technique requires more than just positioning, so here's what you do next:

If you are recording into a digital audio workstation (DAW) that has an M-S Decoder insert, which many do, simply record the side mic to one side of a stereo channel and the mid mic to the other, making note of which is which. Bring up your decoder insert, and it will split the figure-eight mic L-R, reversing the phase of one, and place your mid mic centre (such decoders usually have a mic-reverse function to ensure you're splitting the signal of the side mic and not the mid mic). Boom: big stereo image. If you're recording the old-fashioned way, split the signal of your mid mic to two channels on your mixer or mic preamp, reverse the phase of one, and patch these two to your recording device, later to be panned L-R in the mix. Record the mid mic straight to one channel, and position it in the middle. Note that you can adjust the width of the stereo field by bringing the L-R channels further toward or away from centre, but if you bring them entirely to centre their signals disappear completely, because the reverse-phase images cancel each other out. The mid mic sound remains, however. It's a fascinating and rather complex sonic phenomenon, and one worth exploring.

Dual mono pair

Strictly speaking, a true stereo image should capture identical left and right images of a sound source, as the above techniques do. If you use two different mics, and/or place two mics in very different and unequal positions around the sound source, you aren't really recording in stereo, but in "dual mono".

Which is not to rule out such techniques at all, because they can often yield great results. Consider that an acoustic guitar produces very different tones from different parts of its body and neck anyway, as discussed above, and it's clear that you might get some interesting results from placing different mics at different points around the guitar, and either blending them entirely together in mono, or positioning them L-R to some degree across the stereo field of your final mix. Look back at the single-mic positions discussed above and consider that you can use a combination of any two of these. Even when used in "pseudo stereo" – that is, two differently-recorded points of the guitar panned in stereo – you can often yield a big and sonically pleasing sound from this technique. Of course, you need to be aware of phase cancellation issues with such techniques, and do what you can to minimize them.

Corner loading

This one was passed to me the recording-engineer friend Huw Price, who is also the author of *Recording Guitar and Bass* (Backbeat Books, 2002). A reflective corner – you'll find plenty in your own house, apartment or studio – naturally emphasizes the low frequencies of any sound played into it. Sit with your guitar aiming into a corner, and place two identical or at least similar mics, one either side of your (or the guitarist's) head, also aiming into the corner. Play, record and check out the full, rich sound it captures. You can also use this technique with just one mic for a fat-bottomed mono recording.

Experiment with these and any other positions you can think of, and see what works for you. Again, as with recording guitar amplifiers, the "best" sound won't be a universal, but will depend on what works when you hear the guitar in the full mix, if it's a full band track.

RECORDING DIRECT

Traditionally, recording direct, or DI'ing for short (for "direct injection") was mainly the preserve of electric bass, although studio guitarists recording pop tracks have often used the technique too, to capture clean, snappy tones. In the old days, you just plugged into a DI box that converted your high-impedance guitar signal to a low-impedance signal, went from there to a mixing board or preamp unit, and connected that to the recorder. These days, the same technique can be useful for recording a pure, unadulterated guitar signal for processing at a later stage, and there are advantages to not tying yourself to a particular amp or effects sound too early in the process. Recording this way can also feel a little "cold" and naked, too, though, and sometimes it's hard to get the right vibe – and therefore to play your best – without a little more tonal mojo going on at the time of tracking.

Players DI'ing today have a lot more options, thanks to the plethora of processors, amp simulators and multi-FX units available, the majority of which offer some form of DI output for recording direct to your digital interface or multi-track tape machine (as discussed in Chapter 5). The majority of notable pro guitarists today still mike up guitar amps because this remains the most reliable means of achieving the tones they seek, but more and more professionals are turning to DI-ready units with built-in effects and amp sims, too. DI'ing in this way particularly offers plenty of benefits to the guitarist working in a home studio, though. Chief among these are the elimination of noise that might disturb neighbours and housemates, the elimination of the need for a quality microphone and the understanding of mic placement techniques, and the convenience of tapping the myriad ready-made tones that such units often provide.

Direct-injection recording really is just about as simple as it sounds. If your unit offers a DI output, simply connect this to one of your interface's line inputs (or a pair, if it's configured as two stereo outs), and match output and input levels carefully between units to make sure you're not overloading the signal. Once you've got the units working together, it's just a matter of dialling up the sound you want for the track, and going at it. As handy as these DI-ready multi-FX and amp sim units are, however, it can be tempting to overuse the cranked amp and effects sounds that they offer. If you're playing a guitar track that will need to blend well with other instruments in a final band mix, you might want to err on the side of restraint and consider putting further effects on in your DAW at a later stage, rather than saddling yourself with sounds that can't be changed down the road (which takes us back to one of the more compelling reasons for old-school DI'ing in the first place).

In-the-box guitar processing

Another form of DI recording for guitar that is becoming more and more popular these days eliminates the need for an external FX or amp-modelling unit and keeps it all in the box, using computer-based simulation programs available as plug-ins in your DAW to attain your sounds. Many of these can be played through "live" with no perceivable delay, rather than merely applied to recorded tracks after the fact, so you get the sound and feel required to produce the best performance.

One of the most popular of these programs is Amp Farm, a software plug-in produced by leading modelling amp manufacturer Line 6. Amp Farm goes beyond digital simulations of dozens of classic and vintage amps and effects to offer interchangeable speaker and cabinet simulations, and even simulations of several classic recording microphones. Native Instruments' Guitar Rig plug-in offers a similarly broad range of sounds, with bonus features such as a virtual control room in which to tweak your digitally emulated sound before committing it to disk.

Many other packages include simpler plug-in "channel strip" processors that still provide a lot of sonic power. Although they don't have the depth of sounds and features that Amp Farm or Guitar Rig provide, UAD's Nigel, ReWire's GT Player and Waves' iGTR do provide a lot of sounds in a very user-friendly format, for very little financial outlay. Most of these can also be used, with the proper interface, to perform live in real time, too, by patching through a PA system rather than a traditional guitar amp.

Parallel-path recording

Another pro trick is to employ parallel-path recording, a technique similar to that discussed in relation to dual amp set-ups in Chapter 5. This usually involves recording one track of a real guitar amp miked-up, and one track of a direct

To get a big, loud guitar sound at home, or in a small studio, you're probably better off using a smaller amp, such as the Fender Champ (above) or a Vox AC4 (below).

signal from the guitar, with no amp or effects, but other dual-path options are available, such as one pure path, and one DI'd from a processor or amp simulator.

To achieve this, use a traditional DI box and take its low-impedance output to the interface, and its high-impedance parallel output to your guitar amp. This parallel-path approach gives you one (hopefully) good genuine amp sound to work with, and the "safety" of a pure guitar signal that you can process differently later, or blend in with the amp tone.

Cranked-up amps at low volumes

One dilemma perpetually faced by the home recordist is that of achieving cranked-up electric guitar tones at volumes low enough to keep neighbours and housemates happy. Many of the DI techniques already discussed provide great solutions here, but plenty of guitarists still want to record real amps with real mics in real rooms. What do you do? Well, there are several possible solutions.

The first of these often involves simply rethinking your needs size-wise, and using a much smaller amp to record with than you would normally use to perform live on stage. This might seem like a major comedown from your visions of mammoth tone, but professional guitarists have done it this way for years. Whatever fire-breathing monsters they used on stage, guitar greats such as Jimmy Page, Eric Clapton, Brian May, Keith Richards, Pete Townshend, Dave Davies and even sometimes Jimi Hendrix all crafted some classic tones from diminutive, low-watt amps in the studio – amps that in many cases wouldn't even be loud enough for a small gig, but that sound phenomenal fired up with a good studio microphone in front of them.

The fact is, there's a juxtaposition of logic afoot when you get down to recording, which flips our sonic senses on their heads and determines that, in fact, in the very refined and often enclosed environment of the studio, small amps can easily be made to sound very big, whereas big amps often sound disappointingly small. There are a few interrelated factors behind this, which bear some further examination.

Most players who have any gigging or recording experience with tube amps realize that every model has its "sweet spot", the volume level where it really starts to give up the good stuff, and that spot is usually close to halfway up on the Volume or Gain control, and sometimes beyond. Big 50-watt or 100-watt (or even many 30-watt) amps that kick out righteous tones in a 200 to 500-seat club or hall when you get them up somewhere between 11 o'clock and 2 o'clock on the dial just don't sound anything like you want them to when they're reined in at 8 o'clock in a smaller room. Crank them up to the sweet spot regardless in a smaller room, and the confined space just doesn't let the sound blossom the way it wants to in order to sound its best. Whack a 4-watt amp like a Fender Champ, Vox AC4 or Dr Z Mini-Z up to its sweet spot, however, and it will bloom in just about any room, without rattling the hinges or floor studs besides.

Hand in hand with the first point, the best studio microphones tend to be extremely sensitive, and are engineered to handle less-than-extreme volume levels. Yes, you can put a Shure SM57 or similarly robust dynamic mic in front of just about anything and it can take it, but many of the best engineers prefer to tap the sonic splendours of high-end condenser mics or, more and more these days, lush, warm sounding ribbon mics. A cranked 50-watter will overload the front end of a sensitive condenser mic and result in a mushy track that is distorted in all the wrong ways, and even a cranked 30-watter might blow the thin metal film element in a ribbon mic. Get your little beauty sounding its best, though, and you can put either of these microphone types right up on it without fear, to make the most of a high-end mic translating the performance of a dynamic tube amp operating right within its sweet spot.

Thirdly, say you do find a room to record in where you can ratchet up that 100-watter without fear of reprisal, and a microphone willing to handle it (certainly some name artists do record this way, of course). As often as not, the results on tape, or hard drive, aren't anywhere near as "big" sounding as the effort you undertook to capture it. Recording a big, loud amp without extreme attention to details such as microphone technique (which often requires multiple mics, skilfully and strategically positioned), the application of studio compression and other esoteric tools in the experienced engineer's arsenal, too often translates to a rather flat, characterless mush in the track. In short, it's simply a lot easier to make a small amp sound good, and once you get it down in the track, physical size becomes irrelevant. What really matters is crafting a lively, original tone that sits well in the mix, and comes back out of the listener's speakers sounding as big as you want it to sound.

If you only have access to a larger amp, though, and need to tame its output for recording purposes, there are a few things you can do. Some of these involve purchasing pieces of equipment designed and manufactured specifically for the purpose of making loud amps quieter, while others require modification to an existing amplifier.

Output attenuators

These devices "soak up" some of the wattage coming out of your tube amp before it hits the speaker, thereby reducing your overall volume level. The benefit is that they let you turn an amp up to the setting where its tubes start to cook, in sonic terms, and produce the tone you're seeking to achieve, while shedding a large proportion of the volume that usually comes hand-in-hand with that tone. Several different makes and models are available, and most provide switching for different levels of output attenuation (volume cut), while some also offer DI outputs that tap a signal from this amp-output tone to feed directly to a mixing desk or recording interface. Be aware, however, that running an amp hot with an attenuator attached will strain tubes and other components more than running the same amp at low volumes, because even though you're hearing less volume from the speaker, the amp itself is still operating at a level intended to produce a lot of noise. Also, heavy attenuator use will change the perceived tone of an amp slightly, for two reasons: first, with less wattage hitting the speakers, said speakers will react slightly differently, and therefore sound differently; second, our ears perceive frequencies differently at different volume levels, so the "same tone" won't sound the same at 92dB as it does at 120dB. Still, these can be useful devices, and plenty of players make good use of them.

Power reduction modifications

There are a handful of mods that a qualified amp tech can perform to provide a variable reduction in a tube amp's output levels. One simple operation involves installing a pentode/triode switch, which can change your output tubes' operating mode, as desired, from their usual pentode mode to triode mode (actually a "mock-triode" mode), which cuts their output by about half in wattage terms. This simple, reversible mod can be performed on most tube amps, retaining their full-power alongside an instant-half-power mode, but it is certainly work for a trained professional. More invasive modifications come in the form of a handful of voltage-based power reduction circuits that can be added to many amps. One of the best known of these, London Power's Power Scaling, works within the power section of your tube amp to scale down voltages supplied to the tubes, allowing them to hit their tonal sweet spot at lower volume levels. Again, this one is a job for a qualified professional. Neither of these mods, whether simple or complex, should be undertaken lightly and without due consideration of the ways in which it might devalue an amplifier. Such mods will almost certainly void the warranty on any new amp, too.

Tube converters

The output levels of amps using large 6L6 or EL34 output tubes can be knocked down by fifty percent with the use of tube converters that allow them to run on smaller EL84 output tubes. These plug-in devices, found in the forms of THD's Yellow Jackets and TAD's Tone Bones, require no internal modification, and simply plug into the sockets that normally carry the larger, more powerful tubes. They have built-in sockets to receive nine-pin EL84s, along with the internal components required to convert the voltage and bias levels to those that these lower-powered tubes can safely run on. As output tubes do play a major part in shaping the voice of any tube amp, these converters (and the change to EL84s) will also alter the tone of any amp using them, and not just the overall volume, but this is a change that some players intentionally seek for its own sake.

Isolation cabinets

Taking the form of a guitar speaker sealed in a soundproof box, iso cabs offer another means of running your amp at full tilt without producing much – possibly any – sound in the room. For recording purposes, professionally made iso cabs include a microphone mount and output alongside the speaker input, so you can just plug in, crank up and go. Popular units are manufactured by Demeter, Randall and AxeTrak. In addition to muffling your volume levels, these do also change your overall tone somewhat, since the speaker producing it is now enclosed in a much smaller space than any room you might normally record in, and speakers react – and sound – very different in different sized rooms, with different amounts of air space around them. Still, if it's a compromise, it's one that has allowed many rockers in particular to record mega-cranked lead tones without worrying about the flashing blue lights pulling up in front of the premises.

MIXING & MASTERING

This is a book about playing and understanding the guitar, and a chapter that is aimed primarily at recording the guitar, but it's worth knowing a little about other aspects of completing a recording project if you are to take that guitar playing successfully from studio to distribution. To that end, let's take a quick look at some basics of mixing and mastering. These are subjects that have entire books written about them, and each is an art unto itself, but a brief primer here can at least introduce you to the theories of these skills.

Mixing is the process of adjusting the volume, pan (stereo placement) and EQ levels of all recorded tracks, and playing them back simultaneously to bounce them to a master recording. Essentially, you're mixing all tracks together at their desired relative levels to create the best blend of the overall sound of the band playing together. In the most basic possible scenario, with all recorded tracks sounding fine just as they stand, mixing can be as simple as that: pan each track to the point where you want it to appear in the stereo field, adjust its level so it has the correct prominence in the final mix, and adjust its EQ (if necessary) so it sits in the right place in the overall frequency range of the full-band performance. In most cases, however, the task of mixing also involves applying several layers of effects and processing to individual tracks to get them sounding right even before you start adjusting levels to place them in the mix, and this really is the more time-consuming part of the process.

If you're recording and mixing in the digital realm and staying entirely, or even mostly, in the box, you will apply most of this processing in the form of plug-ins used in individual channels or in auxiliary channels to which a number of tracks are grouped and fed (via a "bus" or "send" track – a sort of detour route for a track's sound). For example, you might want to apply a little compression to both your lead and rhythm guitar tracks, but differing amounts, while giving them similar amounts of plate reverb.

A compressor plug-in would be loaded into the individual tracks of each and set to its appropriate level, then, after the compressor insert, each track might be routed via a stereo bus to an aux track that has been loaded with a stereo reverb plug-in. Drum tracks might also have their own individual EQ and compression inserts, but be grouped in their own aux track for reverb and other global effects. In analogue recording and mixing (or digital mixing that runs "outside the box"), actual hardware processors are employed in these functions, and connected to your mixer's track and auxiliary channels via patch cables. Once again, the digital realm makes this job quicker, easier and cleaner for the home recordist.

In the old days, the final mix was done live, playing the multi-track recording back in real time and adjusting levels as you went – pushing the guitar up for the solo, muting the vocal track to keep unwanted noise out of instrumental passages and so on and so forth. The process usually required running pass after pass, and bringing extra hands in to man faders and knobs, until all changes were done just right while the multi-track was rolling, and the master deck was recording. Today, even the most basic DAWs have automated mix functions, which enable you to set and save all changes in levels, pan, EQ, effects and more – either in real time or in a graphic editing window – and then bounce the final mix to disk without need of touching a single function on your virtual mixer.

While a mix is recorded to a master tape, the task of mastering is a separate function applied after the mix has been completed. When albums were still released on vinyl discs, mastering involved cutting the groove to a master disc used for pressing vinyl discs, and in the process, adjusting aspects of its compression, EQ and overall volume levels. Mastering no longer involves the cutting (other than when a band still releases on vinyl), but is still a crucial final step in completing any professional recording, and should be considered an essential part of any ambitious home recording, too.

Good professional mastering engineers are often known to have the sharpest ears in the business, and they put the final punch, sheen and shimmer on a recording. The mastering process involves running the final mix of a song through an array of high-quality EQs, compressors, limiters and sometimes even a little global reverb, to achieve the best ratio of volume and dynamics and the ideal overall frequency range for the track, in an effort to ensure that it sounds its best for a range of potential listening environments.

Even now, in the digital age, professional mastering engineers tend to run digital mixes through outboard devices to accomplish these tasks, listening on extremely sensitive, high-end monitors in an acoustically designed studio. For the home or project studio, DIY mastering is often performed with software mastering plug-ins. These can even be inserted into a master fader channel while mixing, but home mastering is often best accomplished by running your best final stereo mix back through the DAW and tweaking with the mastering software.

Whatever gear you use, the most important tools of the mastering process are your ears and a neutral listening environment. The goal is to produce a lively, dynamic recording, with degrees of punch or warmth or aggression appropriate to the material, and no overtly obtrusive frequencies that might distract the listener from the performance (such as a bass that's too boomy or too far forward, highs from cymbals and guitars that are harsh and grating, and so forth). Think of mastering as putting the icing on the cake: it can really help to make a great final product, but if the cake is only mediocre in the first place, it can't render it a dessert fit for a king.

history of the GUITAR

An underdog among stringed instruments for many centuries, the guitar has grown – over just the course of the last century – to be the most widely played musical instrument in the world. In previous centuries the lute, and related stringed and fretted instruments from which the guitar evolved, were rarely afforded the respect of classical instruments such as the violin, viola and cello, and were more the realm of vagabonds, Gypsies and travelling minstrels – performers who were largely looked down upon in their day. In the mid-to-late nineteenth century and the early part of the twentieth, the guitar was still lagging behind the banjo and mandolin in the popularity stakes among folk instruments, and its limited volume-producing capabilities kept it towards the back of the bandstand right up into the 1930s. But gradually, steadily, it began its move towards the front.

THE RISE OF THE GUITAR

It's difficult to say exactly why the guitar's popularity began to increase. On one front, the quest of many players and makers in the 1920s and 30s to get their guitars louder helped to bring the instrument centre stage. National's resonator guitars, in production from 1927, were much louder than acoustic guitars, and helped plenty of early players to be heard. Early experiments with amplified guitars in the late 1920s and early 30s – conducted most prominently by Stromberg-Voisinet, ViviTone (headed by former Gibson designer Lloyd Loar) and Rickenbacker – shone a light on a new path. Established guitar maker Gibson took the ball in the mid-30s and ran with it, producing the first mass-manufactured electric guitars. From that point on, guitars would have no trouble competing with trumpets and sax in terms of volume.

This proliferation of the electric guitar boosted the popularity of guitars in general. The guitar's greater prominence in the big-band setting won it more recognition, for acoustic guitars too. Meanwhile, microphones and sound-support (PA) systems improved, so it became easier for a performer to use an acoustic guitar on stage – several decades before add-on pickups for acoustics became popular. The guitar's relatively low acoustic output no longer limited its applications, and the sky was the limit.

At the same time, more and more players were discovering the sheer versatility of the instrument. The guitar was more portable than the piano, more versatile than the banjo or mandolin, and a much better instrument for self-accompaniment than the violin because you could easily strum it and sing at the same time. While it never became the single dominant instrument in the jazz world, it gradually became a bigger part of the popular music scene both in the US and in Europe. Through the course of the 1940s and 50s the guitar became a leading voice in blues, country and folk music, and it was set to explode when rock'n'roll came along.

Rock'n'roll was born with a guitar in its hands. Perhaps bands made up of piano, saxophone and drums could have generated some of the same attitude but it's the guitar, and the electric guitar in particular, that's always been the engine of rock'n'roll. Just as amplification enabled the guitar to compete with the trumpet and sax in a big-band setting, it allowed a couple of six-string guitars, along with a bass and a drum set, to stand in for an entire horn section. Where a big sixteen-piece band was required to power a dance in a large hall in the 1920s, 30s and 40s, the three or four-piece combo was more than capable of the task in the 50s. The impact and convenience of smaller line-ups shot rock'n'roll on its way, and the popularity of the guitar along with it.

It was to be several decades before the first guitar naysayers were heard. In the 1980s, several pundits sounded the death knell for the guitar, or at least proclaimed its dethronement, when the synthesizer and other forms of electronic instrumentation swept popular music. Suddenly electronic keyboards that had largely just (badly) mimicked pianos and organs in years past were capable of tapping a near-limitless palette of polyphonic sounds. The humble guitar seemed unable to compete. It continued churning away regardless, however, in garages, basements and underground clubs, and more prominently in the hands of stadium rockers who were still rooted to the powerful six-string (though they might have adopted synths in supporting roles). The synthesizer certainly established a voice that remains with us to this day, but after what we might call its honeymoon period, during which the novelty of its sound briefly gripped much of the music world, it proved ultimately unmatched to the task of dethroning the guitar as the driving force of rock. While post-punk and indie bands never wavered from the six-string cause, rockers like Guns N' Roses brought the guitar thundering back to the platinum-selling fold in the late 80s, and grungers like Nirvana consolidated its status as the noisemaker supreme in the early 90s.

Made in Seville: the label on an authentic De Torres guitar.

In the intervening years, the guitar's status has remained relatively solid. Instrument sales are occasionally troubled by videogaming or the net, but neither these nor the guitar-light arrangements of hip-hop, rap or chart pop have dented it. According to *The Music Trades*' 2010 Industry Census, worldwide sales of guitars have risen from 681,762 units in 1992 to 2,991,260 units in 2009. And this was a recession-year figure that was slightly down from pre-recession sales of 3,302,670 in 2007. Having earned a ticket to the dance some sixty years ago, the guitar clearly isn't going away in a hurry.

THE MAJOR PLAYERS

Guitar-making was practised for many centuries in Europe, and notably gained most respect as a classical instrument, thanks in large part to Spanish luthier Antonio de Torres. Working from 1850 to 1890, Torres made only an estimated 320 guitars in his lifetime, but his advances in the craft earned him the title "father of the modern classical guitar", and his designs would influence nearly all other makers in one way or another.

But, these significant developments in classical guitar-making aside, the guitar as we best know it today was developed largely in the United States by craftsmen who had emigrated from Europe in the nineteenth century. Orville Gibson and Leo Fender were both American born, but Christian Friedrich Martin – the founder of the longest-established of the major American guitar brands – was another German émigré. Of the other great patriarchs of today's big guitar names, Adolph Rickenbacker was born in Switzerland, Friedrich Gretsch in Germany, Anastasios Stathopoulo (Epiphone) in Greece, John Dopyera (National) in the former Czechoslovakia and Alfred Dronge (Guild) in Poland.

Martin

C.F. Martin began making guitars in New York City soon after his arrival in the United States in 1833, but relocated to Cherry Hill and then Nazareth, Pennsylvania, where the Martin company has remained ever since. Martin's success was well deserved, and the company's longevity achieved through hard work, and not mere chance. C.F. Martin played a big part in modernizing the flat-top guitar from around the middle of the nineteenth century. First he eliminated much of the instrument's ornamentation in favour of constructional advances that improved its tone and feel. Then he improved the bracing structure of the top so that it could eventually support steel strings. These would greatly increase the instrument's volume, way beyond that of strings made of gut.

The lynchpin of C.F. Martin's design efforts was his development of the X-brace, still the standard today on flat-top acoustic guitars. It gave the guitar's top (soundboard) both greater strength and greater freedom of

The old master: Spanish luthier Antonio de Torres.

movement than the rudimentary "ladder bracing" systems widely in use before. Martin's sturdy X allowed the use of both thinner braces and a thinner top, and greatly increased the resonance of the soundboard in the process, opening up the voice of the instrument.

Having set a standard for the guitar in the Civil War-era US, Martin led the way into the twentieth century, with others such as Washburn, Ditson, Kay and Harmony largely following the Pennsylvania company's lead – albeit lagging somewhat behind it. In 1917 Martin established what is perhaps the most abiding image of the acoustic guitar today with the advent of the dreadnought. This wide-waisted flat-top with somewhat squared shoulders was first manufactured by Martin to be sold under the Ditson brand, but was sold by Martin under its own name in 1931 after Ditson ceased trading.

Best known in the form of the mahogany bodied D-18, rosewood bodied D-28 and ultra-fancy D-45 (all of which have spruce tops), Martin's dreadnought remains the preferred instrument of countless bluegrass, country and acoustic-rock artists, and its shape is mirrored in one form or another by almost every maker of steel-string flat-top acoustic guitars working today.

Meanwhile, other body styles that echo Martin's pre-dreadnought models have seen a resurgence. The petite parlour-bodied O-18 and O-28 models have experienced a renewed popularity (a trend jumped on by several other manufacturers), while mid-sized OO-, OOO- and larger Grand Concert models all remain in production. Although Martin suffered at the nadir of the guitar's popularity in the early 1980s, producing only three thousand units in 1982, the company regained its health later that decade under the leadership of C.F. Martin IV. The sixth generation of the Martin family to oversee the business, he was appointed CEO in 1986. The five hundred thousandth guitar in the company's history was completed in 1990 and production of Martins has outstripped any previous pace over the past twenty years, with the millionth guitar completed in 2004.

Gibson

Another long-established American guitar-maker, Gibson is known for working to a template that is very different to that of Martin's flat-top, but no less innovative. The company was founded by Orville Gibson, who single-handedly invented the archtop guitar in the 1890s, working alone in his back-room shop in Kalamazoo, Michigan.

Following the lead of violin and cello makers who'd worked this way for centuries before him, Gibson carved the arched tops of his guitars from solid wood, striving to achieve the best ratio of strength to resonance. By the 1920s and early 30s, the archtop acoustic had become the most popular form of instrument with professional jazz and dance band guitarists. From 1922 onwards, the necks of these guitars were more stable – and more easily adjusted – than ever before, thanks to Gibson designer Lloyd Loar's invention of the truss rod, a steel rod enclosed in a chamber within the guitar's neck that could be adjusted to relieve string pressure and counteract any resultant bowing.

Gibson would eventually follow Martin with its own successful line of flat-top acoustic guitars, but its archtop was the one that gave the guitar a real boost. The ES-150, released in 1936 and taken up by seminal jazz artist Charlie Christian soon afterwards, was the first production electric guitar from a major manufacturer. In fact, it was really just a simplified version of Gibson's acoustic archtops, only with a blade pickup mounted in the neck position.

While continuing to advance the format throughout the next decade and a half, Gibson nevertheless retained a heavy dose of tradition in its designs, consistent in the glued-in necks, F-holes, arched tops and bound bodies and necks that most of its guitars shared. It was perhaps this same sense of tradition that caused the company to turn down Les Paul's ideas for the production

Charlie Christian, godfather of jazz guitar, played a Gibson archtop on most of his recordings.

of a solidbodied guitar in the late 1940s, something Gibson avoided until Fender made a splash with its Esquire and Broadcaster (later Telecaster) in 1950.

Still, the Les Paul Model that emerged two years later would become one of the most influential solidbodies of all time, and was but the first of several Gibson innovations of the solidbody era. It was initially sold in 1952, with a neck angle that was too shallow for the trapeze bridge that was fitted to it, necessitating the awkward arrangement of having to wrap the strings under the bridge bar in 1952. The Les Paul was updated with a one-piece wraparound bridge late in 1953, and received Gibson's new, fully adjustable Tune-o-matic bridge in 1956 (a unit devised by company president Ted McCarty himself for use on the first Les Paul Custom of 1954). All the while the goldtop Les Paul Model carried a pair of single-coil P-90 pickups.

The move to a sunburst finish on the Les Paul in 1958 (following the addition of humbucking pickups in 1957) might have seemed like a nod toward tradition for Gibson, but it signalled the demise of the original run of the model, which was deleted from the catalogue in 1960, replaced in 1961 by a guitar that would become best known as the SG.

It's odd, with hindsight, to think that a sunburst Les Paul Standard – which would eventually become guitar of choice for Eric Clapton, Jimmy Page, Paul Bloomfield and countless others – could be considered too radical for acceptance by the guitar community. The more unusual creations in the Modernist series – the Flying V and Explorer– were also initially short-lived. But one major Gibson innovation made a major splash right from the start, perhaps precisely because it combined the traditional with the modern. The ES-335, released in 1958, had an arched top (pressed from laminated maple), a pair of F-holes and a certain amount of airspace within its body.

It also, however, had two deep cutaways that afforded easy access to all 22 frets, a thinline body and a solid maple block running down the centre. The latter, and the use of Gibson's relatively new Tune-o-matic bridge that it enabled, made the ES-335 much more feedback resistant than any traditional archtop electric, and also gave it more tonal clarity and better sustain, properties that helped it become an instant hit with a wide variety of players.

Following further envelope-pushing efforts in the form of the stylish "reverse-bodied" Firebird of 1963, Gibson eventually found its biggest successes by relying on established solid and semi-solid designs. The single-cutaway Les Paul, styled after the original one, returned in 1968 (though with P-90 pickups at first, mini-humbuckers later and finally full-sized humbuckers in the 1970s). The SG that had replaced the Les and the ES-335 both remained popular from their release until the present day. Following the gradual shift of production from Kalamazoo to Nashville, Tennessee, and several changes of ownership – the last taking place in 1986 following the company's near demise at the hands of parent company Norlin – Gibson is now going strong once again.

A taut, bright, clean guitar tone was key to the sound of 1980s guitar band Echo & The Bunnymen. Singer Ian McCulloch (right) plays a Gibson semi-acoustic, while Will Sergeant (middle) plays a Fender Strat.

The Explorer is one of the more unusual of guitar shapes – but that didn't stop Johnny Winter playing some mean blues-rock boogie on it.

Reissues of more radical creations such as the Flying V and Explorer have become favourites with heavy rockers, while revolutionary new models such as the Robot Series guitars, with automated tuning systems, and digital-capable Dark Fire and Dusk Tiger models, address the needs of adventurous players of the twenty-first century.

Gibson's archtop acoustic-electrics, though less of a staple than they were in the 1930s to early 50s, remain standards of the jazz world, and all the while, Gibson's own flat-top acoustics, which hit their stride in the 1930s, have won many fans and posted some strong competition for Martin. Meanwhile, sister-company Epiphone, purchased by Gibson in 1957, has long provided a successful budget brand to the company, and today produces several Asian-made guitars that mirror traditional Gibson models in style and features.

Kele Okereke of Bloc Party and his Fender Tele.

Fender

If he had done nothing more than unveiling the first successful, mass-produced solidbody electric guitar in 1950, his place in guitar history would have been assured. But Leo Fender's manufacturing of the guitar that was briefly called the Esquire, then Broadcaster, then finally Telecaster, was just the first of several innovations that this Californian would bring to the musical instrument world.

   Already recognized as a forward-looking amplifier designer and manufacturer after establishing a company under his own name in 1946, Leo Fender was learning to tap into the needs of professional musicians working near his shop in the Fullerton district of Los Angeles, and to use their input to shape his designs. He managed to find answers to many of these performer's guitar needs in the pre- and early rock'n'roll years.

   Although its wood-plank appearance and screwed-together construction was at first derided by some in the industry, the Telecaster offered instant solutions to many of the difficulties that amplified guitarists were facing in 1950. Its solid ash body greatly reduced the feedback that plagued most musicians who tried to play their hollowbodied archtop acoustic-electrics through loud amplifiers, while also improving the sustain and clarity of the electric guitar's tone. In addition, its narrow pickups, steel bridge plate and brass saddles – along with the solid body and one-piece maple neck – all worked in combination to offer a brighter, more cutting tone than that found from any electric guitar widely available before 1950. It helped many a guitarist in an ongoing struggle to cut through the mix in a big-band situation.

Aside from any tonal considerations, the Telecaster's "bolt-on" neck and hardware (actually affixed by screws) made it easy to service and repair, as well as more affordable to manufacture than elaborate glued-together hollowbodied archtop guitars with set necks. Once the initial scorn faded, others in the industry looked around and realized that musicians were taking up this new canoe paddle with enthusiasm, and actually playing it. And it sounded good.

In 1954 Fender hit another one out of the park with the release of the Stratocaster. Arguably the world's most influential electric guitar design, copied directly and indirectly by countless makers large and small over the past fifty-plus years, the Stratocaster brought several then-revolutionary new ideas to the floor. Its three single-coil pickups provided a wider variety of voices, and its contoured body, with deep recesses where the player's ribcage and right forearm met the body's back and front respectively, made it extremely comfortable to play. More significant than both of these combined, perhaps, was its ingenious new "Synchronized Tremolo", a vibrato system that combined bridge and tailpiece into one unit and offered a smooth, broad down-bend that many major players soon employed to dramatic effect.

In the late 1950s and early 60s Fender released two more significant models. With its rosewood fingerboard, broader single-coil pickups, offset body design and more complex electronics, the Jazzmaster of 1958 was aimed at the type of player it was named after. But it really caught fire more with the burgeoning surf scene, and, much later, many indie and punk players. The Jaguar of 1962, however, was marketed to surf guitarists right from the start, and its narrower, brighter pickups and shorter scale length (24" compared to Fender's standard 25.5") seemed to hit the mark with some success, although neither it nor the Jazzmaster – each Fender's top-of-the-line model for a time – ever outstripped the Telecaster or Stratocaster in the popularity stakes.

Meanwhile, Fender's amplifier production continued apace, and although this is a history of guitar manufacturers, it's worth noting that the company unveiled several developments both in the circuitry and cabinet design of new models between the mid-1950s and mid-60s that have continued to influence amplifier manufacturers to this day.

In January 1965 the sale of Fender to the Columbia Broadcasting Systems (CBS) entertainment conglomerate was completed, a milestone in the company's history that created the common "pre-CBS" delineation that is now used to denote the more desirable vintage Fender models manufactured prior to 1965. Many enthusiasts also consider the post-CBS years to mark a gradual decline in the quality of Fender instruments, a situation generally attributed to the large corporation's efforts to ramp up production to meet the guitar boom of the late 60s. As the guitar market briefly receded in the late 1970s and early 80s, CBS's lack of investment in Fender sent the company to an all-time low of production and quality.

The early 1980s did give birth to the Squier brand, however, which would be a successful budget arm of Fender in years to come. But otherwise the company's fortunes were at their lowest ebb. Fender was sold again in 1985, to a group of investors and Fender managers, and under the careful guidance of this team soon began to recover its considerable former strengths.

Today, thankfully, the Fender Musical Instruments Corporation is again one of the world's leading guitar and amplifier manufacturers, and has long reaffirmed its foothold in the market both by producing accurate reissue versions of its most popular guitars and amps from the 50s and 60s, and by designing contemporary and "modified" renditions of these alongside several countless new models, all of which address the broad and varied needs of guitarists today.

PJ Harvey has played a number of different guitars, but here she's using a Fender Jaguar – an instrument much loved by grunge, indie and surf bands the world over.

Rickenbacker

The early history of Rickenbacker guitars is interwoven with the history of the electric guitar in general. Swiss émigré Adolph Rickenbacker founded a tool-and-die operation in Los Angeles in the 1920s, and soon found himself doing work for local guitar makers, among them National, which used metal bodies (and other parts) for its resophonic acoustic guitars. Rickenbacker's associations with National, and in particular, National employees George Beauchamp and Paul Barth – who were working to develop a functional electric-guitar pickup at the time – lured him more deeply into the guitar business, and as amplification of the instrument became a practical reality in the early 30s, Rickenbacker was right there to put his name on the product.

Rickenbacker, Beauchamp, Barth and a few others formed the Ro-Pat-In company in 1931, the name of which was very sensibly changed in 1934 to the rather more catchy Electro String Instrument Company. But most of the time the brand name given to their lap-steel and "Spanish" electric guitars was Rickenbacker (though at first the name was given the Germanic "Rickenbacher", with an "h").

Early Rickenbackers were made in minimalist shapes from a variety of materials, with bodies and necks of wood, bakelite or aluminum, but all carried Beauchamp and Barth's distinctive "horseshoe" pickup, a unit that is beloved of many lap-steel players to this day.

These cumbersome pickups continued to appear on more conventionally shaped Rickenbacker electric guitars into the mid-1950s. Having been sold to Francis Hall in 1953, however, the Rickenbacker's look would soon begin to change further. In late 1957 and early 58, the guitars began carrying Rickenbacker's famous bright, jangly "toaster-top" single-coil pickups, while the body and neck designs also evolved into those we know from the company's golden age in the late 50s and 60s.

From the short-scale 325 played by John Lennon, and the 360/12 electric twelve-string played by George Harrison and Roger McGuinn, to the Export Model 1998s and the British-market 330s and 360s smashed by Pete Townshend, these are the guitars we tend to think of when we think "Rickenbacker". The arrival of the hotter Hi-Gain pickup in 1969, aka the "button top", addressed some players' needs for a hotter, meatier sound, and landed on Rickies played by the likes of Paul Weller with The Jam and Peter Buck with R.E.M.

Today, Rickenbacker continues to manufacture guitars that carry variations of both pickup types, including several reissue-style models that capitalize on the success of instruments originating from the 60s and a number of artist signature models that follow similar designs.

Gretsch

After manufacturing drums, banjos and other instruments in New York City and nearby Brooklyn from 1883, Gretsch entered the guitar market in the late 1930s, largely as a rival to Gibson and Epiphone (then still separate companies). Through the 1940s Gretsch specialized in archtop electric guitars, producing models that were sometimes quite fancy but occasionally lacked in overall quality when compared to its upmarket competitors.

As the rock'n'roll boom of the 50s dawned, however, Gretsch capitalized on the new genre in a big way, though initially it promoted its electric guitars by using the name of a particularly famous country picker. Having launched what it promoted as a "solid-bodied" guitar in 1953, the semi-solid Duo Jet, in the wake of Fender and Gibson's early success in that market, Gretsch got a bigger boost by signing Chet Atkins to put his name to the hollowbody archtop electric 6120 model in 1954, officially released early in 55. By endorsing both the Chet Atkins Hollow Body and its "solid" partner, the Duo Jet-like Chet Atkins Solid Body, Atkins helped to bring the Gretsch name to the

Pete Doherty loves his Ricky.

forefront of popular music. His association with the brand, in addition to Gretsch's pioneering use of bright alternative colours and Bigsby vibrato tailpieces all helped to land these Brooklyn-made instruments in the hands of formative rock'n'rollers such as Eddie Cochran, Cliff Gallup, Bo Diddley, Duane Eddy and eventually the Beatle George Harrison.

In the late 50s Gretsch again found itself rivalling Gibson in the effort to put a humbucking pickup into production. Although both companies had designs in the works around the same time, Gibson's PAF humbucker arrived on guitars a little ahead of Gretsch's Filter'Tron, which was unveiled to the trade in the summer NAMM show of 1957 and replaced the DeArmond 200 (aka DynaSonic) on up-market Gretsch models from 1958. Gretsch remained the choice of many major players throughout the 60s, and the brand even seemed for a time to have weathered its sale to Baldwin in 1967 relatively unscathed.

The subsequent moves to one production facility after another beneath the Baldwin umbrella, however, and the final departure from the Brooklyn plant in 1972 slowly took their toll. Gretsch appeared to lose touch with players' needs through much of the 70s, and a steady decline was capped by Baldwin's sale of the company back to the Gretsch family in 1985, when Fred Gretsch III took up the reins.

In 1989 Fred Gretsch III launched a range of Japanese-made guitars based largely on vintage models from the 50s and early 60s, and these greatly helped the brand to recover much of its earlier popularity. In 2002 the Fender Musical Instrument Corp took over the manufacturing and distribution of Gretsch guitars, and has further expanded the line-up of Japanese-made instruments, while occasionally offering high-end US-made models alongside a successful line of budget-friendly guitars in the Gretsch Electromatic series. More than fifty years after their first arrival in the catalogue, models such as the semi-solid Duo Jet and hollowbodied 6120 are again among the most popular Gretsch guitars on the market.

OTHER MAKERS

It's not all about the Big Five guitar brands. Plenty of others have established their names, and made a significant impact on the market. Guild, founded in 1953, has been much respected for both its acoustic and electric output, with Starfire, Bluesbird and X-Series electrics being particularly popular. The company survived financial difficulties and changes of ownership over the years to end up being bought by Fender Musical Instruments Corp in 1995. For a time, Fender revived many classic acoustic and electric designs, and added a range of high-end archtops designed by luthier Robert Benedetto. But sadly the company ceased production of Guild instruments in the first decade of the twenty-first century.

After leaving his own company in the hands of new owners CBS, Leo Fender eventually found his way to the position of president of Music Man Inc (now Ernie Ball/Music Man) in 1975, and contributed designs to the company, whose Silhouette, Axis and Albert Lee models are among the company's most popular offerings today. From Music Man, Fender moved on to establish G&L in 1979 (the initials short for "George and Leo", accounting for partner and former Fender colleague George Fullerton, who departed the company in 1986). At G&L, Leo Fender pioneered a new range of pickup designs, many of which had been inked on his drawing board while he was still retained as a CBS consultant with Fender in the late 60s.

He also established a number of vaguely Fender-like models, most notably the popular, Tele-like ASAT model (briefly named Broadcaster, before Fender's objections). Following Fender's death in 1991, G&L was sold to music electronics company BBE, which currently maintains a broad line-up of US-made G&L guitars, alongside an Asian-made Tribute series. Meanwhile makers such as Dean, Kramer, Jackson, Charvel and Hamer – all established in the mid-to-late 70s – have addressed the needs of plenty of players seeking alternatives to the major electric-guitar brands, and rockers in particular.

In Europe, electrics marketed in the 50s and 60s by companies such as Selmer and Futurama were often the down-market alternatives for players who couldn't get their hands on rare US-made Fenders and Gibsons, and although they often sought to ape these brands they were rarely even close enough to be dubbed copies. Guitars made by Framus and Hagstrom in Germany and Sweden respectively, however, were often excellent instruments in their own right, and the latter in particular have landed in the hands of plenty of name artists over the years. Across the channel, British brands Burns and Vox established several iconic models in the 60s, while electric makers Patrick Eggle and FretKing and acoustic makers Lowden and Brook have all won plaudits in more recent years.

Canadian guitar makers, while expressing themselves in several excellent original electric designs from the Godin company, have largely made themselves heard in the acoustic market. Larrivée, founded in Toronto by Jean Larrivee in 1968 and currently located in Vancouver, offers a popular line-up of high-end flat-top guitars made to original designs that are often more inspired by classical-guitar shapes than those coined by Martin and Gibson. Reaching a somewhat broader market, the La Patrie, Norman and Seagull brands of the LaSiDo company offer steel-string and classical acoustic guitars at a broad range of prices.

Johnny Borrell of Razorlight and his Gretsch.

Japanese makers, already rivals to cheaper US guitars of the 60s and early 70s, proved in the late 70s that they could compete with the up-market brands, too, as instruments made by Ibanez, Yamaha, Aria and a few others presented what seemed a quantum leap in design and quality over what had been seen from Asian factories just ten years before. Yamaha was an early frontrunner, with its SG2000 solidbody and SA2000 semi-acoustic winning over several former Gibson players. Its Pacifica Series made a splash in the lower-priced markets, while several of the company's acoustic guitars have been longstanding successes. Ibanez has grown from being primarily a copy guitar company to being a leading maker of original hotrodded "superstrats" and other models aimed at shred-metal players, among which its Steve Vai-endorsed JEM series and Joe Satriani-endorsed JS series have been particularly successful.

On the acoustic and electric fronts respectively, US makers Taylor and Paul Reed Smith (PRS) have both been major players in their respective fields and have boomed tremendously since their cottage-industry roots of the mid- to late-70s. Based in Stevensville, Maryland, after many years in Annapolis, PRS produces a wide range of designs that are considered by many to combine some of the best elements of the Gibson and Fender templates, while copying neither. The tone and versatility of these instruments has won the company a long list of professional endorsees, including David Grissom, Carlos Santana, Dave Navarro, Mark Tremonti and many others.

From El Cajon, California, Taylor crafts a range of acoustic guitars that have won many fans over the past thirty years. The company's body shapes occasionally echo the dreadnought and Grand Concert styles originated by Martin, but never entirely mirror them, and many clever and creative features in Taylor's instruments – including a variety of alternative wood types, service-friendly neck attachments and advanced pickup and electronic systems – have all proved a boon to a growing roster of professional players. Signature models for Dave Matthews, Taylor Swift, Jason Mraz and Serj Tankian attest to just a handful of the hundreds of name artists using Taylor guitars, and a recent expansion into electric guitars promises to broaden this forward-looking company's reach in the near future.

Amid all the large manufacturers, a great many smaller and custom makers are continually working to advance the craft, while rarely receiving the broader recognition they deserve. Whether it's an electric from Nik Huber, Roger Giffin, Don Grosh, Saul Koll, John Suhr or Stefan D'Pergo; a flat-top acoustic from Dana Bourgeois, Andy Manson or J.W. Gallagher; an archtop from Steven Andersen, Robert Benedetto or John Monteleone; or a classical guitar from Thomas Humphrey, Robert Ruck or Paulino Bernabé, such one-man or small-shop makers often provide some of the best luthiery work available anywhere, at any price.

Resources

There are millions of books, DVDs and websites out there that can help take your guitar playing right up into the stratosphere. And the last few years has seen an explosion in the number of tuition videos cropping up on YouTube – you can now find plenty of guitar lessons in all styles entirely for free there. This section features a selection of books and DVDs we would recommend, followed by a chord directory which covers all the guitar chords which are commonly used (and a few which aren't).

Guitar instruction

Books

Hal Leonard Guitar Method (book & CDs) Will Schmid & Greg Koch (Hal Leonard, 2002)
How to Write Songs on Guitar Rikky Rooks (Backbeat Books, 2009)
Music Theory for Guitarists: Everything You Ever Wanted to Know But Were Afraid to Ask Tom Kolb (Hal Leonard, 2005)
Totally Interactive Band Bible (book, CD & DVD) Rod Fogg (Thunder Bay Press, 2007)
Totally Interactive Guitar Bible (book, CDs & DVD) Dave Hunter & others, feat. Dave Gregory (Thunder Bay Press, 2006)
The Ultimate Guitar Chord Chart various authors (Hal Leonard, 1999)

DVDs

Complete Rock Guitar Method: Beginning Rock Guitar, Lead & Rhythm feat. various presenters (Alfred Publishing, 2003)
Fifty Jazz Licks You Must Know! feat. Frank Vignola (Guitar Lab, 2009)
Fifty Licks Country Style feat. Troy Dexter (Hal Leonard, 2003)
Guitar World: How to Play Hard Rock and Heavy Metal Guitar feat. various presenters (Alfred Publishing, 2009)
House of Blues Beginner: Blues Guitar Level 1 with John McCarthy (Rock House Method, 2005)
Jimmy Bruno: No Nonsense Jazz Guitar feat. Jimmy Bruno (Hot Licks, 2005)
John Petrucci – Rock Discipline feat. John Petrucci (Warner Brothers, 2002)
Johnny Hiland: Chicken Pickin' Guitar feat. Johnny Hiland (Hot Licks, 2006)
The Rock House Method: Learn Rock Guitar feat. John McCarthy (Rock House Method, 2005)
Ronnie Earl: Blues Guitar With Soul feat. Ronnie Earl, dir. Arlen Roth (Hot Licks, 2005)
Arlen Roth's 150+ Acoustic Hot Licks for Rock, Blues, Country, Rockabilly and R&B Guitar feat. Arlen Roth (Hot Licks, 2006)

History
Books

Acoustic Guitars: The Illustrated Encyclopedia Tony Bacon & Dave Hunter (Thunder Bay Press, 2009)
American Guitars: An Illustrated History Tom Wheeler (Harper Resource, 1992)
Electric Guitars: The Illustrated Encyclopedia Tony Bacon & Paul Day (Thunder Bay Press, 2006)
Guitar: Music; History; Players Richard Chapman (Dorling Kindersley, 2003)
Star Guitars: 101 Guitars that Rocked the World Dave Hunter (Voyageur Press, 2010)
With Strings Attached: The Art and Beauty of Vintage Guitars Jonathan Kellerman (Ballentine Books, 2008)

Technical
Books

Guitar Electronics for Musicians Donald Brosnac (Omnibus Press, 2009)
The Guitar Pickup Handbook: The Start of Your Sound Dave Hunter (Backbeat Books, 2008).
The Guitar Player Repair Guide Dan Erlewine (Backbeat Books, 2007)
The Guitar Sourcebook: How to Find the Sounds You Like Dave Hunter (Backbeat Books, 2006)
The Player's Guide to Guitar Maintenance Dave Burrluck (Balafon Books, 2000)

Amps & effects
Books

All About Vacuum Tube Guitar Amplifiers Gerald Weber (Hal Leonard, 2009)
Amps! The Other Half of Rock'n'Roll Ritchie Fliegler (Hal Leonard, 1993)
The Guitar Amp Handbook: Understanding Tube Amplifiers and Getting Great Sounds Dave Hunter (Backbeat Books, 2005)
Guitar Effects Pedals: The Practical Handbook Dave Hunter (Backbeat Books, 2004)
Introduction to Guitar Tone and Effects David M. Brewester (Hal Leonard, 2003)
A History of Marshall: The Illustrated History of the Sound of Rock Michael Doyle (Hal Leonard, 1993)
The Soul of Tone: Celebrating 60 Years of Fender Amps Tom Wheeler (Hal Leonard, 2007)
Stompbox: A History of Guitar Fuzzes, Flangers, Phasers, Echoes and Wahs Art Thompson (Backbeat Books, 1997)
The Tube Amp Book: Deluxe Revised Edition Aspen Pittman (Backbeat Books, 2003)
Vox Amplifiers: The JMI Years Jim Elyea (History For Hire Press, 2009)

For a reminder of how to read chord diagrams, see pp.17–18 in Chapter 1.

C chords

C# Chords

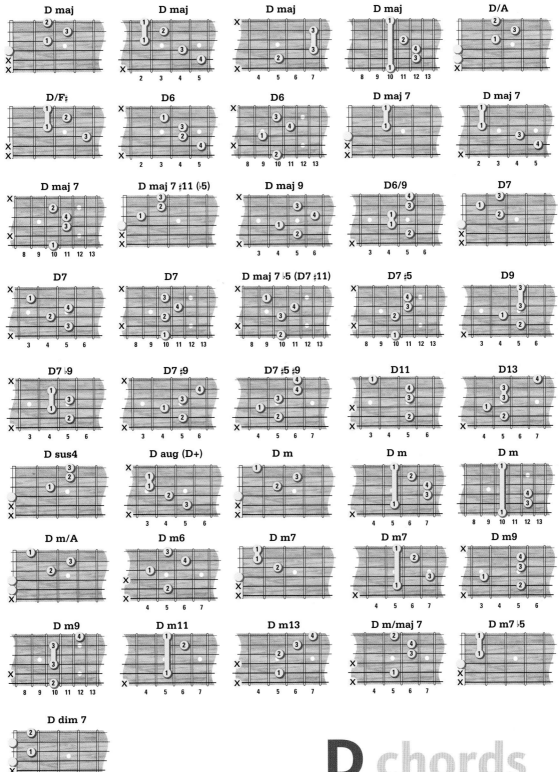

D chords

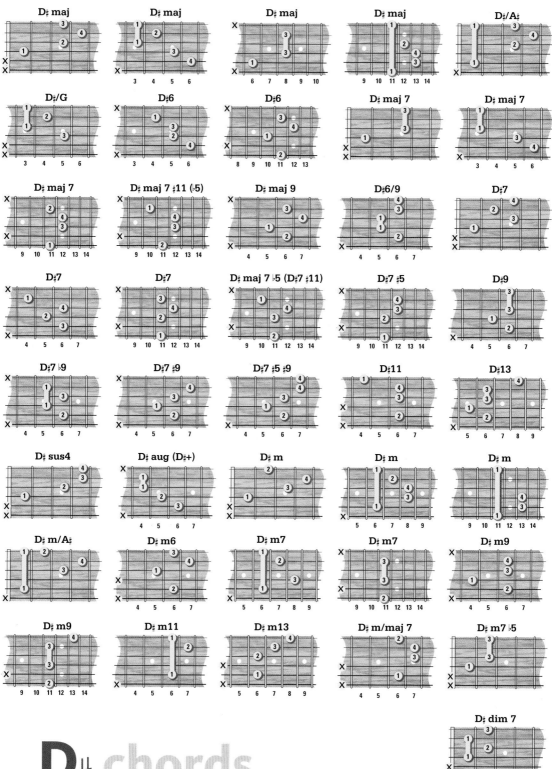

D♯ chords

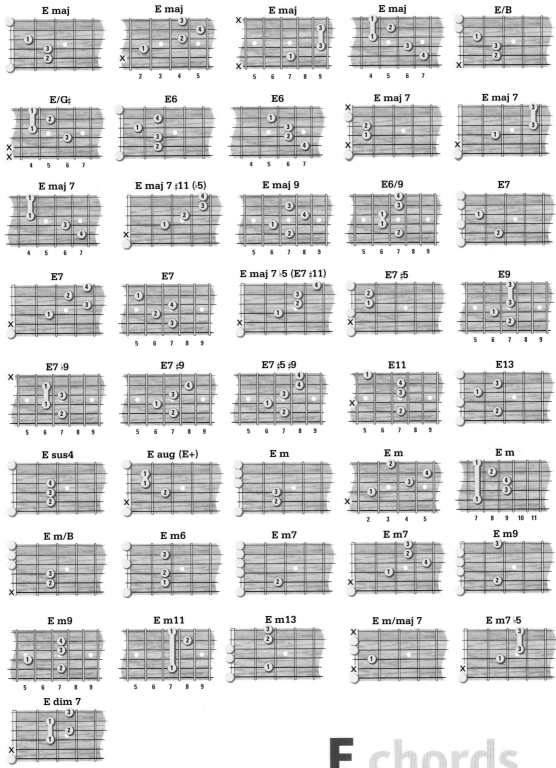

E chords

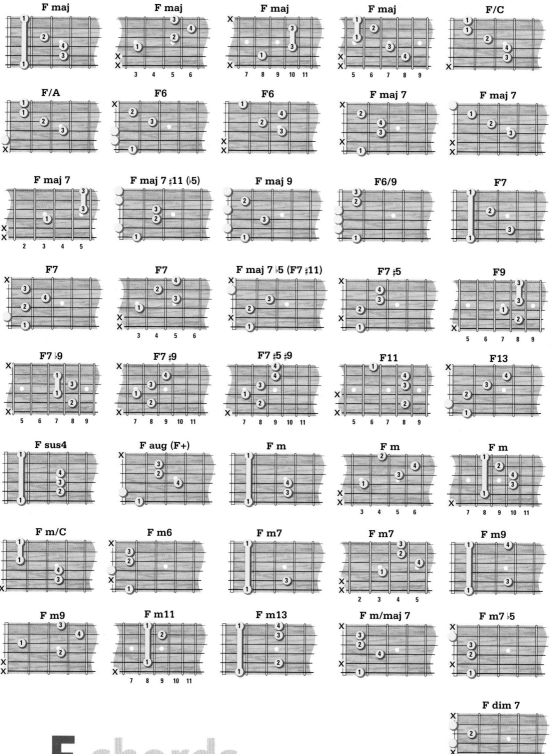

F chords

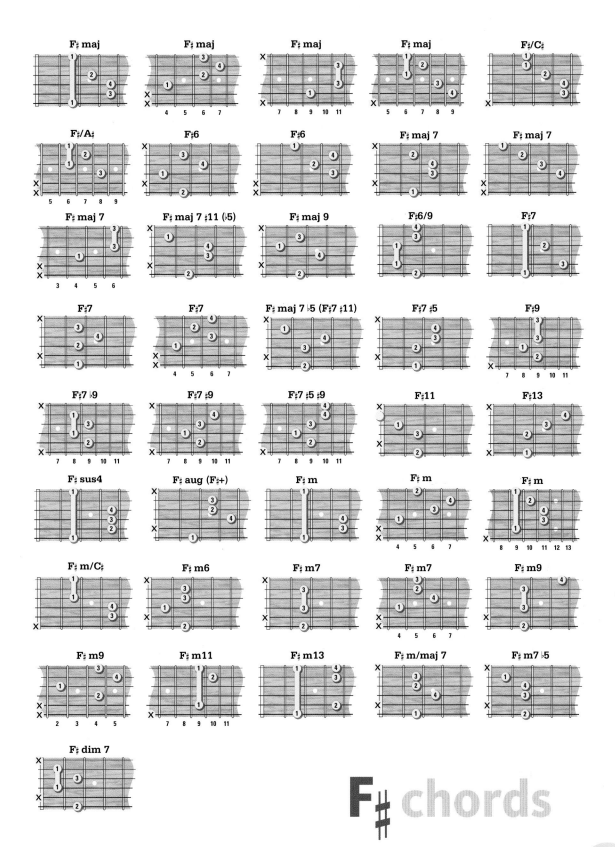

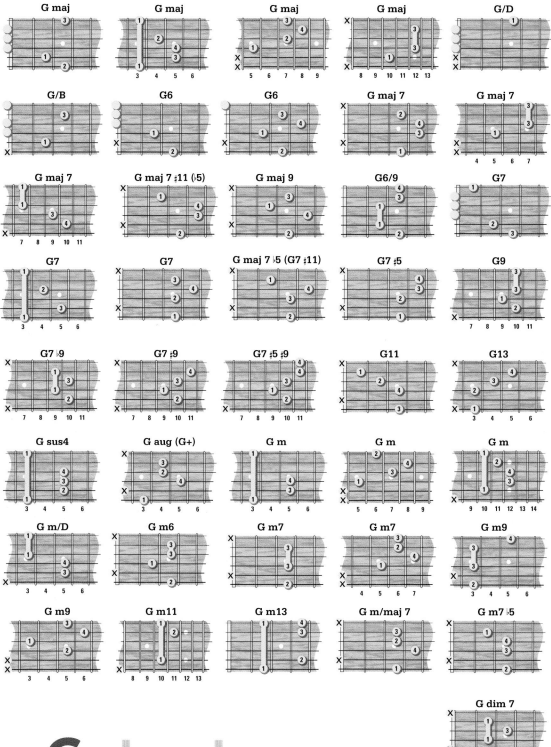

G chords

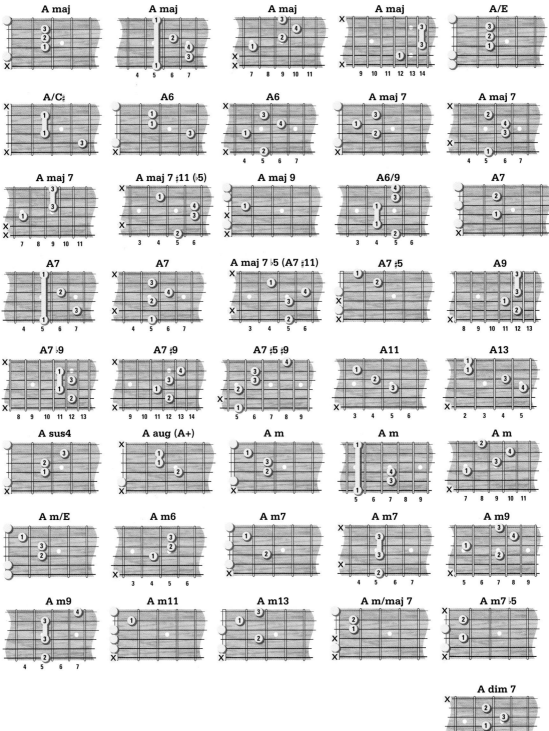

A chords

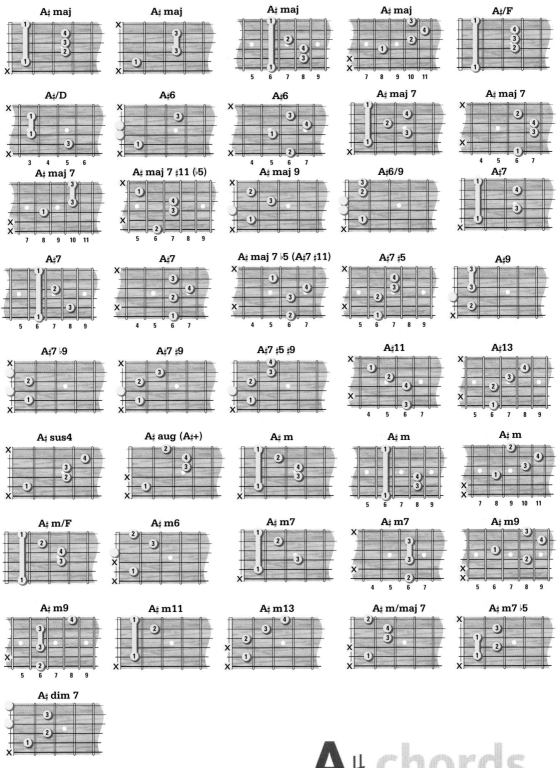

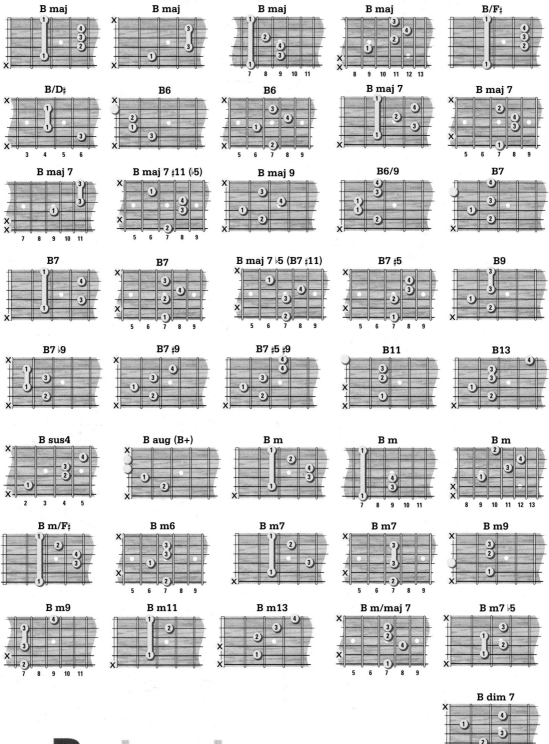

B chords

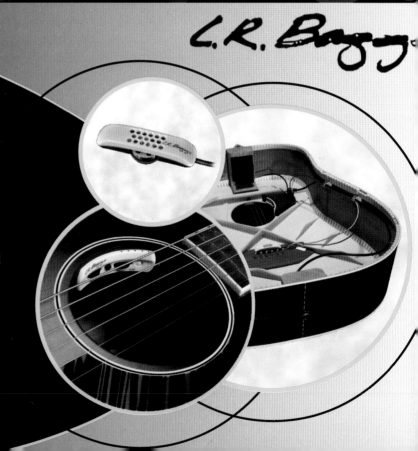

Index

DynaSonic 49, 50, 68

E

ebony 28, 31, 34
echo effects 259
Echoplex 189, 194
echo units 189
Eddy, Duane 202
effects pedals 149–156, 185–195, 238, 240
Eggle 46
electric guitars (basics) 8–10
Electro-Harmonix 191, 193
Englemann 26
EQ 195, 249, 271
Ernie Ball 46

F

Facebook 235
faders 249
Fairchild compressors 250
fan strut 31
Fender 45, 46, 47, 49, 67, 68, 281, 284, 286
  Backstage 180
  Bassman 170, 171, 173
  Broadcaster 40, 41, 48
  Bronco 224
  Esquire 41, 200
  Jazzmaster 224, 282
  JMP50 173
  Mustang 220
  Stratocaster 38, 41, 42, 47, 55, 56, 58, 67, 68, 204, 216, 281
  Telecaster 38, 40, 41, 48, 54, 67, 212, 281
  Telecaster Thinline 45
  Tweed 172
  Tweed Deluxe 171
  Twin Reverb 171, 173
Fender, Leo 276, 286
fingerboard 25, 31, 39, 40, 67, 68
fingerpicks 126, 163
fingerstyle 120–126
FireBox 246
FireStudio 246
FireWire connections 248

flamenco 31, 32
flangers 191
flatpicking 23
flat-top 5, 21, 22, 23, 25, 28, 29, 32, 33, 37
Fleetwood Mac 31
floating bridges 54
Floyd Rose tremolo 58, 67
folk 29
Framus 59
Fret-King 46
frets 59, 60
Frisell, Bill 42
Froggy Bottom 25
Fulltone 189, 192
fuzz pedals 149, 150, 189, 190, 212, 213
Fuzz-Tone 189, 190

G

gain 170
Gallup, Cliff 45
GarageBand 246
gating 249
Gibson 22, 33, 37, 42, 44, 45, 46, 47, 49, 50, 56, 58, 67, 68, 277
  ES-150 43
  ES-175 44
  ES-335 43
  ES-350T 43
  Explorer 219
  GA-40 Les Paul Amp 173
  J-200 21, 28
  Les Paul 37, 42, 47, 55, 67, 206, 209, 212, 278
  SG 42, 67
  Super Jumbo 21
Gibson, Orville 276
gigs 235
Gilmour, David 57
G&L 46
gliss 14
golpeador 32
Gordon-Smith 46
Graydon, Jay 187
Greenwood, Jonny 221
Gretsch 44, 45, 46, 49, 50, 53, 58, 59, 68, 285
  Duo Jet 44

S

saddle 9, 67
sample rate 247, 248
Santa Cruz 22
Santana, Carlos 288
sapele 28
Satriani, Joe 190
scales
   blues scale 113, 115
   major pentatonic scale 115
   minor pentatonic scale 109, 115
   minor scales 103
"Scarborough Fair" 101
Schaller 60
secondhand equipment 196
secondhand guitars 56, 63
semi-solid guitars 44
set-up 78
Setzer, Brian 51
Sex Pistols, The 227
Seymour Duncan 51
Shadows, The 204
shuffle 111
Shure
   SM57 252, 254, 260, 263, 264, 269
   SM58 252, 253, 263
Silver Jet 44
single-coil pickups 47, 51
single-note playing 82, 97–100
Siouxsie & the Banshees 191
Sitka spruce 26
slap-back echo 202
Slash 194
slide guitar 139–154
slides 165
Smiths, The 192, 217
Smoky Amps 180
Sola Sound/Colorsound 189, 190
solidbodies 41, 57, 278
solid-state amplifiers 167, 179
songwriting 232
Son House 139
soundboard 5, 33
sound engineers 239
soundhole 5, 25, 31

speakers 177–178
   monitor speakers 245, 255, 258
   rotary speakers 192
speaking length 5
Sperzel 60
spruce 26, 31, 32
steel guitars 28, 59
stereo pedals 150
Sting 31
stompboxes 185
stopbar tailpiece 57
Stray Cats, The 51
stringing 72–75
strings 160–162
   acoustic 160
   coated 160
   electric 161
   gauges 161
   phosphor bronze 160
strumming 82–83
Summers, Andy 191
sunburst 38
sus chords 89–90
Swift, Taylor 288
sycamore 32

T

tailpieces 53, 58
Talking Heads 227
Tankian, Serj 288
tap plate 32
Taylor 22, 25, 28, 288
TC Electronics Nova System 183, 250
thermionic valves 169
TonePros 56
Torres, Antonio de 31
Townshend, Pete 50, 206, 269
trapeze tailpieces 33, 54
tremolo 192
Tremonti, Mark 288
triplets 15, 16
Trower, Robin 192
truss rods 25, 66, 277
tube converters 270
tube distortion 169

Picture Credits